FIRST EDITION

TABLE OF CONTENT

BIRDS OF NORTH AMERICA

INDEX

INTRODUCTION

What is Birdwatching?

Birdwatching, also known as birding, is the recreational observation of wild birds in their natural habitats. It involves identifying birds by sight and sound, often utilizing binoculars and field guides. While primarily a leisure activity enjoyed by people of all ages and skill levels, birdwatching also contributes significantly to citizen science and ornithological research through the collection of valuable data on bird distribution, migration patterns, behavior, and population trends. Dedicated birdwatchers, sometimes referred to as "birders," often develop a deep knowledge of avian ecology and conservation, and may actively participate in monitoring programs and conservation efforts.

Why This Guide?

This indispensable resource provides in-depth general descriptions for **201 Bird Species**, covering essential identification characteristics such as appearance, feeding strategies, distinctive sounds, nesting habits, geographical range, differentiating between similar species and migratory patterns.

The guide further enhances accuracy with **high-resolution photographs** showcasing the distinct plumage variations of males, females, and juveniles.

Plan your birding excursions effectively using the included **range maps** detailing species distribution across North America. Immerse yourself in the auditory world of birds with convenient scannable QR codes that link directly to **360 songs and calls**.

Beyond identification, the engaging "**Did You Know?**" section unveils captivating facts, adding a layer of wonder and knowledge to your birdwatching pursuits.

Bird Anatomy

Bird anatomy represents a highly specialized and remarkably efficient adaptation for aerial locomotion and diverse ecological niches. Characterized by a unique suite of skeletal modifications, including pneumatic bones, a fused vertebral column (synsacrum), and a keeled sternum, the avian body plan is lightweight yet structurally robust. The forelimbs are transformed into wings, featuring elongated and fused metacarpals and digits supporting flight feathers crucial for lift, thrust, and control.

The respiratory system is exceptionally advanced, employing a unidirectional flow of air through parabronchi and air sacs, ensuring a constant supply of oxygen vital for the high metabolic demands of flight. The digestive system is streamlined with a beak replacing teeth, a crop for food storage, a gizzard for mechanical breakdown, and rapid processing to minimize weight.

Internally, birds possess a four-chambered heart ensuring complete separation of oxygenated and deoxygenated blood, supporting their high activity levels. Their nervous system exhibits a relatively large cerebellum for coordination and balance, and highly developed visual and auditory senses crucial for navigation, foraging, and social interactions.

Furthermore, avian anatomy displays significant diversity across species, reflecting adaptations to varied diets, habitats, and lifestyles.

Beak morphology, foot structure, plumage characteristics, and internal organ systems all exhibit remarkable variations that underscore the evolutionary success and ecological breadth of this fascinating class of vertebrates. A comprehensive understanding of bird anatomy is fundamental to fields ranging from ornithology and veterinary medicine to paleontology and biomechanics.

Getting Started with Birdwatching

Embarking on the journey of birdwatching, or birding, is an enriching experience that connects you with the natural world in a profound way. It requires minimal upfront investment and offers a lifetime of discovery, from your own backyard to the most remote corners of the globe.

A practical guide to taking your first steps:

1. Cultivate Awareness: The most crucial starting point is simply paying attention. Begin by observing the birds you encounter daily – in your garden, local park, or even through your window. Notice their size, shape, colors, and behaviors. Listen for their songs and calls. This initial awareness will naturally spark curiosity and lay the foundation for more focused observation.

2. Arm Yourself with Basic Tools: While sophisticated equipment can enhance the experience later, you can start with just a few essentials:

- **Binoculars:** A good pair of binoculars is your primary tool for bringing distant birds into clear view. For beginners, an 8x42 or 10x42 model is often recommended. The first number indicates magnification, and the second is the objective lens diameter (which affects light-gathering ability). Look for comfortable handling and clear optics.
- **Field Guide:** A reliable field guide, either a physical book or a mobile app, is essential for identification. Choose a guide specific to your geographic region, featuring clear illustrations or photographs and concise descriptions of key field marks, habitat, and vocalizations.
- **Notebook and Pen/Pencil:** Keeping a record of your sightings is a valuable practice. Note the date, time, location, species (if known), and any interesting behaviors observed. This not only helps you track your progress but also contributes to citizen science efforts later on.

3. Learn Basic Identification Skills: Start with common and easily recognizable birds in your area. Focus on key identification features:

- **Size and Shape:** Is it robin-sized, sparrow-sized, or larger? Is it slender or stocky? Note the shape of the beak, tail, and wings.
- **Plumage:** Pay attention to the colors and patterns of the feathers. Where are the different colors located? Are there any distinctive markings like wing bars, eye rings, or streaks?
- **Behavior:** How does the bird move? Does it hop, walk, or climb? How does it feed? Does it forage on the ground, in trees, or in flight?
- **Habitat:** Where did you see the bird? Different species prefer different environments (forests, wetlands, grasslands, etc.).

- **Vocalization:** Learn to distinguish common bird songs and calls. Many field guides and online resources offer audio recordings.

4. Explore Local Birding Spots: Discover areas in your vicinity known for bird activity. This could include parks, nature reserves, lakeshores, or even quiet residential streets with mature trees. Visiting diverse habitats will expose you to a wider variety of species.

5. Join the Birding Community: Connecting with other birdwatchers can significantly accelerate your learning. Consider:

- **Local Birding Clubs:** These groups often organize field trips, workshops, and presentations, providing excellent opportunities to learn from experienced birders.
- **Online Forums and Social Media Groups:** These platforms allow you to ask questions, share sightings, and connect with enthusiasts globally.
- **Guided Bird Walks:** Participating in a guided walk led by an expert can provide invaluable insights into identification techniques and local birdlife.

6. Be Patient and Observant: Birdwatching requires patience. Birds may not always be readily visible. Take your time, move slowly and quietly, and use your senses to detect their presence. Learn to scan your surroundings methodically.

7. Respect Birds and Their Environment: Always prioritize the well-being of birds and their habitats. Observe from a distance to avoid disturbance, never approach nests, and refrain from using artificial calls or feeders in a way that could harm birds or alter their natural behavior. Follow ethical birding guidelines.

8. Embrace Lifelong Learning: Bird identification is a continuous learning process. Don't be discouraged if you can't identify every bird you see. Enjoy the process of discovery, celebrate each new species you learn, and allow your passion for birds to grow.

How to Identify Birds

Bird identification, or bird identification, is a multifaceted process requiring a systematic and observant approach to distinguish between various avian species. It involves the comprehensive evaluation of a suite of characteristics, both visual and auditory, in conjunction with contextual information. A skilled observer integrates these elements to arrive at an accurate species determination.

Key Methodological Components:

1. **Visual Characteristics:** This involves meticulous examination of the bird's physical attributes, including:

- **Size and Shape:** Overall body dimensions (length, wingspan), body proportions (relative size of head, tail, legs), and characteristic silhouettes (e.g., upright stance of a heron, streamlined shape of a swallow).
- **Plumage:** Detailed analysis of feather coloration, patterns (streaks, bars, spots), and the distribution of these markings across different body regions (head, back, breast, wings, tail). Attention is paid to variations based on age, sex, and seasonal plumage.
- **Bill Morphology:** Shape, size, and color of the beak, which often reflects the bird's diet and foraging strategy (e.g., long and probing for nectar, short and conical for seeds, hooked for predation).
- **Legs and Feet:** Length, color, and structure of the legs and feet, indicating habitat preference and locomotion (e.g., long legs for wading, strong talons for grasping).
- **Bare Parts:** Color and appearance of the eyes, orbital rings, and any exposed skin.
- **Flight Pattern:** Observation of wing shape during flight, wingbeat frequency and depth, and characteristic flight behaviors (e.g., soaring, flapping, gliding, hovering).

2. **Auditory Characteristics:** Identification through vocalizations is a critical skill, often providing the primary or confirming evidence:

   - **Song:** Complex and often repeated vocalizations, typically associated with territorial defense and mate attraction. Songs exhibit species-specific patterns, pitch, rhythm, and tonal qualities.
   - **Calls:** Shorter and often simpler vocalizations used for various purposes, including alarm, contact, and feeding. Different call types within a species can provide further identification clues.

3. **Contextual Information:** Understanding the surrounding environment and the bird's behavior enhances identification accuracy:

   - **Habitat:** The type of environment where the bird is observed (e.g., forest, grassland, wetland, urban area) can significantly narrow down potential species.
   - **Geographic Location and Season:** Knowledge of species distribution and migratory patterns helps to exclude unlikely candidates.
   - **Behavior:** Observing foraging techniques, social interactions, nesting habits, and other behaviors can provide valuable clues.

Process of Identification:

The identification process typically involves a systematic approach:

1. **Initial Observation:** Note the overall impression of the bird, including size, shape, and general color.
2. **Detailed Examination:** Focus on specific visual features, listening attentively for vocalizations.
3. **Comparison with Resources:** Utilize field guides (physical or digital), online databases, and recordings of songs and calls to compare observed characteristics with known species.
4. **Consideration of Context:** Integrate habitat, location, season, and behavior into the identification process.
5. **Elimination:** Systematically rule out species that do not match the observed characteristics.
6. **Confirmation:** When possible, obtain multiple lines of evidence (visual and auditory) to confidently identify the species.

Professional Considerations:

Accurate bird identification requires ongoing learning, keen observational skills, and familiarity with regional avifauna. Professionals in fields such as ornithology, ecology, conservation, and wildlife management rely on precise identification for research, monitoring, and conservation efforts. The use of standardized terminology and adherence to rigorous observation protocols are essential for maintaining data quality and ensuring reliable species determinations.

Bird Behavior and Ecology

Bird Behavior and Ecology is a dynamic and interdisciplinary field that investigates the intricate relationships between avian species and their environment, encompassing the diverse array of actions, interactions, and adaptations that shape their survival, reproduction, and distribution. This discipline delves into the proximate and ultimate causes of bird behaviors, exploring how genetic predispositions, physiological mechanisms, and environmental pressures interact to influence foraging strategies, social dynamics, communication systems (including vocalizations and visual displays), mate choice, parental care, territoriality, migration patterns, and anti-predator tactics.

Ecologically, this field examines how birds interact with biotic (e.g., other organisms, vegetation) and abiotic (e.g., climate, habitat structure) components of their ecosystems. Research in bird ecology focuses on understanding population dynamics, community structure, species interactions (including competition, predation, mutualism, and parasitism), habitat selection and use, the impact of environmental change (such as habitat loss, climate change, and pollution) on avian populations, and the role of birds in ecosystem functioning (e.g., seed dispersal, pollination, insect control).

A strong understanding of bird behavior and ecology is crucial for effective conservation efforts, wildlife management, and ecological research. By elucidating the behavioral responses of birds to environmental stressors and the ecological roles they play, this field provides critical insights for mitigating threats, restoring habitats, and promoting the long-term persistence of avian biodiversity. Researchers and practitioners in this area employ a wide range of methodologies, including field observations, experimental manipulations, physiological measurements, genetic analyses, and spatial modeling, to unravel the complexities of avian life and their vital connections within the natural world.

Bird Habitats

North America exhibits a remarkable diversity of bird habitats, shaped by its vast latitudinal and longitudinal expanse, varied topography, and complex climate patterns. These habitats range from the Arctic tundra and boreal forests of the north to the tropical rainforests of Central America, encompassing grasslands, deserts, mountains, coastlines, and a multitude of freshwater and saltwater ecosystems in between. Each habitat type supports a unique avian community, with species adapted to specific vegetation structures, food sources, and environmental conditions.

Key Habitat Types and Characteristics:

- **Forests and Woodlands:** Representing the most widespread habitat, these include coniferous boreal forests, temperate deciduous forests, oak-hickory woodlands, and coastal redwood forests. They offer diverse vertical stratification, providing niches for various bird species that forage, nest, and seek shelter in the canopy, understory, and forest floor. Examples include woodpeckers, warblers, owls, and thrushes.
- **Grasslands and Prairies:** Vast expanses of grasses and herbaceous vegetation, supporting ground-nesting birds like sparrows, meadowlarks, and prairie chickens. The structure and composition of grasslands vary from shortgrass to tallgrass prairies, influencing the avian species present.
- **Wetlands:** Including marshes, swamps, bogs, and fens, these water-saturated environments are crucial for waterfowl, shorebirds, wading birds, and various songbirds. They provide essential breeding, feeding, and resting areas, particularly during migration. Examples include herons, egrets, ducks, and rails.
- **Deserts and Aridlands:** Characterized by low precipitation and sparse vegetation, these habitats host specialized bird species adapted to survive harsh conditions, such as roadrunners, cactus wrens, and various raptors.
- **Tundra and Alpine Regions:** Found in the far north and at high elevations, these treeless environments with low-growing vegetation support birds like ptarmigans, snow buntings, and various shorebirds during their breeding season.

- **Coasts and Shorelines:** Dynamic interfaces between land and sea, providing critical habitat for seabirds, shorebirds, and waterfowl. Habitats range from sandy beaches and rocky shores to estuaries and mangrove forests. Examples include gulls, terns, sandpipers, and pelicans.
- **Lakes, Ponds, and Rivers:** Freshwater aquatic ecosystems that support a variety of waterbirds, including ducks, geese, loons, and kingfishers, as well as riparian species along their edges.
- **Shrublands and Thickets:** Transitional habitats with low-growing woody vegetation, important for species like thrashers, towhees, and some warblers that prefer dense cover for nesting and foraging.
- **Urban and Suburban Habitats:** Human-modified landscapes that can support a surprising diversity of birds adapted to these environments, such as pigeons, sparrows, starlings, and robins, often utilizing parks, gardens, and built structures.

Ecological Significance:

North American bird habitats are integral to the continent's biodiversity and ecosystem functioning. Birds play crucial roles as pollinators, seed dispersers, insectivores, and scavengers, contributing to plant reproduction, pest control, and nutrient cycling. The health and diversity of these habitats directly influence the abundance and distribution of bird populations, which serve as indicators of environmental change.

Conservation Challenges:

Many North American bird habitats face significant threats from human activities, including habitat loss and fragmentation due to urbanization, agriculture, forestry, and resource extraction. Climate change is also altering habitat suitability and species distributions. Conservation efforts are crucial to protect and restore these vital ecosystems and ensure the long-term survival of North America's diverse avian fauna. These efforts involve habitat protection through the establishment of protected areas, habitat restoration and management, sustainable land-use practices, and addressing the impacts of climate change. Collaborative initiatives across the United States, Canada, and Mexico, such as the North American Bird Conservation Initiative (NABCI), are essential for addressing the conservation needs of migratory birds and their shared habitats across the continent.

Birds Reproductive Strategies

Bird's reproductive success hinges on a complex interplay of behaviors and physiological adaptations encompassing nest construction, egg production and incubation, elaborate courtship rituals, and precise mating. These processes are crucial for the continuation of bird species and exhibit remarkable diversity across the avian class.

Nesting: Nesting behavior is fundamental for providing a secure environment for egg incubation and the rearing of young. Birds exhibit a wide array of nest-building strategies, influenced by factors such as habitat, predator pressure, and species-specific requirements.

- **Nest Construction:** Birds utilize diverse materials, including twigs, grasses, leaves, mud, feathers, and even human-made items, to construct nests of varying complexity. Nest architecture ranges from simple scrapes in the ground to elaborate woven cups, domed structures, and cavity nests in trees or cliffs. The selection of nest site and building materials often reflects an intricate balance between insulation, camouflage, stability, and accessibility for parental care.

- **Nest Function:** The primary function of a nest is to protect eggs and developing chicks from predation, environmental extremes (temperature, moisture), and physical damage. Nest design can influence incubation efficiency and the microclimate experienced by the developing embryos.

Eggs: Bird eggs are a testament to evolutionary adaptation, providing all the necessary resources for embryonic development within a protective shell.

- **Egg Morphology:** Avian eggs exhibit considerable variation in size, shape, color, and markings, both within and between species. Eggshell composition is primarily calcium carbonate, providing structural integrity while allowing for gas exchange. Pigmentation, resulting from the deposition of pigments like biliverdin and protoporphyrin, can serve for camouflage, species recognition, and even thermoregulation. Egg shape can be correlated with factors such as clutch size, nesting environment, and flight efficiency of the parent.

- **Clutch Size and Incubation:** The number of eggs laid in a single nesting attempt (clutch size) varies greatly among species and can be influenced by factors like food availability, parental investment capacity, and predation risk. Incubation, the process of maintaining eggs at an optimal temperature for embryonic development, is typically performed by one or both parents. Incubation strategies range from continuous brooding to intermittent incubation, with incubation periods varying depending on egg size and species.

Courtship: Prior to mating, birds often engage in elaborate courtship rituals that serve to attract a mate of the correct species and assess their fitness.

- **Displays and Signals:** Courtship behaviors can involve a combination of visual, auditory, and tactile signals. Males often display vibrant plumage, perform intricate dances or aerial maneuvers, offer food gifts, and produce complex songs or calls to attract females. These displays can signal genetic quality, foraging ability, territorial control, and overall health.

- **Mate Choice:** Females typically play a crucial role in mate selection, evaluating male displays and characteristics to choose a partner that will maximize their reproductive success. Factors influencing mate choice can include the intensity and complexity of displays, physical attributes, and the quality of resources or nesting sites controlled by the male.

Mating: The culmination of successful courtship is mating, which involves the transfer of sperm from the male to the female to fertilize the eggs.

- **Copulation:** The physical act of mating in birds, known as copulation, typically involves a brief cloacal contact between the male and female. While some species form long-term pair bonds and mate monogamously, others exhibit polygamous mating systems, where individuals mate with multiple partners.

- **Pair Bonds and Parental Care:** The duration and nature of pair bonds vary significantly among bird species. Monogamous pairs may cooperate in nest building, incubation, and the care of young. In polygamous systems, parental care responsibilities may be skewed towards one parent, often the female. The level of parental investment is a key factor influencing offspring survival and ultimately, the reproductive success of the parents.

How to use this book

This guide is designed to introduce you to the fascinating world of birdwatching, equipping you with the fundamental knowledge and skills needed to embark on your avian adventures. The first section, lays the groundwork for your journey, covering essential concepts and practical tips to get you started.

Section two provides comprehensive information on individual bird species, designed to enhance your identification skills and deepen your understanding of bird behavior. Each species account follows a standardized format, allowing for quick access to key details.

General Description This section outlines general knowledge about a species and also provide a distinction of both sexes.

Feeding This section provides information on the bird's diet and foraging behavior. Understanding a bird's feeding habits can help you predict where to find it and observe its behavior. Details may include preferred food sources (insects, seeds, fruits, etc.), foraging techniques, and typical feeding habitats.

Vocalization/Sounds This section describes the bird's vocalizations, including songs, calls, and other sounds. Descriptions may include phonetic representations, comparisons to other species' vocalizations, and notes on the context in which sounds are produced. Bird songs and calls are crucial for identification, especially in dense vegetation or when visual observation is difficult.

Range This section outlines the bird's geographic distribution, including breeding, wintering, and migratory ranges. Understanding a bird's range is essential for determining its likelihood of occurrence in a specific location.

Migration This section describes the bird's migration patterns, including timing, routes, and destinations. Many bird species undertake seasonal migrations, moving between breeding and wintering grounds. Knowing a bird's migration patterns can help you predict its presence in a particular area at different times of the year.

Similar Species This section provides detailed comparisons between the target species and other similar species, highlighting key differences in plumage, size, shape, and behavior. Many bird species share similar characteristics, making identification challenging. Pay close attention to these comparisons, as they are crucial for accurate identification.

Section three is your primary tool for accurate bird identification in the field. It combines detailed photographic representations of male, female, and juvenile plumages with comprehensive range maps to help you narrow down possibilities based on location and appearance.

Visual Comparisons Each species entry includes high-quality photographs showcasing the distinct plumages of adult males, adult females, and juveniles. These variations are crucial for accurate identification, as many species exhibit significant sexual dimorphism (differences between males and females) and age-related plumage changes.

Carefully observe the following features in each photograph:

- **Overall shape and size:** Note the bird's silhouette, body proportions, and relative size compared to other birds you may have seen.
- **Plumage patterns and colors:** Pay close attention to the distribution of colors, patterns (streaks, spots, bars), and any distinctive markings on the head, wings, tail, and body.
- **Bill and leg shape and color:** These features can be highly diagnostic, especially for species that are otherwise similar in plumage.
- **Eye color and pattern:** Note the color of the iris and any eye rings or superciliary lines.

Range Maps

Geographic Distribution: Each species entry includes a range map that illustrates the bird's typical geographic distribution. These maps are essential for narrowing down potential identifications based on your location.

- **Understanding the Map Key:** Familiarize yourself with the map key, which typically indicates breeding, wintering, and migratory ranges.
- **Focus on Your Location:** Identify your current location on the map. If the species is not within its indicated range, it is less likely to be the bird you are observing.
- **Seasonal Considerations:** Consider the time of year. Some species have different ranges during breeding and wintering seasons. Pay attention to the seasonal indicators on the map to determine if the species is likely to be present in your area during your observation.

Range Overlap: Be aware that the ranges of different species may overlap. In these cases, you will need to rely more heavily on visual identification to distinguish between similar species.

Rare Sightings: Keep in mind that range maps depict typical distributions. Rare sightings outside of these ranges can occur, but these are less likely.

Section four is designed to enhance your birdwatching experience by providing instant access to the vocalizations of many featured species. Recognizing bird songs and calls is a crucial skill for identification and location, often revealing the presence of a bird before it is visually spotted.

QR CODES

Locate the QR Code: Throughout the species accounts in this book, you will find small, square QR codes associated with specific birds. These are located below species photographs.

Prepare Your Device: You will need a smartphone or tablet with a camera and a QR code scanning application. Most modern smartphones have a built-in QR code scanner within the camera app. If not, you can download a free QR code scanner from your device's app store.

Scan the Code:

- Open your QR code scanning application or your device's camera.
- Position your device's camera over the QR code, ensuring it is within the frame displayed on your screen.
- Hold the device steady until the code is recognized.
- Your device will typically display a notification or link. Tap on this link to be redirected to the associated audio file.

Listen and Learn:

- The link will open a web page or audio player containing the bird's song or call.
- Listen carefully to the vocalization. Pay attention to the pitch, rhythm, and any distinctive patterns.
- Repeat the audio as needed to familiarize yourself with the sound.
- If possible, listen to the audio while observing the image of the bird in the book, or better yet, while observing the bird in the field.

Field Application:

- Once you are familiar with the vocalization, listen for it during your birdwatching excursions.
- Try to match the sounds you hear with the audio samples from the book.
- This will help you identify birds that may be hidden from view.
- Remember that bird vocalizations can vary slightly due to region, age, and individual variation.

Tips for Optimal Use:

- **Ensure a Stable Internet Connection:** The QR codes link to online audio files. A stable internet connection is required for seamless playback.
- **Adjust Volume:** Adjust your device's volume to a comfortable level, especially in noisy environments. Consider using headphones for better clarity.
- **Practice Regularly:** Consistent practice is key to improving your bird song and call recognition skills.
- **Use in Conjunction with Visual Identification:** Combine audio identification with visual cues to confirm your sightings.

Section five "Did You Know?", is designed to enrich your birdwatching experience by providing fascinating and often surprising facts about the birds you've encountered. It goes beyond simple identification, offering insights into the unique behaviors, adaptations, and natural histories of various species. Treat this section as a collection of avian trivia, perfect for deepening your understanding and sparking conversation during your birding adventures.

Contextual Learning:

- **Connect to Field Observations:** After identifying a bird using the species accounts in the earlier sections, refer to the "Did You Know?" entry for that species. This contextual approach reinforces learning and helps you appreciate the bird beyond its visual characteristics.
- **Enhance Species Understanding:** The facts presented often highlight specific adaptations or behaviors relevant to the bird's ecology. For example, if you observe a woodpecker drumming on a tree, the "Did You Know?" section might explain the purpose of this behavior (territorial marking, foraging, etc.).

Independent Exploration:

- **Browse for Intrigue:** Even without immediate field observations, you can peruse the "Did You Know?" section for general avian knowledge. This can spark your interest in specific species or behaviors, encouraging you to seek them out during your next birdwatching trip.
- **Expand Your Avian Vocabulary:** The facts may introduce you to specialized terms related to bird biology, such as "nictitating membrane" or "lek." Understanding these terms will enhance your ability to read and comprehend ornithological literature.

PIGEONS AND DOVES

Pigeons and doves belong to the bird family *Columbidae*. While often used interchangeably, there isn't a strict scientific distinction between them. Generally, the terms "dove" and "pigeon" are used to refer to smaller and larger species within the family, respectively.

General Characteristics:

- **Body Shape:** They typically have stout bodies with short necks and slender bills that often have a fleshy cere (a soft, waxy covering) at the base.
- **Wings and Flight:** They possess strong wings and are capable of swift and direct flight. Some species are highly agile fliers.
- **Legs and Feet:** Their legs are short and sturdy, with four toes – three pointing forward and one pointing backward (anisodactyl arrangement) – adapted for perching and walking.
- **Plumage:** Their plumage is generally soft and dense, often in shades of grey, brown, white, or iridescent colors. Males and females often have similar plumage, though some species exhibit sexual dimorphism.
- **Vocalization:** Their characteristic calls are soft, cooing sounds. The specific calls vary between species.
- **Diet:** They are primarily granivorous (seed-eating), but their diet can also include fruits, berries, insects, and other small invertebrates depending on the species and habitat.
- **Social Behavior:** Many species are social birds, often forming flocks, especially when foraging or roosting.
- **Nesting:** They typically build simple, flimsy nests made of twigs and other available materials, often in trees, on cliffs, or in human-made structures.
- **Reproduction:** They usually lay one or two white eggs per clutch. Both parents typically incubate the eggs and care for the young (squabs or chicks).
- **Parental Care:** Pigeon and dove parents produce "crop milk," a nutritious secretion from the lining of their crop, to feed their young during the first few days of life. This is a unique characteristic within the bird world.

Key Points:

- **Global Distribution:** Pigeons and doves are found worldwide, except for the extreme polar regions. They inhabit a wide variety of habitats, including forests, grasslands, deserts, and urban environments.
- **Adaptability:** Many species, particularly the rock pigeon (*Columba livia*) and its feral descendants, are highly adaptable to human-modified landscapes and thrive in urban areas.
- **Historical and Cultural Significance:** Pigeons have a long history of association with humans. They have been domesticated for various purposes, including:
    - **Messenger Pigeons:** Historically used to carry messages over long distances due to their strong homing instincts.
    - **Food Source:** Some species are raised for their meat (squab).
    - **Sport and Hobby:** Fancy pigeons are bred for their unique appearances and behaviors, and racing pigeons are trained for competitive flying.
    - **Symbolism:** Doves, particularly white doves, are often used as symbols of peace, love, and purity in various cultures and religions.
- **Ecological Roles:** In their natural habitats, pigeons and doves play roles in seed dispersal and serve as a food source for predators.
- **Conservation Status:** The conservation status of pigeons and doves varies greatly. While some species, like the rock pigeon, are abundant, others face threats from habitat loss, hunting, and introduced predators, leading to their endangerment. Examples include the Passenger Pigeon (now extinct due to human activities) and various island endemic species.
- **Homing Instinct:** Many pigeon species possess a remarkable ability to navigate back to their home loft over long distances, a phenomenon that is still not fully understood but likely involves a combination of magnetic senses, visual cues, and olfactory navigation.
- **Diversity:** The *Columbidae* family is diverse, comprising over 300 species exhibiting a wide range of sizes, colors, and behaviors.

Mourning Dove - *Zenaida macroura*

Mourning Dove is a common and widespread North American bird, recognized by its slender body, small head, and long, pointed tail. These doves are generally attired in soft shades of brown and gray, with black spots on their wings and a dark mark on their cheeks. Males tend to exhibit a pinkish hue on their breasts and a bluish-gray crown, while females are typically duller in coloration. Juveniles resemble adults but display white-tipped feathers.

FEEDING, they are primarily ground feeders, consuming seeds and grains, and they often gather in flocks, especially during migration and in winter.

SOUNDS Their distinct vocalizations include a soft, mournful "coo," from which they derive their name, and a sharp, whistling sound produced by their wings in flight.

RANGE & MIGRATION Their range spans across North America, from southern Canada through the United States and into Mexico. Northern populations are migratory, moving southward in the fall and returning northward in the spring, while southern populations may be resident.

SIMILAR SPECIES that can be confused with the mourning dove, include other dove species, such as the Inca Dove, and the Common Ground Dove.

Male

Female

Juvenile

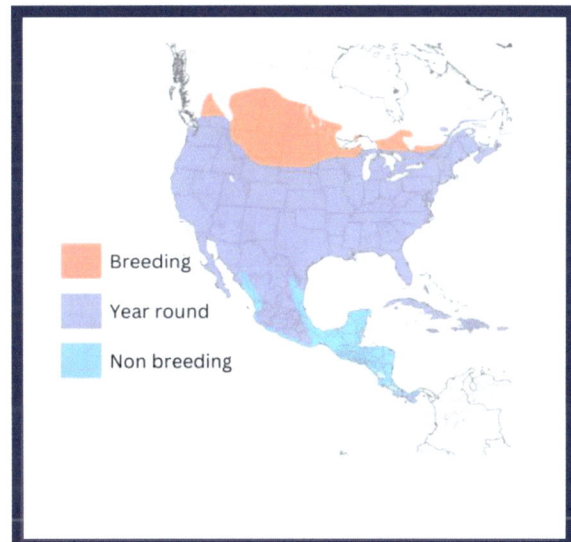

Breeding

Year round

Non breeding

Song

DID YOU KNOW....

Beyond their mournful coo, their wings produce a distinct high-pitched whistling sound during flight, especially on takeoff and landing.
This sound is thought to help communicate danger to other doves in the flock.

They exhibit unusual bathing behaviors. They will lie flat on the ground or a low branch, leaning to one side and stretching out a wing for up to 20 minutes during sun or rain.

When trying to distract predators from their nest, the adult Mourning Dove will perform a "broken-wing" display, fluttering on the ground.

Band-tailed Pigeon- *Patagioenas fasciata*

Band-tailed Pigeon, North America's largest native pigeon, exhibits a soft blue-gray plumage above and a purplish-gray below, distinguished by a white crescent on the back of its neck and a pale gray band at the tip of its tail. Adult males and females share similar plumage, though subtle differences may exist. Juveniles lack the distinctive white neck crescent and display light scalloping on their back feathers.

FEEDING These pigeons forage for fruits, nuts, seeds, and occasionally insects, often in large flocks, navigating treetops with surprising agility.

SOUNDS Their vocalizations consist of a slow, low-pitched, two-note "coo" that resembles an owl's hoot.
HABITAT & RANGE They inhabit mature forests, oak woodlands, and semi-open areas, with a range spanning western North America, including the Pacific Coast and mountainous regions.

MIGRATION Their migration patterns are influenced by food availability, leading to nomadic movements.
SIMILAR SPECIES Similar in size to the Rock Pigeon, they can be distinguished by the white neck crescent and the band on its tail.

Adults

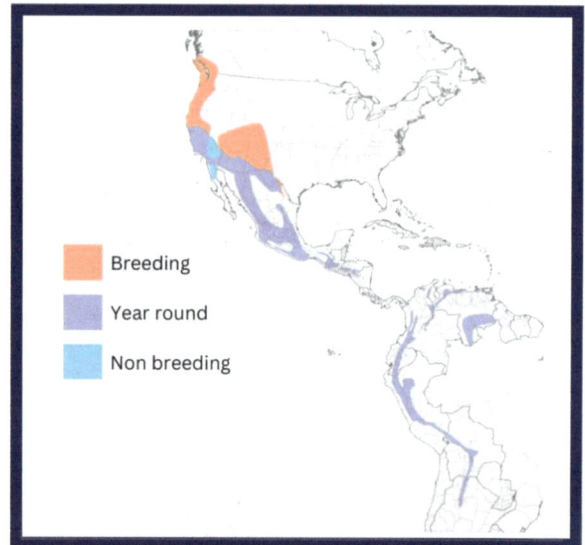
Juvenile

Breeding

Year round

Non breeding

Song   Call

DID YOU KNOW....

It holds the title of the largest pigeon species native to North America, noticeably bigger than the familiar Rock Pigeon and Mourning Dove.

The Band-tailed Pigeon is the closest living relative to the extinct Passenger Pigeon. This close genetic link has even led to the rediscovery of a Passenger Pigeon louse species that was thought to be extinct, found on Band-tailed Pigeons.

There are two distinct breeding populations: the Pacific Coast subspecies and the Interior or Four Corners subspecies, with limited overlap in their breeding ranges.

White-tipped Dove - *Leptotila verreauxi*

White-tipped Dove, is a ground-dwelling dove characterized by its plump body, short, rounded tail, and relatively small head. Adults exhibit a pale undercarrlage, transitioning from a grayish-pink breast to a frosty gray belly, with brown wings and a subtle white tipping on the outer tail feathers, which is most visible during flight. Close observation may reveal a green iridescence on the neck and breast. Regarding distinctions between sexes, there are not very distinct visual differences between male and female white tipped doves. Juvenile birds will resemble the adults, but may have less distinct colorations.

FEEDING These doves primarily forage on the ground in open woodlands and shrubby areas, feeding mainly on seeds, but also incorporating insects and berries into their diet.

SOUNDS Their vocalizations consist of a deep, drawn-out, descending coo, a low-pitched sound that distinguishes them from other dove species.

RANGE & MIGRATION Their range in North America is generally limited to South Texas, and they are primarily non-migratory.

HABITAT They prefer habitats with dense undergrowth, such as woodland edges, thickets, and areas near water.

SIMILAR SPECIES include other doves within the Leptotila genus, such as the Gray-fronted Dove, which can be differentiated by subtle differences in plumage and habitat preference.

Adult

Adult

Juvenile

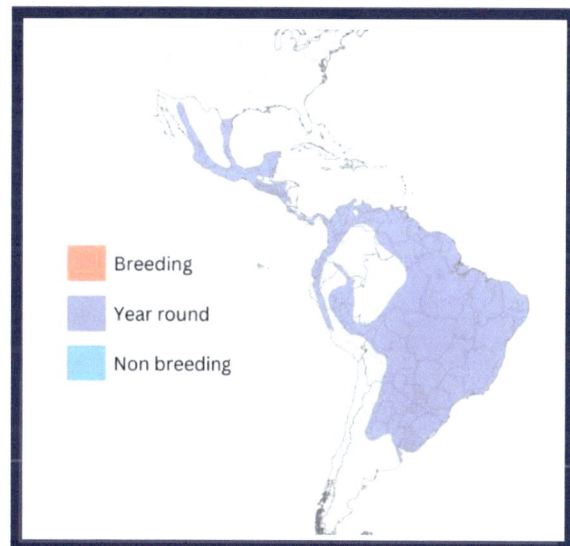

Breeding

Year round

Non breeding

Song

DID YOU KNOW....

Unlike many other doves and pigeons, the White-tipped Dove is known to keep its nest exceptionally clean.

The White-tipped Dove is considered the most widespread dove species in the Americas.

Birders unaware of their presence may be startled when a White-tipped Dove flushes, as their wings produce a quite audible whistling noise during takeoff.

Spotted Dove - *Spilopelia chinensis*

The Spotted Dove, is an introduced species in North America, primarily found in limited areas of Southern California. Generally, these medium-sized doves exhibit a light brown body with pinkish underparts and a distinctive black neck patch heavily spotted with white. Distinguishing between sexes can be difficult, as males and females appear very similar. Juveniles have a duller plumage and the spotted neck patch is less defined.

FEEDING It consist mainly of foraging on the ground for seeds and grains, and they are frequently seen in suburban environments, parks, and agricultural areas.

SOUNDS They produces a strong, rolling cooing song, sometimes with a harsher middle tone.

RANGE & MIGRATION They are considered permanent residents within their established North American range and do not exhibit migratory patterns there.

SIMILAR SPECIES in the region include the Mourning Dove and the White – winged Dove, which can be distinguished by their differing plumage and the absence of the Spotted Dove's characteristic neck patch.

Adult

Juvenile

Adult

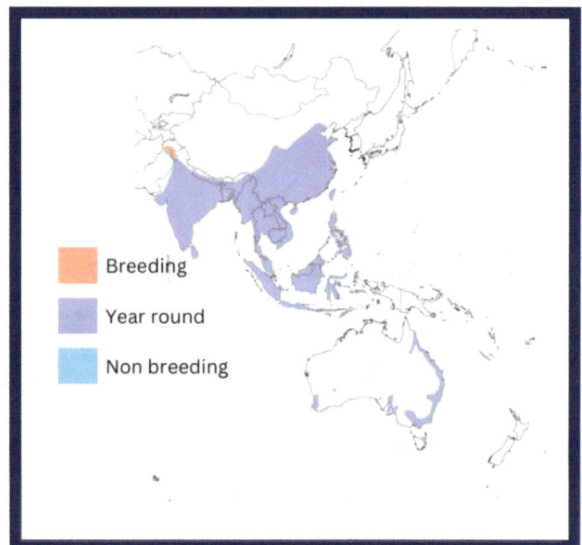

Breeding

Year round

Non breeding

DID YOU KNOW....

Native to southern Asia, the Spotted Dove has been introduced to various parts of the world, including Australia, New Zealand, Mauritius, parts of North America (like California and Hawaii), and some Pacific Islands. These introduced populations have successfully established themselves.

In parts of China it is considered a delicacy and may be found on restaurant menus.

They have been observed taking baths in the rain by leaning to one side and raising a wing to allow the rainwater to clean their feathers. They also preen, scratch, and use bird baths.

Song

Common Ground Dove - *Columbina passerine*

Common Ground Dove, North America's smallest dove, is a diminutive bird with a sandy brown overall coloration and distinctive dark spots on its wing coverts. In flight, It reveals rich rufous patches on its wings. Males are distinguished by a pinkish wash on their head, neck, and chest, along with bluish crowns, while females exhibit a duller plumage. Juveniles resemble adults but display lighter breast scaling.

FEEDING These doves are primarily ground feeders, consuming seeds and grains, with occasional insects.

SOUNDS Their vocalizations consist of quiet, moaning coos, and they also produce a "wut-wut" call when threatened.

HABITAT & RANGE They inhabit open woodlands, desert areas, and even urban landscapes across the southern United States, extending into Central America and the Caribbean.

MIGRATION They are generally non-migratory, remaining within their range year-round.

SIMILAR SPECIES may include other small doves or sparrows, but the Common Ground Dove's distinctive plumage and calls aid in identification.

Adult

Adult

Juvenile

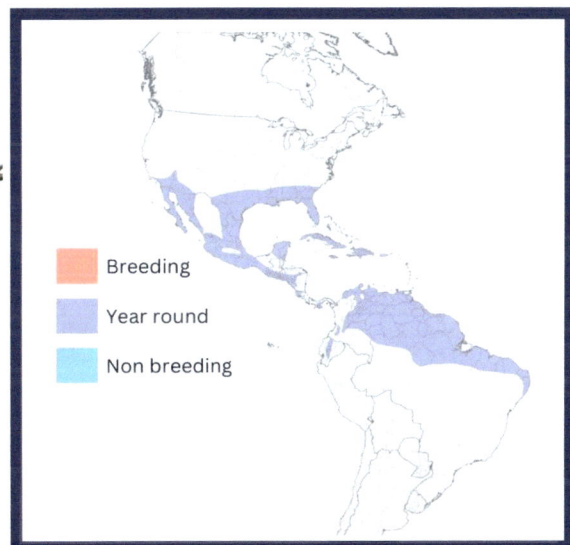

Breeding

Year round

Non breeding

Song

DID YOU KNOW....

It holds the title of the smallest dove found in North America, being only about the size of a house sparrow.

They typically form strong, monogamous pair bonds that can last for several years and even across multiple breeding seasons.

When they take flight, they reveal a flash of rich, reddish-brown (rufous) patches on their underwings, a feature not easily seen when they are perched or on the ground.

FALCONS

Falcons are captivating birds of prey belonging to the family Falconidae. They are renowned for their incredible speed, agility, and hunting prowess.

General Characteristics:

- **Body Shape:** Falcons typically possess a streamlined, aerodynamic body shape built for speed. They have long, pointed wings that are relatively narrow, allowing for efficient and rapid flight. Their tails are usually moderately long and tapered, aiding in maneuverability.
- **Size:** Falcon species exhibit a significant range in size. Some of the smallest falcons are only slightly larger than songbirds, while the largest can rival the size of some hawks.
- **Plumage:** Their plumage varies greatly depending on the species and habitat, often featuring combinations of brown, black, white, gray, and rufous. Some species have distinctive markings like facial "moustaches" or barring on their underparts.
- **Head and Beak:** Falcons have relatively large heads with prominent, forward-facing eyes providing excellent binocular vision crucial for judging distances when hunting. Their beaks are strongly hooked with a sharp tomial tooth (a notch on the upper mandible) that helps them sever the spinal cord of their prey.
- **Talons:** They possess strong feet with sharp, curved talons used for grasping and killing prey. Their toes are anisodactyl, with three toes pointing forward and one pointing backward, providing a secure grip.
- **Flight:** Falcons are masters of aerial flight. They are capable of incredibly fast dives, known as stoops, reaching speeds of over 200 mph in some species like the Peregrine Falcon. They also exhibit agile and swift horizontal flight, often using rapid wingbeats.
- **Vocalization:** Their calls are typically sharp and often described as "kek-kek-kek" or similar variations.

Key Points:

- **Apex Predators:** Most falcons are apex predators in their respective ecosystems, meaning they are at the top of the food chain and have few natural predators as adults.
- **Carnivorous Diet:** Falcons are strictly carnivorous, primarily feeding on birds, small mammals, reptiles, and insects, depending on their size and habitat.
- **Hunting Techniques:** They employ various hunting techniques, including:
  - **Stooping:** High-speed dives to strike prey in mid-air or on the ground.
  - **Pursuit:** Chasing prey in agile, direct flight.
  - **Perch Hunting:** Waiting on a high perch to ambush unsuspecting prey.
- **Nesting Behavior:** Falcons do not typically build elaborate nests. They often nest in scrapes on cliff ledges, tree cavities, or abandoned nests of other birds. Some species will also utilize artificial nest boxes.
- **Parental Care:** Both parents usually participate in incubating the eggs and caring for the young (eyases). The young typically fledge (leave the nest) after several weeks.
- **Global Distribution and Diversity:** With nearly 40 recognized species, falcons exhibit significant diversity in size, appearance, habitat preference, and hunting strategies across the globe.
- **Ecological Importance:** As predators, falcons play a vital role in regulating populations of their prey species, contributing to the balance of their ecosystems.
- **Conservation Status:** While some falcon species are thriving, others face threats such as habitat loss, pesticide contamination (historically, particularly DDT), and illegal trade. Conservation efforts are crucial for the long-term survival of vulnerable species.
- **Cultural Significance:** Falcons have held cultural significance throughout history, often symbolizing nobility, speed, and power. They have been used in falconry for centuries, demonstrating the close relationship between humans and these magnificent birds.

American Kestrel - *Falco sparverius*

The American Kestrel, North America's smallest falcon, exhibits a striking color pattern. Males showcase blue-gray wings, a rufous back, and a rufous tail with a black terminal band, accompanied by a pinkish-tan underside often with dark spotting. Females, conversely, display rufous wings, back, and tail, all marked with dark barring, and a cream-colored underside with dark streaks. Juveniles resemble females, gaining their adult plumage as they mature.

FEEDING These falcons are opportunistic hunters, primarily feeding on insects, small mammals, and birds, employing a "sit-and-wait" or hovering hunting strategy.

SOUNDS Their vocalizations include a rapid, high-pitched "klee-klee-klee" call.

HABITAT & RANGE They occupy a wide range of habitats, from open fields and grasslands to urban areas, across North America, extending into Central and South America.

MIGRATION While some populations are resident, others, particularly those in northern regions, migrate southward during winter.

SIMILAR SPECIES include other small falcons like the Merlin, but the Kestrel's smaller size, distinct plumage, and characteristic hovering behavior aid in identification.

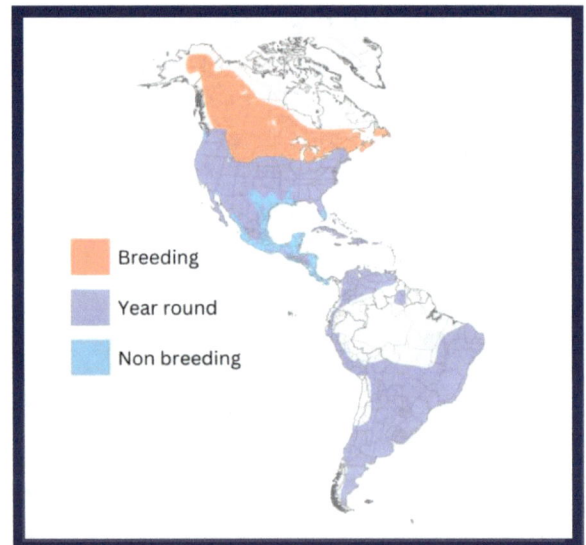

Male

Female

Juvenile

Breeding
Year round
Non breeding

Call

Juvenile Call

DID YOU KNOW....

It holds the title of the smallest falcon species found in North America. It is roughly the size of a Blue Jay or a Mourning Dove

They have two black spots on the back of their heads, known as ocelli ("little eyes" in Latin). The widely accepted theory is that these spots act as "false eyes," potentially deterring predators or aggressive songbirds from attacking them from behind.

They can see ultraviolet (UV) light. This ability is believed to aid them in hunting by making the urine trails of small mammals, like voles, more visible.

Crested Caracara - *Caracara plancus*

Crested Caracara is a striking raptor, a unique member of the falcon family, that exhibits a blend of hawk and vulture-like behaviors. Adults are easily recognized by their black cap, white neck and cheeks, and yellow-orange facial skin and legs. Juveniles, in contrast, display a browner plumage and lack the vibrant colors of adults. While males and females are generally similar in appearance, subtle size differences may exist.

FEEDING This opportunistic bird forages on the ground as readily as it does in the air, consuming a diverse diet of carrion, small mammals, reptiles, insects, and even birds.

SOUNDS Their vocalizations include harsh, cackling calls.

HABITAT & RANGE They inhabit open country, including grasslands, pastures, and deserts, primarily in the southern United States, particularly Texas and Florida, and extending southward through Central and South America.

MIGRATION They are mostly non-migratory, maintaining territories year-round.

SIMILAR SPECIES While related to falcons, their ground-foraging habits and scavenging behavior set them apart, though they may be confused with vultures or other raptors from a distance.

Adult

Adult

Juvenile

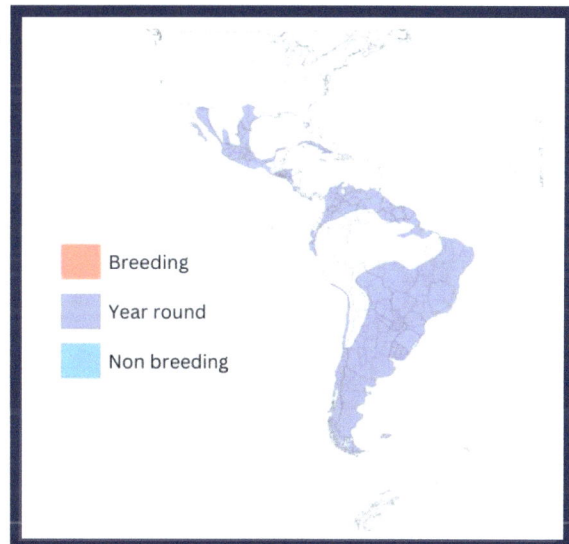

Breeding

Year round

Non breeding

Call 1

Call 2

DID YOU KNOW....

The bare skin on its face and throat can change from yellow-orange to reddish depending on its mood and social context.

Unlike most raptors that primarily hunt in the air, the Crested Caracara frequently walks or runs on the ground to find food.

They can live for a relatively long time for a bird of prey, with the oldest recorded individual living over 21 years in the wild.

Aplomado Falcon - *Falco femoralis*

Aplomado Falcon is a striking raptor characterized by its long, pointed wings and long tail, exhibiting a sleek and agile build. Adults display a distinctive plumage, with a dark gray back, a black and white facial pattern, a white chest, a black band across the mid-belly, and an orange lower belly. Females are typically larger than males. Juveniles resemble adults but show streaked underparts and a paler lower belly.

FEEDING These falcons are primarily aerial hunters, preying on small birds and large insects, and they also take lizards and small mammals.

NESTING They do not build their own nests, instead utilizing abandoned nests of other birds.

SOUNDS Their vocalizations include a series of rapid, high-pitched calls.

RANGE & MIGRATION Historically, their range in North America included the grasslands of the southwestern United States, but populations severely declined. Current populations in the U.S. are primarily the result of reintroduction efforts, concentrated in areas of southern Texas and New Mexico. Globally, their range extends through Central and South America. While they are generally considered resident birds, some localized movements may occur.

SIMILAR SPECIES include the American Kestrel and the Peregrine Falcon, but the Aplomado Falcon's unique color patterns and body structure distinguish it.

Adult
Adult
Juvenile

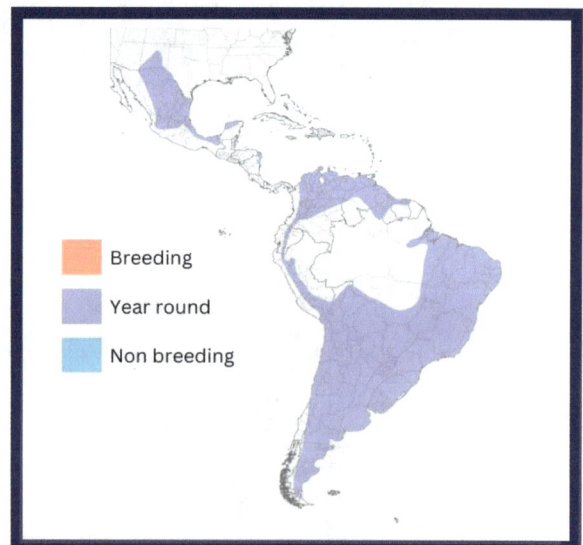

Breeding

Year round

Non breeding

Call 1

Call 2

DID YOU KNOW....

The name "Aplomado" comes from the Spanish word "aplomado," meaning "lead-colored," referring to the blue-gray plumage on its back and wings.

They often hunt in pairs or even family groups. One bird will flush out the prey while the other intercepts it, increasing their hunting success.

In Brazil, Aplomado Falcons have been observed following Maned Wolves and catching birds that the wolves flush from the vegetation.

Merlin - *Falco columbarius*

Merlin, a small and agile falcon, is found across North America, displaying distinct characteristics between sexes and age groups. Adult males are recognized by their bluish-gray backs and heavily streaked underparts, while females exhibit a darker brown coloration with similar streaking. Juveniles resemble adult females.

FEEDING They are primarily aerial predators, specializing in hunting small to medium-sized birds, with their diet also including insects and small mammals. Their flight is rapid and direct, enabling them to pursue prey with great efficiency.

SOUNDS Their vocalizations include a rapid series of "ki-ki-ki" notes, used particularly when alarmed.

HABITAT They occupy a wide range of habitats, from open woodlands and grasslands to coastal areas and increasingly, urban environments.

MIGRATION They exhibit migratory patterns, with populations breeding in northern regions moving south for the winter.

SIMILAR SPECIES, such as the American Kestrel, can be distinguished by differences in size, plumage, and facial markings.

Male

Female

Juvenile

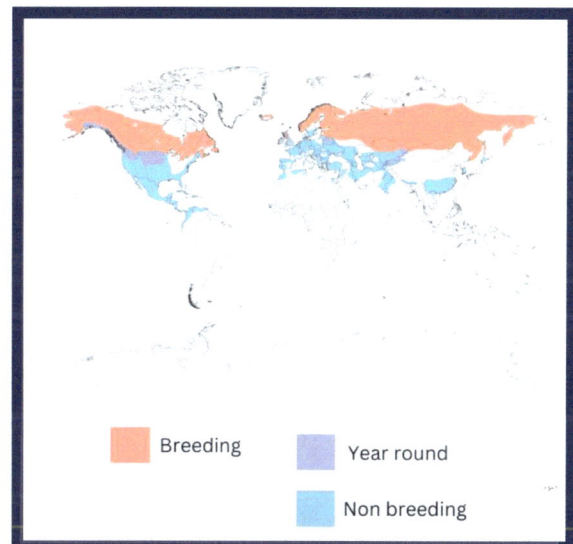

Breeding
Year round
Non breeding

Call 1

Call 2

DID YOU KNOW....

In medieval falconry, Merlins were specifically associated with ladies of the court. Noblewomen would fly them in pursuit of skylarks.

Despite being fierce predators, their flight pattern somewhat resembles that of a pigeon, which is why they were historically nicknamed "Pigeon Hawks." Their scientific name, columbarius, also refers to pigeons.

When there is a surplus of food, Merlins may cache (hide) prey at the nest or in nearby vegetation to eat later.

Peregrine Falcon - *Falco peregrinus*

Peregrine Falcon, a powerful and swift raptor, is characterized by its slate-blue to blackish back and wings, a pale underside with dark barring, and a distinctive dark "moustache" mark below its eyes. These birds are renowned for their incredible speed, particularly during their aerial dives, or "stoops," where they can reach speeds exceeding 200 mph. Females are noticeably larger than males, a common trait among raptors. Juveniles display a browner plumage with streaking rather than barring on their underparts.

FEEDING Peregrine Falcons are primarily aerial predators, specializing in hunting medium-sized birds, which they capture in mid-flight.

SOUNDS Their vocalizations are typically harsh, rapid "kak-kak-kak" calls, especially when defending their territory or during courtship.

HABITAT They have a wide distribution across North America, inhabiting a variety of environments, from urban areas with tall buildings to coastal cliffs and mountain ranges.

MIGRATION Some populations are migratory, moving south for the winter, while others are resident year-round.

SIMILAR SPECIES include other falcons, such as the Prairie Falcon and Merlin, but the Peregrine's size, dark moustache, and powerful build help distinguish it.

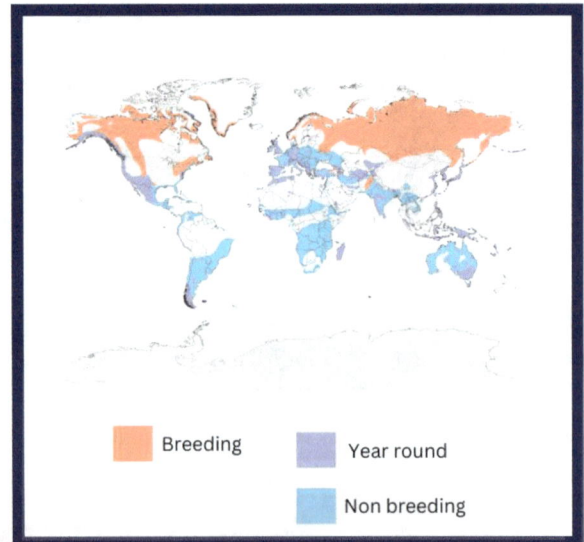

Adult

Adult

Adult

Juvenile

Breeding

Year round

Non breeding

Call 1

Call 2

DID YOU KNOW....

During their incredibly fast dives (stoops), Peregrine Falcons produce tears that are thicker than normal, almost like maple syrup. This helps prevent their eyes from drying out due to the high speeds and wind pressure.

When attacking larger prey, Peregrine Falcons often tuck their talons close and strike with a closed foot, essentially "punching" the prey out of the air with enough force to stun or kill it instantly.

They have one of the most widespread natural distributions of any bird species, found on every continent except Antarctica. This has earned them the nickname "wandering falcon."

Prairie Falcon - *Falco mexicanus*

Prairie Falcon is a medium-to-large falcon found in western North America, characterized by its pale brown upperparts and light underparts with dark streaks. Distinguishing features include a dark "moustache" stripe, a dark patch behind the eye, and dark markings in the "armpits" of their wings. Males are generally smaller than females, but their plumage is otherwise similar. Juveniles exhibit streaked underparts and a slightly different coloration compared to adults.

FEEDING These falcons are skilled predators, primarily feeding on small mammals, birds, and reptiles, which they capture through swift, powerful flight.

SOUNDS Their vocalizations consist of harsh, rapid "kree-kree-kree" calls, particularly around the nest.

HABITAT They inhabit open, arid environments, including grasslands, deserts, and rocky areas.

RANGE & MIGRATION Their range extends from southern Canada to northern Mexico. While some populations may exhibit short-distance movements, they are largely non-migratory.

SIMILAR SPECIES When identifying this bird, similar species such as the Peregrine Falcon and Merlin should be considered, but the Prairie Falcon's distinct markings and habitat preferences help distinguish it.

Adult
Adult
Juvenile

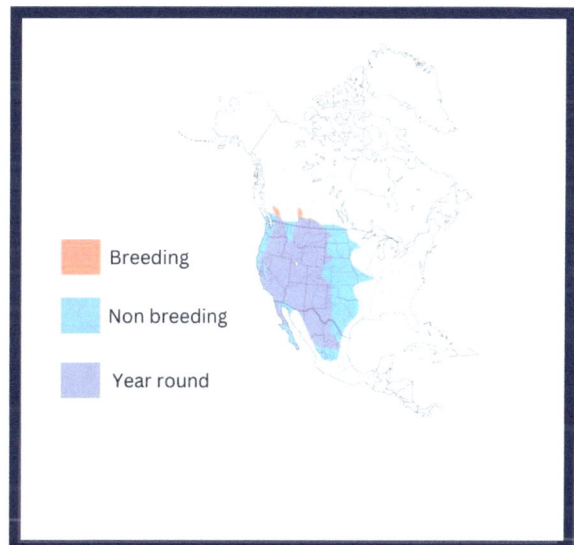

Breeding

Non breeding

Year round

Call 1

Call 2

DID YOU KNOW....

Unlike the Peregrine Falcon, which is famous for its high-altitude dives, the Prairie Falcon often hunts with rapid, maneuverable flight close to the ground, surprising prey by using terrain to stay hidden.

During their powerful strikes, Prairie Falcons have been known to hit prey with such force that they can literally separate the head from the body.

They are highly regarded and frequently used in the sport of falconry.

Gyrfalcon - *Falco rusticolus*

The Gyrfalcon, the largest falcon in the world, is a powerful bird of prey inhabiting Arctic regions of North America. These falcons exhibit a range of color morphs, from nearly pure white to dark gray, with females being notably larger than males. They possess the characteristic falcon shape, with long, pointed wings and a long tail. Juveniles display a streaked plumage.

FEEDING, they are primarily predators of birds, especially ptarmigan, but they also hunt waterfowl and small mammals. Their hunting strategy involves both aerial pursuits and surprise attacks from perches.

SOUNDS While typically silent outside of the breeding season, they produce harsh "kak-kak-kak" calls and other vocalizations near their nests, which they defend aggressively.

RANGE & MIGRATION Their range primarily encompasses the Arctic tundra, with occasional winter movements southward into northern parts of the United States and southern Canada. They may move southward in the winter months, but are primarily a non-migratory bird.

NESTING They utilize cliff faces for nesting, often using old nests from other birds.

SIMILAR SPECIES Distinguishing them from similar species, such as Peregrine Falcons, requires careful observation of their larger size, bulkier build, and broader, less sharply pointed wings.

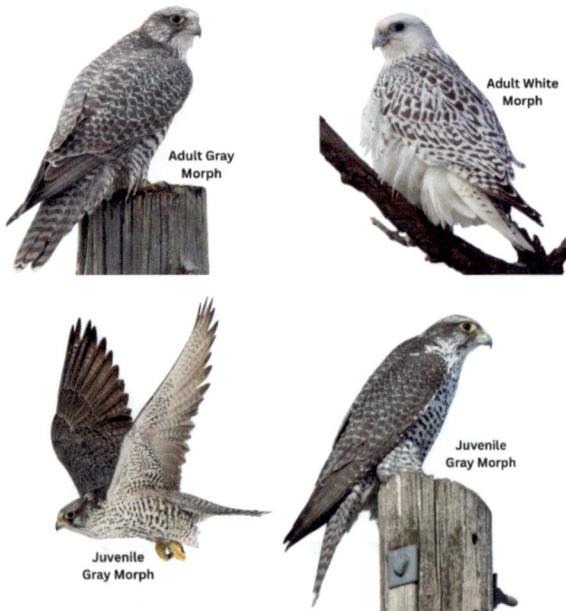

Adult Gray Morph

Adult White Morph

Juvenile Gray Morph

Juvenile Gray Morph

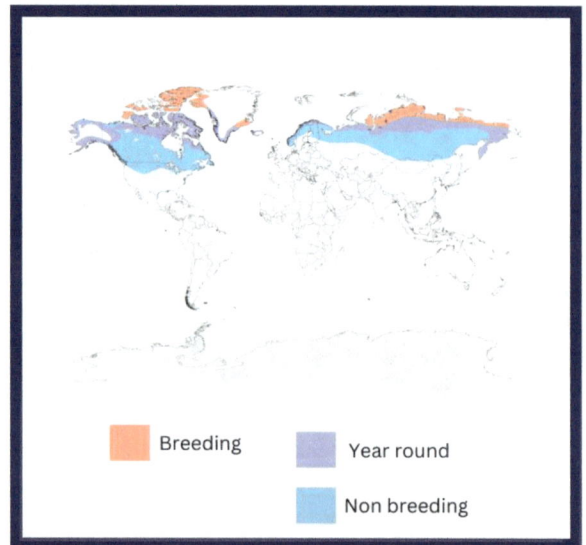

Breeding

Year round

Non breeding

Call 1

Call 2

DID YOU KNOW....

It holds the title of the world's largest falcon species. Females are notably larger than males, sometimes weighing almost twice as much.

Historically, in the Middle Ages, Gyrfalcons were so highly prized that only royalty was permitted to hunt with them. Even today, the white morph is sometimes referred to as the "bird of kings".

It is typically the earliest nesting raptor in the Arctic, sometimes beginning nest defense as early as late January.

HAWKS AND EAGLES

Hawks and eagles are both birds of prey (raptors) belonging to the family *Accipitridae*. They share several general characteristics but also have key differences.

General Characteristics:

- **Carnivorous:** Both hawks and eagles are primarily meat-eaters.
- **Sharp Talons:** They possess strong feet with sharp, curved claws (talons) used for grasping and killing prey.
- **Hooked Beaks:** Their beaks are strong and sharply hooked, ideal for tearing flesh.
- **Excellent Eyesight:** Both groups have exceptional vision, crucial for spotting prey from great distances. Their visual acuity is far superior to that of humans.
- **Powerful Flight:** They are strong fliers, capable of soaring, gliding, and rapid pursuit of prey.
- **Nest Building:** They build nests, often called eyries, typically in high places like tall trees or cliffs.
- **Sexual Dimorphism:** In most species, the females are larger than the males.

Key Points:

Eagles:

- **Size:** Generally larger and heavier than hawks, with greater wingspans. Some are among the largest flying birds.
- **Build:** Typically have a more robust and powerful build.
- **Flight:** Often soar for extended periods with minimal flapping, utilizing their broad wings to ride air currents. Some species can dive at very high speeds.
- **Prey:** Tend to hunt larger prey, including mammals, large birds, fish, and sometimes even deer or other ungulates. Some species also scavenge.
- **Talons:** Possess very strong talons with a powerful grip.
- **Head and Beak:** Often have larger heads with a more pronounced and heavier hooked beak.
- **Habitat:** While varied, many eagle species are found in open areas, near water sources, or in mountainous regions that can support larger prey.
- **Vocalization:** Often have high-pitched whistling or chirping calls.
- **Nests:** Build very large and sturdy nests that they may use and add to for many years.

Hawks:

- **Size:** Generally smaller and lighter than eagles, with a wider range of sizes among different species.
- **Build:** Can range from slender and agile to more stout, depending on their hunting style.
- **Flight:** Often involve more flapping flight, especially the accipiters (like sharp-shinned and Cooper's hawks) which are agile fliers in wooded areas. Buteos (like red-tailed hawks) soar more but typically at lower altitudes than eagles.
- **Prey:** Primarily hunt smaller prey such as rodents, small birds, reptiles, and insects.
- **Talons:** Strong, but generally less massive than those of eagles, suited for their smaller prey.
- **Head and Beak:** Tend to have more delicate heads and neater, though still hooked, beaks compared to eagles.
- **Habitat:** Found in a wider variety of habitats, including forests, fields, grasslands, and even urban areas, reflecting the diversity of their prey.
- **Vocalization:** Often have hoarse, piercing screams or calls.
- **Nests:** Build nests that vary in size but are generally smaller than eagle nests and may be built annually or seasonally.

Distinguishing between Hawks and Eagles:

While size is a primary indicator, other factors like wing shape, flight patterns, habitat, and prey can help differentiate between them, especially when size comparison is difficult in flight. Eagles often have broader, longer wings suited for soaring, while hawks can have more rounded or pointed wings depending on their flight style.

Red-tailed Hawk - *Buteo jamaicensis*

Red-tailed Hawk is a large, robust bird of prey with a broad wingspan, widely distributed across North America. Adults are typically recognized by their reddish-brown tail, though this feature is absent in juveniles, which display brown-barred tails. Plumage varies considerably, with light and dark morphs existing. Generally, they exhibit a dark brown back and a lighter underside with a streaked belly band. Females are typically larger than males. Juveniles resemble adults but have brown banded tails.

FEEDING These hawks are opportunistic predators, primarily feeding on small mammals, but also taking birds, reptiles, and amphibians.

SOUNDS Their characteristic call is a raspy, descending scream, often used in film and television to represent the sound of other raptors.

HABITAT They inhabit diverse environments, from open fields and grasslands to woodlands and urban areas.
MIGRATION While some northern populations migrate south during winter, many Red-tailed Hawks are year-round residents within their range.

SIMILAR SPECIES include other Buteo hawks, such as the Swainson's Hawk and the Ferruginous Hawk, but the Red-tailed Hawk's variable plumage and vocalizations aid in identification.

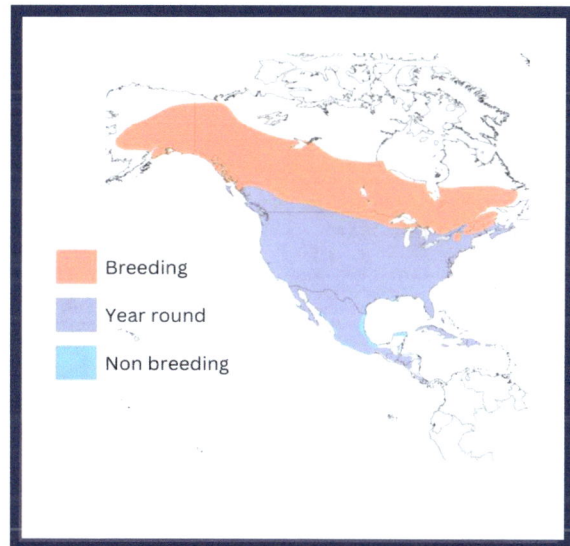

Adult Dark Morph

Adult Light Morph

Juvenile Light Morph

Juvenile Dark Morph

- Breeding
- Year round
- Non breeding

Adult Call

Juvenile Call

DID YOU KNOW....

Historically, they were sometimes called "chickenhawks," but this is misleading as they rarely prey on birds as large as adult chickens.

They have a clear inner eyelid called a nictitating membrane that cleans and protects their eyes, especially while they are grappling with struggling prey.

Due to their intelligence and relatively sociable nature, Red-tailed Hawks are a popular choice for falconry, though they are typically used for hunting terrestrial game like rabbits rather than fast-flying birds.

Common Black Hawk - Buteogallus anthracinus

Common Black Hawk is a medium-sized raptor characterized by its predominantly dark plumage, broad wings, and a short tail with a distinctive white band. Adult birds display a sleek, black coloration with yellow legs and a yellow base to their black bill. While males and females share similar plumage, females tend to be slightly larger. Juvenile Common Black Hawks exhibit a streaked brown appearance, differing significantly from the solid black of adults.

FEEDING These hawks are typically found near water sources, where they primarily feed on aquatic prey such as crabs, crayfish, fish, and frogs. They will also consume other small vertebrates, and insects.

SOUNDS Their vocalizations include a series of piping whistles.

RANGE Their range extends from the southwestern United States through Central America and into parts of South America.

HABITAT They prefer riparian habitats.

MIGRATION May vary, with some populations, particularly those in the northernmost parts of their range, exhibiting migratory behavior.

SIMILAR SPECIES to consider for identification include the Zone-tailed Hawk, and the Great Black Hawk, though careful observation of plumage and habitat can typically distinguish them.

Adult

Adult

Juvenile

Juvenile

Breeding

Year round

Non breeding

Call 1

Call 2

DID YOU KNOW....

Unlike many hawks that hunt solely from perches or while soaring, Common Black Hawks are known to wade in shallow water, sometimes fluttering their wings to startle fish and other aquatic prey, then herding them into shallower areas for easier capture

There has been documented natural hybridization between a Common Black Hawk and a Red-shouldered Hawk (Buteo lineatus) in California. Hybridization between different genera of hawks is considered rare.

They are known to abandon nesting sites if there is too much human disturbance or if the surrounding riparian habitat is altered or developed.

Broad-winged Hawk - *Buteo platypterus*

Broad-winged Hawk is a compact, medium-sized raptor inhabiting forested regions of North America. Adults exhibit a dark brown back, a reddish-brown head and chest, and barred underparts, with a distinctive dark tail featuring a broad white band. While males and females share similar plumage, slight size differences may occur. Juveniles display a lighter brown coloration with coarse streaking on the underparts and a tail with numerous narrow bands.

FEEDING These hawks are opportunistic predators, feeding on a varied diet of small mammals, amphibians, reptiles, insects, and occasional birds, hunting primarily from perches.

SOUNDS Their characteristic vocalization is a high-pitched, piercing whistle.

MIGRATION They breed in deciduous and mixed forests across eastern North America, undertaking a long migration to Central and South America for the winter, often forming large flocks known as "kettles" during their southward journey.

SIMILAR SPECIES include other Buteo hawks, such as the Red-shouldered Hawk, but the Broad-winged Hawk's smaller size, distinct tail pattern, and habitat preferences aid in identification.

Adult Dark Morph

Adult Light Morph

Juvenile Light Morph

Juvenile Dark Morph

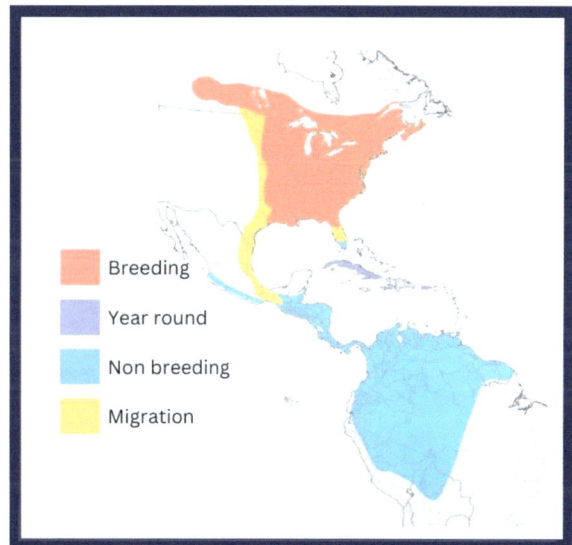

Breeding

Year round

Non breeding

Migration

Call

DID YOU KNOW....

Unlike most North American raptors, Broad-winged Hawks are highly gregarious during migration. They gather in massive flocks, sometimes numbering in the thousands, called "kettles." These flocks soar together on thermal air currents, creating a spectacular swirling vortex in the sky.

They are among the first North American raptors to begin their southward migration, often leaving their breeding grounds as early as August.

They engage in impressive aerial courtship rituals involving high-soaring, cartwheels, and dives to attract a mate. Pairs may even lock talons in mid-air and spiral downwards.

Ferruginous Hawk - *Buteo regalis*

Ferruginous Hawk, a large raptor endemic to North America's open country, exhibits a robust build with broad, long wings and a fan-shaped tail. This hawk displays two color phases: a more common pale phase with rusty orange markings and a white underbelly, and a less frequent dark phase with predominantly dark brown plumage. While there are size differences, distinguishing between males and females by sight alone can be difficult. Juveniles typically have less intense coloring than adults.

FEEDING These hawks are specialized predators, primarily targeting small mammals like ground squirrels and jackrabbits, employing "sit-and-wait" or soaring hunting techniques.

SOUNDS Their vocalizations are typically harsh, high-pitched screams or calls.

HABITAT They inhabit grasslands, shrublands, and deserts across western North America.

RANGE & MIGRATION Breeding range extend from southern Canada to the southwestern United States, and winter range reach into northern Mexico. Migration varies, with some populations moving seasonally while others remain relatively sedentary.

SIMILAR SPECIES include other Buteo hawks, particularly the Red-tailed Hawk and the Rough-legged Hawk, but the Ferruginous Hawk's large size and distinctive leg feathering help with identification.

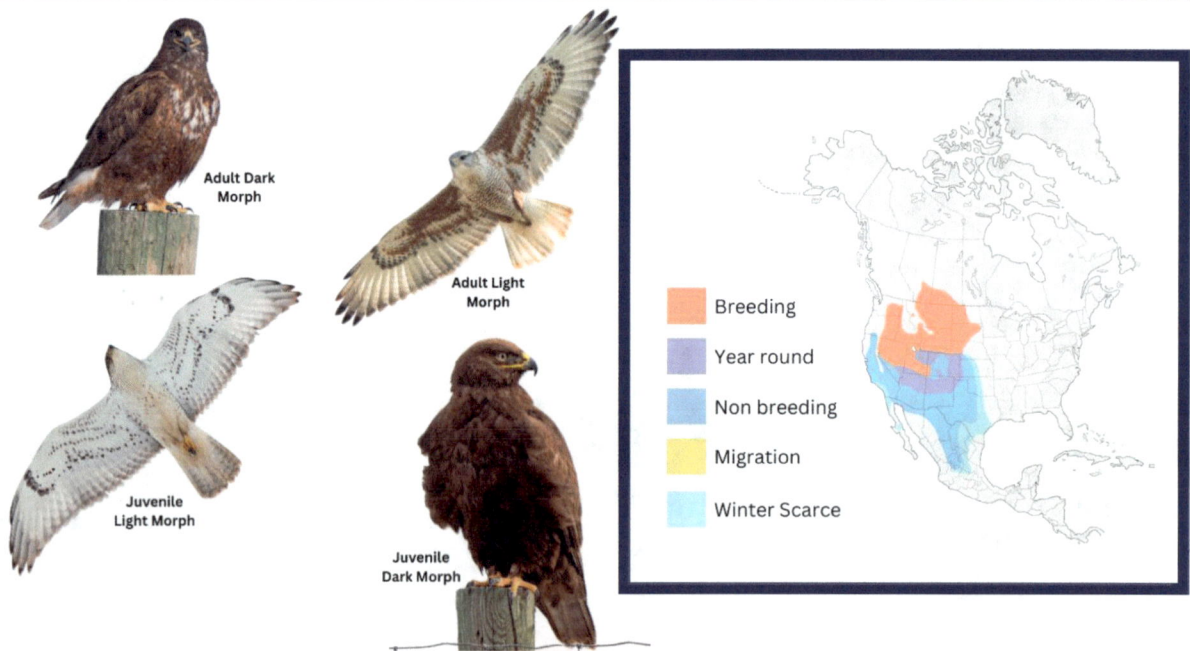

Adult Dark Morph

Adult Light Morph

Juvenile Light Morph

Juvenile Dark Morph

- Breeding
- Year round
- Non breeding
- Migration
- Winter Scarce

Call 1

Call 2

DID YOU KNOW....

The Ferruginous Hawk is the largest hawk in the Buteo genus found in North America, even bigger than the well-known Red-tailed Hawk. Its substantial size can sometimes lead to it being mistaken for an eagle.

Along with the Rough-legged Hawk and the Golden Eagle, the Ferruginous Hawk is one of the only North American raptors to have feathers covering its legs all the way down to its toes. This "booted" appearance is a distinctive feature.

The name "ferruginous" comes from the Latin word "ferrugo," meaning rust. This refers to the rusty or reddish-brown coloration seen on the back and legs of the more common light-morph individuals.

Gray Hawk - *Buteo plagiatus*

Gray Hawk, is a medium-sized raptor characterized by its pale gray plumage. Adult Gray Hawks exhibit a solid, unpatterned gray on their upper parts, with a lighter gray and white underside, and a distinctive black tail marked with three white bands. Males and females share similar plumage, though females are typically larger. Juveniles display a contrasting appearance with dark brown upperparts, a pale-banded brown tail, and brown-spotted white underparts, along with a brown-streaked buff head and neck.

FEEDING These hawks primarily feed on lizards and snakes, but also consume small mammals, birds, and frogs, often hunting from a perch or during a low glide.

SOUNDS Their vocalizations include a shrill, whistled "kleee-ooo" call.

HABITAT They inhabit open woodlands and forest edges.

RANGE & MIGRATION They range from the southwestern United States through Mexico and into Central America. They are generally non-migratory within their core range.

SIMILAR SPECIES Distinguishing Gray Hawks from similar species, like juvenile Broad-winged or Red-shouldered Hawks, involves observing their bolder facial patterns, paler underwings, and the unique white patch at the base of their uppertail.

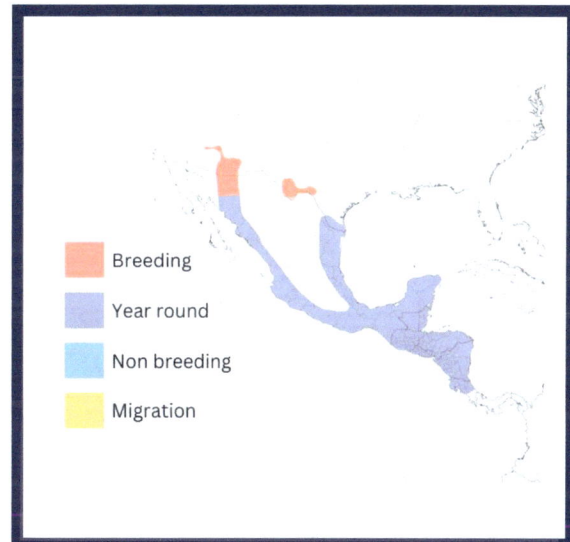

Adult

Adult

Juvenile

Juvenile

Breeding

Year round

Non breeding

Migration

Adult Call

Juvenile Call

DID YOU KNOW....

While most Buteo hawks are found in temperate regions, the Gray Hawk is primarily a tropical species. Its breeding range just barely extends into the southern parts of Arizona, Texas, and occasionally New Mexico in the United States.

Its previous common name was the "Mexican Goshawk" due to its more slender body, relatively long tail, and agile flight, which are reminiscent of true goshawks (genus Accipiter). However, genetically, it is more closely related to other Buteo hawks.

They are adept at snatching lizards from the ground or even plucking them off tree trunks in flight.

Northern Harrier - *Circus hudsonius*

The Northern Harrier is a slender, medium-sized raptor easily identified by its distinctive white rump patch and owl-like facial disc, which aids in its keen hearing. Adult males are a striking pale gray above and white below with black wingtips, while adult females are larger and exhibit brown plumage with buffy underparts and brown streaking. Juveniles resemble females but have a more cinnamon-colored underside.

FEEDING These hawks are known for their low, gliding flight over open fields and marshes as they hunt for prey, which primarily consists of small mammals, particularly voles, but also includes birds, reptiles, and insects.

SOUNDS Their vocalizations are relatively infrequent, but they may produce a series of "ke-ke-ke" calls when alarmed.

RANGE & MIGRATION They have a wide range across North America, breeding in northern regions and migrating to southern areas for the winter, though some remain resident year-round.

HABITAT They favor open habitats like grasslands, marshes, and agricultural fields.

SIMILAR SPECIES might include other hawks, but the harrier's unique flight style, white rump, and facial disc provide clear distinguishing features.

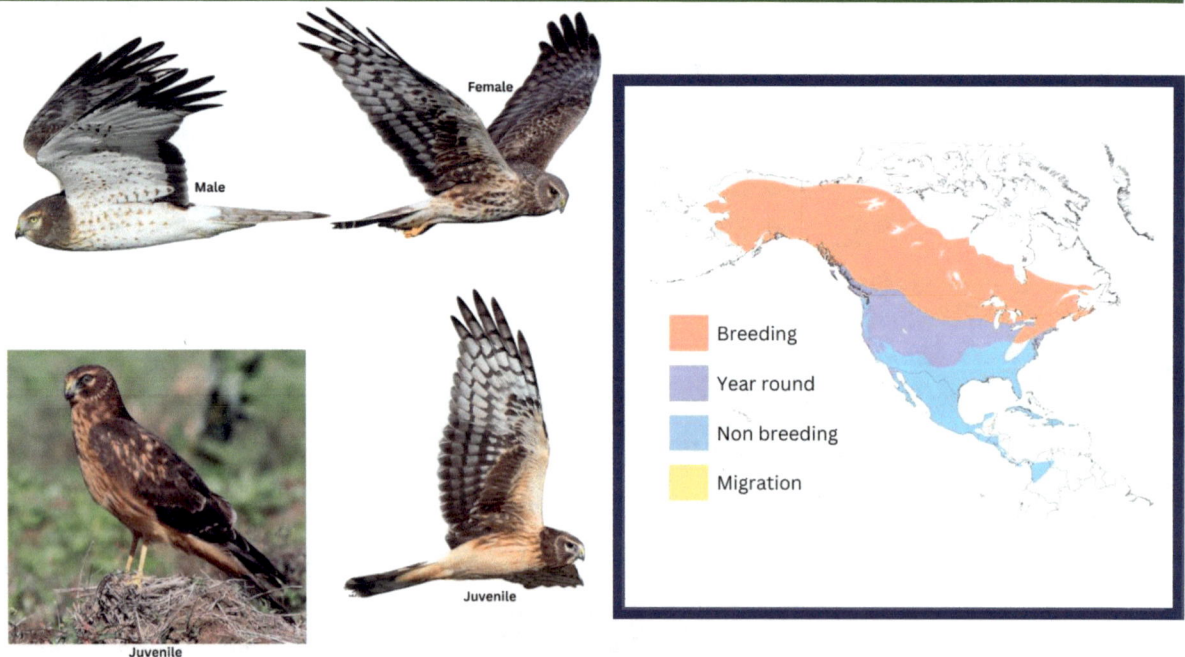

Male

Female

Juvenile

Breeding

Year round

Non breeding

Migration

Juvenile

Male Call

Female Call

DID YOU KNOW....

They possess a facial disc of feathers similar to owls, which helps them to funnel sound to their ears. This adaptation allows them to hunt effectively by sound, locating prey hidden in dense vegetation.

While they primarily hunt small mammals and birds, Northern Harriers have been observed subduing larger prey, such as rabbits and ducks, by drowning them in water.

The name "harrier" comes from an older word, "harrower," meaning "something that pursues and destroys," reflecting their hunting style.

Red-shouldered Hawk - *Buteo lineatus*

Red-shouldered Hawk is a medium-sized raptor, a Buteo, characterized by its slender build and relatively long tail. Adult Red-shouldered Hawks display a striking plumage with reddish-brown barring on their underparts, dark and white checkered wings, and the namesake reddish "shoulders." Males and females exhibit similar plumage, though females tend to be slightly larger. Juveniles are primarily brown above with pale underparts streaked with brown.

FEEDING These hawks are adapted to forested environments, where they hunt a variety of prey, including small mammals, amphibians, reptiles, and occasionally birds. Their primary hunting strategy involves perching and watching for prey, or soaring over their territory.

SOUNDS The Red-shouldered Hawk's vocalizations are distinctive, most notably a loud, clear "kee-aah" scream.

HABITAT They inhabit deciduous and mixed forests across eastern North America and along the Pacific coast in California.

MIGRATION While some northern populations may migrate, many Red-shouldered Hawks are resident within their territories year-round.

SIMILAR SPECIES include the Red-tailed Hawk and Broad-winged Hawk, but the Red-shouldered Hawk's distinct plumage and habitat preferences aid in identification.

Adult

Adult

Juvenile

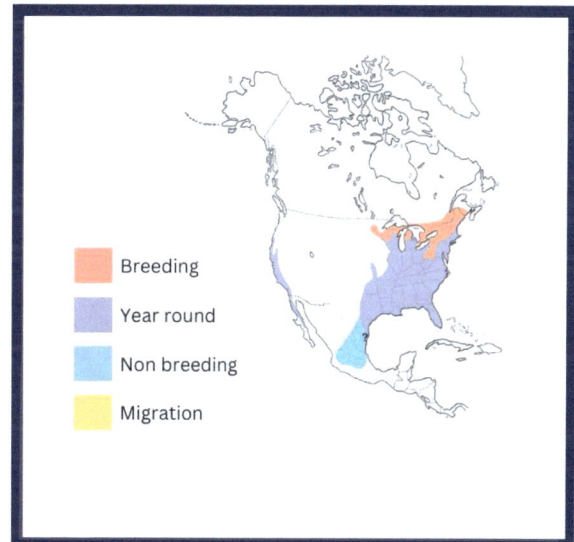

Breeding

Year round

Non breeding

Migration

Call 1

Call 2

DID YOU KNOW....

Their courtship involves impressive aerial displays. Pairs will fly together, sometimes even rolling over on their backs and briefly flying upside down.

They have been observed working together with crows, which are often considered enemies, to chase away larger predators like Great Horned Owls and Red-tailed Hawks that might prey on their eggs or young.

In the southern parts of their range, particularly in Florida, Red-shouldered Hawks can begin nesting as early as January.

Rough-legged Hawk - *Buteo lagopus*

The Rough-legged Hawk, a medium-large raptor, is distinguished by its feathered legs, a crucial adaptation for its Arctic habitat. These hawks exhibit varied plumage, with both light and dark morphs, and are recognizable by their dark carpal patches and a dark band on their white tail. Females tend to be larger and have browner plumage with more prominent belly markings. Juveniles display less distinct plumage patterns.

FEEDING These hawks primarily feed on small rodents, particularly voles and lemmings, and are known for their ability to hover while hunting.

SOUNDS Their vocalizations are relatively infrequent, consisting of whistles and calls, especially during breeding season.

RANGE & MIGRATION They breed in the Arctic tundra of North America and Eurasia, migrating southward to southern Canada and the northern United States during winter.

HABITAT They favor open country, such as grasslands and agricultural fields, during their non-breeding season.

SIMILAR SPECIES include other Buteo hawks, but the Rough-legged Hawk's feathered legs and hovering behavior are key identifying features.

Adult Male Light Morph

Adult Female Light Morph

Juvenile Light Morph

Juvenile Dark Morph

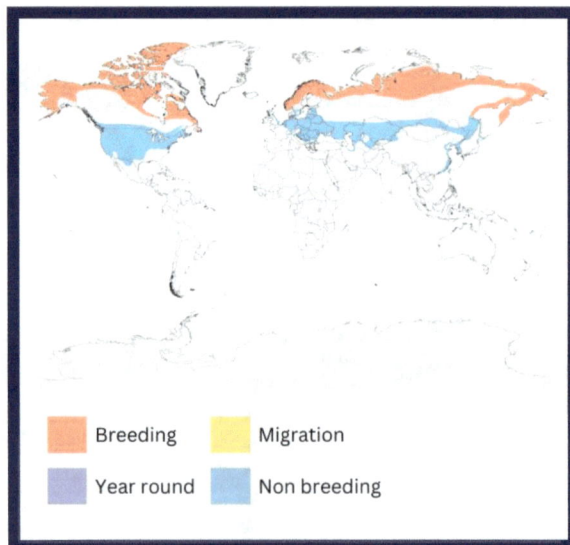

Breeding Migration

Year round Non breeding

Call

DID YOU KNOW....

As their name suggests, Rough-legged Hawks are one of the few North American raptors (along with the Ferruginous Hawk and Golden Eagle) to have feathers extending all the way down their legs to their toes.

They are known to steal prey from other birds, including Northern Harriers, Red-tailed Hawks, American Kestrels, and even other Rough-legged Hawks

They are strictly Arctic and subarctic breeders, nesting primarily on cliffs, rocky outcrops, or riverbanks in the tundra and taiga regions of North America and Eurasia.

Sharp-shinned Hawk - *Accipiter striatus*

Sharp-shinned Hawk is North America's smallest accipiter, characterized by its slender build, short, rounded wings, and a long, square-tipped tail. Adult Sharp-shinned Hawks display a bluish-gray upper plumage, with underparts exhibiting narrow, reddish-orange horizontal barring. Males are notably smaller than females, with a more intense reddish-orange barring. Juvenile birds are brown above and streaked with brown on their white underparts.

FEEDING These hawks are specialized predators of small birds, which they capture with swift, agile flights through dense woodland.

SOUNDS Their vocalizations are typically a series of rapid, high-pitched "kik-kik-kik" calls, especially when alarmed.

HABITAT & RANGE They inhabit forested regions across North America, with a broad range that extends from Canada to Central America.

MIGRATION Many populations undertake migrations, moving southward during the winter.

SIMILAR SPECIES Distinguishing them from similar species, particularly the Cooper's Hawk, requires careful observation of size, head shape, and tail characteristics.

Adult

Adult

Juvenile

Juvenile

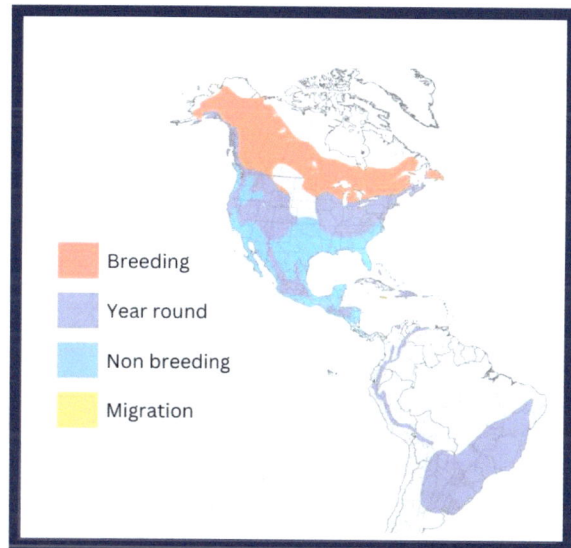

Breeding

Year round

Non breeding

Migration

Call 1

Call 2

DID YOU KNOW....

Unlike some other raptors that soar high and dive, Sharp-shinned Hawks are ambush predators. They often hunt by stealthily flying low through dense vegetation, using natural cover to get close to their prey before bursting out in a sudden, swift attack. This "dash-and-grab" style is highly characteristic

Their relatively short, rounded wings and long tail give them exceptional maneuverability in the air. They can twist and turn with incredible speed and precision as they pursue their prey through dense forests and thickets. This agility is crucial for catching fast-flying songbirds

Short-tailed Hawk - *Buteo brachyurus*

Short-tailed Hawk is a relatively small buteo characterized by two distinct color morphs: a dark morph, which is more prevalent in Florida, and a light morph. Both morphs have dark upperparts, but the light morph displays clean white underparts, while the dark morph is predominantly dark with white barring on the flight feathers. Juveniles exhibit streaked or spotted underparts.

FEEDING This hawk primarily preys on birds, capturing them through spectacular aerial dives.

SOUNDS Its vocalizations are not frequently heard, but they include a high-pitched squeal.

RANGE The Short-tailed Hawk's range in North America is limited, primarily found in Florida, with very small populations in southern Arizona, and they are also found through central and South America.

MIGRATION They are not known to have large migration patterns, but in Florida they may have some regional movement.

HABITAT They favor habitats such as cypress swamps, forests near open areas, and mangrove forests.

SIMILAR SPECIES include the Broad-winged Hawk, but the Short-tailed Hawk's behavior, such as its frequent high soaring and kiting, and plumage differences aid in distinguishing it.

Adult Light Morph

Adult Dark Morph

Adult Dark Morph

Juvenile Dark Morph

Breeding

Year round

Non breeding

Migration

Call

DID YOU KNOW....

Unlike many hawks that hunt from a perch, Short-tailed Hawks frequently employ a hunting technique called "kiting" or "aerial still-hunting." They face into the wind with wings spread, using updrafts to hover almost motionlessly at great heights (often between 75-250 meters), patiently scanning for prey below.

Despite their specialized hunting techniques, studies suggest a relatively low hunting success rate, with only around 11% of observed stoops resulting in a successful capture.

Unlike many Buteo hawks that are often seen perched in the open, Short-tailed Hawks are rarely observed perching. They spend the majority of their day soaring and hunting.

Swainson's Hawk - *Buteo swainsoni*

Swainson's Hawks are medium-sized raptors characterized by their long, pointed wings and relatively long, narrow tails, making them adept at soaring and migration. They exhibit a wide range of plumage variations, or morphs, from light to dark. Males and females are generally similar in appearance, though females are typically slightly larger. Juveniles display a streaked breast and a lighter overall coloration compared to adults. The species is known for its distinct light and dark morphs, with light morphs presenting a pale underside and dark bib, while dark morphs can be almost entirely black.

FEEDING They are opportunistic feeders, primarily consuming insects, especially grasshoppers during the breeding season. They also prey on small mammals, reptiles, and birds.

SOUNDS Their vocalizations are typically a series of high-pitched whistles or screams.

RANGE & MIGRATION They breed across western North America, from southern Canada to the southwestern United States, and undertake one of the longest migrations of any North American raptor, wintering in South America, particularly in the grasslands of Argentina.

SIMILAR SPECIES include other *Buteo* hawks, such as Red-tailed Hawks and Ferruginous Hawks, but Swainson's Hawks are distinguished by their longer, more pointed wings, narrower tails, and their unique migration patterns.

Adult Light Morph

Adult Dark Morph

Juvenile Light Morph

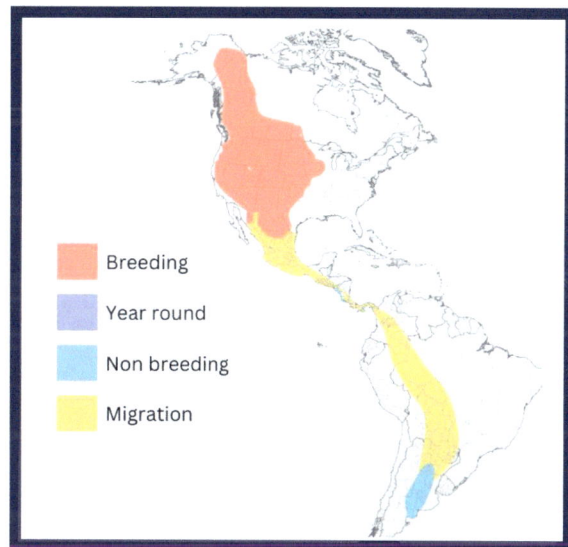

Breeding

Year round

Non breeding

Migration

Call

DID YOU KNOW....

They undertake one of the longest migrations of any North American raptor, traveling up to 12,000 miles roundtrip from their breeding grounds in North America to their wintering grounds in Argentina

Unlike most raptors that primarily eat vertebrates, during their migration and in their South American wintering grounds, Swainson's Hawks switch to a diet consisting almost entirely of insects, especially grasshoppers and dragonflies, earning them the nickname "grasshopper hawk" or "locust hawk."

Unlike some other raptors that follow coastlines or mountain ridges during migration, Swainson's Hawks primarily follow an inland route between continents.

White-tailed Hawk - *Geranoaetus albicaudatus*

White-tailed Hawk is a large raptor characterized by its broad wings and, as its name suggests, a prominent white tail, often featuring a thin black subterminal band. Adults display a light gray to white plumage on their underparts, with darker gray backs and wings. Males and females are generally similar in appearance, though females tend to be slightly larger. Juveniles exhibit a mottled brown and white plumage, transitioning to adult coloration over several years. This hawk exhibits two primary color morphs: a light morph, which is most common, and a dark morph, which is much rarer and displays a sooty brown overall plumage.

FEEDING They are primarily predators of rodents, rabbits, and other small mammals, but also take birds, reptiles, and insects.

SOUNDS Their vocalizations are typically a series of high-pitched whistles or screams.

RANGE This hawk's range extends from the southern United States, specifically Texas and parts of the Gulf Coast, southward through Central and South America.

MIGRATION While generally non-migratory, some individuals may undertake local movements in response to food availability.

SIMILAR SPECIES include other large hawks, such as the Red-tailed Hawk or Swainson's Hawk, but the White-tailed Hawk's distinctive white tail and overall plumage, especially in the light morph, help distinguish it.

Adult Light Morph

Adult Dark Morph

Juvenile Dark Morph

Juvenile Light Morph

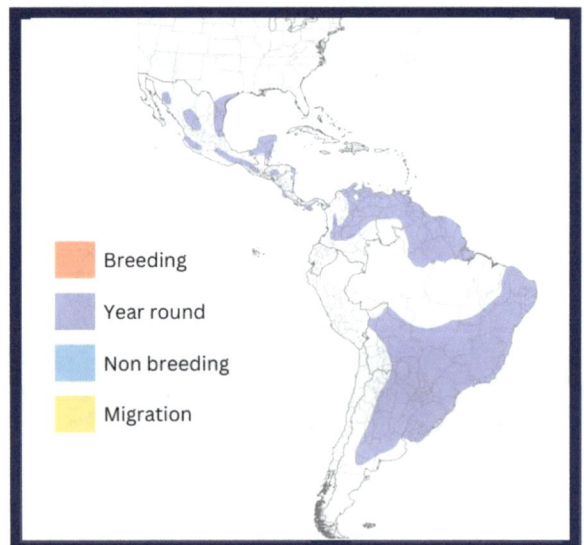

Breeding

Year round

Non breeding

Migration

Adult Call

Juvenile Call

DID YOU KNOW....

This hawk is frequently observed "kiting," which means it hovers almost motionlessly in the air against the wind for extended periods while hunting. This behavior is particularly suited to its open grassland and savanna habitats.

Unlike many raptors, White-tailed Hawks often incorporate an especially long stick into their nest structure for no apparent functional purpose.

During courtship, both the male and female may land on the ground, and the male will engage in a peculiar behavior of tugging at grass blades and weeds.

Zone-tailed Hawk - *Buteo albonotatus*

The Zone-tailed Hawk, a medium-sized raptor, is known for its remarkable mimicry of Turkey Vultures in flight, often soaring with wings held in a shallow "V" shape and rocking from side to side. This behavior likely aids in its hunting strategy. Adults display dark plumage with a single white band on the tail, hence the name. Males and females are virtually indistinguishable in plumage, though females tend to be slightly larger. Juveniles are similar to adults but have more pale mottling on their underparts and multiple pale bands on the tail, which diminish with age.

FEEDING They are primarily predators of birds, small mammals, and reptiles, often ambushing their prey from soaring flight.

SOUNDS Their vocalizations are typically quiet, consisting of high-pitched whistles and calls, rarely heard.

HABITAT They inhabit arid woodlands, canyons, and riparian areas in the southwestern United States, Mexico, and Central and South America.

MIGRATION Their migration patterns are complex; some populations are resident, while others, particularly those in the northern portions of their range, migrate south for the winter.

SIMILAR SPECIES include Turkey Vultures, which they closely resemble in flight, and other dark-plumaged hawks, but the Zone-tailed Hawk's distinctive tail band and flight style help in identification.

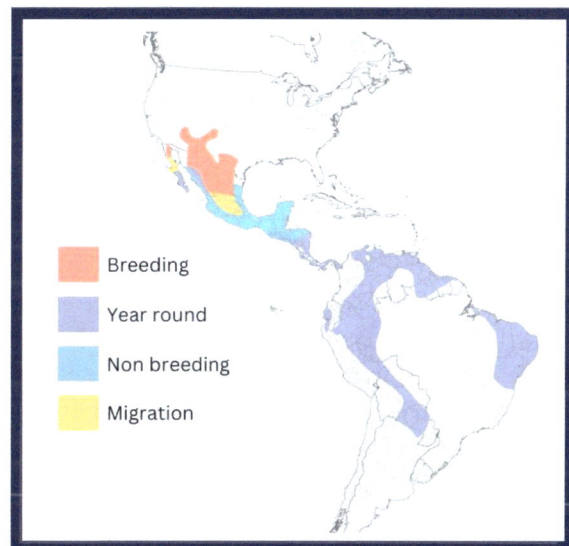

- Breeding
- Year round
- Non breeding
- Migration

Call

DID YOU KNOW....

The Zone-tailed Hawk exhibits remarkable mimicry of the Turkey Vulture in flight. It soars with its wings held in a slight dihedral (V-shape) and rocks from side to side, just like a vulture.

This hawk is an opportunistic feeder and will take advantage of various hunting strategies. Besides the "vulture mimicry" low-altitude surprise attacks, they also hunt from perches and sometimes chase and capture flying birds.

Unusually for a hawk, the Zone-tailed Hawk is one of the few that frequently stalks other birds as prey.

OWLS

Owls are fascinating nocturnal birds of prey belonging to the order Strigiformes. They are found on every continent except Antarctica and exhibit a remarkable diversity in size, habitat, and hunting strategies.

General Characteristics:

- **Nocturnal Predators:** Most owl species are primarily active at night, possessing exceptional adaptations for hunting in low-light conditions.
- **Sharp Talons and Powerful Feet:** Their strong feet are equipped with sharp, curved talons used for grasping and killing prey.
- **Hooked Beaks:** Owls have strong, hooked beaks ideal for tearing flesh.
- **Forward-Facing Eyes:** Unlike most birds, owls have large, forward-facing eyes that provide excellent binocular vision, crucial for judging distances accurately when hunting. This fixed eye position necessitates their remarkable neck mobility.
- **Exceptional Hearing:** Owls possess highly developed hearing, often with asymmetrical ear placement. This allows them to pinpoint the location of prey with incredible accuracy, even in complete darkness. Some species have facial discs that help funnel sound towards their ears.
- **Silent Flight:** Many owl species have specialized feather structures with soft fringes that disrupt airflow, allowing for virtually silent flight. This stealth is essential for ambushing prey.
- **Wide Range of Sizes:** Owls vary dramatically in size, from the tiny Elf Owl (around 5 inches tall) to the massive Eurasian Eagle-Owl (reaching up to 28 inches in length).
- **Diverse Plumage:** Their plumage provides excellent camouflage, blending in with their surroundings. Colors range from browns and grays to whites and blacks, often with intricate patterns.
- **Solitary Hunters:** While some species may roost in groups, owls are generally solitary hunters.
- **Carnivorous Diet:** Owls are carnivores, feeding on a variety of prey including small mammals (mice, voles, rabbits), birds, insects, reptiles, amphibians, and fish, depending on the species and habitat.
- **Vocalizations:** Owls are known for their distinctive hoots, but they also produce a variety of other sounds, including screeches, whistles, barks, and hisses, used for communication, territorial defense, and courtship.

Key Points:

- **Adaptations for Nocturnal Hunting:** Their large eyes, exceptional hearing, and silent flight are key adaptations that make them highly successful nocturnal predators.
- **Ecological Importance:** Owls play a vital role in controlling populations of rodents and other small animals, helping to maintain ecosystem balance.
- **Diversity and Habitat:** The wide variety of owl species reflects their adaptation to diverse habitats, from dense forests and grasslands to deserts and urban areas.
- **Conservation Concerns:** Some owl species face threats due to habitat loss, deforestation, pesticide use, and human persecution. Conservation efforts are crucial for their survival.
- **Cultural Significance:** Owls have held various symbolic meanings in different cultures throughout history, often associated with wisdom, mystery, and sometimes bad omens.
- **Lack of Crop and Gizzard:** Unlike many other birds, owls lack a crop (for temporary food storage) and their gizzard has relatively weak muscles. They typically swallow small prey whole or tear larger prey into chunks, and indigestible materials like bones and fur are regurgitated in the form of pellets.
- **Sexual Dimorphism:** In some owl species, females are larger and sometimes more brightly colored than males.
- **Nesting Habits:** Owls nest in a variety of locations, including tree cavities, abandoned nests of other birds, rock crevices, and even on the ground, depending on the species. They typically lay a clutch of white eggs.

American Barn Owl - *Tyto furcata*

American Barn Owl, is a medium-sized owl easily recognized by its distinctive heart-shaped facial disc and pale coloration. It is a nocturnal predator that employs silent flight to hunt in open habitats. General coloration includes a light face and underparts, varying from white to buff, and buffy-brown upperparts with dark speckling. While subtle differences exist, distinguishing males from females can be difficult, although females tend to be slightly larger and may exhibit more spotting. Juveniles are covered in white down, gradually developing the adult plumage. There are variations in the coloration of barn owls across their range, but the basic form is consistent.

FEEDING They are specialized hunters of small mammals, particularly voles, relying on their exceptional hearing to locate prey in darkness.

SOUNDS Their primary vocalization is a drawn-out, raspy screech, a sound quite different from the typical hooting of other owls. They also produce various other sounds, including clicks and hisses.

RANGE & MIGRATION They are found throughout North America, extending into Central and South America. While some populations may exhibit localized movements, they are generally considered non-migratory.

SIMILAR SPECIES are relatively few within their range, with their unique facial disc and vocalizations serving as key identifiers.

Adult

Adult

Juvenile

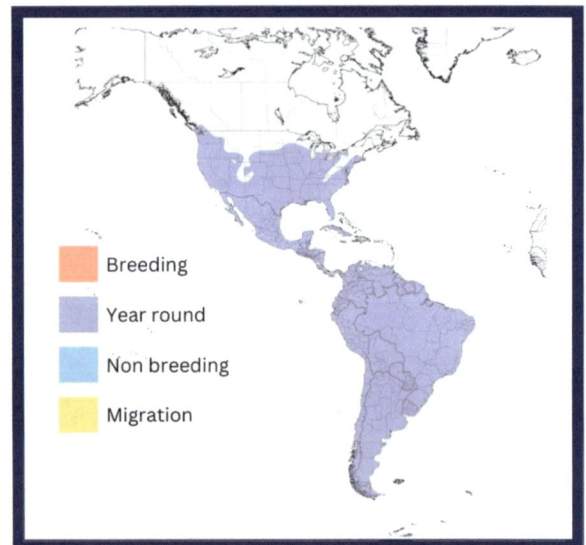

Breeding

Year round

Non breeding

Migration

Adult Call

Juvenile Call

DID YOU KNOW....

Until 2024, the Barn Owl was considered a single, widespread species found on every continent except Antarctica. However, ornithologists split it into three distinct species. The American Barn Owl is now recognized as being restricted to the Americas.

While Barn Owls have excellent low-light vision, their ability to locate prey by sound alone is the best of any animal ever tested. They can catch mice in complete darkness or when hidden by vegetation or snow, relying solely on their auditory senses.

They swallow their prey whole, including bones, fur, and other indigestible material. About twice a day, they regurgitate these remains in the form of pellets

Barred Owl - *Strix varia*

Barred Owl, is a large, striking owl found throughout much of North America. It is characterized by its round head, lack of ear tufts, and distinct barred plumage, with horizontal barring on the neck and chest and vertical streaks on the belly. Females are typically larger than males. Juveniles exhibit a reddish-brown coloration with buff barring.

FEEDING They are opportunistic predators, primarily feeding on small mammals like voles, but also consuming birds, amphibians, reptiles, and even invertebrates.

SOUNDS Their most recognizable vocalization is a series of loud, resonant hoots, often described as "who cooks for you? who cooks for you all?" They also produce a variety of other calls, including barks, screams, and duets between mated pairs.

RANGE Their range extends across eastern North America and, increasingly, into the Pacific Northwest, where it has expanded significantly.

MIGRATION They are generally non-migratory, remaining within their territories year-round.

SIMILAR SPECIES A similar species is the Spotted Owl, with which it competes in the western portions of its range, and hybridization has been recorded.

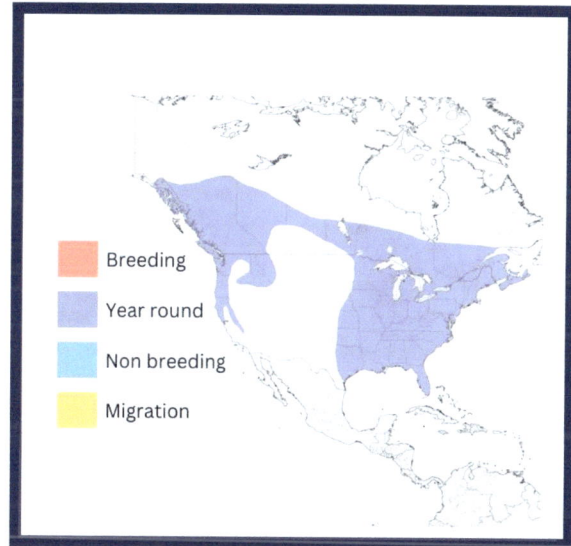

Adult

Adult

Juvenile

- Breeding
- Year round
- Non breeding
- Migration

Song

Juvenile Call

DID YOU KNOW....

Unlike most other owl species that have yellow eyes, the Barred Owl has distinctive dark brown eyes, giving them a soulful appearance. Only a few other North American owl species share this trait.

A Barred Owl's right ear is positioned slightly higher than its left ear. This asymmetrical ear placement helps them pinpoint the exact location of prey by processing sound from two different angles.

Unlike many owls, Barred Owls have been observed wading into shallow water to hunt for fish and crayfish.

Boreal Owl - *Aegolius funereus*

Boreal Owl, a resident of North America's boreal forests, is a small, elusive owl characterized by its dark brown plumage with white spotting, and a distinct grayish-white facial disc framed by a dark border. They possess bright yellow eyes, contributing to their distinctive appearance. Females are generally larger than males. Juveniles have a darker, more uniformly brown plumage compared to adults.

FEEDING Primarily nocturnal, Boreal Owls are sit-and-wait predators, feeding mainly on small mammals, particularly voles, but also taking other small rodents and occasional birds.

SOUNDS Their vocalizations include a series of rapid, low-pitched hoots, especially during the breeding season.

HABITAT & RANGE They inhabit dense coniferous forests across northern North America, extending into mountainous regions further south.

MIGRATION While not considered highly migratory, they may exhibit irruptive movements in response to fluctuations in prey availability.

SIMILAR SPECIES include the Northern Saw-whet Owl, which can be distinguished by subtle differences in plumage and size.

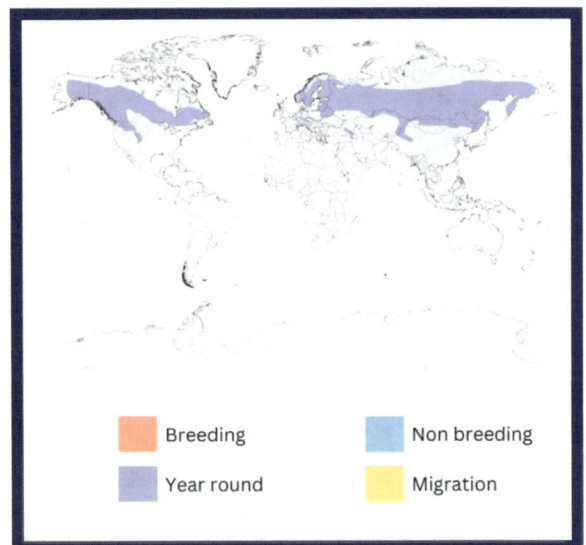

Adult

Adult

Juvenile

| Breeding | | Non breeding |
| Year round | | Migration |

Song

Call

DID YOU KNOW....

They are primarily "sit-and-wait" predators, meaning they perch silently on low branches or tree trunks, scanning for prey with their exceptional hearing and then swooping down swiftly.

Male Boreal Owls attract females by leaving food inside potential nesting cavities. If the female approves of the location and the offering, she is more likely to stay and breed.

In Europe, the Boreal Owl is often known as Tengmalm's Owl, named after the Swedish naturalist Peter Gustaf Tengmalm.

Burrowing Owl - *Athene cunicularia*

The Boreal Owl is a small, nocturnal owl characterized by its large, rounded head and yellow eyes, inhabiting boreal and mountainous coniferous forests across North America. Males are generally smaller than females, and both exhibit a dark brown to grayish-brown plumage with white spotting. Juveniles have a similar appearance to adults, but with more muted coloration.

FEEDING They are primarily carnivorous, relying on small mammals, particularly voles, as their main food source.

SOUNDS Their vocalizations include a series of rapid, high-pitched toots, used primarily by males during the breeding season, and other various calls.

RANGE & MIGRATION They are found in the northern regions of North America, extending from Alaska to eastern Canada, and also in some mountainous areas further south. While some populations may exhibit small-scale seasonal movements in response to food availability, they are generally considered to be primarily sedentary rather than truly migratory.

HABITAT These owls prefer dense coniferous forests, often with mature or dead trees that provide suitable nesting cavities.

SIMILAR SPECIES include the Northern Saw-whet Owl, which can be distinguished by its different facial pattern and calls.

Adults

Adult

Juvenile

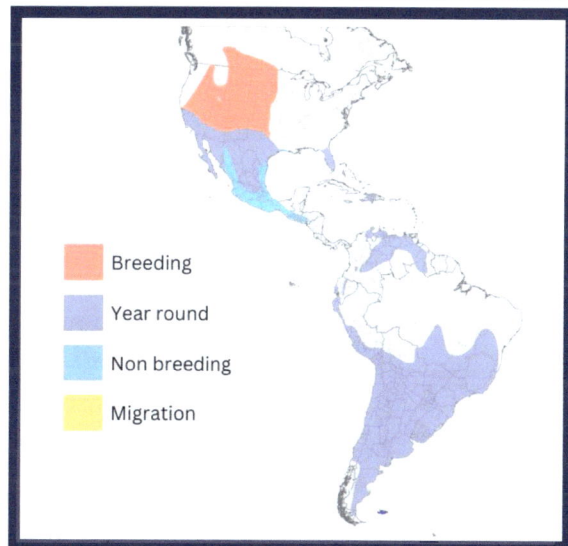

Breeding

Year round

Non breeding

Migration

Song

Adult Call

DID YOU KNOW....

Unlike most owls that nest in trees, Burrowing Owls are the only North American owl species that primarily nests and roosts underground in burrows.

Compared to other owls, they have notably long legs. This adaptation isn't just for their characteristic upright stance; it allows them to run quickly on the ground to chase after prey.

When threatened, young Burrowing Owls can produce a surprisingly accurate vocal mimicry of a rattlesnake's rattle. This startling sound can deter potential predators from investigating their burrow.

Eastern Screech-Owl - *Megascops asio*

Eastern Screech-Owl is a small, stocky owl with prominent ear tufts and yellow eyes, found throughout eastern North America. They exhibit two primary color morphs, gray and reddish-brown (rufous), providing excellent camouflage. Females are typically larger than males. Juveniles resemble adults but may have more subtle plumage.

FEEDING They are highly adaptable predators, consuming a diverse diet of small mammals, birds, insects, amphibians, and reptiles.

SOUNDS Their vocalizations include a distinctive, haunting "whinny" or tremolo, as well as softer trills and hoots.

MIGRATION They are non-migratory, maintaining year-round territories in a variety of habitats, including deciduous and mixed woodlands, suburban areas, and even urban parks, as long as there are suitable nesting cavities.

HABITAT They prefer areas with trees, and will use natural cavities, old woodpecker holes and nest boxes.

SIMILAR SPECIES include other small owls, but the Eastern Screech-Owl's unique vocalizations and color variations help distinguish it.

Adult Red Morph

Adult Gray Morph

Juvenile

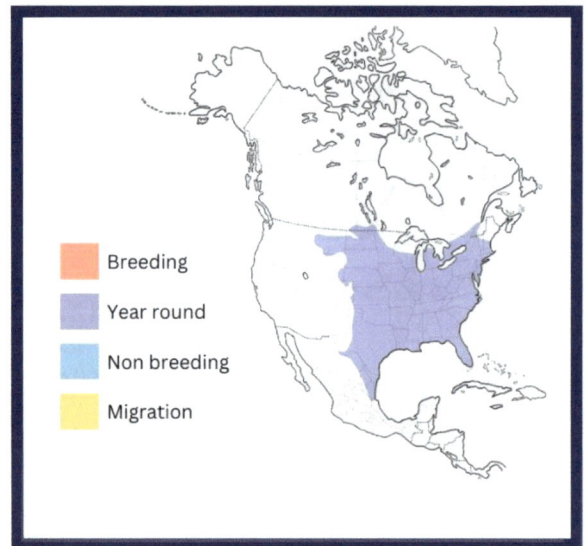

Breeding

Year round

Non breeding

Migration

Song 1

Song 2

DID YOU KNOW....

Despite their name, the Eastern Screech-Owl's most common calls are not screeches.

They have been observed bringing live blind snakes into their nest cavities. These small, non-venomous snakes then feed on ants, flies, and other insects that can infest the nest, essentially acting as a natural pest control for the owl's home.

When feeling threatened, an Eastern Screech-Owl will employ a unique defense mechanism. It will stretch its body upwards, tighten its feathers close to its body, and raise its ear tufts to appear as a broken branch or snag, making it less noticeable to predators.

Elf Owl - *Micrathene whitneyi*

Elf Owl, North America's smallest owl, is a diminutive bird with a grayish-brown plumage, highlighted by pale yellow eyes and distinctive white "eyebrows." Males and females are similar in appearance, though females tend to be slightly larger. Juveniles resemble adults.

FEEDING These nocturnal owls primarily feed on insects, especially scorpions and moths, but also take small vertebrates.

SOUNDS Their vocalizations include a series of high-pitched yips and chuckles, with males producing more complex songs than females.

RANGE & HABITAT They inhabit arid regions of the southwestern United States and Mexico, favoring desert scrub, woodlands, and canyons, often nesting in abandoned woodpecker cavities, particularly in saguaro cacti.

MIGRATION Elf Owls are partial migrants, with many populations wintering in central Mexico.

SIMILAR SPECIES are few due to their very small size, but the owl's unique vocalizations and habitat preferences help to distinguish them.

Adult

Adult

Juvenile

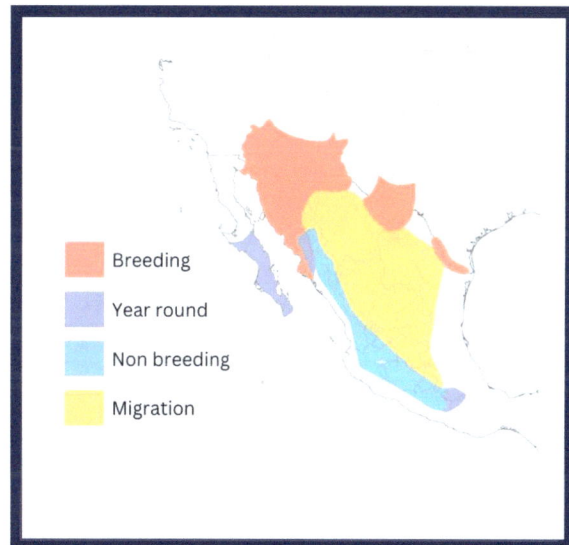

Breeding

Year round

Non breeding

Migration

Song

Call

DID YOU KNOW....

The Elf Owl holds the title of the smallest owl species globally and is also considered one of the smallest raptors overall. It's only about 5-6 inches tall, roughly the size of a sparrow or a small can of beans, and weighs less than a golf ball (around 1.2-1.9 ounces).

While most owls prey on small mammals, the Elf Owl's diet consists mainly of insects and other arthropods like moths, beetles, crickets, grasshoppers, and scorpions. Remarkably, they often remove the stinger from scorpions before eating them.

Ferruginous Pygmy-Owl - *Glaucidium brasilianum*

Ferruginous Pygmy-Owl, a small and diurnal owl, is characterized by its compact build, relatively long tail, and distinctive "false eyes" on the back of its neck. Its plumage is generally rusty-brown, with pale underparts streaked with brown. Males and females are visually similar, though females tend to be slightly larger. Juveniles resemble adults but exhibit a more barred pattern on their underparts.

FEEDING This owl is a predator, primarily hunting small birds, insects, reptiles, and mammals.

SOUNDS Its song is a series of rapid, high-pitched toots, often described as a "toot-toot-toot" rhythm, and it also produces sharp alarm calls.

RANGE & MIGRATION The Ferruginous Pygmy-Owl's range in North America is limited to the southern regions of Texas and Arizona, extending southward into Mexico and Central and South America. They are generally non-migratory, remaining within their territories year-round.

HABITAT Their preferred habitats include thorn scrub, woodlands, and riparian areas, particularly those with dense vegetation.

SIMILAR SPECIES may include other small owls, but the Ferruginous Pygmy-Owl's diurnal habits, long tail, and distinct vocalizations help to differentiate it.

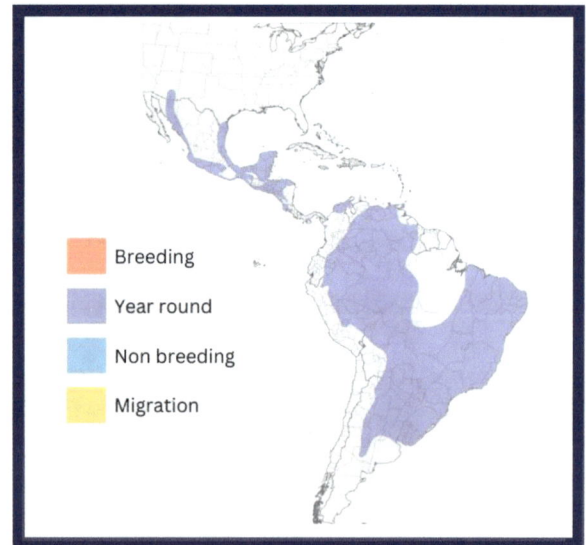

Adult

Adult

Juvenile

Breeding

Year round

Non breeding

Migration

Song

Call

DID YOU KNOW....

Unlike most owls that are nocturnal, the Ferruginous Pygmy-Owl is frequently active during the day, especially at dawn and dusk (crepuscular). This allows it to exploit different prey than strictly nocturnal owls.

It has two dark patches on the back of its head that resemble eyes, complete with whitish borders. These "ocelli" are thought to confuse potential predators or even prey, possibly making the owl appear to be watching them even when it isn't.

Despite its small size (roughly 6-7 inches long), it possesses surprisingly large feet and sharp talons, enabling it to capture and carry prey that can be up to twice its own weight.

Flammulated Owl - *Psiloscops flammeolus*

Flammulated Owl is a small, nocturnal owl characterized by its reddish-brown plumage, dark eyes, and small ear tufts. Its name derives from the subtle, flame-like markings on its face and underparts. Males and females are virtually indistinguishable in appearance, although females may be slightly larger. Juveniles resemble adults but have a more uniformly gray plumage.

FEEDING They are primarily insectivorous, feeding almost exclusively on moths and other nocturnal insects.
SOUNDS Their song is a low, hollow "hoot" or "boop," often repeated at intervals, and they produce soft clicks or chitters as alarm calls.

HABITAT & RANGE They inhabit mature coniferous forests, particularly ponderosa pine and Douglas-fir forests, in mountainous regions of western North America, extending from southern British Columbia down through the western United States and into Mexico.

MIGRATION They are migratory, moving south to Mexico and Central America for the winter.

SIMILAR SPECIES include the Western Screech-Owl, but the Flammulated Owl can be differentiated by its smaller size, darker eyes, and distinct vocalizations, as well as its preference for higher elevation coniferous forests.

Adult

Adult

Juvenile

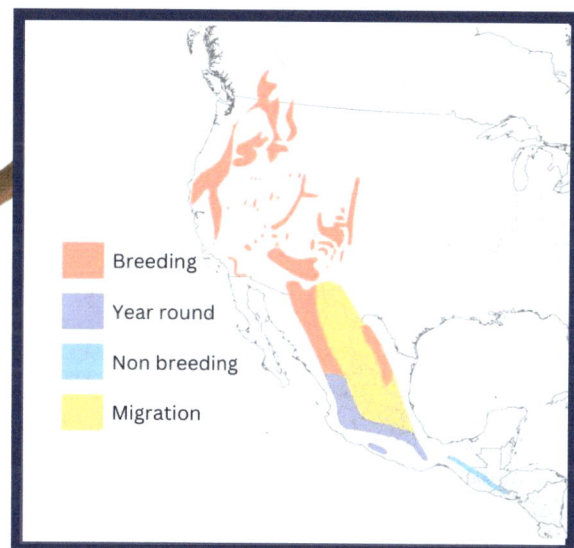

Breeding

Year round

Non breeding

Migration

Song

Call

DID YOU KNOW....

Unlike most small owls that possess yellow eyes, the Flammulated Owl has dark brown eyes. This is a key identifying feature.

Its name refers to the subtle, flame-like streaks of reddish-brown feathers that run down its back and across its facial disc, providing excellent camouflage against pine bark

This owl is a cavity nester but doesn't create its own holes. It almost exclusively uses abandoned woodpecker cavities, particularly those made by Northern Flickers and Pileated Woodpeckers, making it dependent on the presence of these other bird species.

Great Gray Owl - *Strix nebulosa*

Great Gray Owl, the largest owl species by length in North America, is a striking bird with a silvery-gray plumage marked by fine white, gray, and brown streaking. It possesses a large, rounded head, prominent yellow eyes, and a distinctive large facial disk that aids in its exceptional hearing. While appearing large due to its fluffy feathers, it is relatively light in weight. Males and females are similar in appearance, though females tend to be slightly larger. Juveniles resemble adults but may have a slightly different feather pattern.

FEEDING These owls are primarily predators of small mammals, especially voles, and they are adapted to hunt in dense boreal forests. Their hunting strategy involves listening intently from a perch and then swooping down to capture prey, even beneath deep snow.

SOUNDS Their vocalizations include deep, booming hoots used for territorial defense, particularly during the breeding season.

HABITAT & MIGRATION They inhabit coniferous forests across northern North America and Eurasia, often near open areas like meadows or bogs. While they are generally non-migratory, they may move southward in years of low prey availability, a phenomenon known as irruption. Their habitat consists of mature forests with openings that support their prey.

NESTING They do not build their own nests, but rather they use abandoned nests of other large birds or cavities in trees.

SIMILAR SPECIES include the Great Horned Owl and Barred Owl, but the Great Gray Owl's size, facial disk, and habitat preferences distinguish it.

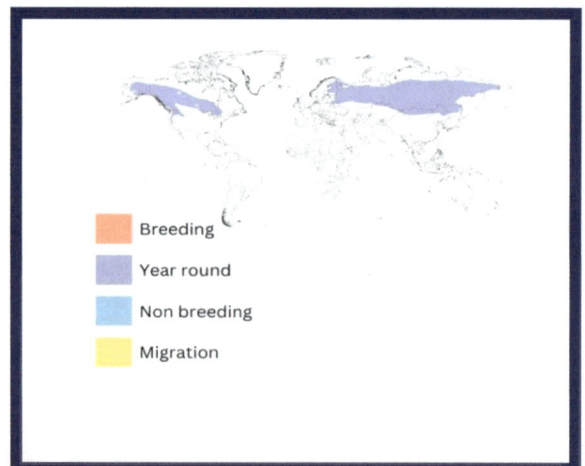

Adult
Adult
Juvenile

Adult Song   **Juvenile Call**

Breeding

Year round

Non breeding

Migration

DID YOU KNOW....

This is the tallest owl species in North America, reaching up to 33 inches in height. However, much of this is fluffy feathers, making it surprisingly lightweight. It weighs considerably less than the Great Horned Owl and Snowy Owl, which have smaller body lengths but greater mass.

Due to its silent flight and ability to blend seamlessly with the bark of coniferous trees, it's often called the "Phantom of the North" or "Great Gray Ghost," making it elusive to spot.

They possess the largest facial disk of any raptor. This impressive disk of feathers acts like a parabolic dish, funneling even the faintest sounds to their ears, crucial for detecting prey under snow.

Great Horned Owl - *Bubo virginianus*

Great Horned Owl is a large, powerful bird of prey recognizable by its prominent ear tufts and yellow eyes. Their plumage is typically mottled gray-brown, providing excellent camouflage. Females are generally larger than males. Juveniles are covered in fluffy down, with a distinct contrast between their lighter head and darker facial disc.

FEEDING These owls are apex predators, with a varied diet including mammals, birds, reptiles, and even insects.

SOUNDS They are known for their deep, resonant "who-who-who-who" hoot, which serves as a territorial declaration. They also produce a variety of other sounds, including hisses and clicks.

HABITAT Found throughout North, Central, and South America, they inhabit a wide range of environments, from forests and deserts to urban areas. Their preferred habitats include woodlands, forests, and areas with a mix of open spaces and trees.

MIGRATION They are primarily non-migratory, maintaining territories year-round.

SIMILAR SPECIES may include other large owls, such as the Barred Owl or Snowy Owl, but the Great Horned Owl's distinct ear tufts and vocalizations aid in identification.

Male

Female

Juvenile

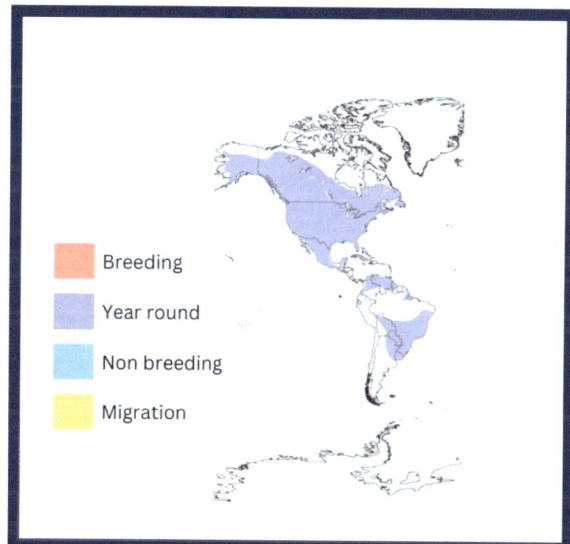

Breeding

Year round

Non breeding

Migration

Song

Female Call

DID YOU KNOW....

The prominent feather tufts on their heads, which give them their name, are not related to their hearing. They are believed to play a role in camouflage by breaking up the owl's outline, and they can also be used in communication and display.

Their flight is nearly silent due to specialized serrations on the leading edge of their wing feathers. These break up the airflow, reducing turbulence and noise, allowing them to ambush prey effectively.

They are among the earliest nesting birds in North America. They often begin nesting in January or February, and it's not uncommon for them to be incubating eggs while snow still covers the ground.

Long-eared Owl - *Asio otus*

Long-eared Owl, a slender and cryptic bird, is characterized by its prominent, closely set ear tufts and a striking orange facial disk. These medium-sized owls exhibit a mottled brown plumage, providing excellent camouflage in their preferred habitats. While males and females appear similar, females may display heavier streaking. Juveniles produce distinctive begging calls, aiding in their detection.

FEEDING They are primarily nocturnal hunters, feeding on small mammals, particularly voles, and occasionally birds.

SOUNDS Their vocalizations include low, hooting sounds during courtship and a variety of shrieks and barks when alarmed.

HABITAT They inhabit a wide range across North America, favoring areas with a mix of dense forests for roosting and open fields for hunting. Their habitat commonly consists of forest edges, woodlands, and areas with thickets.

MIGRATION They are partially migratory, with some individuals moving south during harsh winters or in response to prey availability.

SIMILAR SPECIES include the Short-eared Owl and the Great Horned Owl, but differences in ear tuft size, facial disk coloration, and habitat preferences help distinguish them. Long eared owls do not build their own nests, and instead use abandoned nests of other birds.

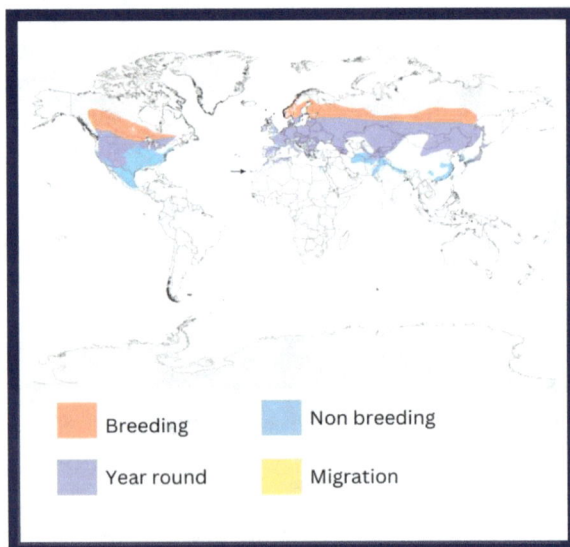

Male

Female

Juvenile

Breeding

Non breeding

Year round

Migration

Adult Call

Juvenile Call

DID YOU KNOW....

When threatened in its day roost, the Long-eared Owl will raise its ear tufts, compress its feathers tightly against its body, and freeze in a stiff, upright posture. This makes it resemble a tree branch or bark, an effective camouflage tactic. This "tall-thin position" has earned it the nickname "cat owl" in the past.

Unlike many owls that are solitary, especially outside the breeding season, Long-eared Owls are unusually social and often roost in groups. These groups can range from a few individuals to over 100 owls in dense cover, potentially for safety in numbers.

Northern Hawk Owl - *Surnia ulula*

Northern Hawk Owl is a medium-sized owl that exhibits hawk-like behaviors, primarily hunting during the day. Its distinguishing features include a long, pointed tail, a relatively small head, and yellow eyes. Both males and females share a similar plumage of dark brown with white spotting on their backs and white underparts with dark barring, though females tend to be slightly larger. Juveniles display a more grayish-brown coloration with less distinct white markings.

FEEDING These owls are primarily predators of small mammals, particularly voles, but they also consume other rodents and birds.

SOUNDS Their vocalizations include a series of rapid, high-pitched trills and whistles, varying in tone and duration.

HABITAT & RANGE They inhabit boreal forests and taiga regions across northern North America, extending into Eurasia. Their preferred habitat consists of coniferous forests interspersed with open areas, such as clearings and bogs.

MIGRATION While generally non-migratory, they may exhibit irruptive movements southward during winters with scarce prey.

SIMILAR SPECIES that may cause confusion include certain hawks, but the Hawk Owl's unique combination of owl and hawk characteristics aids in identification.

Male

Female

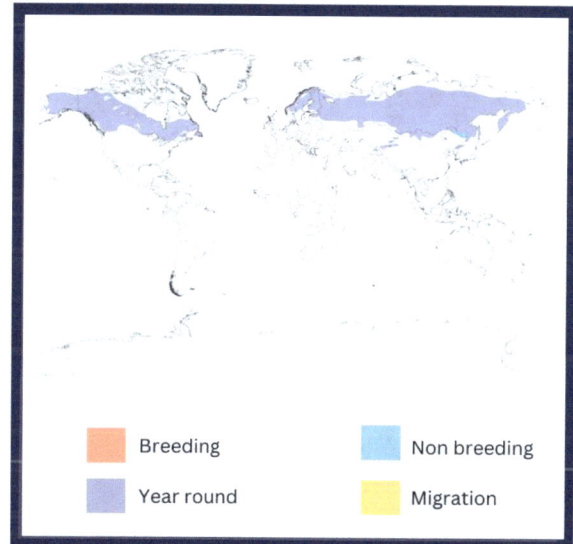

Breeding   Non breeding

Year round   Migration

Juvenile

Song   Call

DID YOU KNOW....

It strongly resembles a hawk in its overall shape, with a long, tapered tail and relatively small head for an owl. Its flight style, a mix of quick wingbeats and glides, also evokes that of a hawk

Unlike many nocturnal owls with specialized feathers for silent flight, the Northern Hawk Owl's wingbeats are quite audible, similar to a hawk's. This is because silent flight isn't as crucial for a daytime predator

When prey is abundant, Northern Hawk Owls will cache surplus food, such as mice, in tree crevices, holes, or dense spruce boughs for later consumption.

Northern Pygmy-Owl - *Glaucidium gnoma*

The Northern Pygmy-Owl is a small, fierce predator found in western North America. It is characterized by its compact size, streaked underparts, and a distinctive pair of black spots on the back of its neck that resemble eyes. While there are slight variations, distinguishing between male and female plumage is difficult, though generally females can be slightly larger. Juveniles resemble adults but may have slightly softer plumage.

FEEDING These owls are diurnal, hunting primarily during the day, and their diet consists of small birds, mammals, and insects.

SOUNDS Their vocalizations include a series of high-pitched, evenly spaced "toots."

HABITAT They inhabit a range of forested environments, favoring coniferous and mixed woodlands, particularly those with mature trees.

RANGE & MIGRATION Their range extends from southwestern Canada through the mountainous regions of the western United States and into Mexico. They are generally year-round residents within their range, with limited migration.

SIMILAR SPECIES might include other small owls, but the Northern Pygmy-Owl's daytime activity and distinctive calls aid in identification.

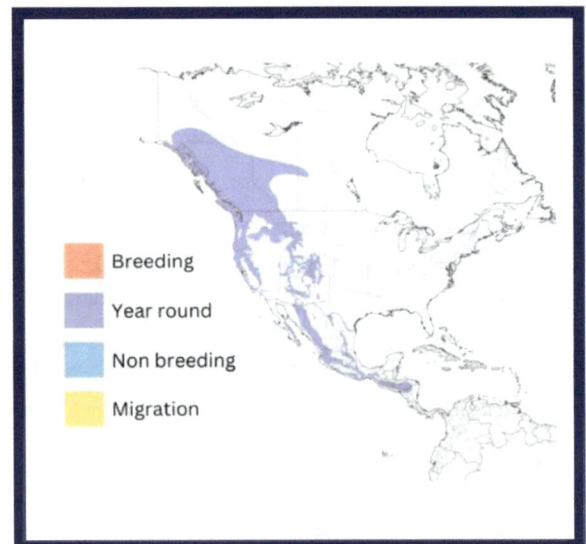

Male

Female

Juvenile

Juvenile

Breeding

Year round

Non breeding

Migration

Song

Juvenile Call

DID YOU KNOW....

It has dark, oval spots on the back of its neck that resemble eyes, possibly to deter predators or mobbing songbirds from attacking from behind.

Despite being one of the smallest owls in North America, it is a fierce predator known to attack and kill prey much larger than itself, including birds up to three times its weight and even chickens.

Pairs of Northern Pygmy-Owls have been known to "sing" to each other or perform duets. Interestingly, both males and females have the same pitch of voice.

Short-eared Owl - *Asio flammeus*

Short-eared Owl is a medium-sized owl characterized by its mottled brown and buff plumage, striking yellow eyes, and small, often barely visible, ear tufts. It is a diurnal and crepuscular hunter, frequently seen flying low over open fields. Males and females are very similar in appearance, with females typically slightly larger and heavier. Juveniles are distinguished by their downy plumage and darker facial disks.

FEEDING These owls are primarily predators of small mammals, particularly voles, but they also take birds and insects.

SOUNDS Their vocalizations include a raspy "kree-ah" call, a series of hoots during courtship, and snapping sounds made with their mandibles when threatened.

RANGE They have a wide range, inhabiting open habitats across North America, including grasslands, tundra, marshes, and agricultural fields.

MIGRATION They exhibit nomadic and migratory behavior, with movements influenced by prey availability. Some populations are resident, while others undertake long-distance migrations, particularly in northern regions.

HABITAT They prefer open areas with low vegetation.

SIMILAR SPECIES include the Long-eared Owl, which has longer ear tufts and a different vocalization, and the Barn Owl, which has a heart-shaped facial disk.

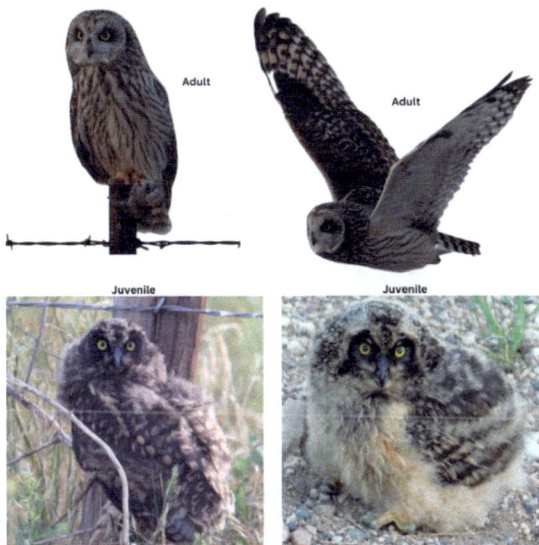

Adult | Adult
Juvenile | Juvenile

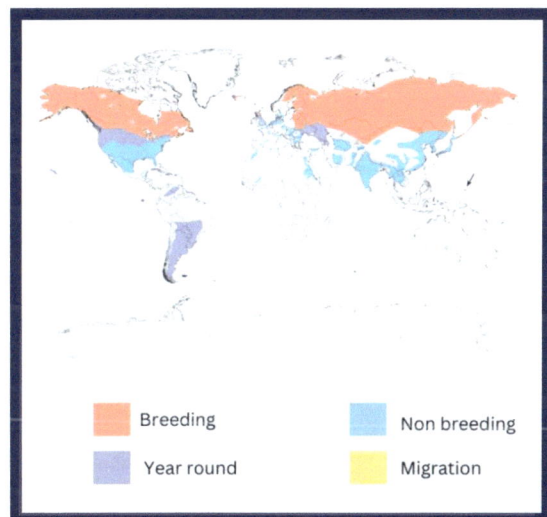

Breeding — Non breeding — Year round — Migration

Call **Song**

DID YOU KNOW....

Its flight is often described as buoyant, floppy, and erratic, sometimes compared to that of a moth or bat. They have irregular wingbeats and glide with their wings held horizontally.

Unusually for an owl, the Short-eared Owl nests on the ground in open areas. The female creates a simple scrape in the soil, lining it with grass and feathers.

The "ear tufts" that give the owl its name are very short and often held flat against the head, making them inconspicuous unless the owl is alert or defensive.

Snowy Owl - *Bubo scandiacus*

Snowy Owl is a large, striking owl easily recognized by its predominantly white plumage and bright yellow eyes, adaptations that serve it well in its Arctic habitat. Adult males are typically almost entirely white, while females and juveniles display dark barring or spotting. Juveniles have heavier dark markings than adult females.

FEEDING These owls are primarily carnivores, with lemmings forming a significant portion of their diet, though they also hunt other small mammals and birds. Unlike many owls, Snowy Owls are diurnal, hunting both day and night, especially during the continuous daylight of Arctic summers.

SOUNDS Their vocalizations include a variety of hoots, barks, and hisses, used for territorial defense and mating.

HABITAT They inhabit the Arctic tundra, nesting on the ground in open areas.

RANGE & MIGRATION Their range spans the northernmost regions of North America and Eurasia. They are nomadic, with their migration patterns heavily influenced by food availability. They may move southward in winter, sometimes in large numbers called irruptions, when prey is scarce in the Arctic.

HABITAT Their habitat consists primarily of open tundra, but during winter, they may be found in open fields, grasslands, and coastal areas.

SIMILAR SPECIES include other large owls, but the Snowy Owl's distinctive white plumage and yellow eyes make it relatively easy to identify.

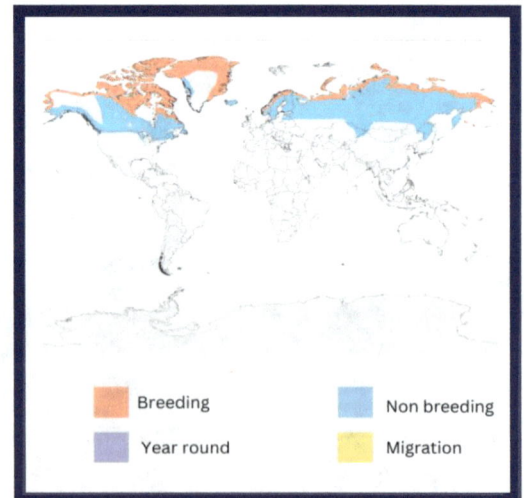

Male

Female

Juvenile

Juvenile

Breeding   Non breeding

Year round   Migration

Song   Call

DID YOU KNOW....

They are are the heaviest owl species in North America due to their dense plumage required for Arctic temperatures.

Male Snowy Owls become progressively whiter as they age, while females retain more dark barring throughout their lives. The whitest owls are typically older males.

They have been observed using a unique hunting method called the "sweep," where they catch prey in the talons of one foot while flying low.

Western Screech-Owl - *Megascops kennicottii*

Western Screech-Owl, a small, stocky owl with prominent ear tufts and yellow eyes, inhabits western North America. Its plumage varies, typically displaying gray-brown tones with intricate streaks and mottling that provide excellent camouflage. Males and females exhibit similar plumage, though females are slightly larger. Juveniles resemble adults but have softer, fluffier down.

FEEDING These owls are nocturnal predators, primarily feeding on insects and small vertebrates like rodents and birds.

SOUNDS Their vocalizations consist of a series of accelerating hollow "toot" notes, often described as a bouncing ball sound, rather than a screech.

HABITAT & RANGE They reside in a variety of habitats, including woodlands, forests, and suburban areas, throughout western North America, ranging from southern Alaska down through Mexico. They prefer habitats with cavities for nesting, such as tree holes and nest boxes.

MIGRATION They are generally non-migratory, remaining within their territories year-round.

SIMILAR SPECIES include the Eastern Screech-Owl, which is found in eastern North America, and other small owls, but their distinct vocalizations and geographic ranges help differentiate them.

Adult

Adult

Juvenile

Juvenile

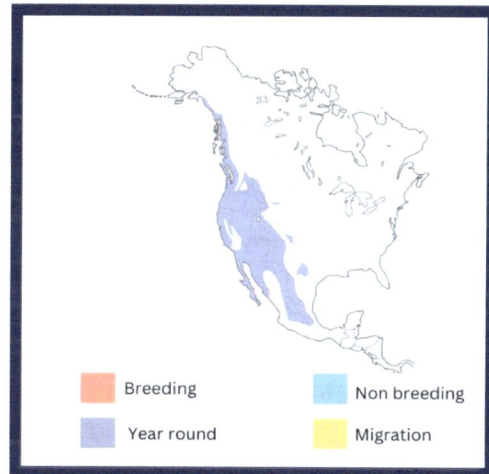

Breeding

Non breeding

Year round

Migration

Song

Call

DID YOU KNOW....

Unlike its name suggests, the Western Screech-Owl doesn't screech. Its most distinctive call is a series of 5-9 short, whistled hoots that speed up towards the end, resembling a bouncing ball.

In duets between a mated pair, the female's calls are higher-pitched than the male's, despite the female typically being larger.

When threatened, they will stretch their body, tighten their feathers, and freeze, effectively resembling a branch and making them very difficult to spot.

WOODPECKERS

Woodpeckers are fascinating birds belonging to the family Picidae, characterized by their unique adaptations for a life spent primarily on trees.

General Characteristics:

- **Specialized Bills:** Woodpeckers possess strong, chisel-like bills adapted for drilling into wood. The bill's tip is constantly sharpened by their pecking action.
- **Long, Barbed Tongues:** They have remarkably long, often barbed, and sticky tongues used to extract insects and larvae from the holes they create. In some species, the tongue can extend several inches beyond the bill.
- **Zygodactyl Feet:** Most woodpeckers have zygodactyl feet, with two toes pointing forward and two pointing backward. This arrangement provides a strong grip for clinging to vertical surfaces like tree trunks. Some species have only three toes.
- **Stiff Tail Feathers:** Their tail feathers, particularly the central ones, are stiff and strong, providing support and balance as they climb and peck.
- **Adaptations for Climbing:** Short, strong legs and sharp claws, combined with their zygodactyl feet and stiff tails, enable woodpeckers to move vertically up tree trunks with agility.
- **Skull Adaptations:** To withstand the impact of repeated pecking, woodpeckers have several unique skull adaptations, including a thick but compressible skull, a hyoid bone that wraps around the brain, and a small brain with minimal cerebrospinal fluid. These features help absorb shock and prevent brain damage.
- **Nostril Protection:** Bristly feathers or specialized sacs around their nostrils help filter out wood dust and debris during drilling.
- **Undulating Flight:** Many woodpecker species exhibit a characteristic undulating flight pattern, flapping their wings in bursts followed by short glides with wings folded.
- **Vocalizations and Drumming:** While they have various calls, woodpeckers are also known for their "drumming" – a rapid pecking on resonant surfaces like dead trees or even man-made structures. Drumming serves as a territorial display and a way to attract mates.
- **Cavity Nesters:** Woodpeckers are primary cavity excavators, meaning they create their own nest holes in trees, usually in dead or decaying wood. These abandoned cavities are then used by many other bird species and small mammals.
- **Varied Diets:** While primarily insectivorous, feeding on wood-boring insects, ants, beetles, and caterpillars, woodpeckers also consume fruits, nuts, seeds, and tree sap, depending on the species and season. Sapsuckers have a specialized diet of tree sap and the insects trapped within it.

Key Points:

- **Ecological Importance:** Woodpeckers play a crucial role in forest ecosystems by controlling insect populations and creating nesting sites for other wildlife.
- **Adaptations to Niche:** Their unique physical and behavioral adaptations allow them to exploit food sources and habitats that are inaccessible to most other birds.
- **Communication:** Drumming is a vital form of communication for territorial defense and mate attraction.
- **Conservation Status:** While many woodpecker species are common, some face threats due to habitat loss and degradation, making conservation efforts important.
- **Human Interactions:** Woodpeckers can sometimes come into conflict with humans by drumming on buildings or excavating holes in wooden structures in search of insects or nesting sites. Sapsuckers can also damage trees by drilling numerous sap wells.
- **Diversity:** With around 180 species worldwide, woodpeckers exhibit a wide range of sizes, colors, and ecological roles. Examples include the large Pileated Woodpecker, the colorful Red-headed Woodpecker, and the ground-foraging flickers.

Acorn Woodpecker - *Melanerpes formicivorus*

Acorn Woodpecker is a striking, medium-sized woodpecker characterized by its bold black, white, and red plumage, most notably a white face and forehead, a black back, and a red cap on males. These woodpeckers are known for their unique acorn-storing behavior. Males possess a full red cap, while females have a black forehead separating the red cap from the white face. Juveniles have a brownish-gray cap and less distinct plumage compared to adults.

FEEDING Their primary food source is acorns, which they meticulously store in "granary" trees, but they also consume insects, sap, and fruits.

SOUNDS Their vocalizations include a variety of raucous calls, most notably a "waka-waka" sound, and they engage in drumming on trees.

RANGE & MIGRATION They are found throughout oak woodlands in the western and southwestern United States, extending into Mexico and Central America. The Acorn Woodpecker is generally non-migratory, remaining within its range year-round.

HABITAT They prefer oak woodlands and mixed oak-conifer forests.

SIMILAR SPECIES include other *Melanerpes* woodpeckers, such as the Lewis's Woodpecker and the Red-headed Woodpecker, but the Acorn Woodpecker's distinctive facial pattern and acorn-storing behavior set it apart.

Female

Male

Juvenile

Juvenile

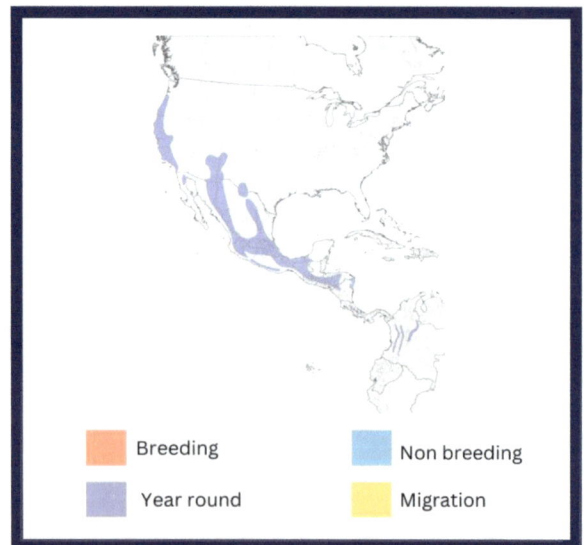

Breeding

Non breeding

Year round

Migration

Group Call

DID YOU KNOW....

They are famous for creating and maintaining "granary trees" or other wooden structures (like utility poles or buildings) filled with thousands of individually drilled holes, each holding a single acorn. These granaries can be used for generations by a family group. A single granary can contain up to 50,000 acorns.

In groups with multiple females laying eggs in the same nest cavity, the females will often remove and eat each other's eggs until they all start laying around the same time. This strange behavior ensures that no single female's offspring has a hatching advantage

Arizona Woodpecker - *Dryobates arizonae*

The Arizona Woodpecker is a distinctive bird of the southwestern United States and Mexico, characterized by its predominantly brown back, a feature that sets it apart from many other North American woodpeckers. This compact woodpecker displays heavily spotted underparts and a prominent white cheek patch. Adult males possess a small red patch on the rear of their crown, which is absent in females. Juveniles exhibit a duller plumage with heavier markings.

FEEDING They primarily forage for insects, particularly beetle larvae, by climbing tree trunks and branches, scaling or prying off bark, and excavating into wood. They also consume fruits, acorns, and seeds. Their vocalizations include sharp "peek" calls and rasping, descending rattle calls.

RANGE Their range is restricted to the pine-oak woodlands of southeastern Arizona, southwestern New Mexico, and the Sierra Madre Occidental of Mexico.

MIGRATION They are generally non-migratory, although they may exhibit altitudinal movements in response to food availability.

HABITAT Their preferred habitat consists of open woodlands, particularly pine-oak forests at mid-elevations.

SIMILAR SPECIES can include other woodpeckers, but the Arizona Woodpecker's solid brown back and distinctive facial pattern help distinguish it.

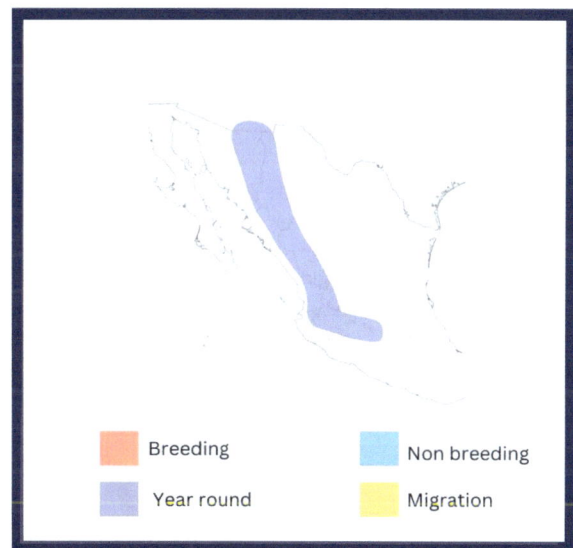

Male

Female

Juvenile Male

Juvenile Female

Breeding
Non breeding
Year round
Migration

Call

Juvenile Call

DID YOU KNOW....

The Arizona Woodpecker is the only woodpecker in the United States with a completely brown back. Most other North American woodpeckers have black and white plumage on their backs.

This woodpecker often forages in a distinctive manner, spiraling upwards around a tree trunk, much like a Brown Creeper. After reaching a certain height, it will fly to the base of another tree and repeat the process.

Compared to some other woodpecker species, the Arizona Woodpecker is often described as being quieter, both in its calls and drumming.

American Three-toed Woodpecker - *Picoides dorsalis*

American Three-toed Woodpecker is a medium-sized woodpecker primarily found in coniferous forests across North America. It is characterized by its black and white barred back, black wings, and white underparts with blackish barring on the flanks. Males are distinguished by a yellow crown patch, while females have a solid black crown. Juveniles resemble adults but typically exhibit a yellow crown patch as well.

FEEDING They primarily feed on insects, especially wood-boring beetle larvae, which they extract by flaking bark from dead or dying trees.

SOUNDS Their vocalizations include soft, "pik" calls and slow drumming patterns.

HABITAT They inhabit mature or old-growth boreal conifer forests, particularly those with spruce, fir, and pine trees, and are often found in areas disturbed by fire or insect outbreaks.

MIGRATION While they are generally non-migratory, they may exhibit nomadic movements in response to food availability, particularly in areas with abundant insect populations.

SIMILAR SPECIES include the Black-backed Woodpecker, from which they can be distinguished by the American Three-toed Woodpecker's barred back and more prominent white markings.

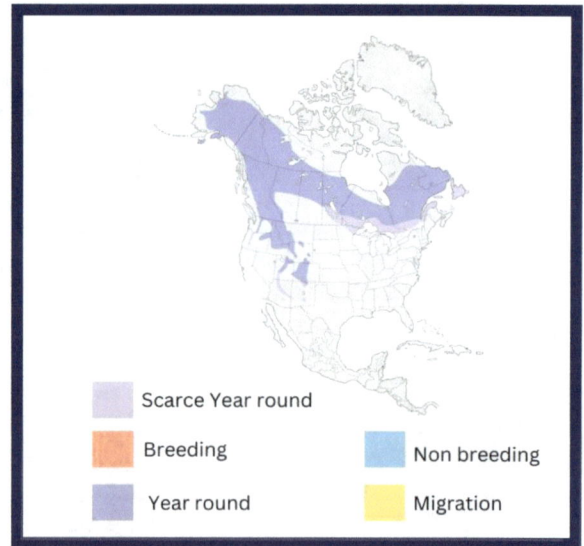

Male

Female

Juvenile

Call

Juvenile Call

Scarce Year round

Breeding

Year round

Non breeding

Migration

DID YOU KNOW....

As its name suggests, this woodpecker has only three toes on each foot (two forward, one backward), unlike most woodpeckers which have four. This adaptation is thought to provide a stronger grip for scaling bark, its primary foraging technique, though it might slightly reduce climbing agility.

They are unique in their primary foraging method, which involves flaking or scaling off bark in sideways swipes to reveal beetle larvae underneath, rather than drilling deeply into the wood like many other woodpeckers. This leaves distinctive patterns on dead and dying trees.

While they only have three true toes, they can rotate their outer (fourth) toe backward to some extent, which effectively mimics a three-toed stance and aids in gripping vertical surfaces.

Black-backed Woodpecker - *Picoides arcticus*

Black-backed Woodpecker is a medium-sized woodpecker characterized by its solid black back and white underparts with black barring on the flanks. Males are distinguished by a yellow crown patch, while females have a solid black crown. Juveniles resemble adults but may have a duller yellow crown patch.

FEEDING These woodpeckers are specialized feeders, primarily consuming the larvae of wood-boring beetles, particularly those found in recently burned forests. Their feeding habits make them crucial to the ecology of these post-fire environments.

SOUNDS Their vocalizations include sharp "chip" notes and drumming, which can be distinguished by a trailing off at the end, similar to the American Three-toed Woodpecker.

HABITAT They inhabit boreal and montane coniferous forests across North America, with a strong affinity for recently burned areas. Their habitat is closely tied to areas with high densities of dead or dying trees, particularly conifers.

MIGRATION While they are generally non-migratory, they may move in response to changes in food availability, often following outbreaks of bark beetles or recent wildfires.

SIMILAR SPECIES include the American Three-toed Woodpecker, which shares a similar habitat and some physical characteristics, but can be distinguished by differences in plumage and vocalizations.

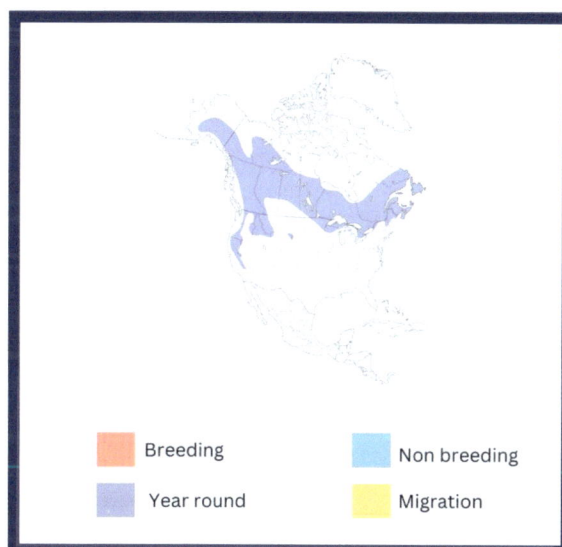

Male

Female

Juvenile

Breeding

Year round

Non breeding

Migration

Call

Juvenile Call

DID YOU KNOW....

This woodpecker has a strong association with recently burned forests. They are often one of the first bird species to colonize these areas, attracted by the abundance of wood-boring beetle larvae that thrive in fire-damaged trees. This specialization makes them somewhat nomadic, as they follow the cycle of forest fires.

In addition to typical woodpecker calls and drumming, the Black-backed Woodpecker has a unique agonistic call described as a "wet-et-ddd-eee-yaaa" or "scream-rattle-snarl." This call is often associated with a hunched posture and wing-spreading display during territorial encounters.

Downy Woodpecker - *Dryobates pubescens*

Downy Woodpecker, North America's smallest woodpecker, is a common sight in woodlands and backyards. It displays a black and white plumage, with a heavily spotted or barred pattern on its wings and back. Males are easily identified by a small red patch on the back of their head, while females lack this marking. Juveniles resemble adults but often have a reddish or yellowish tinge to their head feathers.

FEEDING These woodpeckers are primarily insectivorous, foraging for insects, larvae, and eggs on tree trunks and branches. They also consume seeds and berries.

SOUNDS Their vocalizations include a sharp "pik" call and a rapid, descending series of "pik" notes, along with a drumming sound produced by tapping on wood.

RANGE & MIGRATION They can be found throughout most of North America, from southern Canada to Florida and Texas. While some northern populations may move slightly southward in winter, they are generally considered non-migratory.

HABITAT Their preferred habitats include deciduous and mixed woodlands, orchards, and suburban areas.

SIMILAR SPECIES The Downy Woodpecker is often confused with the slightly larger Hairy Woodpecker, but the Downy's smaller size, shorter bill, and finer barring on its outer tail feathers help distinguish it.

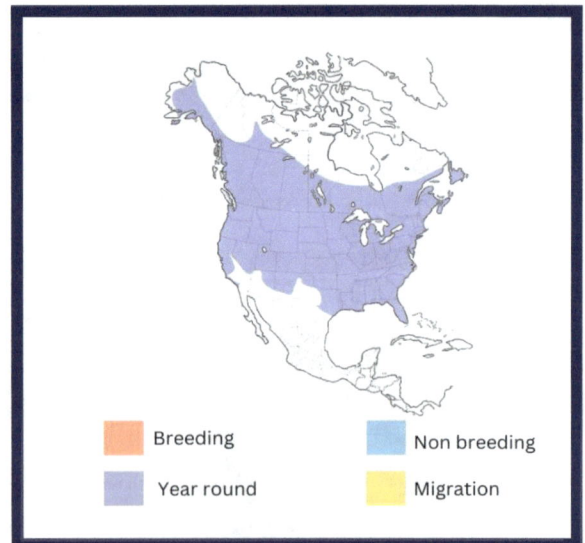

Male

Female

Juvenile

| Breeding | Non breeding |
| Year round | Migration |

Adult Call **Juvenile Call**

DID YOU KNOW....

While it holds the title of the smallest woodpecker in North America (measuring only about 5.5 to 7 inches long), there are many smaller woodpecker species found in other parts of the world, particularly the piculets.

Male and female Downy Woodpeckers often forage in different parts of the same tree. Males tend to feed on smaller, higher branches, while females are more often found on the trunk and larger, lower branches. This reduces competition between the pair.

In accordance with Bergmann's rule (which states that animals in colder climates tend to be larger), Downy Woodpeckers in northern Canada are about 12% larger than those in Florida.

Gila Woodpecker - *Melanerpes uropygialis*

Gila Woodpecker is a medium-sized woodpecker primarily found in the arid regions of the southwestern United States and Mexico. They exhibit a pale brown to gray overall plumage, with barred black and white patterns on their back and wings. Adult males are distinguished by a small red cap on the crown, while females lack this red marking. Juvenile Gila Woodpeckers resemble females but often display duller plumage and less distinct barring.

FEEDING Their diet consists mainly of insects, especially ants and beetles, supplemented with fruits, seeds, and nectar. They are also known to consume saguaro cactus fruit.

SOUNDS Their vocalizations include a series of sharp "pik" calls and a rattling drum on resonant surfaces like cacti.

HABITAT They inhabit desert scrub, saguaro cactus forests, and riparian woodlands, adapting well to urban environments.

MIGRATION The Gila Woodpecker is generally a non-migratory resident within its range.

SIMILAR SPECIES include the Ladder-backed Woodpecker, which shares a similar range and habitat, but can be distinguished by its more extensive black and white ladder-like barring on the back and wings, and the Golden-fronted Woodpecker, which is found more easterly, and has a golden nape and forehead.

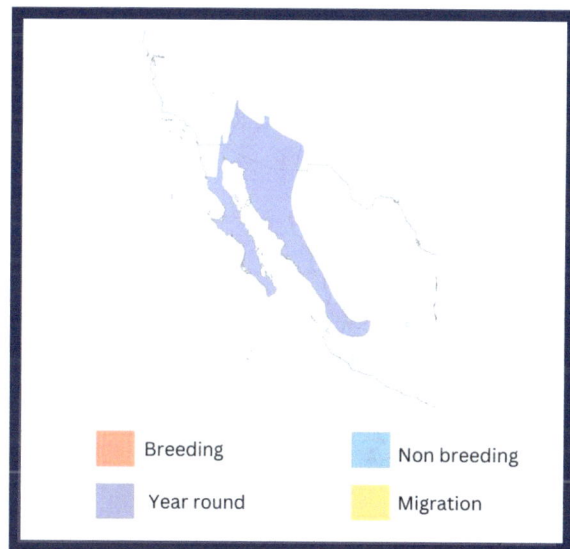

Male

Female

Juvenile

Breeding

Non breeding

Year round

Migration

Call

Rattling Drum

DID YOU KNOW....

Unlike most woodpeckers that nest in dead trees, Gila Woodpeckers are well-adapted to the arid environments they inhabit and frequently excavate their nest cavities in living saguaro cacti. This makes them crucial "architects" of the desert, as their abandoned nest holes are later used by a variety of other desert creatures, including Elf Owls, Purple Martins, and Cactus Wrens

They have adapted to human presence and are known to visit backyard hummingbird feeders to drink the sugary water. They have also been observed stealing dog food left out on porches.

Golden-fronted Woodpecker - *Melanerpes aurifrons*

Golden-fronted Woodpecker is a medium-sized woodpecker characterized by its barred black-and-white back and a buffy-brown overall coloration. Males are distinguished by a red crown and a golden-yellow forehead, while females possess a golden-yellow nape and forehead, but lack the red crown. Juveniles are duller in plumage, displaying fine streaking on the crown and breast, and faint coloration on the nape.

FEEDING These woodpeckers are omnivorous, feeding on insects and larvae, fruits, nuts, and seeds, foraging by gleaning, pecking, and probing on tree trunks and branches.

SOUNDS Their vocalizations include loud "churr" calls and drumming, especially during territorial displays and courtship.

HABITAT They inhabit open woodlands, brushlands, and semi-open areas, including urban and suburban parks, primarily in Texas and Oklahoma, extending southward into Mexico and Central America. Their habitat strongly includes areas with mesquite, oak, and cottonwood trees.

MIGRATION They are generally non-migratory, remaining within their range year-round.

SIMILAR SPECIES include the Red-bellied Woodpecker, with which they may share habitat, but they can be distinguished by their distinct head patterns and coloration.

Male

Female

Juvenile

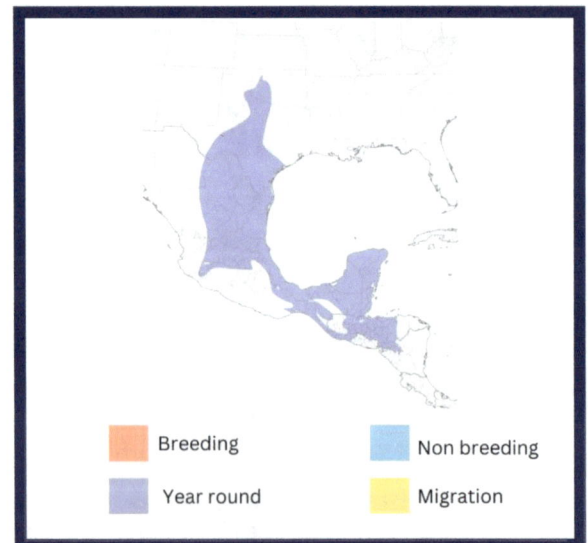

🟧	Breeding	🟦	Non breeding
🟪	Year round	🟨	Migration

Call

Drumming

DID YOU KNOW....

They are true omnivores with a highly varied diet that changes with the seasons and location. They eat a significant amount of both insects (adults and larvae, including grasshoppers, beetles, ants) and plant matter (fruits, nuts, acorns, corn).

Uniquely, adult Golden-fronted Woodpeckers have been observed providing small rocks and snail shells to their nestlings. The snail shells are believed to be a source of calcium, crucial for growing young birds, while the rocks may aid in digestion (grit). This provisioning of non-food items for a nutritional or physiological benefit is noteworthy.

Hairy Woodpecker - *Dryobates villosus*

Hairy Woodpecker is a medium-sized woodpecker characterized by its striking black and white plumage. Its wings are black with white spotting, and a bold white stripe runs down its back. Males can be distinguished by a red patch on the back of their heads, which is absent in females. Juveniles are similar to adults, but young males will display a red coloration on the top of their heads.

FEEDING They are primarily insectivorous, foraging for wood-boring beetle larvae, ants, and other insects by drilling into tree trunks and branches. They also supplement their diet with seeds, nuts, and berries.

SOUNDS Their vocalizations include a sharp "peek" call and a rapid drumming sound.

RANGE & MIGRATION They are found throughout much of North America, inhabiting mature forests, woodlands, and even suburban areas with trees. While they are mainly permanent residents, some northern populations may move southward or to lower elevations during harsh winters.

HABITAT Their preferred habitat consists of areas with mature trees, both living and dead, providing ample foraging and nesting sites.

SIMILAR SPECIES include the Downy Woodpecker, which is significantly smaller and has a proportionally smaller bill, and also has spots on its outer tail feathers.

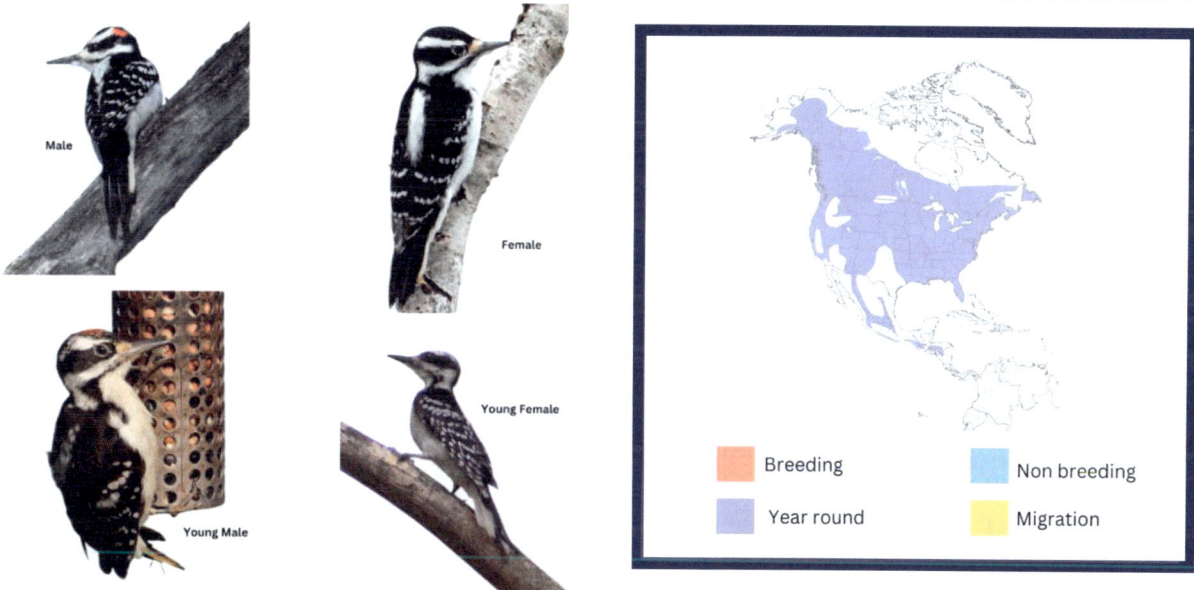

Male

Female

Young Male

Young Female

Breeding
Year round
Non breeding
Migration

Call

Drumming

DID YOU KNOW....

Despite being significantly larger than its very similar-looking cousin, the Downy Woodpecker, the Hairy Woodpecker is still considered a medium-sized woodpecker. This size difference is a key identification feature, along with the Hairy's longer bill (about the length of its head)

They seem to listen for the loud sounds of the larger woodpecker excavating and then investigate the deep holes left behind, feeding on insects that the Pileated Woodpecker might have missed.

While their diet is primarily insects, Hairy Woodpeckers will occasionally drink sap from the wells drilled by sapsuckers. They have also been recorded pecking into sugarcane to drink the sugary juice.

Ladder-backed Woodpecker - *Dryobates scalaris*

Ladder-backed Woodpecker is a small, striking woodpecker found primarily in arid regions of North America, characterized by its distinctive black and white ladder-like barring on its back. Both sexes exhibit this pattern, but males are easily identified by their bright red nape patch, which is absent in females. Juveniles are similar to females but display duller plumage and often show some red on their crowns.

FEEDING These woodpeckers specialize in foraging for insects, particularly beetles, ants, and larvae, which they extract from dead or dying trees and cacti.

SOUNDS Their vocalizations include a sharp "pik" call and a rapid, descending rattle, rather than a true song.

HABITAT They inhabit dry scrublands, deserts, and open woodlands, favoring areas with mesquite, cacti, and other desert vegetation.

MIGRATION They are generally non-migratory, remaining within their range year-round, which extends from the southwestern United States down into Mexico.

SIMILAR SPECIES include other small woodpeckers like the Downy Woodpecker and Nuttall's Woodpecker, but the Ladder-backed Woodpecker's distinct barring and arid habitat preference help distinguish it.

Male

Female

Juvenile

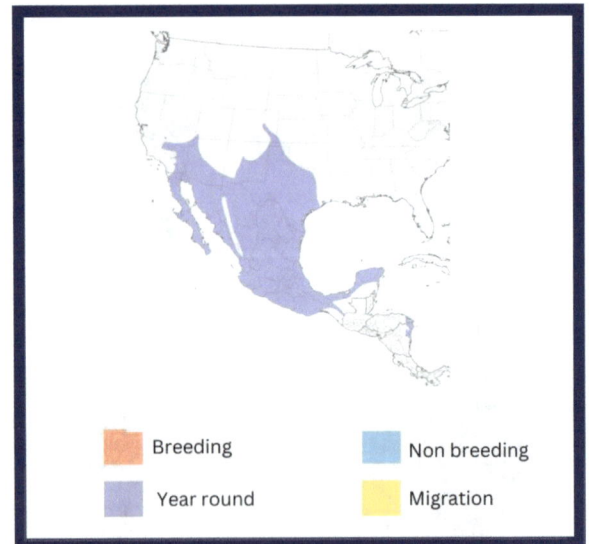

Breeding

Non breeding

Year round

Migration

Call 1

Call 2

DID YOU KNOW....

It thrives in deserts, desert scrub, thorn forests, and even uses cacti like the Joshua tree and agave for foraging and nesting. This adaptation allows it to occupy niches where other woodpeckers are less common.

Interestingly, Ladder-backed Woodpeckers in the southern parts of their range tend to have noticeably smaller bills compared to those found further north.

These woodpeckers are quite agile and can often be seen twisting, turning, balancing with their wings open, and even hanging upside down to reach food.

Northern Flicker - *Colaptes auratus*

Northern Flicker is a large, brown woodpecker that distinguishes itself by frequently foraging on the ground, primarily for ants and beetles. They exhibit a characteristic black-scalloped pattern on their backs and a noticeable white rump patch that flashes during flight. Variations exist, with "Yellow-shafted" flickers in the east displaying yellow underwings and a black "mustache" on males, while "Red-shafted" flickers in the west have reddish underwings and a red "mustache." Females of both variations generally have duller plumage and lack the distinct mustache. Juveniles resemble adults but often have a less defined pattern.

FEEDING Their diet consists mainly of insects, particularly ants, but they also consume fruits, berries, and seeds.

SOUNDS They produce a variety of vocalizations, including loud, ringing calls and a series of rapid "wicka-wicka" notes. They also engage in drumming, a form of communication and territorial display.

RANGE & MIGRATION These birds inhabit a wide range of open woodlands, forest edges, and even urban areas across North America, extending from Alaska and Canada down to Central America. Northern Flickers in the northern parts of their range are migratory, moving south for the winter, while those in southern regions may remain year-round.

HABITAT They prefer habitats with a mix of trees and open ground for foraging.

SIMILAR SPECIES could include other woodpeckers, but the Northern Flicker's ground-feeding behavior and distinctive plumage help to differentiate it.

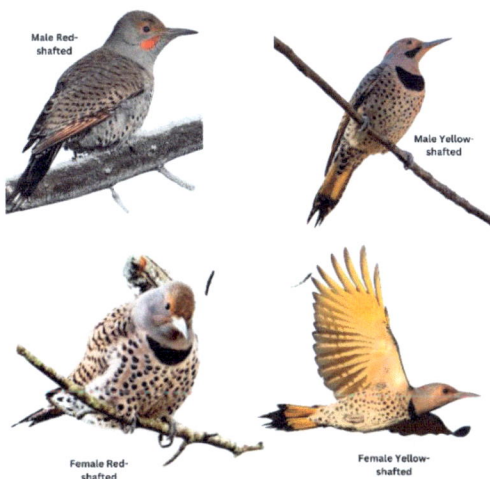

Male Red-shafted

Male Yellow-shafted

Female Red-shafted

Female Yellow-shafted

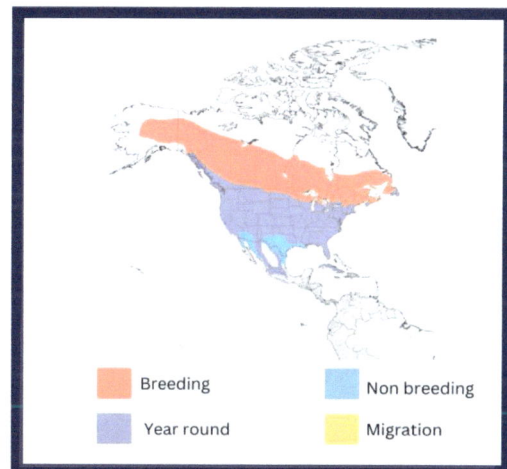

Breeding

Non breeding

Year round

Migration

Adult Call

Juvenile Call

DID YOU KNOW....

Unlike most woodpeckers that primarily forage on tree trunks and branches, the Northern Flicker spends a significant amount of its time feeding on the ground. They have a slightly curved bill that helps them dig in the soil for their favorite food: ants.

To aid in catching ants, Northern Flickers have large salivary glands that produce sticky saliva. Each time their tongue extends, it gets coated with this glue-like substance, making it easier to trap their tiny prey.

The Northern Flicker has an astonishing number of regional or folk names – over 120 have been documented! These names often refer to their appearance (like "Yellowhammer" for the yellow underwings) or their behavior.

Pileated Woodpecker - *Dryocopus pileatus*

Pileated Woodpecker is a strikingly large bird, nearly crow-sized, characterized by its predominantly black plumage, bold white stripes on its face and neck, and a prominent flaming-red crest. Males are distinguished by a red stripe on their cheek, while females have a black forehead. Juveniles are similar to adults but have a duller crest.

FEEDING They primarily feed on insects, particularly carpenter ants, which they extract from decaying wood by excavating distinctive rectangular holes.

SOUNDS Their vocalizations include loud, ringing "kuk-kuk-kuk" calls and a characteristic drumming on trees.
HABITAT & MIGRATION They inhabit mature forests, both deciduous and coniferous, throughout much of North America, and are generally non-migratory, maintaining territories year-round. Their preferred habitat consists of areas with abundant dead and dying trees.

SIMILAR SPECIES are few due to their large size, but the Ivory-billed Woodpecker, now likely extinct, was the most closely related.

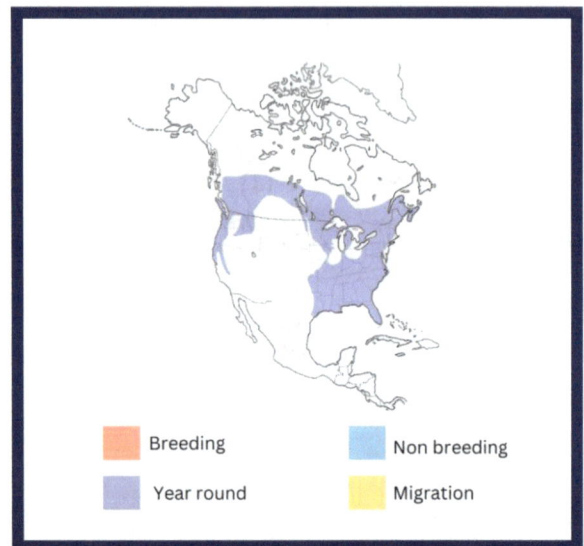

Male

Female

Juvenile

Breeding

Non breeding

Year round

Migration

Call

Juvenile Call

DID YOU KNOW....

Unlike most woodpeckers that create round holes, the Pileated Woodpecker leaves behind distinctively rectangular or oblong holes in trees as it excavates for its primary food, carpenter ants. These excavations can be so large and deep (sometimes a foot or more long) that they can occasionally cause small trees to break in half.

Its loud, ringing calls and drumming can sound surprisingly similar to the calls attributed to the possibly extinct Ivory-billed Woodpecker, leading some to mistake one for the other based on sound alone.

Compared to other woodpeckers, the Pileated Woodpecker's drumming is relatively slow, often starting slowly, accelerating in the middle, and then trailing off at the end. This can be a distinguishing characteristic.

Red-bellied Woodpecker - *Melanerpes carolinus*

Red-bellied Woodpecker is a medium-sized woodpecker characterized by its striking black and white barred back and wings. Adult males are easily identified by their bright red cap that extends from the forehead to the nape, while females have a red nape and a grayish crown. Both sexes have a pale, often reddish, wash on their bellies, though this is frequently faint and not the most reliable identifying feature. Juveniles exhibit duller plumage with less distinct barring and a brownish-gray cap.

FEEDING These woodpeckers are omnivorous, consuming insects, nuts, fruits, and seeds, often storing food in crevices for later use.

SOUNDS Their vocalizations include a rolling "churr" call and a sharp "chik" note, as well as drumming on resonant surfaces.

MIGRATION & RANGE They are non-migratory and are found throughout the eastern United States, from southern Canada down to Florida and Texas.

HABITAT They prefer deciduous forests, woodlands, and suburban areas with mature trees.

SIMILAR SPECIES include the Golden-fronted Woodpecker, which has a more golden nape and forehead, and the closely related Gila Woodpecker, which is primarily found in the southwestern United States and has less intense barring.

Male

Female

Juvenile

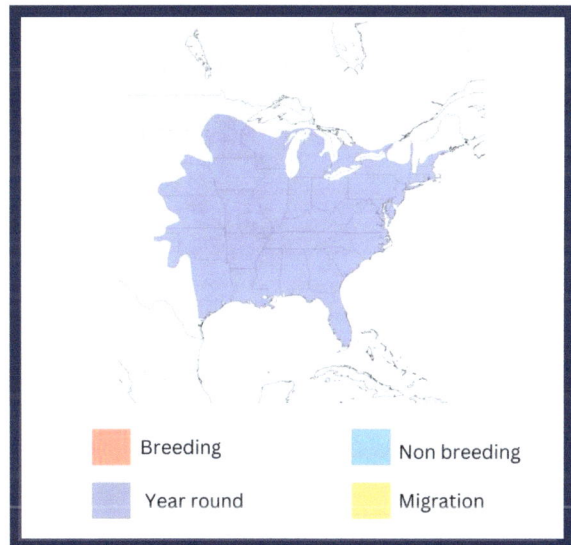

Breeding	Non breeding
Year round	Migration

Call 1   Call 2

DID YOU KNOW....

Despite its name, the red on its belly is typically a pale reddish or pinkish wash and is not always easily visible. The most prominent red coloration is on the head of the male.

Their tongue is exceptionally long, nearly two inches past the tip of their beak, with a barbed tip, which helps them extract insects from crevices.

Males primarily forage on tree trunks, while females tend to forage more on tree limbs and higher up in the trees.

Red-headed Woodpecker - *Melanerpes erythrocephalus*

The Red-headed Woodpecker is a striking, medium-sized woodpecker easily recognized by its entirely crimson head, white underparts, and large white wing patches against a black back and wings. Both male and female adults display this vivid plumage, making them visually identical. Juveniles, however, have a grayish-brown head and back with developing white wing patches, gradually acquiring the adult's vibrant coloration.

FEEDING These woodpeckers are omnivorous, consuming insects, nuts, seeds, berries, and even the eggs and young of other birds. They are known for catching insects in flight and storing nuts in tree crevices.

SOUNDS Their vocalizations include a sharp "tchur" call and a rolling drum on resonant wood, though they are less vocal than some other woodpecker species.

HABITAT They inhabit open woodlands, particularly those with dead trees and snags, as well as orchards, parks, and agricultural areas across much of eastern North America, extending westward into parts of the Great Plains.

MIGRATION Red-headed Woodpeckers exhibit varying migration patterns, with northern populations typically migrating southward during winter, while southern populations may remain resident year-round.
SIMILAR SPECIES include the Red-bellied Woodpecker and the Golden-fronted Woodpecker, but the Red-headed Woodpecker's fully red head is a key distinguishing feature.

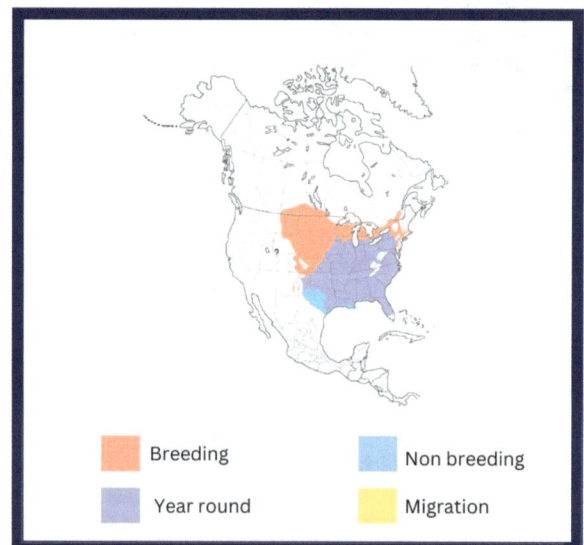

Adult

Adult

Juvenile

| Breeding | Non breeding |
| Year round | Migration |

Adult Call

Juvenile Call

DID YOU KNOW....

Unlike most woodpeckers with some red on the head, the Red-headed Woodpecker has a completely crimson-red head, neck, and upper breast, making it instantly recognizable. This vibrant red contrasts sharply with its pure white underparts and black back and wings with prominent white secondary feathers.

While they do drill for insects, Red-headed Woodpeckers are more adept at catching insects in flight than many other woodpeckers. They often perch and then fly out to snatch flying insects, exhibiting flycatcher-like behavior.

Uniquely among woodpeckers, they often perch perpendicular (sideways) to small branches, more like a songbird than the typical lengthwise grip of other woodpeckers.

Yellow-bellied Sapsucker - *Sphyrapicus varius*

Yellow-bellied Sapsucker is a distinctive North American woodpecker characterized by its black and white plumage, with a notable white stripe along its folded wings. Males possess a red crown and throat, while females have a red crown and a white throat. Juveniles display a brownish wash and a finely spotted crown.

FEEDING These sapsuckers are known for their unique feeding habits, drilling rows of shallow holes, or "sapwells," in trees to consume sap, insects trapped within, and the cambium layer.

SOUNDS Their vocalizations include mewing calls and a distinctive, stuttered drumming pattern.

HABITAT, RANGE & MIGRATION They inhabit deciduous and mixed forests, particularly favoring areas with birch and maple trees, and their range spans across much of eastern North America, with migration to the southern United States, Central America, and the Caribbean during winter. They are the only eastern North American woodpecker that is fully migratory.

SIMILAR SPECIES include other sapsuckers, such as the Red-naped and Red-breasted Sapsuckers, which can be distinguished by differences in head and throat coloration.

Male

Female

Juvenile

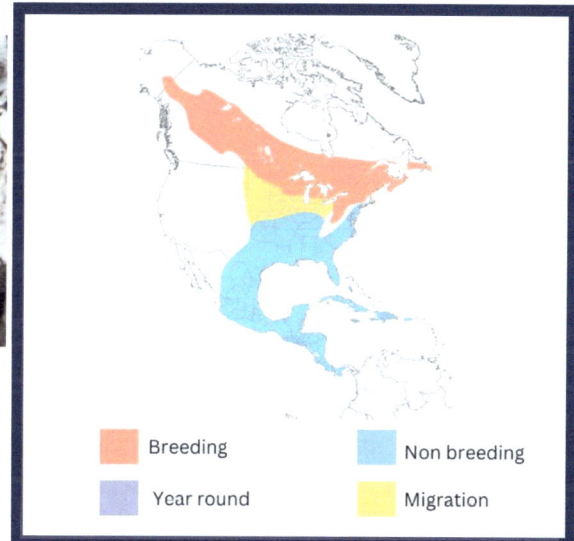

Breeding | Non breeding
Year round | Migration

Adult Call

Juvenile Call

DID YOU KNOW....

They drill neat rows of shallow holes, called "sap wells," in the bark of trees. These wells aren't just for the sapsucker; they attract insects and other birds, like hummingbirds, which also feed on the oozing sap, making the sapsucker a crucial resource provider in its ecosystem.

Interestingly, female Yellow-bellied Sapsuckers tend to migrate farther south in the winter than males.

Their drumming pattern is less of a continuous roll and more of an irregular, staccato series, sometimes described as sounding like Morse code. This makes their drumming quite distinctive from other woodpeckers

WRENS

Wrens are a fascinating group of small, active songbirds belonging to the family *Troglodytidae*. They are found primarily in the New World, with only a few species occurring in the Old World (these are often referred to as "true wrens").

General Characteristics:

- **Small Size:** Most wrens are quite small, typically ranging from about 9 to 17 cm (3.5 to 6.7 inches) in length. They often appear plump or rounded in shape.
- **Short Wings and Tail:** They possess short, rounded wings, which allow for agile flight in dense vegetation. Their tails vary in length but are often held cocked upright, a characteristic posture.
- **Cryptic Plumage:** Their feathers are generally dull in color, often in shades of brown, gray, black, and white. This cryptic coloration provides excellent camouflage in their preferred habitats. Some species may have barring, speckling, or other subtle patterns.
- **Strong Legs and Feet:** Wrens have strong legs and feet adapted for clinging to branches, twigs, and other surfaces as they forage.
- **Energetic and Active:** They are highly active birds, flitting and hopping through undergrowth, searching for food. Their movements are often quick and jerky.
- **Loud and Complex Songs:** Despite their small size, wrens are known for their surprisingly loud and often complex songs. Males use these songs to attract mates and defend territories. Each species has a distinct song, and some males can have a repertoire of different song types.
- **Varied Habitats:** Wrens occupy a wide range of habitats, including forests, woodlands, scrublands, marshes, rocky areas, and even suburban gardens. Their specific habitat preferences vary depending on the species.
- **Insectivorous Diet:** The majority of wrens are primarily insectivorous, feeding on insects, spiders, and other small invertebrates. Some larger species may occasionally take small frogs or lizards, and some may eat berries or seeds, especially during the non-breeding season.
- **Diverse Nesting Habits:** Wrens exhibit diverse nesting behaviors. Some species build elaborate, domed nests with a side entrance, while others nest in cavities such as tree holes, rock crevices, or even man-made structures. Males of some species may build multiple "dummy" nests to attract females.
- **Monogamous or Polygynous:** Mating systems vary among wren species. Some are monogamous, forming pair bonds that may last for a single breeding season or longer. Others, particularly those where males build multiple nests, can be polygynous, with one male mating with several females.

Key Points:

- **New World Dominance:** The vast majority of wren species are found in the Americas, highlighting their evolutionary success in this region.
- **Ecological Importance:** Wrens play a role in controlling insect populations within their ecosystems.
- **Indicator Species:** Due to their sensitivity to habitat changes, wrens can sometimes serve as indicator species, reflecting the health of their environment.
- **Vocal Powerhouses:** Their disproportionately loud and intricate songs are a defining characteristic and crucial for communication and territorial defense.
- **Adaptability:** The variety of habitats they occupy demonstrates their adaptability to different environmental conditions.
- **Conservation Status:** While many wren species are common and widespread, some face threats due to habitat loss and degradation, highlighting the importance of conservation efforts.

Cactus Wren - *Campylorhynchus brunneicapillus*

Cactus Wren, the largest wren in North America, is a robust bird well-adapted to arid environments. It displays a brown upper plumage with white streaks, a prominent white eyebrow, and a heavily spotted breast. Males and females are visually similar, while juveniles exhibit paler underparts and less distinct spotting.

FEEDING These wrens primarily forage on the ground, consuming insects, spiders, and occasionally fruits and seeds.

SOUNDS Their song is a loud, raspy series of chirps, often described as a sputtering sound, and they also produce various harsh calls.

RANGE & MIGRATION They reside in the desert regions of the southwestern United States and northern Mexico, favoring habitats with dense cactus and thorny shrubs. They are non-migratory, maintaining territories year-round.

HABITAT Their preferred habitat is within arid regions containing cacti, such as Saguaro and Cholla.

SIMILAR SPECIES may include other wren varieties, but the Cactus Wren's larger size, bold markings, and distinctive vocalizations readily distinguish it.

Adult

Adult

Juvenile

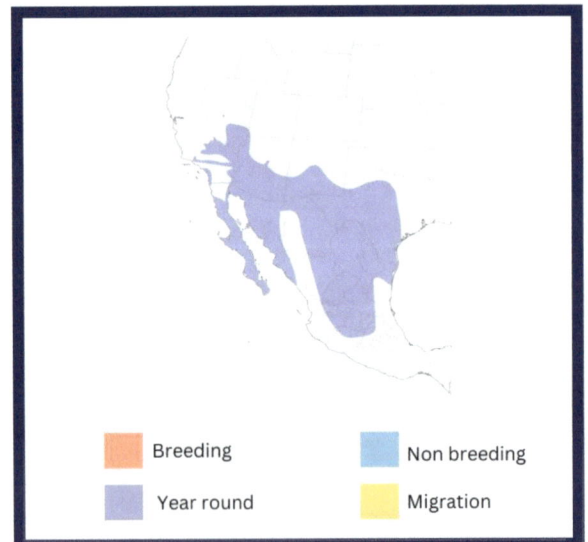

Breeding

Non breeding

Year round

Migration

Song
Call

DID YOU KNOW....

Both male and female Cactus Wrens build large, football-shaped nests with a tunnel-like entrance. These bulky structures, about 7 inches in diameter and 12 inches long, offer protection from predators and the harsh desert climate.

True to their name, they overwhelmingly prefer to build their nests in cacti, especially cholla, saguaro, and prickly pear, or other thorny desert plants like mesquite and palo verde, gaining protection from the spines.

Cactus Wrens strategically orient the entrance of their nests depending on the time of year. For nests built during hot months, the entrance faces the prevailing afternoon breeze for cooling, while those built in cooler months face away from cold winds to retain warmth.

Canyon Wren - *Catherpes mexicanus*

Canyon Wren, is a slender, long-tailed wren adapted to rocky environments throughout western North America. It displays a subtle, mottled gray-brown plumage, a pale throat and chest, and a long, slightly down-curved bill. Males and females are virtually indistinguishable in appearance, with no significant differences in plumage. Juveniles resemble adults but may have slightly softer, less defined markings.

FEEDING These wrens are primarily insectivorous, foraging for insects and spiders among rocks and crevices.
SOUNDS Their song is a series of descending, clear, liquid notes, often echoing through canyons and rocky ravines, and they also produce a sharp "chip" call.

RANGE & MIGRATION They are found in arid and semi-arid regions, particularly in canyons, rocky cliffs, and boulder fields, from southern British Columbia through the western United States and into Mexico. Canyon Wrens are generally non-migratory, remaining within their territories year-round.

HABITAT Their preferred habitat is characterized by steep, rocky slopes and cliffs, providing ample nesting and foraging opportunities.

SIMILAR SPECIES, such as other wrens, may be distinguished by their different habitat preferences and distinct vocalizations.

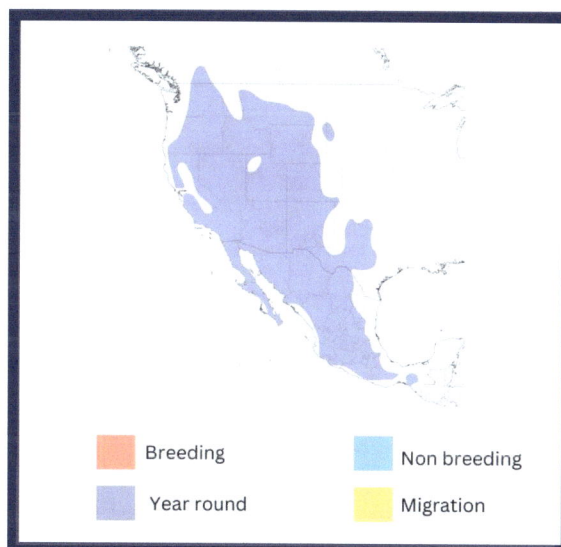

Breeding

Year round

Non breeding

Migration

Song

Call

DID YOU KNOW....

Its scientific name Catherpes comes from Greek words meaning "to creep," perfectly describing how it navigates its rocky habitat. It has a flattened skull and its vertebral column attaches higher on the skull than most birds, allowing it to probe deep crevices for insects without bumping its head

The Canyon Wren is not known to drink water directly. It likely obtains all the moisture it needs from its insect prey.

It has been observed stealing insects trapped in spiderwebs or even pilfering insects stored in wasp nests.

Carolina Wren - *Thryothorus ludovicianus*

Carolina Wren is a small, energetic songbird characterized by its warm brown plumage, prominent white eyebrow stripe, and upturned tail. It possesses a robust build and a relatively long, decurved bill. Males and females are virtually indistinguishable in appearance, displaying the same plumage patterns. Juveniles resemble adults but exhibit a duller coloration and less distinct eyebrow stripe.

FEEDING These wrens are primarily insectivorous, foraging for insects and spiders among dense vegetation and on the ground.

SOUNDS Their vocalizations are loud and varied, featuring a series of clear, ringing phrases, often described as "tea-kettle, tea-kettle, tea-kettle," and they also produce a variety of chattering and scolding calls.

RANGE & MIGRATION They are non-migratory and inhabit the eastern half of the United States, extending from southern Canada down to Mexico, favoring dense undergrowth in woodlands, thickets, and suburban gardens.

HABITAT Their preferred habitat includes brush piles, fallen logs, and overgrown areas.

SIMILAR SPECIES include other wren species, particularly the Bewick's Wren, but the Carolina Wren's loud song and overall warmer coloration help to differentiate it.

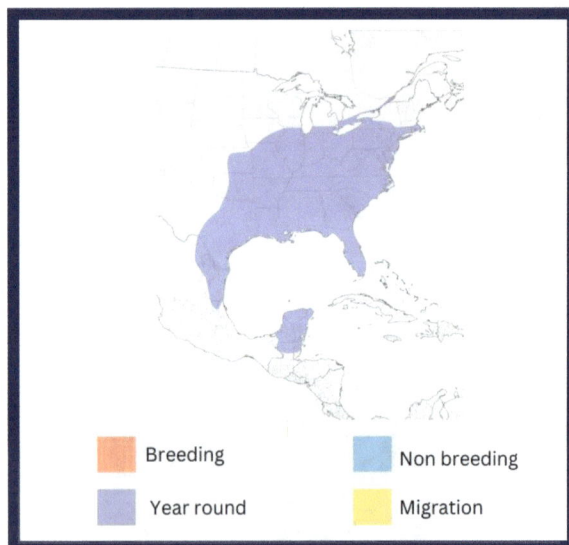

Adult

Adult

Juvenile

Breeding

Non breeding

Year round

Migration

Song

Call

DID YOU KNOW....

Despite their small size (about 5.5 inches long), male Carolina Wrens possess an exceptionally large repertoire of songs, with some individuals known to sing up to 40 different variations. They can sing almost constantly throughout the day, sometimes up to 3,000 times!

While only the male Carolina Wren sings the loud, clear songs, the female often contributes with a rapid, chattering trill, creating a duet.

A peculiar habit of Carolina Wrens is the frequent incorporation of shed snakeskin into their nest structure. The reason for this is not entirely clear, but it's speculated it might deter predators.

Northern House Wren - *Troglodytes aedon*

Northern House Wren is a small, active songbird with a drab, grayish-brown plumage, a slightly paler underside, and faint barring on its wings and tail. It possesses a relatively long, thin, slightly decurved bill. Males and females are virtually indistinguishable by plumage alone, although males may be slightly larger. Juveniles are similar to adults but have a duller coloration and less distinct barring.

FEEDING These wrens are primarily insectivorous, foraging for insects and spiders on the ground and in vegetation.

SOUNDS Their songs are a rapid, bubbly series of notes, often delivered with great enthusiasm, while their calls include a sharp "churr" or "scold."

RANGE & MIGRATION They are widely distributed across North America, breeding throughout much of the continent and migrating south for the winter. The northern populations travel to the southern United States and Mexico during the colder months.

HABITAT Their preferred habitats include open woodlands, forest edges, brushy areas, and suburban gardens, often near human habitation.

SIMILAR SPECIES might include other wrens, such as the Winter Wren or Bewick's Wren, but the Northern House Wren's song, habitat preferences, and overall appearance help to distinguish it.

Adult

Adult

Juvenile

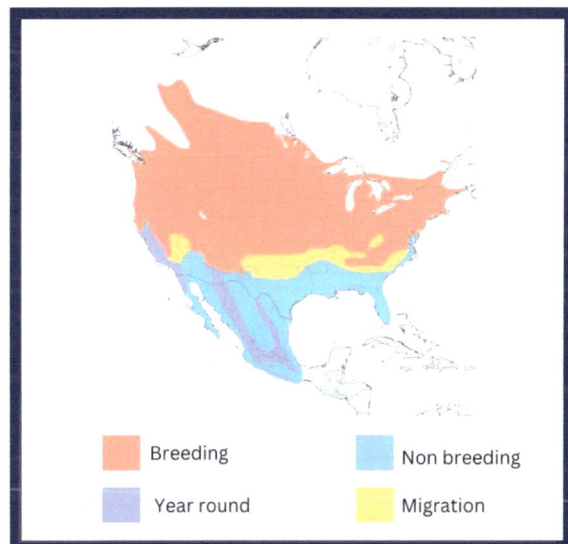

Breeding

Non breeding

Year round

Migration

Song

Call

DID YOU KNOW....

Male Northern House Wrens are industrious builders. They often start constructing multiple incomplete "dummy" nests within their territory to attract a female. The female then inspects these options and chooses one to complete and lay her eggs in.

To combat nest parasites like mites, Northern House Wrens frequently incorporate spider egg sacs into their nest material. Once the spiderlings hatch, they prey on the mites, acting as tiny pest control within the wren's nest.

While generally solitary, Northern House Wrens will sometimes gather in communal roosts during cold winter nights to conserve warmth

Marsh Wren - *Cistothorus palustris*

Marsh Wren is a small, secretive songbird found in North American wetlands. Adults exhibit a brown upper plumage with a dark cap and a white eyebrow stripe, and they possess a distinct white and black streaked back. Males and females share similar plumage, though males are often slightly larger. Juvenile birds resemble adults but have less distinct markings.

FEEDING These wrens primarily consume insects and spiders, foraging among the dense vegetation of their marsh habitats.

SOUNDS The male Marsh Wren is known for its complex, gurgling song, used to establish territory and attract mates, and they also produce various sharp, buzzy calls.

RANGE & MIGRATION Their range spans across North America, with populations found in both coastal and inland marshes. Migration patterns vary; some populations are year-round residents, while others migrate south for the winter.

HABITAT They favor habitats with tall, dense vegetation like cattails, bulrushes, and reeds, within both freshwater and saltwater marshes.

SIMILAR SPECIES include other wrens, particularly the Sedge Wren, but the Marsh Wren's preferred habitat and vocalizations aid in distinguishing it.

Adult

Adult

Juvenile

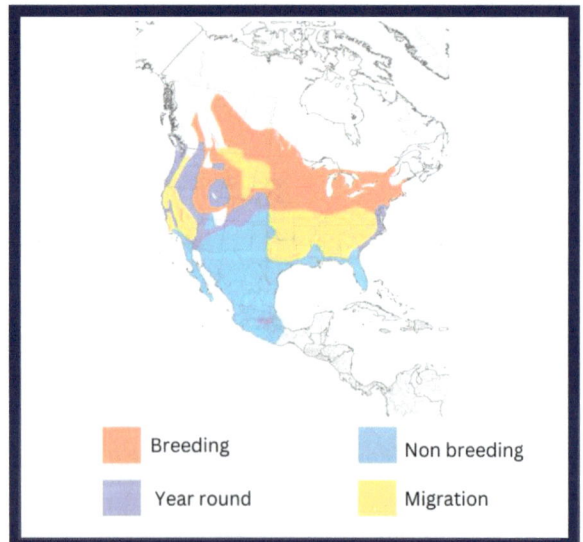

| Breeding | Non breeding |
| Year round | Migration |

Song

Call

DID YOU KNOW....

Marsh Wrens exhibit polygyny. A successful male with a desirable territory and impressive nest-building skills can have multiple females nesting within his territory at the same time. Each female typically raises her brood independently.

Both male and female Marsh Wrens can be fiercely territorial. They have been observed destroying the eggs and even the nestlings of other Marsh Wrens and other bird species nesting nearby, possibly to reduce competition for resources.

Unlike many songbirds that primarily sing during the day, male Marsh Wrens are known to sing both day and night, especially during the breeding season, to establish and defend their territories and attract mates.

Pacific Wren - *Troglodytes pacificus*

Pacific Wren is a very small, compact bird characterized by its overall brown plumage, with darker barring on its wings, tail, and underparts. It maintains a short, often cocked tail, and exhibits a pale eyebrow. Sexes are visually similar. Juveniles resemble adults, but may have less distinct barring.

FEEDING These wrens are primarily insectivorous, foraging among dense undergrowth for insects and spiders.

SOUNDS Their song is a complex, rapid series of musical trills and chatters, a distinctive sound in their forested habitats. They also produce sharp "kit-kit" call notes.

RANGE & MIGRATION They are found in the western regions of North America, particularly in old-growth evergreen forests, and also in various other forested habitats, including riparian areas. While they are mainly resident birds, some populations, particularly those in interior regions, may move short distances southward during the winter.

HABITAT They favor habitats with dense understory, such as old-growth forests, areas with fallen logs, and thickets near streams.

SIMILAR SPECIES to be aware of include the Winter Wren, from which it was recently separated, and the House Wren, but differences in song and subtle plumage variations help distinguish them.

Adult

Adult

Juvenile

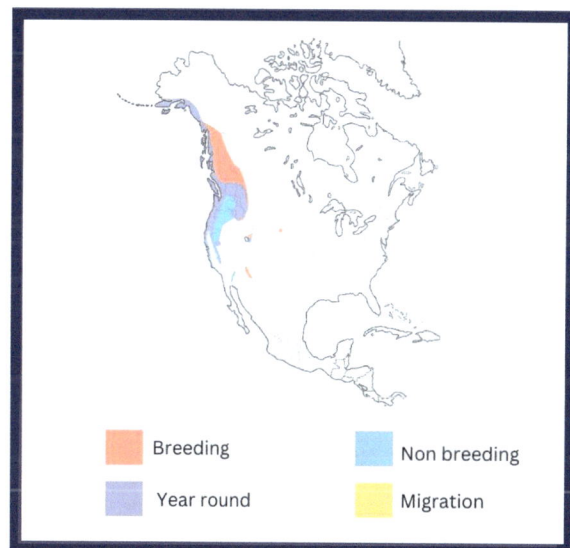

Breeding

Non breeding

Year round

Migration

Song

Call

DID YOU KNOW....

Pacific Wrens possess an incredibly complex and varied song, far out of proportion to their small size. What's truly unique is that these songs exhibit regional "dialects." Birds in different geographic areas have distinct song patterns that are learned, not entirely innate. This cultural transmission of song is a fascinating area of study.

Despite being one of the smallest songbirds in their range, Pacific Wrens are remarkably hardy and can survive in cold, damp environments, including dense forests and rocky coastal areas.

They often show strong site fidelity, meaning they tend to return to the same breeding and wintering territories year after year.

Sedge Wren - *Cistothorus stellaris*

Sedge Wren, a small and secretive bird, is characterized by its streaked brown back, pale underparts, and a lightly streaked breast. Both males and females share similar plumage, making visual sex differentiation difficult in the field. Juveniles resemble adults but display a more buffy coloration and less distinct streaking.

FEEDING These wrens primarily forage on the ground or within dense vegetation, feeding on insects and spiders.

SOUNDS Their song is a dry, rapid series of buzzy notes, often described as sounding like a sewing machine, while their calls include sharp, short notes.

RANGE & MIGRATION The Sedge Wren's breeding range extends across portions of the northern and central United States and southern Canada, and they winter in the southeastern United States. They are migratory, moving south during the colder months.

HABITAT Their preferred habitat consists of wet meadows, sedge meadows, and other grassy areas with dense vegetation.

SIMILAR SPECIES include other small wrens, especially the Marsh Wren, but the Sedge Wren's drier habitat preference and distinctive song aid in identification.

Adult

Adult

Juvenile

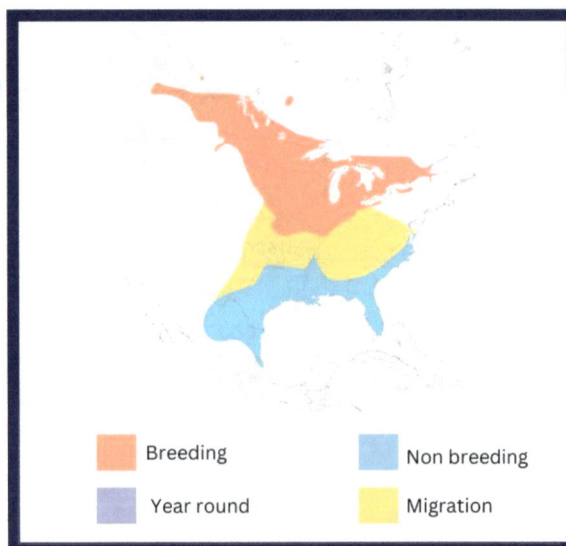

| Breeding | Non breeding |
| Year round | Migration |

Song

Call

DID YOU KNOW....

Unlike many territorial birds that return to the same breeding grounds year after year, the Sedge Wren is a nomadic breeder in North America. They will move to areas with suitable moist meadows and grasslands and may not return to the same location the following year if conditions aren't right.

Some Sedge Wrens in North America are thought to have a unique double brooding strategy. They may raise their first brood in the northern part of their breeding range and then migrate further south within their breeding range to raise a second brood in late summer.

The male's song is quite distinctive and has been described as sounding like two pebbles tapping together or the rattling of a bag of marbles. It starts with a few sharp, separate notes before launching into a rapid, dry trill.

Winter Wren - *Troglodytes hiemalis*

Winter Wren is a very small, brown songbird characterized by its short, cocked tail and a subtle pale eyebrow. Its plumage is a dark reddish-brown with faint dark barring on the underparts and wings. Males and females are very similar in appearance, while juveniles tend to be darker overall.

FEEDING These wrens are insectivores, foraging for insects, spiders, and other small invertebrates primarily on the ground among dense vegetation.

SOUNDS Their song is a complex, high-pitched series of trills and warbles, remarkably loud for such a small bird, while their call is a sharp, dry "chimp."

HABITAT They inhabit dense, moist forests, particularly those with abundant downed logs, thick undergrowth, and mossy areas, favoring coniferous or mixed forests.

RANGE & MIGRATION Their breeding range extends across boreal North America, and they migrate to the southern United States for the winter. Migration patterns can vary, with some populations being sedentary.

SIMILAR SPECIES include the House Wren, which is generally lighter in color and has a longer tail.

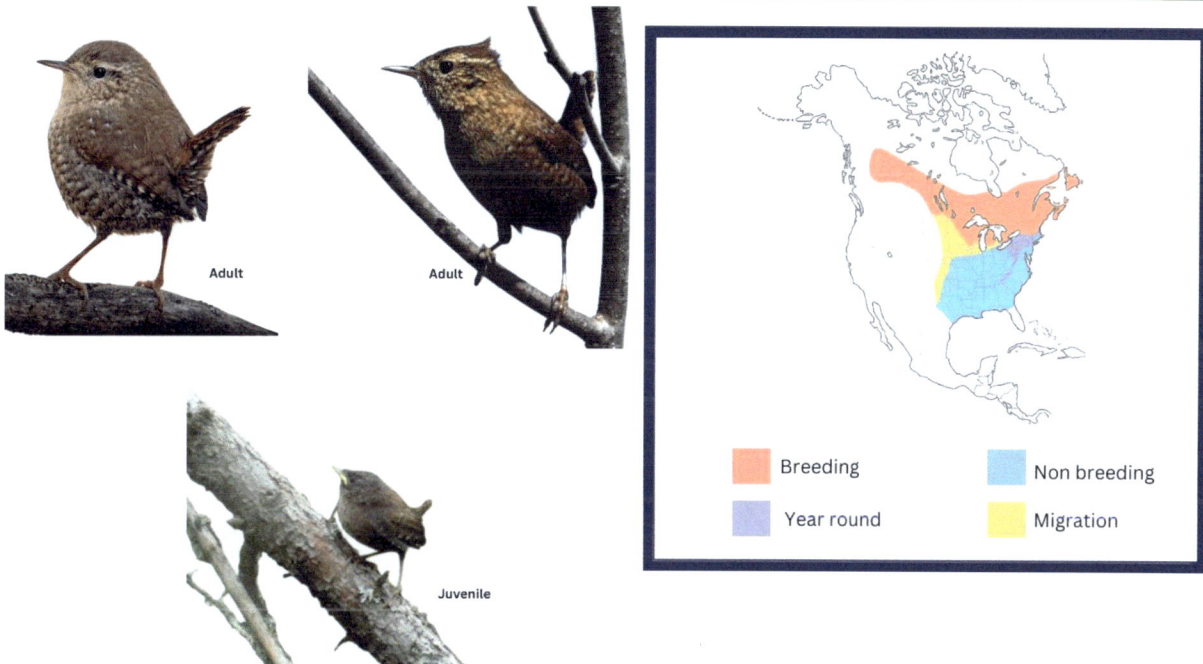

Adult

Adult

Juvenile

Breeding

Non breeding

Year round

Migration

Song

Call

DID YOU KNOW....

Despite being one of the smallest songbirds in North America (weighing only about 8-12 grams and measuring 8-12 cm in length), the Winter Wren possesses an incredibly loud and complex song. Per unit weight, their song delivery is said to be 10 times more powerful than a crowing rooster.

Due to its small, round body, short tail that is often held erect, and its habit of scurrying and hopping along the ground and through dense undergrowth, the Winter Wren is sometimes described as looking like a "dark brown flying mouse."

These tiny birds often exhibit a characteristic behavior of bobbing their entire body up and down, almost like they are doing squats, as they nervously look around while foraging in the forest understory.

HUMMINGBIRDS

Hummingbirds are a fascinating group of small birds found exclusively in the Americas. They belong to the family Trochilidae and exhibit a remarkable array of adaptations that allow them to thrive on nectar and small insects.

General Characteristics:

- **Size:** They are among the smallest of birds, with most species ranging from 3 to 5 inches in length. The bee hummingbird of Cuba is the smallest bird in the world, weighing less than a dime.
- **Flight:** Hummingbirds are exceptional fliers, being the only birds capable of true hovering flight. They can also fly forwards, backwards, sideways, and even upside down. Their wings beat incredibly fast (20-80 times per second, and up to 200 times per second while diving), creating the characteristic "humming" sound from which they get their name.
- **Metabolism:** They possess the highest metabolism of any non-insect animal. To fuel their rapid wing movements and high heart rates (up to 1200 beats per minute during flight), they need to consume large amounts of food frequently.
- **Diet:** Their primary food source is nectar from flowers, which they extract with their long, slender bills and specialized tongues. They also eat small insects for protein.
- **Tongue:** Their tongues are long, forked, and often have fringed edges to efficiently lap up nectar. They can lick 10-15 times per second while feeding.
- **Coloration:** Many male hummingbirds (and sometimes females) have iridescent plumage with brilliant, metallic colors. These colors are not due to pigments but result from the microscopic structure of their feathers, which refract light.
- **Bills:** Hummingbird bills are adapted to the flowers they feed on and can vary greatly in length and shape, sometimes being straight, curved, or even upturned.
- **Feet:** Their feet are small and weak, primarily used for perching and not for walking or hopping.
- **Brain Size:** Proportionally, hummingbirds have the largest brains of any bird, allowing for excellent spatial memory to remember flower locations and migration routes.

Key Points:

- **Pollination:** Hummingbirds are important pollinators for many plant species, especially those with tubular flowers.
- **Migration:** Many hummingbird species are migratory, undertaking long journeys between breeding and wintering grounds. Some, like the Ruby-throated Hummingbird, can fly non-stop across the Gulf of Mexico.
- **Torpor:** To conserve energy during cold nights or when food is scarce, hummingbirds can enter a state of torpor, a deep sleep-like state where their metabolic rate and body temperature drop significantly.
- **Nesting:** Female hummingbirds typically build small, cup-shaped nests made of plant down, spider webs, and other soft materials. They usually lay only two tiny eggs.
- **Solitary Nature:** Hummingbirds are generally solitary and territorial, often fiercely defending their feeding areas.
- **Lack of Smell:** They have a poor sense of smell but possess excellent color vision, especially for red and orange flowers.
- **Diversity:** There are over 330 species of hummingbirds, found throughout the Americas, with the greatest diversity in the tropics.
- **Vulnerability:** Some hummingbird species are facing threats due to habitat loss, climate change, and the use of pesticides.

Allen's Hummingbird - *Selasphorus sasin*

Allen's Hummingbird is a small hummingbird known for its vibrant plumage and energetic flight. Males display a brilliant iridescent orange-red throat, a green back, and a rufous wash on the flanks. Females and juveniles are primarily green above with a grayish-white underbelly, often with some rufous on the flanks and tail. Juvenile males will gradually acquire the vibrant throat.

FEEDING These hummingbirds are nectar feeders, relying on flowers and supplemental feeders, and also consume small insects for protein.

SOUNDS Allen's Hummingbirds produce a distinctive buzzing sound with their wings during flight and a sharp "chip" call. Males perform elaborate aerial displays accompanied by a high-pitched buzz and a series of sharp, metallic chips.

RANGE & MIGRATION Their breeding range is primarily along the coastal California and some coastal Oregon, with a separate population on the Channel Islands. During migration, they move south to winter in central and southern Mexico.

HABITAT They favor coastal scrub, chaparral, and open woodlands, and are also found in suburban gardens with flowering plants.

SIMILAR SPECIES include the Rufous Hummingbird, with which they often overlap in range and are difficult to differentiate, especially females and juveniles. The primary differences lie in the tail feather shape and subtle plumage details, and sometimes by the timing of migration.

Male

Female

Juvenile

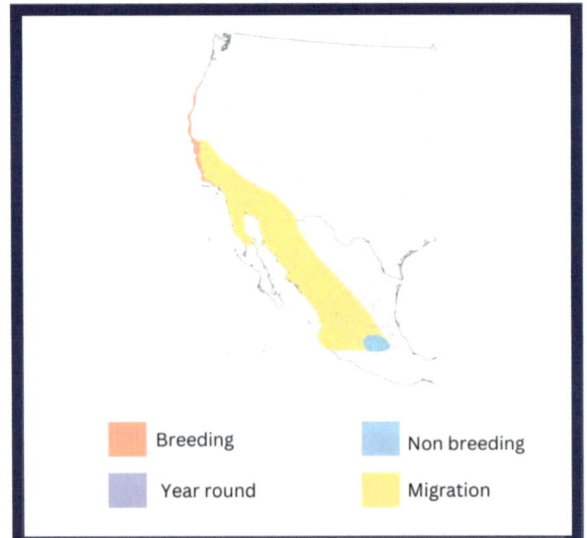

Breeding | Non breeding
Year round | Migration

Display Chips

Call

DID YOU KNOW....

The migratory males are some of the earliest northbound migrants, returning to their breeding grounds as early as January, likely to coincide with the early blooming flowers in their coastal habitat.

During their impressive J-shaped courtship dive (from up to 100 feet high), the males produce a sharp, high-pitched squealing sound with their tail feathers at the bottom of the dive.

Female Allen's Hummingbirds may build new nests on top of old ones or even take materials from old nests to construct a new one in a different location

Anna's Hummingbird - *Calypte anna*

Anna's Hummingbird, a small, stocky hummingbird, is a year-round resident of the Pacific coast of North America. It is known for its remarkable ability to withstand cold temperatures, allowing it to expand its range northward. The male Anna's Hummingbird is easily recognized by its vibrant rose-pink gorget and crown, which flash brilliantly in sunlight. Females and juveniles exhibit a more subdued plumage, with a green back and grayish underparts, often with a few red spots on the throat. Juveniles are similar to females, developing their adult plumage over time.

FEEDING These hummingbirds are primarily nectarivores, feeding on the nectar of flowers, and they also consume small insects and spiders for protein.

SOUNDS Their song is a series of scratchy, buzzy notes, and they produce a sharp "chip" call.

RANGE & MIGRATION They are found from British Columbia, Canada, south to Baja California, Mexico, with their range expanding inland. They are largely non-migratory, though some altitudinal movements may occur.

HABITAT Their preferred habitats include urban gardens, open woodlands, and chaparral.

SIMILAR SPECIES might include other hummingbirds like the Allen's Hummingbird, but Anna's Hummingbird's robust build, round head, and distinctive song and gorget help distinguish it.

Male

Female

Juvenile

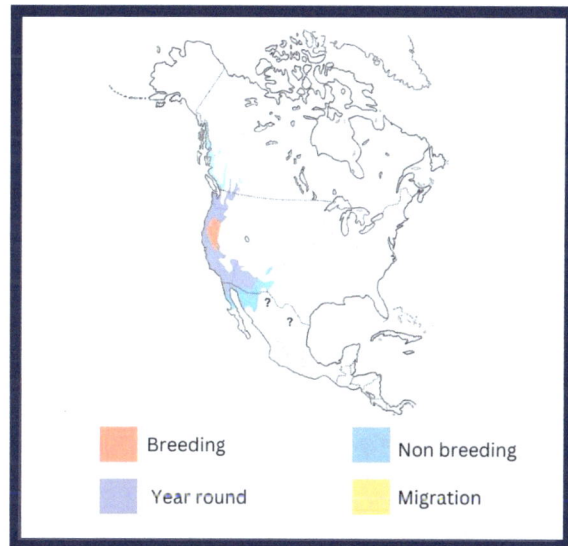

Breeding   Non breeding

Year round   Migration

Song   **Call**

DID YOU KNOW....

The male Anna's Hummingbird is the only North American hummingbird species with a gorget (iridescent throat patch) that extends up and over its entire head, like a shimmering helmet. In most other species, the gorget is limited to the throat area.

They have readily adapted to urban and suburban environments, thriving on introduced plant species like eucalyptus and the nectar provided in backyard feeders. This adaptability has significantly contributed to their range expansion

On rare occasions, bees and wasps can become impaled on the thin bill of an Anna's Hummingbird, tragically leading to the bird's starvation.

Berylline Hummingbird - *Saucerottia beryllina*

Berylline Hummingbird, a vibrant resident of the southwestern United States and Mexico, is a medium-sized hummingbird characterized by its brilliant emerald-green plumage. Both males and females share this overall coloration, though males may exhibit a slightly more intense green. Distinguishing between sexes visually can be difficult, but typically, females may display a slightly duller coloration. Juvenile birds resemble females, often with a more muted green and some buffy feather edges.

FEEDING These hummingbirds primarily feed on nectar from flowering plants, supplementing their diet with small insects caught in flight.

SOUNDS Their vocalizations consist of high-pitched, thin chips and trills, often difficult for the human ear to discern.

RANGE & MIGRATION Their range in North America is limited, primarily found in southeastern Arizona and southwestern New Mexico, extending south into Mexico. They are generally considered residents within their range, with some altitudinal movements in response to food availability, rather than a true migration.

HABITAT Their preferred habitat includes oak woodlands, canyons, and mountain slopes, particularly areas with abundant flowering plants.

SIMILAR SPECIES in their range include other green hummingbirds like the Broad-billed Hummingbird and the Violet-crowned Hummingbird, but the Berylline Hummingbird's overall green coloration and subtle plumage differences help distinguish it.

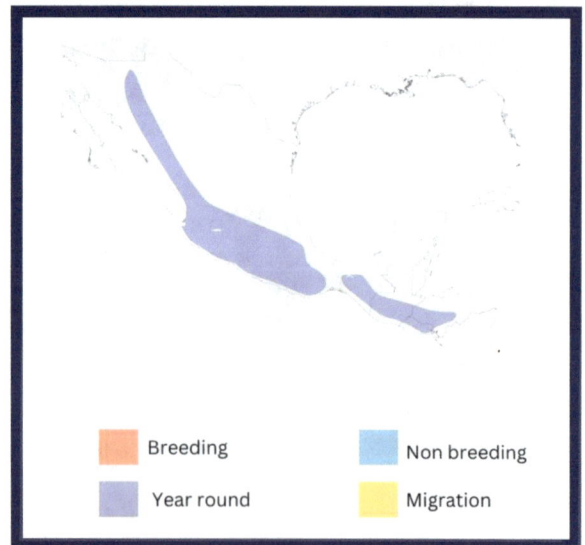

Adult

Adult

Juvenile

Song

Call

Breeding

Non breeding

Year round

Migration

DID YOU KNOW....

Its common name comes from the mineral beryl, as its predominantly green coloration closely resembles the sea-green gem.

In addition to hawking for insects in the air, they have been observed picking arthropods directly from spider webs

The female builds a solid cup nest made of plant fibers bound with spiderweb and often camouflages the exterior with lichens

Black-chinned Hummingbird - *Archilochus alexandri*

Black-chinned Hummingbird, a small and agile bird, is characterized by its iridescent green back and flanks. Males possess a black chin and throat, which appears a deep purple in bright light, along with a dark, forked tail. Females and juveniles exhibit a duller green back, a whitish throat, and a rounded tail with dark subterminal bands and white tips. Juveniles are similar to females, but often show buffy fringes on their head and back feathers.

FEEDING These hummingbirds are primarily nectar feeders, utilizing their long, slender bills to extract nectar from flowers, and they also consume small insects and spiders for protein.

SOUNDS Their vocalizations include a series of dry, buzzy chips and a high-pitched, thin "seep" call. During courtship, males perform elaborate displays with a buzzing sound created by their wings.

RANGE & MIGRATION They breed in western North America, ranging from British Columbia south through the western United States and into Mexico, and migrate south to Mexico for the winter.

HABITAT They favor semi-open habitats, including canyons, woodlands, deserts, and suburban gardens, especially areas with flowering plants.

SIMILAR SPECIES include the Ruby-throated Hummingbird, which has a more eastern range, and Anna's Hummingbird, which has a reddish throat in males and is a year-round resident in much of its range.

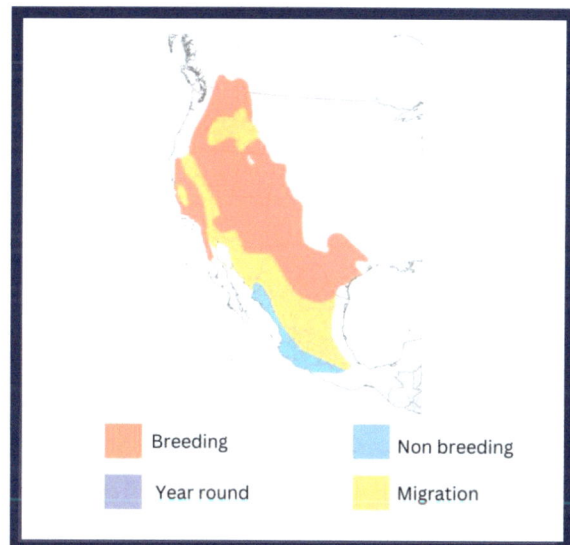

Breeding

Non breeding

Year round

Migration

Call

DID YOU KNOW....

During courtship, the male performs a dramatic "pendulum" display, flying back and forth in wide U-shaped arcs, often producing a whirring sound at the bottom of each dive.

The Black-chinned Hummingbird was found to have the smallest known genome of all living amniotes (vertebrates that lay their eggs on land or retain the fertilized egg within the mother), with only 0.91 pg (910 million base pairs).

This species is known to hybridize with several other hummingbird species, including Anna's, Lucifer, Broad-tailed, and Costa's Hummingbirds.

Broad-billed Hummingbird - *Cynanthus latirostris*

Broad-billed Hummingbird is a vibrant, medium-sized hummingbird characterized by its namesake broad, red bill, ideal for feeding on tubular flowers. Males exhibit a striking iridescent green plumage with a deep blue throat, while females are generally duller green above and grayish below, often showing a faint green wash on their flanks. Juveniles resemble females but may have buffy fringes on their head and neck feathers.

FEEDING These hummingbirds are primarily nectarivores, feeding on nectar from a variety of flowering plants, but they also consume small insects for protein.

SOUNDS Their songs are a series of high-pitched, thin chips and trills, and they produce sharp, dry chip calls.

RANGE & MIGRATION Their range extends from the southwestern United States, primarily Arizona and New Mexico, southward into Mexico. They are partial migrants, with some populations moving south during the winter months, although many remain within their breeding range.

HABITAT They prefer habitats such as canyons, riparian woodlands, and oak forests, often near flowering plants.

SIMILAR SPECIES include other hummingbird species, but the Broad-billed Hummingbird's distinctive bill and plumage, especially the male's blue throat, help distinguish it.

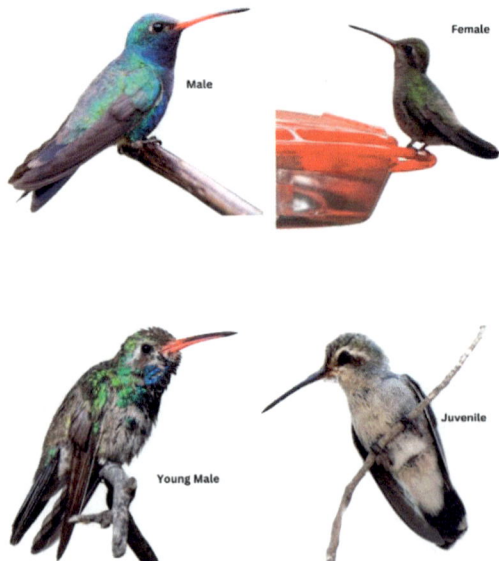

Male   Female

Young Male   Juvenile

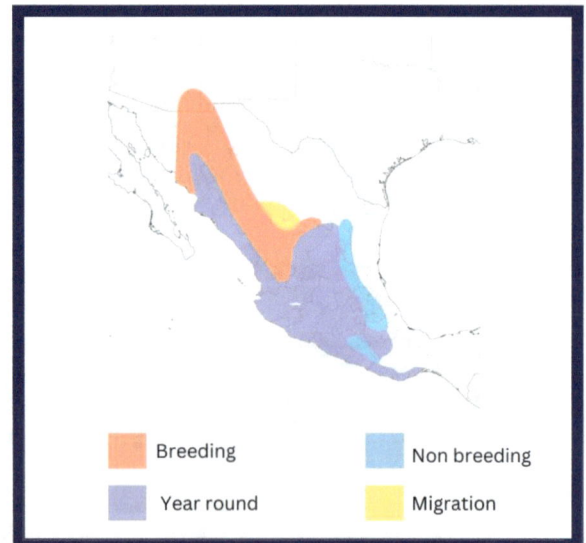

- Breeding
- Non breeding
- Year round
- Migration

Song

Call

DID YOU KNOW....

Despite its name, the "broad-billed" refers to the base of the bill being relatively wide, not necessarily the entire bill. It could have easily been named for its vibrant colors, like "Cobalt Firebill" or "Metallic Emerald."

Adult males sometimes have a hint of "cobwebs" at the base of their upper beak.

During courtship, the male performs a unique "pendulum display" flight in front of the female, hovering and flying in repeated arcs from side to side.

Broad-tailed Hummingbird - *Selasphorus platycercus*

Broad-tailed Hummingbird, a medium-sized hummingbird found in western North America, is recognized by its namesake broad tail feathers. Males are particularly striking, showcasing a vibrant rose-pink gorget that flares during courtship displays, along with a green back and flanks. The male also produces a distinct metallic trill with its wings during flight. Females and juveniles are more subdued, displaying a green back, grayish underparts, and often a slightly rufous wash on the flanks, with a rounded tail that shows white tips on the outer tail feathers. Juveniles resemble females.

FEEDING They primarily feed on nectar from flowers, supplementing their diet with small insects.

SOUNDS Their song is a high-pitched, thin series of chips and trills, and they also produce sharp chip calls.

RANGE & MIGRATION They breed in mountainous regions of the western United States and into Mexico, preferring coniferous forests, meadows, and scrublands at higher elevations. They are migratory, moving south to Mexico and Central America for the winter.

SIMILAR SPECIES include other *Selasphorus* hummingbirds, such as the Rufous Hummingbird and Calliope Hummingbird, but the Broad-tailed Hummingbird's characteristic broad tail and distinctive wing trill help distinguish it.

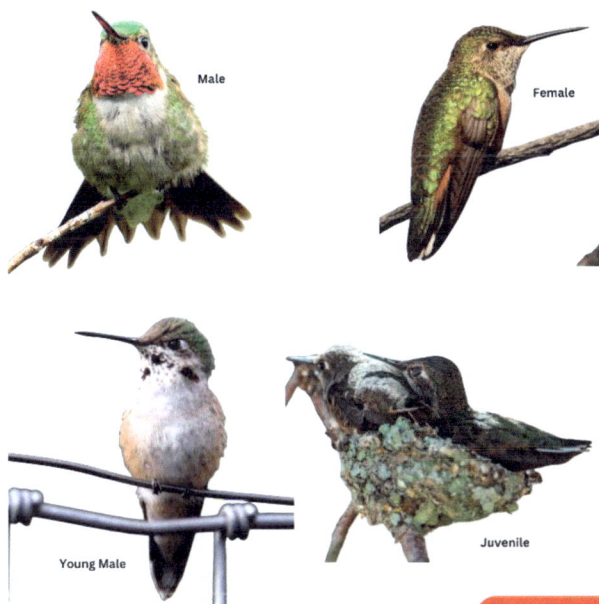

Male

Female

Young Male

Juvenile

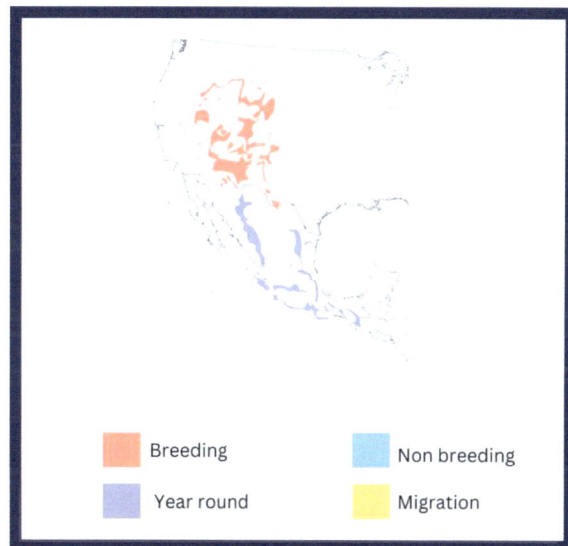

Breeding

Non breeding

Year round

Migration

Call 1

Call 2

DID YOU KNOW....

Interestingly, the specialized wing feathers that create the male's trill wear down over the breeding season. By midwinter, the trill is often inaudible until they grow new feathers before the next breeding season.

Research suggests that males unable to produce this wing trill due to feather manipulation are more likely to lose their territories to more aggressive males, highlighting the importance of this non-vocal communication.

The female constructs a tiny cup-shaped nest using spider webs and plant down, often camouflaged with lichen and moss. The elasticity of the spider silk allows the nest to stretch as the chicks grow.

Buff-bellied Hummingbird - *Amazilia yucatanensis*

Buff-bellied Hummingbird is a medium-sized hummingbird characterized by its distinctive buff-colored belly, from which it derives its name. Adult birds display a bronzy-green coloration on their upperparts, and a notable feature is their straight, bright red bill with a dark tip. Males are further distinguished by an iridescent green throat, which can appear dark in certain lighting conditions. Females exhibit a similar overall plumage, though often with less intense iridescence. Juveniles are recognized by their darker bills and duller, grayish underparts.

FEEDING These hummingbirds primarily feed on nectar from flowers, and they also consume small insects for protein.

SOUNDS Their vocalizations include sharp "chip" sounds and a series of rapid, repeated notes.

HABITAT They inhabit lowland areas, including woodlands, scrublands, and urban gardens, primarily in eastern Mexico and southernmost Texas.

RANGE & MIGRATION Their range extends along the Gulf Coast, and they may disperse northward after the breeding season.

SIMILAR SPECIES that may cause confusion include other hummingbird species, but the Buff-bellied Hummingbird's unique color patterns and red bill are key identifying features.

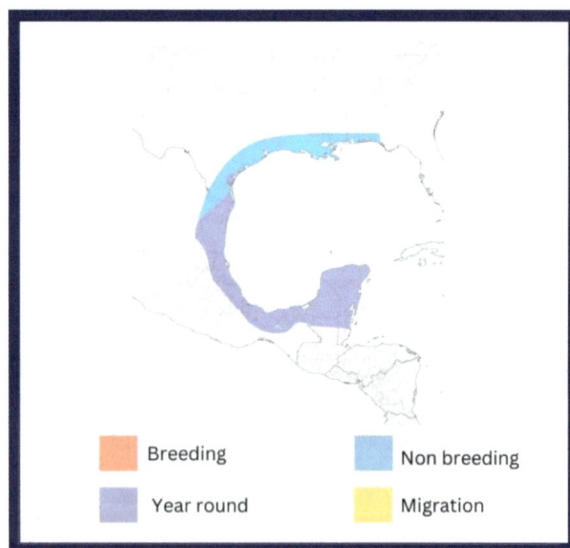

Breeding   Non breeding

Year round   Migration

Song   Call

DID YOU KNOW....

Due to their rapid wing movements and hovering ability around flowers, they can sometimes resemble moths in flight.

Although generally diurnal, Buff-bellied Hummingbirds have been observed feeding at night, particularly nesting females.

Unlike many North American hummingbirds that migrate south for the winter, some Buff-bellied Hummingbirds exhibit a unique northward dispersal along the Gulf Coast of the United States after the breeding season

Calliope Hummingbird - *Selasphorus calliope*

Calliope Hummingbird, the smallest breeding bird in North America, is characterized by its compact size and short tail. Males are easily recognized by their vibrant magenta gorget, which appears as radiating streaks, along with green flanks and a dark tail. Females and juveniles exhibit a more subdued plumage, with green upperparts, whitish underparts, and often a lightly streaked throat; juveniles may have a faint dusky or rusty wash on the flanks.

FEEDING These hummingbirds are primarily nectarivorous, feeding on the nectar of flowers, and they also consume small insects and spiders for protein.

SOUNDS Their songs are a series of high-pitched, thin chips and buzzes, and their calls include sharp "tsip" notes.

RANGE & MIGRATION They breed in mountainous regions of the western United States and Canada, particularly in coniferous forests and subalpine meadows. They are long-distance migrants, wintering in Mexico. During migration, they follow blooming flowers up and down mountain ranges.

HABITAT Their habitat preferences include open coniferous forests, meadows, and scrublands, particularly those with abundant flowering plants.

SIMILAR SPECIES include other *Selasphorus* hummingbirds, such as the Rufous Hummingbird and the Allen's Hummingbird, but the Calliope's small size and distinctive gorget help distinguish adult males.

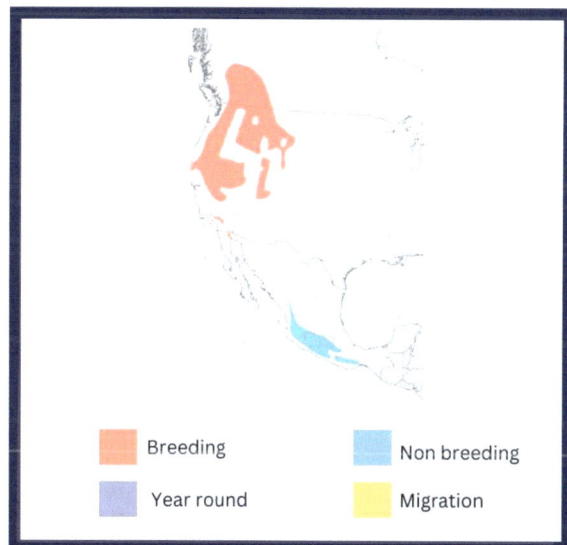

Breeding

Non breeding

Year round

Migration

Call 1   Call 2

DID YOU KNOW....

It holds the remarkable title of the smallest long-distance migratory bird in the world. Despite its tiny size (around 3 inches long), it undertakes an annual round trip migration of up to 5,600 miles between its breeding grounds in western North America and its wintering grounds in southern Mexico.

Its name comes from Calliope, the Greek muse of eloquence and epic poetry, meaning "beautiful voiced." However, its vocalizations are described as rather unmelodic, typically consisting of buzzing and chip sounds.

The female frequently builds her tiny, well-camouflaged nest on the base of an old pine cone or in a tree knot, making it exceptionally difficult to spot as it blends in with the surrounding conifer.

Costa's Hummingbird - *Calypte costae*

Costa's Hummingbird is a small hummingbird primarily found in the arid regions of southwestern North America. This species is known for its distinctive plumage and adaptations to harsh desert environments. The male Costa's Hummingbird is easily recognized by its vibrant purple gorget, which extends into elongated, flared feathers on the sides of its throat, creating a "mustache" effect. The rest of its body is a dull green, with a dark cap. Females, by contrast, are more subdued, exhibiting a grayish-green coloration with pale underparts and a slightly darker cheek patch; they lack the male's vibrant gorget. Juveniles resemble females but may have a buffy tinge to their plumage.

FEEDING These hummingbirds are specialized nectar feeders, relying heavily on desert flowers, particularly those of desert scrub and chaparral plants. They also consume small insects and spiders for protein.

SOUNDS The male Costa's Hummingbird's song is a high-pitched, thin, and metallic series of notes, often described as a "zinging" sound, accompanied by a sharp, high-pitched "tick" call.

RANGE & MIGRATION Their range includes the deserts of southern California, Nevada, Arizona, and Baja California, Mexico. They are partial migrants, moving to lower elevations or coastal areas during the non-breeding season.

HABITAT Their preferred habitat is arid scrublands, chaparral, and desert washes, where they can find an abundance of flowering plants.

SIMILAR SPECIES include Anna's Hummingbirds and Black-chinned Hummingbirds, but the male Costa's unique gorget and the overall arid habitat preference helps to distinguish them.

Male

Female

Juvenile

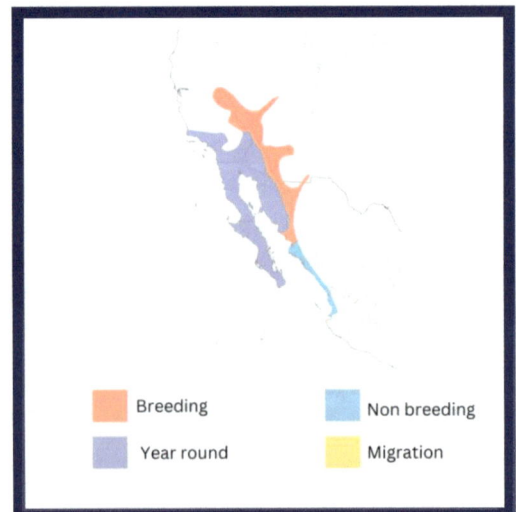

Breeding

Non breeding

Year round

Migration

Call

DID YOU KNOW....

It is named after Louis Marie Pantaleon Costa, Marquis de Beauregard, a French nobleman. Imagine having to say that full name every time!

The male has iridescent violet throat feathers (gorget) that flare out dramatically to the sides during courtship displays, making his head look remarkably like a tiny, shimmering squid or octopus to the observing female.

While they often nest in shrubs in open desert areas, they have also been observed nesting in unusual locations like on sailboats in marinas.

Lucifer Hummingbird - *Calothorax lucifer*

Lucifer Hummingbird, also known as the Lucifer sheartail, is a medium-sized hummingbird characterized by its long, decurved bill. Males are particularly striking, displaying an iridescent magenta gorget and a dark, forked tail, while females exhibit a more subdued, cinnamon-buff coloration on their underparts and a shorter tail. Juveniles resemble females, with potential for some metallic feathers appearing as they mature.

FEEDING These hummingbirds primarily feed on nectar from desert flowers, especially agave, and supplement their diet with small insects and spiders.

SOUNDS Their vocalizations include typical hummingbird chip notes, and males produce snapping sounds with their tail feathers during courtship displays.

RANGE & MIGRATION They inhabit arid, high-elevation regions, primarily in central and northern Mexico, with a limited range extending into the southwestern United States, specifically parts of Texas, New Mexico, and Arizona. They are migratory, moving to central Mexico during the winter months.

HABITAT Their preferred habitat consists of canyons, mountain slopes, and dry washes with desert shrubs and cacti.

SIMILAR SPECIES might include other hummingbird varieties found in the same region, but the Lucifer Hummingbird's distinctive bill shape and male plumage aid in identification.

Male   Female

Juvenile

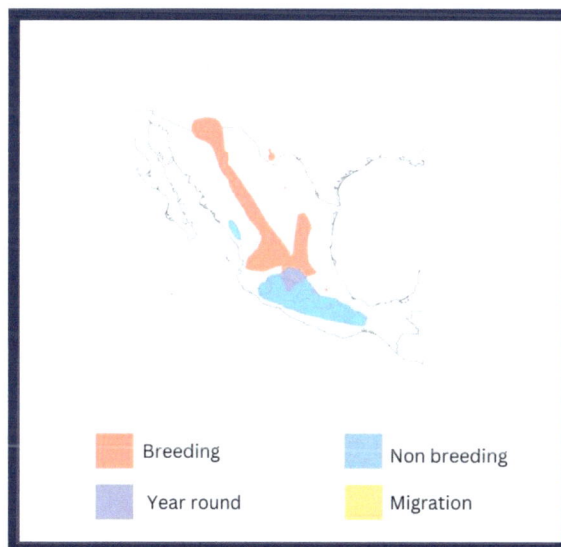

Breeding   Non breeding

Year round   Migration

Call

DID YOU KNOW....

It is the only hummingbird in its range with a distinctly decurved (down-curved) bill. This feature is a key identifier for both males and females of all ages.

It belongs to a group of hummingbirds called "sheartails" due to their deeply forked and narrow tail, although this is most obvious when the male spreads his tail during display.

Unlike other hummingbirds that typically perform courtship displays near feeding areas or perches, the male Lucifer Hummingbird uniquely displays at the female's nest, even while she is building it, laying eggs, or incubating. The purpose of this behavior isn't fully understood.

Mexican Violetear - *Colibri thalassinus*

Mexican Violetear is a medium-sized hummingbird characterized by its vibrant, metallic green plumage and the distinctive violet patch on its cheek. Both male and female Mexican Violetears share this general coloration, though males may exhibit slightly more intense hues. Juveniles are identifiable by their buff-tinged crowns and underparts, and rufous edging on their feathers.

FEEDING These hummingbirds primarily feed on nectar from flowers, supplementing their diet with small insects.

SOUNDS Their vocalizations consist of a repetitive, sharp, dry "tsu-tzeek" sound.

RANGE & MIGRATION They inhabit subtropical to lower temperate forests, woodlands, and scrublands, often at higher elevations. While their core range extends from southern Mexico to Nicaragua, they are occasionally observed as vagrants in the southern and central United States, particularly Texas, and have been recorded as far north as southern Canada. The seasonal movements of this species are not fully understood, but some northern populations may migrate southward or to lower elevations after breeding.

HABITAT They prefer habitats with flowering plants and forest edges.

SIMILAR SPECIES Similar hummingbird species may overlap in range, but the Mexican Violetear's distinctive violet ear patch and vocalizations aid in identification.

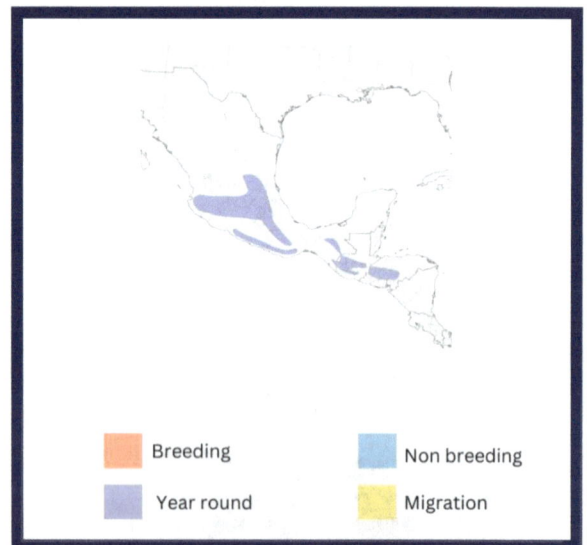

Adult

Adult

Juvenile

Breeding

Non breeding

Year round

Migration

Song

Call

DID YOU KNOW....

It was once considered the same species as the Lesser Violetear (Colibri cyanotus) and together they were known as the "Green Violetear." They are now recognized as distinct species based on differences in their plumage.

Although they forage alone, Mexican Violetears will gather at flowering trees, especially those in coffee-shade Inga trees, indicating a level of social tolerance when food is abundant.

While adult Mexican Violetears primarily feed on nectar, the female will collect a large number of small insects (like fruit flies, mosquitoes, and gnats) to feed her young due to their high nutritional requirements.

Plain-capped Starthroat - *Heliomaster constantii*

Plain-capped Starthroat is a relatively large hummingbird characterized by its long, straight bill and a distinctive white rump patch. Both male and female Plain-capped Starthroats exhibit similar plumage, featuring metallic bronze-green upperparts, a grayish-white underside, and a notable white stripe behind the eye. A key identifying feature is the metallic red to purplish-red gorget, though this can appear dark in low light. Juveniles have a darker, sootier throat.

FEEDING This species primarily feeds on nectar from a variety of flowering plants, often "trap-lining" or defending flower patches. They also supplement their diet with insects, captured by hawking or gleaning.

SOUNDS Vocalizations include sharp chips and high-pitched, slurred "tseep" calls.

RANGE & MIGRATION Their range extends from Mexico down through Central America, with casual appearances in the southern United States, particularly Arizona. They are mainly resident birds, though some northern populations may exhibit local movements.

HABITAT Their preferred habitat encompasses arid to semi-arid landscapes, including woodlands, thorn forests, and open areas with scattered vegetation.

SIMILAR SPECIES may include other larger hummingbirds, but the Plain-capped Starthroat's unique combination of size, bill length, and rump patch aids in identification.

Adult

Adult

Juvenile

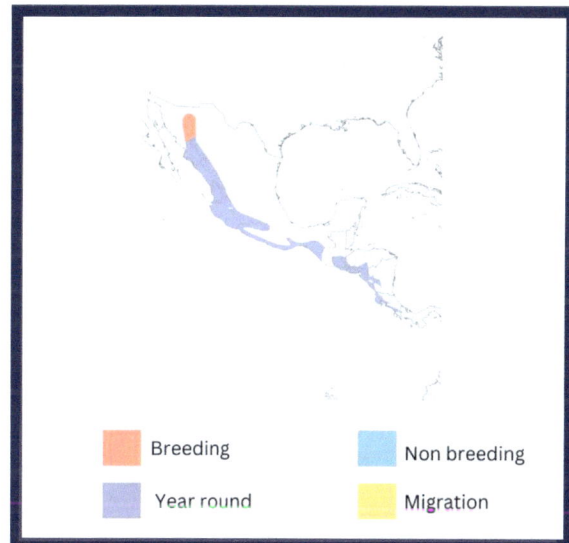

Breeding

Non breeding

Year round

Migration

Call

DID YOU KNOW....

Despite its name, the bright red gorget (throat patch) in males is often difficult to see unless the light catches it at just the right angle. This can make the bird appear relatively dull overall, contrasting with the "flashy" name.

Unlike many hummingbird species, the male and female Plain-capped Starthroats have essentially the same plumage coloration. The main difference is the male's red to purplish-red gorget, which isn't always obvious. Immature birds lack this red coloration

They build a small, shallow cup nest made of plant down and decorated on the outside with lichen. Unusually, they typically place this nest near the tip of a high tree branch.

Rivoli's Hummingbird - *Eugenes fulgens*

Rivoli's Hummingbird, one of the larger North American hummingbirds, is a striking bird characterized by its deep, iridescent green plumage. Males are particularly dazzling, sporting a vibrant violet-blue crown and a glittering emerald green throat. Females are more subdued, displaying a duller green coloration with a grayish-white underbelly and a less pronounced dark mask. Juveniles resemble females but have buffy fringes on their head and body feathers.

FEEDING These hummingbirds are primarily nectar feeders, utilizing their long, slender bills to extract nectar from tubular flowers. They also supplement their diet with small insects caught in mid-air or gleaned from foliage.

SOUNDS Their vocalizations include high-pitched chips and buzzy calls, along with a series of rapid, squeaky notes during courtship displays.

RANGE & MIGRATION Rivoli's Hummingbirds inhabit mountainous regions of the southwestern United States, primarily in Arizona, New Mexico, and Texas, extending south into Mexico and Central America. They are altitudinal migrants, moving to lower elevations during the winter months.

HABITAT Their preferred habitat includes oak-pine woodlands and canyons, especially areas with abundant flowering plants.

SIMILAR SPECIES include other large hummingbirds like the Magnificent Hummingbird, which can be distinguished by subtle differences in plumage and size.

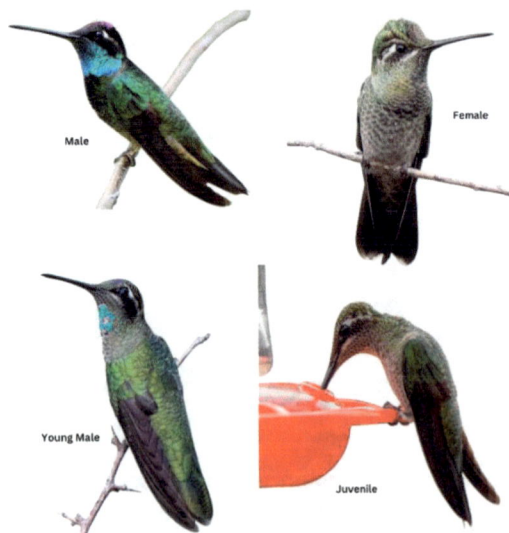

Male

Female

Young Male

Juvenile

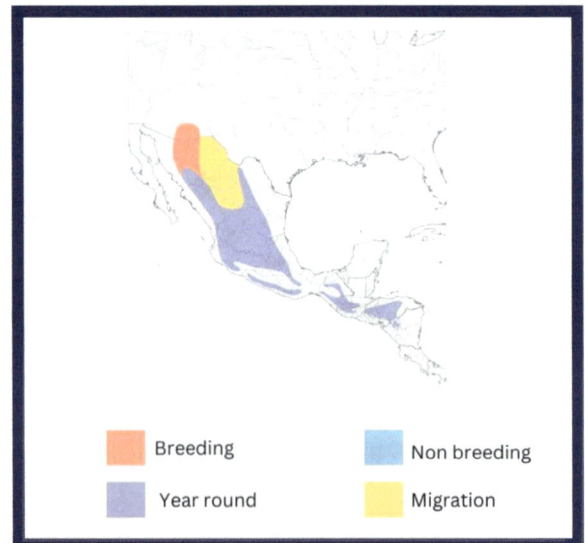

Breeding

Non breeding

Year round

Migration

Call 1

Call 2

DID YOU KNOW....

While many male hummingbirds have brightly colored gorgets (throat patches), the Rivoli's Hummingbird's gorget is a particularly striking emerald green. What makes it unique is that it can appear almost black depending on the angle of the light, showcasing a dramatic shift in color.

For a long time, the Rivoli's Hummingbird was known as the Magnificent Hummingbird (Eugenes fulgens). The name change reflects taxonomic revisions and helps to avoid confusion with other species.

Ruby-throated Hummingbird - *Archilochus colubris*

Ruby-throated Hummingbird is a tiny bird characterized by its vibrant emerald or golden-green back and crown, coupled with gray-white underparts. Male Ruby-throated Hummingbirds are easily identified by their brilliant iridescent red throat, which can appear dark in certain lighting, while females have a white throat. Juveniles resemble females.

FEEDING These hummingbirds primarily sustain themselves by feeding on nectar from flowers, utilizing their long, slender bills, and also consume small insects. Their flight is exceptionally agile, allowing them to hover, fly backward, and change direction rapidly.

SOUNDS While their vocalizations are subtle, they produce quiet chips and a high-pitched, thin chip call.

RANGE & MIGRATION Their breeding range encompasses eastern North America, and they undertake long migrations to wintering grounds in Central America.

HABITAT They favor habitats with abundant flowering plants, including open woodlands, forest edges, and gardens.

SIMILAR SPECIES include other hummingbirds, but the Ruby-throated Hummingbird is the only breeding hummingbird in eastern North America.

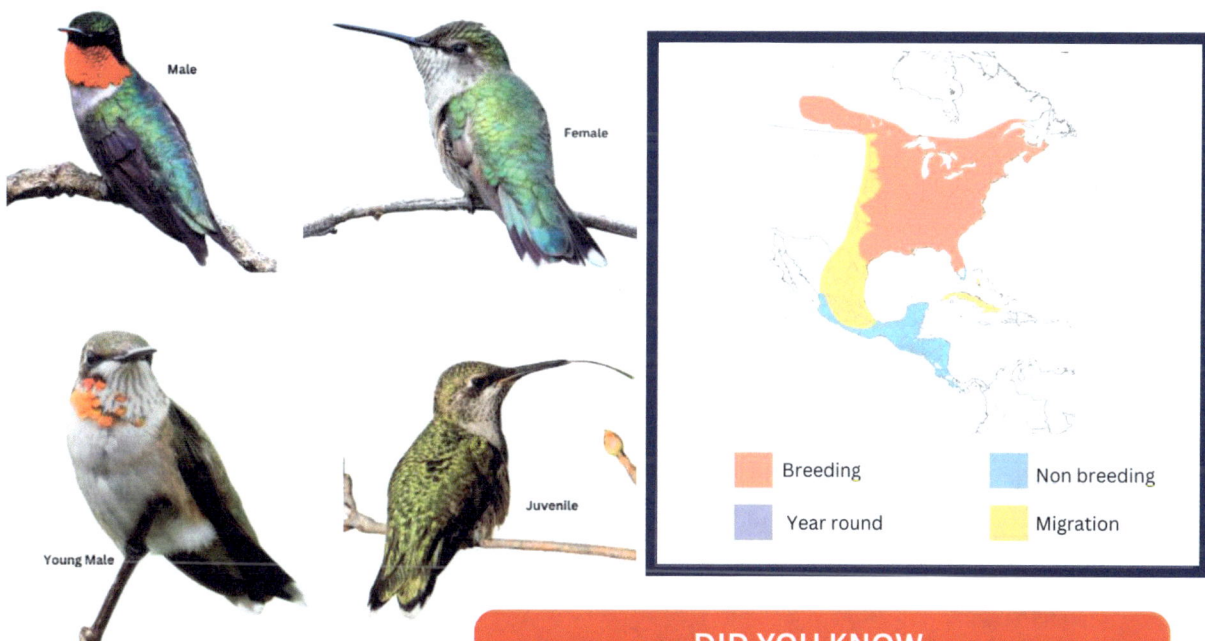

Male

Female

Young Male

Juvenile

Breeding   Non breeding

Year round   Migration

DID YOU KNOW....

It holds the title of the smallest long-distance migratory bird in the world.

Their wings beat at an incredibly high rate, typically 50-75 times per second, but can reach up to 200 beats per second during courtship displays. This rapid wing beat allows them to hover, fly forwards, backward, and even upside down – a maneuverability unique among birds, similar to insects.

Their feet are very small, primarily used for perching. They cannot walk or hop, only shuffle sideways along a branch. However, they can scratch their head by lifting a foot over their wing.

Call 1   Call 2

Rufous Hummingbird - *Selasphorus rufus*

Rufous Hummingbird is a small, energetic bird known for its extensive migrations and fiery plumage. Adult males are particularly striking, displaying a bright orange back and belly, and a vibrant iridescent red throat. Females, in contrast, are primarily green above with rufous-washed flanks and rufous patches in their tail, often with a small orange spot on the throat. Juveniles resemble females.

FEEDING These hummingbirds primarily feed on nectar from flowers, supplementing their diet with small insects caught in mid-air or gleaned from spider webs.

SOUNDS Their vocalizations include sharp chips and trills, and males produce a distinctive buzzing sound during courtship displays.

RANGE & MIGRATION They have a remarkable migratory pattern, breeding in the Pacific Northwest and Alaska, and wintering in Mexico, traveling through the Rocky Mountain region.

HABITAT Their preferred habitats consist of open woodlands, mountain meadows, and shrubby areas, as well as gardens and backyards.

SIMILAR SPECIES, such as Allen's Hummingbirds, can be difficult to distinguish, especially females and juveniles, requiring careful observation of plumage details and range.

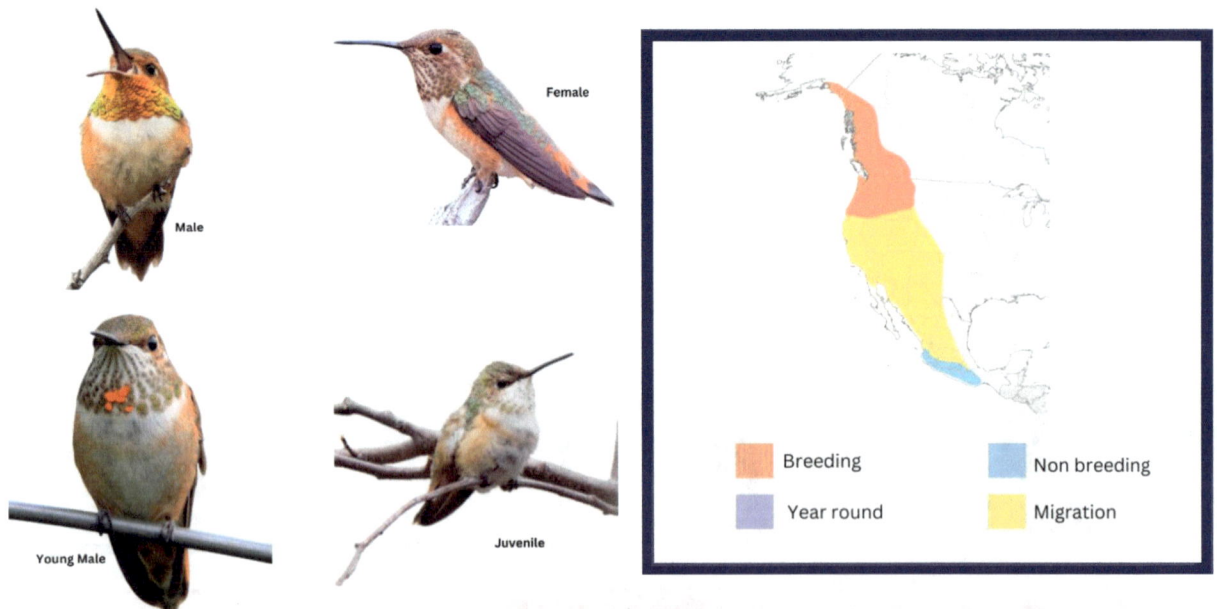

Male
Female
Young Male
Juvenile

Breeding	Non breeding
Year round	Migration

Call 1

Call 2

DID YOU KNOW....

The Rufous Hummingbird undertakes one of the longest migrations of any bird in the world when measured by body length. Their roughly 3,900-mile (one-way) journey from Alaska to Mexico is equivalent to about 78 million of their own body lengths!

This species breeds further north than any other hummingbird in the world, with their breeding range extending into southeastern Alaska.

They possess an exceptional memory for flower locations, remembering where to find nectar sources not only day-to-day but also year-to-year, even if feeders have been moved

Violet-crowned Hummingbird - *Ramosomyia violiceps*

Violet-crowned Hummingbird is a striking bird, easily identified by its clean white underparts and, of course, the glittering violet crown. Both male and female adults share this crown and lack a colorful gorget, a distinguishing feature among North American hummingbirds. They also possess a long, nearly straight bill that is bright reddish-orange with a black tip. Juveniles have a somewhat muted crown, sometimes with a brownish or cinnamon tone.

FEEDING These hummingbirds primarily feed on nectar from flowers, and they readily visit hummingbird feeders. They also supplement their diet with small insects, which they catch in flight or glean from foliage. Their vocalizations include a loud chatter.

RANGE & MIGRATION Their range in the United States is primarily limited to southeastern Arizona and extreme southwestern New Mexico, though they are more widespread in Mexico. While some individuals may migrate further south into Mexico for the winter, others are increasingly being observed year-round in their U.S. range.

HABITAT They favor riparian habitats, particularly canyons with sycamore trees, and also frequent surrounding woodlands and forests.

SIMILAR SPECIES within their range include other Hummingbirds, requiring close observation of key features like bill color, and the presence or absence of a gorget to aid in correct identification.

Adult   Adult

Juvenile

Call

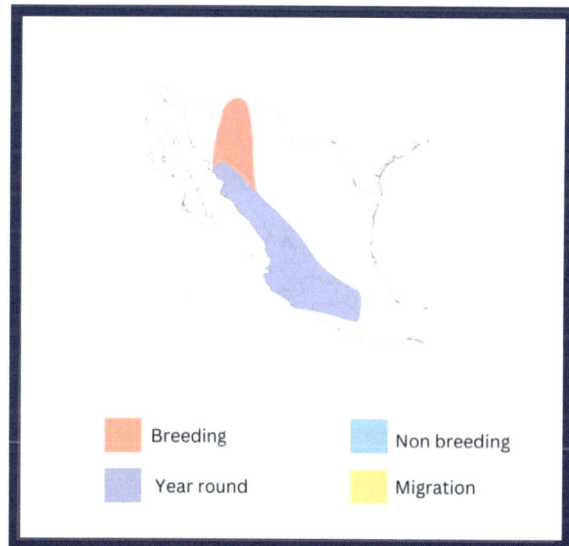

| Breeding | Non breeding |
| Year round | Migration |

DID YOU KNOW....

Unlike most North American hummingbirds, the male Violet-crowned Hummingbird lacks the iridescent, brightly colored throat patch (gorget). Its most striking color is on its crown.

It wasn't until 1959 that the Violet-crowned Hummingbird was confirmed to be nesting in the United States. Before that, it was primarily considered a Mexican species.

Studies have shown that the Violet-crowned Hummingbird tends to be at the top of the "humming order" at nectar sources, often chasing away smaller hummingbird species when food is scarce.

White-eared Hummingbird - *Basilinna leucotis*

White-eared Hummingbird, is a striking hummingbird found in the mountainous regions of North America, particularly in the southwestern United States and Mexico. It is characterized by its vibrant green plumage, a prominent white ear stripe, and a dark mask. Males display a bright red bill and a glittering green throat, while females have a duller green throat and a darker bill. Juveniles resemble females but have buffy fringes on their head and neck feathers.

FEEDING These hummingbirds primarily feed on nectar from flowering plants, favoring tubular blossoms, and supplement their diet with small insects.

SOUNDS Their songs are high-pitched, thin, and often described as a series of rapid, squeaky notes, while their calls include sharp, metallic chips.

HABITAT They inhabit montane pine-oak forests, canyons, and wooded areas, typically at higher elevations.

RANGE & MIGRATION The White-eared Hummingbird's range extends from the southwestern United States south through Mexico and into Central America. They are generally considered altitudinal migrants, moving to lower elevations during colder months, though their movements are not as well-defined as some other hummingbird species.

SIMILAR SPECIES might include other green hummingbirds, but the distinctive white ear stripe and red bill (in males) are key identifying features.

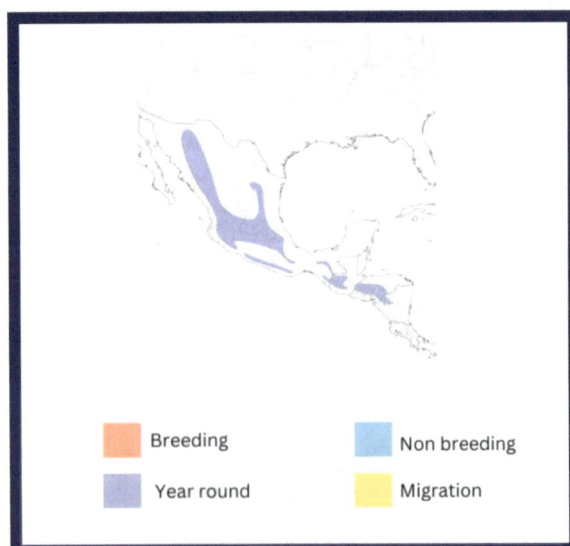

Breeding — Non breeding
Year round — Migration

Song   Call

DID YOU KNOW....

Its most distinctive feature, giving it its name, is a bold, bright white stripe that extends from behind the eye down the sides of its blackish head. This makes it relatively easy to identify compared to other hummingbirds

While the male's head often appears black, in the right light, it can flash a brilliant violet crown and a glittering turquoise-green throat. This iridescent display is often fleeting and depends on the angle of the light.

While they typically nest in trees or shrubs, the female sometimes builds a new nest directly on top of an old one from a previous year.

Xantus's Hummingbird - *Basilinna xantusii*

Xantus's Hummingbird, a striking species, is readily identified by its bold facial pattern and unique plumage. This medium-sized hummingbird features a bright green back, a black mask that extends below the eye, and a white malar stripe. Males display a vibrant rufous or cinnamon-colored tail, while females have a more subdued, often greenish, tail with some rufous edges. Juveniles resemble females but have a duller overall appearance.

FEEDING These hummingbirds are nectarivores, primarily feeding on the nectar of flowering plants, and they also consume small insects for protein.

SOUNDS Their songs are a series of high-pitched, thin chips and trills, and they also produce sharp, metallic calls.

RANGE & MIGRATION Xantus's Hummingbird is primarily found in the southern tip of Baja California Sur, Mexico, making it a relatively localized species within North America. They are generally considered non-migratory, remaining within their limited range year-round.

HABITAT Their preferred habitat includes arid and semi-arid scrublands, canyons, and desert areas with flowering vegetation.

SIMILAR SPECIES include other hummingbirds found in Baja California, such as the Costa's Hummingbird, but the Xantus's Hummingbird's distinctive facial pattern and tail coloration distinguish it.

Male

Female

Juvenile

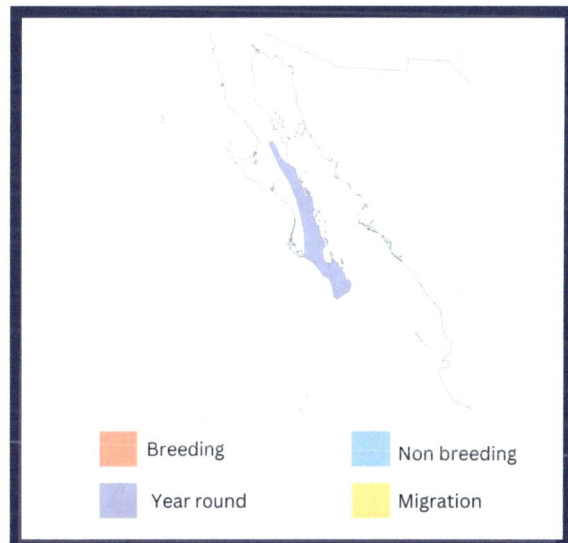

Breeding   Non breeding

Year round   Migration

Call   Song

DID YOU KNOW....

This hummingbird is found nowhere else in the world except the Baja California Peninsula in Mexico. This makes it a true regional specialty.

Its scientific name, Basilinna xantusii, honors John Xantus de Vesey (János Xántus), a Hungarian zoologist who collected the first specimen.

Unlike some species that struggle with habitat changes, the Xantus's Hummingbird has adapted fairly well to human presence within its limited range, even frequenting gardens and feeders.

SWIFTS

Swifts are a fascinating group of highly aerial birds renowned for their incredible speed, agility, and almost entirely airborne lifestyle.

General Characteristics:

- **Order Apodiformes:** Swifts belong to the order Apodiformes, which also includes hummingbirds and treeswifts. The name literally means "footless" in ancient Greek, reflecting their tiny feet which are primarily adapted for clinging to vertical surfaces rather than perching or walking.
- **Aerodynamic Body Shape:** They possess a streamlined, cigar-shaped body with long, slender, and often sickle-shaped wings. This morphology is perfectly adapted for efficient flight and high speeds.
- **Powerful Flight:** Swifts are among the fastest flying birds on Earth. They have strong chest muscles and lightweight bones, allowing for sustained high-speed flight and remarkable aerial maneuvers.
- **Tiny Feet (Pectinate Claws):** Their feet are small with sharp claws that they use to grip onto vertical surfaces like cliffs, trees, and buildings for roosting and nesting. They are not well-suited for walking on the ground. Some species have pectinate claws (comb-like edges) which may aid in clinging to rough surfaces.
- **Wide Gape:** Swifts have a remarkably wide gape, often extending back below their eyes. This allows them to efficiently catch insects in flight, which forms their entire diet.
- **Short Beak:** Despite the wide gape, their beak is typically short and flattened.
- **Dark Plumage:** Most swift species have predominantly dark plumage in shades of brown, black, or gray, often with subtle variations or paler throats or underparts. This may offer camouflage against the sky.
- **Vocalizations:** They are often vocal, producing high-pitched chattering, screaming, or twittering calls, especially in flight and around nesting sites.
- **Precocial or Semi-Precocial Young:** Swift chicks are typically born naked or with sparse down and are relatively helpless, requiring significant parental care.

Key Points:

- **Masters of the Air:** Swifts spend the vast majority of their lives in flight, feeding, drinking (by skimming water surfaces), mating in some species, and even sleeping on the wing.
- **Insectivorous Diet:** Their diet consists entirely of insects and spiders caught in flight. They play a significant role in controlling insect populations.
- **Migration:** Many swift species are migratory, undertaking long journeys between breeding and wintering grounds, often covering thousands of kilometers.
- **Nesting Habits:** Swifts typically nest in crevices, holes in trees, cliffs, or buildings. Some species build nests from saliva, which hardens upon exposure to air (e.g., the edible-nest swiftlets). Others use feathers, moss, and other materials held together with saliva.
- **Adaptations for Aerial Life:** Their entire physiology and morphology are geared towards an aerial existence. They have adaptations like fused vertebrae for stability in flight, powerful wings for speed and endurance, and efficient respiratory systems.
- **Diversity:** There is a significant diversity among swift species in terms of size, plumage, nesting habits, and distribution across the globe, except for the polar regions.
- **Conservation Concerns:** Some swift populations are facing declines due to habitat loss (especially nesting sites), pesticide use reducing insect populations, and climate change affecting migration patterns and food availability.
- **Long Lifespans:** Despite their small size, some swift species are known to have relatively long lifespans. For example, the Common Swift can live for over 20 years.
- **Challenging to Study:** Their high-speed aerial lifestyle makes them challenging birds to study in detail.

Black Swift - *Cypseloides niger*

Black Swift is a large, sooty-black swift found in western North America, recognized by its powerful, streamlined build and shallowly forked tail. Adults of both sexes exhibit identical dark plumage, making them difficult to differentiate visually. Juveniles are similar to adults but may show faint pale feather edging, particularly on the wings.

FEEDING Black Swifts are aerial insectivores, feeding exclusively on insects caught in flight, often at high altitudes.

SOUNDS Their vocalizations are relatively quiet, consisting of high-pitched chirps and chattering sounds, often heard during their spectacular aerial displays.

RANGE & MIGRATION They breed in remote locations, typically near waterfalls or cliffs, from southeastern Alaska and western Canada south through the western United States and into Mexico, with a disjunct population in the Caribbean. They undertake long-distance migrations, wintering in Central and possibly South America, though their precise wintering grounds are still not fully understood.

HABITAT Their breeding habitat is characterized by steep cliffs, often near or behind waterfalls, and forested mountain canyons.

SIMILAR SPECIES, such as Vaux's Swift, are smaller and have paler underparts, while Chimney Swifts have a more pronounced, cigar-shaped body and faster wingbeats.

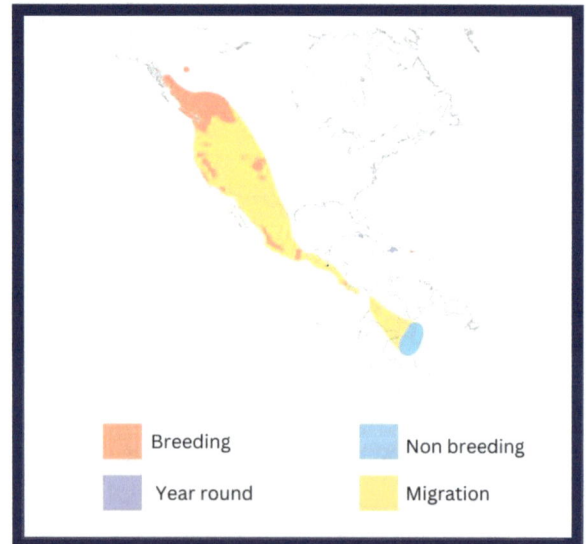

Adult

Adult

Juvenile

Call 1   Call 2

| Breeding | Non breeding |
| Year round | Migration |

DID YOU KNOW....

A significant portion of their nesting sites are located on cliff ledges behind or beside waterfalls. The constant spray keeps the nest moist and potentially offers protection from some predators.

Unlike many other swift species that use saliva to bind their nests, Black Swifts primarily construct their cup-shaped nests from moss and mud, sometimes incorporating ferns or other plant material.

They typically lay only one egg per breeding season, which is unusual for birds of their size and aerial lifestyle. This low reproductive rate makes them particularly vulnerable to population declines.

Chimney Swift - *Chaetura pelagica*

Chimney Swift is a sooty gray, slender bird with long, curved wings and a short, squared tail, often described as a "flying cigar." Males and females are virtually identical in appearance, while juveniles resemble adults but may have slightly less distinct plumage.

FEEDING These aerial insectivores are specialized for catching insects on the wing, consuming a wide variety of flying prey.

SOUNDS Their vocalizations consist of rapid, high-pitched chattering and chipping sounds, particularly during flight.

RANGE & MIGRATION They range across eastern North America during the breeding season, migrating to South America for the winter.

HABITAT Chimney Swifts are uniquely adapted to nesting in vertical structures, historically hollow trees, but now predominantly chimneys, hence their name. They also use air shafts and similar man-made structures.

SIMILAR SPECIES that are aerial insectivores include other swifts, such as Vaux's Swifts in the western part of the continent, but Chimney Swifts are easily distinguished by their sooty gray color and characteristic flight pattern.

Adult

Adult

Juvenile

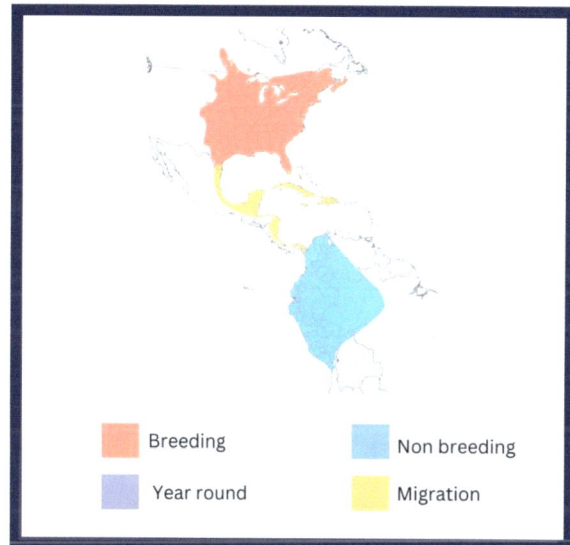

Breeding

Non breeding

Year round

Migration

Call

DID YOU KNOW....

Their body shape is often described as cigar-shaped, and their flight with stiff, acrobatic movements combined with long glides can resemble a bow and arrow.

The shafts of their tail feathers extend into stiff, exposed spines, which they use for extra support when clinging to vertical surfaces. This feature gives them their genus name Chaetura, meaning "spine-tailed." They can have up to seven of these tail spines.

They spend almost their entire lives in flight, even drinking water and collecting nesting materials on the wing

White-collared Swift - *Streptoprocne zonaris*

White-collared Swift is a large, powerful swift characterized by its dark plumage and a distinctive white collar that encircles its neck, broadest at the breast. Adults of both sexes exhibit this striking pattern, with juveniles displaying a duller coloration and grayish-white feather tips.

FEEDING These swifts are aerial insectivores, feeding on insects caught during their continuous flight.

SOUNDS Their vocalizations consist of scratchy, twittering calls, often heard when they gather in large, noisy flocks.

RANGE & MIGRATION They are found across a broad range, from Mexico, through Central and South America, and into the Caribbean, with occasional sightings north of the Mexican border. While generally considered resident, they may make movements to lower elevations during adverse weather.

HABITAT Their habitat preferences include montane and submontane evergreen forests, as well as lowland forests and more open areas, and they nest in colonies within caves, often near or behind waterfalls.

SIMILAR SPECIES include other large swifts, such as the White-naped Swift, requiring careful observation of plumage details for accurate identification.

Adult

Adult

Juvenile

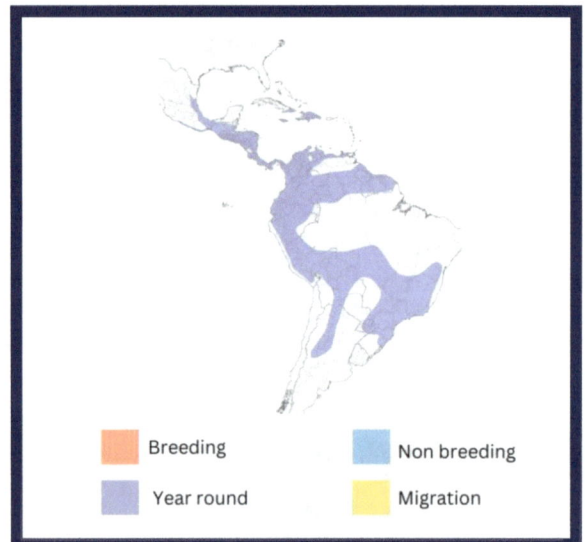

Breeding
Non breeding
Year round
Migration

Call

DID YOU KNOW....

The White-collared Swift is the largest swift species throughout most of its extensive range, which stretches from Mexico through Central and South America (excluding Chile) and includes the Greater and Lesser Antilles and Trinidad.

Flocks of White-collared Swifts create a distinct "wooshing" sound as their large wings beat against the wind during rapid descents, particularly down valleys.

Despite their relatively large size, White-collared Swifts are known for their powerful and fast direct flight, reaching speeds of 70 to 100 kilometers per hour (43 to 62 mph).

TYRANT FLYCATCHERS

Tyrant flycatchers belong to the family Tyrannidae, the largest family of birds in the world with over 400 species found throughout the Americas.

General Characteristics:

- **Size:** They range from very small (6.5-7 cm) to medium-sized (up to 29 cm, excluding long tails in some species).
- **Plumage:** Most species have relatively plain plumage in shades of gray, brown, olive, white, or yellow, often providing camouflage. However, some species exhibit bright colors like red, blue, black, and yellow. Some have crests, which can sometimes be brightly colored or erectile.
- **Bill:** Their bills are typically short, wide, and somewhat flattened, with a slight hook at the tip. Many have bristles (rictal bristles) at the base of the bill, thought to aid in insect capture or protect the eyes. The bill size can vary depending on diet.
- **Legs and Feet:** More arboreal species tend to have weak legs and feet, perching upright.
- **Vocalization:** Their songs are often simple, sometimes described as squeaking, grating, or monotonous whistles. However, vocalizations are crucial for distinguishing between similar-looking species.
- **Diet:** Primarily insectivorous, they are opportunistic feeders, catching flying insects. Some species also consume spiders, caterpillars, berries, fruits, and occasionally small vertebrates.
- **Foraging Behavior:** Many North American species employ a "sallying" feeding style, where they perch and fly out to catch insects in mid-air, returning to the same perch. Tropical species often glean insects from foliage and bark, and some participate in mixed-species foraging flocks.
- **Habitat:** They occupy a wide variety of habitats, from tropical rainforests to deserts and mountains, generally requiring trees with open areas for foraging.
- **Nesting:** Nest types vary and include open cups, domed structures, and hanging bags. Some species nest in holes or even usurp the nests of other birds.
- **Territoriality:** Most tyrant flycatchers are territorial during the breeding season, with some, like kingbirds, being notably aggressive in defending their nesting areas against larger birds.
- **Migration:** Species in temperate climates are often migratory, wintering in the tropics or subtropics.

Key Points:

- **Largest Bird Family in the Americas:** With over 400 species, they represent significant avian diversity.
- **Diverse Morphology and Ecology:** They exhibit considerable variation in size, coloration, bill shape, foraging techniques, and habitat use.
- **Insectivorous Predominantly:** Their diet mainly consists of insects, caught using various aerial and perching strategies.
- **Vocalizations for Identification:** While songs may be simple, they are often key to distinguishing between closely related species with similar plumage.
- **Territorial Behavior:** Many species fiercely defend their breeding territories.
- **Wide Distribution:** Found throughout North and South America, adapting to numerous ecological niches.
- **Not Related to Old World Flycatchers:** Despite the similar name and some superficial resemblances, they belong to a different suborder of Passeriformes (suboscines).

Eastern Phoebe - *Sayornis phoebe*

Eastern Phoebe is a small, unassuming flycatcher with a dark gray-brown upper body and a paler, off-white to light gray underbelly, often showing a slight olive wash. It exhibits a characteristic tail-wagging motion, a key identifier. Males and females are virtually indistinguishable visually, though males may sing more frequently and vigorously. Juveniles resemble adults but have buffy wingbars and a slightly scaled appearance on their upperparts.

FEEDING Eastern Phoebes are primarily insectivorous, catching their prey on the wing with short, darting flights.

SOUNDS Their song is a simple, raspy "fee-bee," with the second syllable often lower in pitch, and they also produce a sharp "chip" call.

RANGE & MIGRATION They are found across eastern North America, from southern Canada down to the Gulf Coast, and westward to the edge of the Great Plains. These birds are migratory, moving south for the winter to the southern United States and Mexico.

HABITAT They prefer habitats near water, such as streams, rivers, and ponds, and are frequently found around bridges, buildings, and other human-made structures, where they often nest on ledges or under eaves.

SIMILAR SPECIES include other *Sayornis* flycatchers like the Black Phoebe and the Say's Phoebe, but their ranges and subtle plumage differences help in distinguishing them.

Adult

Adult

Juvenile

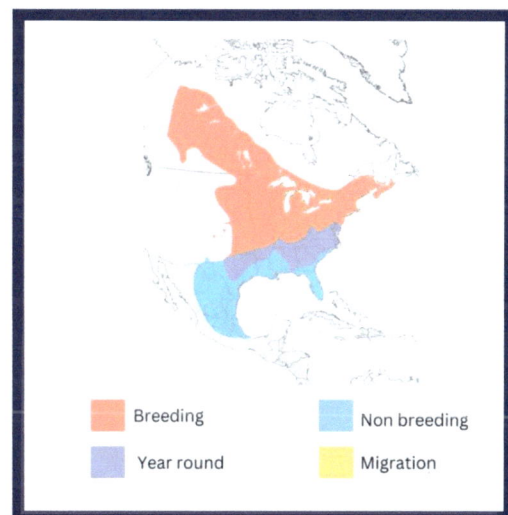

Breeding   Non breeding

Year round   Migration

Song   **Call**

DID YOU KNOW....

In 1804, the Eastern Phoebe became the first bird species in North America to be banded for scientific study. The famous ornithologist John James Audubon used silver thread to mark the legs of nestlings to track their return in subsequent years, proving their site fidelity.

While historically nesting on rock ledges and in caves, Eastern Phoebes have readily adapted to human-made structures. They commonly build nests under eaves of houses, barns, and bridges, even leading to the nickname "bridge pewee." This adaptation has likely contributed to their range expansion.

Female Eastern Phoebes have been observed roosting in their newly built nests even before laying eggs. This behavior is thought to potentially conserve energy.

Black Phoebe - *Sayornis nigricans*

Black Phoebe is a striking, medium-sized flycatcher characterized by its solid black plumage with a bright white belly and undertail coverts. Both male and female Black Phoebes share this distinctive coloration, making them difficult to differentiate visually. Juveniles exhibit a browner tinge to their black plumage and may have faint wing bars.

FEEDING These birds are aerial insectivores, adept at catching insects in mid-flight, often returning to the same perch.

SOUNDS Their song is a series of sharp, repeated "phoebe" notes, and they also produce a sharp "chip" call.

RANGE & MIGRATION They are primarily found in the southwestern United States and along the Pacific coast, extending into Central and South America. They are generally non-migratory within their established range, preferring habitats near water, such as streams, ponds, and even man-made structures like bridges and buildings.

SIMILAR SPECIES Potential confusion could arise with other dark flycatchers, but the Black Phoebe's unique color pattern and preference for riparian habitats make it relatively easy to identify.

Adult

Adult

Juvenile

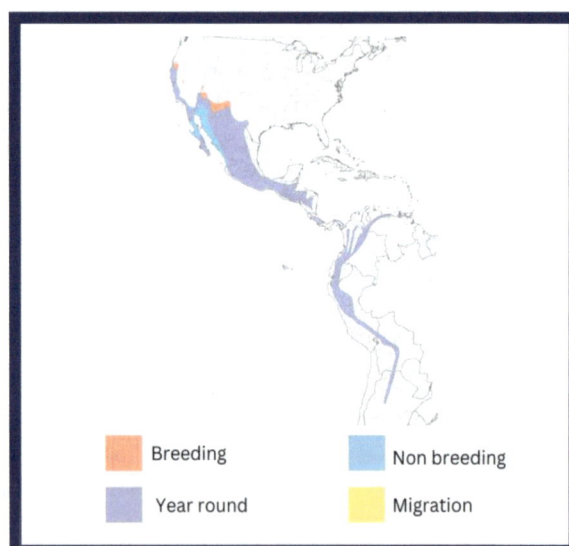

Breeding

Year round

Non breeding

Migration

Song

Call

DID YOU KNOW....

They frequently reuse the same nest site year after year, sometimes even refurbishing an old nest or building a new one directly on top of the previous one. This strong site fidelity highlights their attachment to a successful nesting location.

The female Black Phoebe is solely responsible for the construction (or refurbishment) of the nest, taking 1-3 weeks to complete the task.

During courtship, the male Black Phoebe will show potential nest sites to the female by hovering in front of each for 5-10 seconds. However, the female ultimately makes the final decision on where to build the nest.

Eastern Kingbird - *Tyrannus tyrannus*

Eastern Kingbird is a robust, medium-sized flycatcher characterized by its dark gray to blackish upperparts and bright white underparts, most notably featuring a distinctive white-tipped black tail. While males and females share similar plumage, males may be slightly larger. Juveniles resemble adults but may display slightly duller coloration.

FEEDING These birds primarily feed on insects, which they capture through aerial sallies, and also consume fruits, especially during their winter migration.

SOUNDS Their vocalizations include sharp, buzzing calls and chattering sounds, rather than melodious songs.

RANGE & MIGRATION They breed across much of eastern North America, favoring open habitats such as fields, pastures, and woodland edges, often perching conspicuously on wires or branches. They are migratory, traveling to South America for the winter.

SIMILAR SPECIES include other kingbirds or flycatchers, but the Eastern Kingbird's bold black and white pattern and aggressive behavior are key identifiers.

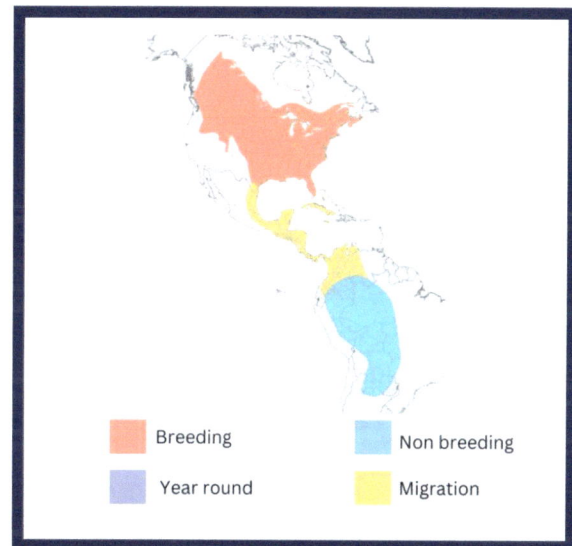

Adult

Adult

Male & Female

Juvenile

Breeding

Non breeding

Year round

Migration

Song

Call

DID YOU KNOW....

Despite its relatively small size, the Eastern Kingbird is known for its aggressive defense of its nest and territory. It will fearlessly attack much larger birds, including hawks, crows, and even herons, dive-bombing and pecking at them until they retreat. This bold behavior has earned it the nickname "tyrant flycatcher."

Unlike many birds, the Eastern Kingbird has a notched or slightly barbed tip on its tongue. This adaptation is believed to help it grip slippery insects more effectively while in flight.

While often nesting in trees and shrubs, Eastern Kingbirds can be quite adaptable in their nest site selection. They have been recorded nesting on fence posts, utility poles, and even in artificial structures.

Scissor-tailed Flycatcher - *Tyrannus forficatus*

Scissor-tailed Flycatcher is a striking bird, easily recognized by its exceptionally long, forked tail, particularly prominent in males. Adult birds exhibit a pale gray head, back, and breast, with salmon-pink flanks and a white underbelly. Males possess significantly longer tails than females, and juveniles have shorter tails and duller coloration, lacking the bright pink hues.

FEEDING These flycatchers are primarily insectivorous, capturing prey on the wing with remarkable agility. Their diet consists mainly of insects, including grasshoppers, crickets, and beetles.

SOUNDS Their vocalizations include a series of chattering and clicking sounds, and they produce calls described as sharp, repeated notes.

RANGE & MIGRATION Their breeding range extends across the south-central United States, from eastern Colorado and Nebraska southward into Texas and western Louisiana. They migrate south for the winter, reaching Central America and occasionally southern Florida.

HABITAT Their preferred habitat is open country, including grasslands, pastures, and roadsides with scattered trees and shrubs, where they can readily perch and hunt.

SIMILAR SPECIES within its range might include other kingbirds, but the Scissor-tailed Flycatcher's distinctive tail makes it easily identifiable.

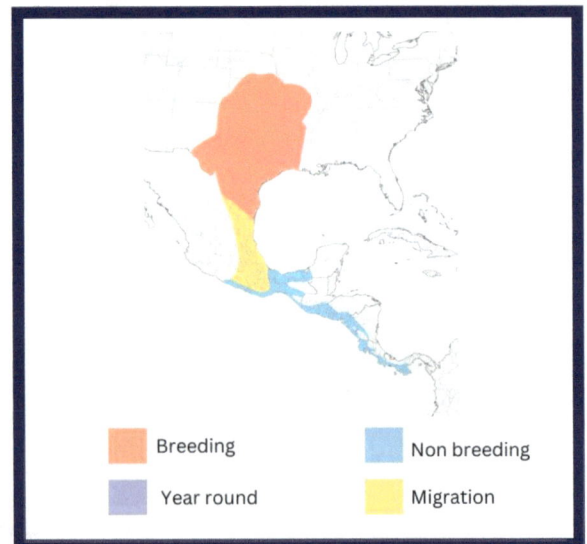

Adult

Adult

Juvenile

Breeding

Non breeding

Year round

Migration

Song

Call

DID YOU KNOW....

The Bobwhite Quail initially won a contest to be Oklahoma's state bird in 1932, but the Scissor-tailed Flycatcher eventually took the title in 1951 due to its diet of harmful insects and its Oklahoma-centered nesting range.

Its former Latin name, Muscivora forficata, and its current one, Tyrannus forficatus, both allude to its distinctive tail. "Forficata" comes from the Latin word "forfex," meaning scissors.

Despite their different appearances, Scissor-tailed Flycatchers are known to hybridize with Western Kingbirds (Tyrannus verticalis), producing fertile offspring.

Great Crested Flycatcher - *Myiarchus crinitus*

Great Crested Flycatcher, a medium-sized bird of eastern North American woodlands, is characterized by its olive-brown upperparts, bright yellow underparts, and distinctive rusty-red tail feathers. Both males and females share similar plumage, making them difficult to distinguish visually. Juveniles exhibit a duller yellow coloration and more subtle rusty tones compared to adults.

FEEDING These flycatchers are primarily insectivorous, capturing prey in mid-air or gleaning them from foliage.

SOUNDS Their vocalizations include a loud, emphatic "wheep!" and a series of rapid, chattering notes.

RANGE & MIGRATION They breed throughout eastern North America, from southern Canada to the Gulf Coast, and migrate south to Central America and northern South America for the winter.

HABITAT These birds prefer deciduous or mixed forests, particularly those with mature trees and open understories, and they are often found near forest edges.

SIMILAR SPECIES include other *Myiarchus* flycatchers, such as the Ash-throated Flycatcher and Brown-crested Flycatcher, which can be differentiated by subtle plumage variations, vocalizations, and range.

Adult

Adult

Juvenile

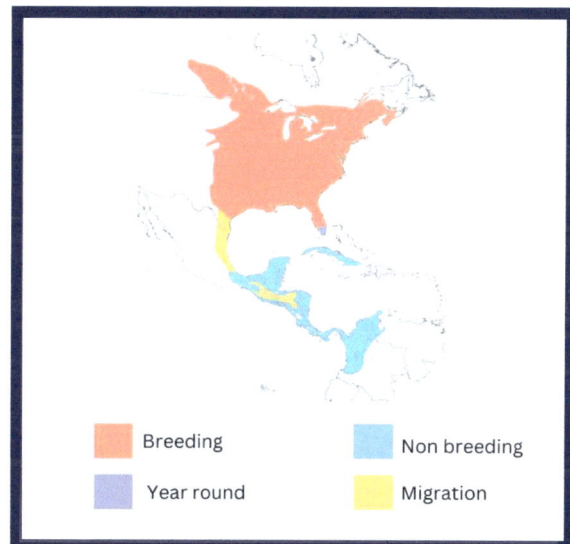

Breeding

Non breeding

Year round

Migration

Dawn Song

Call

DID YOU KNOW....

They are well-known for often incorporating shed snakeskin into their nests. This is a peculiar behavior not commonly seen in other flycatchers. They will also use other similar-looking materials like plastic, cellophane, or onion skins.

While they prefer natural tree cavities or old woodpecker holes, they are surprisingly adaptable and will nest in various unusual locations, including mailboxes, open pipes, buckets, cans, and even crevices in buildings. They also readily use nest boxes.

When perched and searching for prey, they often exhibit a characteristic head-bobbing behavior.

Western Kingbird - *Tyrannus verticalis*

Western Kingbird is a striking flycatcher found across western and central North America, characterized by its bright yellow underparts, gray head, and dark wings and tail with white outer wedges. Both male and female Western Kingbirds share similar plumage, making them difficult to distinguish visually. Juveniles exhibit a paler overall coloration.

FEEDING These birds are primarily insectivorous, catching their prey on the wing or by dropping to the ground. Their diet consists of a variety of insects, including grasshoppers, beetles, and flies.

SOUNDS Their vocalizations include a high, squeaky chatter and sharp, distinct calls.

HABITAT They inhabit open areas such as grasslands, agricultural fields, and deserts with scattered trees and shrubs, often perching conspicuously on wires or fence posts.

RANGE & MIGRATION They are migratory, breeding in North America and wintering primarily in Mexico and Central America.

SIMILAR SPECIES When looking to identify this bird, comparable species to be aware of are, especially the Cassin's Kingbird, and other kingbird species.

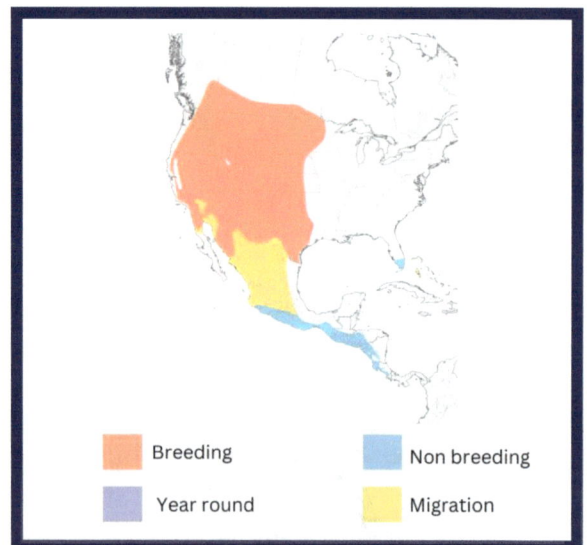

Adult

Adult

Juvenile

Breeding

Year round

Non breeding

Migration

Dawn Song

Call

DID YOU KNOW....

They possess a patch of bright red or crimson feathers on the crown of their heads. However, these feathers are usually concealed by their gray plumage and are only flashed when the bird is agitated, excited, or during territorial displays.

Despite their relatively small size, Western Kingbirds are known for their bold and tenacious defense of their nesting territories. They will fearlessly chase away much larger birds, including hawks, crows, and even ravens, using harsh calls, bill snapping, and their striking red crown display

The Western Kingbird was originally known as the "Arkansas Kingbird." The name was changed to better reflect its broader distribution throughout western North America.

Eastern Wood-Pewee - *Contopus virens*

Eastern Wood-Pewee is a small, flycatcher bird found throughout eastern North America, characterized by its olive-gray upperparts, two pale wing bars, and a pale lower mandible. Both males and females exhibit similar plumage, making visual sexing difficult in the field. Juveniles resemble adults but often have buffy wing bars.

FEEDING These birds are aerial insectivores, capturing insects on the wing with short, sallying flights from a perch.

SOUNDS Their song is a thin, plaintive "pee-a-wee," with the emphasis on the second syllable, and their call is a soft "pip."

RANGE & MIGRATION They breed across the eastern United States and southeastern Canada, migrating to Central and South America for the winter.

HABITAT Their preferred habitat is deciduous and mixed forests, particularly those with an open understory.

SIMILAR SPECIES include other pewees, especially the Western Wood-Pewee, which is difficult to distinguish based on appearance alone, relying heavily on vocalizations for identification.

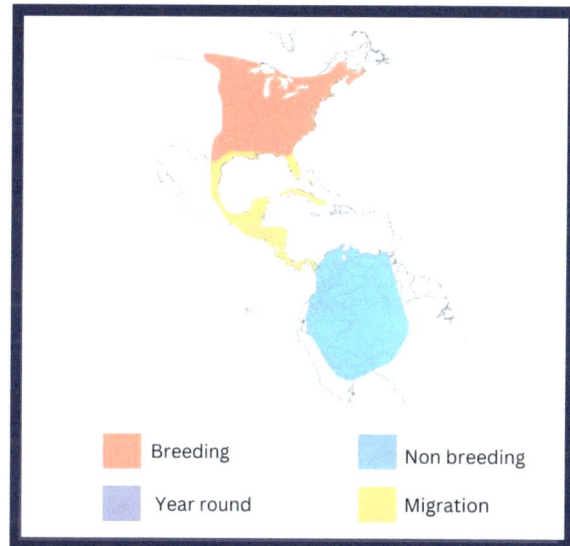

Adult

Adult

Juvenile

Breeding

Non breeding

Year round

Migration

Song

Call

DID YOU KNOW....

While they sing their characteristic "pee-a-wee" throughout the day, male Eastern Wood-Pewees also have a special, faster-paced song they perform at dawn and sometimes dusk, which includes an additional "ahh-d'dee" phrase.

They are highly skilled at catching flying insects in mid-air by sallying out from a perch and then returning to the same spot to eat. They tend to forage higher in the trees compared to some other flycatcher species but lower than others, occupying a specific niche in the forest canopy.

When their nest is disturbed by an intruder, both male and female Eastern Wood-Pewees will give a distinctive, shrill "peeee" call.

Acadian Flycatcher - *Empidonax virescens*

Acadian Flycatcher is a small, olive-green flycatcher of eastern North America, recognized by its relatively large head, prominent eye ring, and two pale wing bars. Both males and females share similar plumage, making visual sexing difficult. Juveniles display a browner hue with buffy wing bars.

FEEDING These birds are primarily insectivorous, capturing prey in mid-air or gleaning them from foliage.

SOUNDS Their song is a sharp, explosive "peet-seet!" or "peet-za!", and they also produce a quiet "pip" call.

RANGE & MIGRATION Acadian Flycatchers breed in mature, deciduous forests with dense undergrowth, particularly in damp areas near streams and ravines. Their breeding range extends from the southeastern Canada southward through the eastern United States. They are a neotropical migrant, wintering in Central and South America.

SIMILAR SPECIES, such as other *Empidonax* flycatchers like the Least Flycatcher and Willow Flycatcher, require careful observation of subtle plumage differences, habitat preferences, and vocalizations for accurate identification.

Adult

Adult

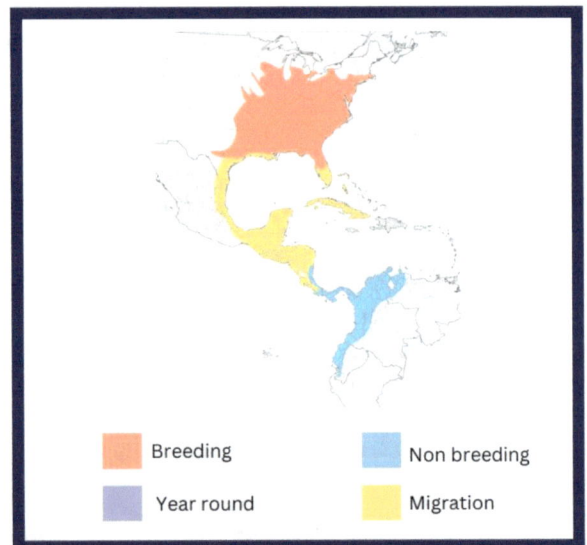

Juvenile

Breeding
Non breeding
Year round
Migration

Dawn Song

Call

DID YOU KNOW....

Their nest is a loosely woven cup, often made of spiderwebs and plant fibers, with distinctive long streamers of plant material hanging down below. This "trashy" appearance might aid in camouflage or distraction.

Unlike most birds that bathe by wading, the Acadian Flycatcher has been observed diving at the water's surface with its chest, then flying to a perch to preen.

They primarily forage by watching from a perch and then making short flights to snatch insects, often from the undersides of leaves. They also hawk insects in mid-air.

Yellow-bellied Flycatcher - *Empidonax flaviventris*

Yellow-bellied Flycatcher, a small and elusive member of the Empidonax flycatcher genus, is characterized by its olive-green upperparts, yellowish underparts, and two prominent white wingbars. Both male and female Yellow-bellied Flycatchers exhibit similar plumage, making visual sexing difficult. Juvenile birds resemble adults but often display buffer wingbars and a more muted yellow coloration.

FEEDING These flycatchers are primarily insectivorous, capturing their prey in mid-air or gleaning insects from foliage.

SOUNDS Their songs consist of a thin, high-pitched "seee-yip" or "per-wee," while their calls include a sharp "pit" or "spit."

RANGE & MIGRATION They breed in boreal forests, particularly in spruce-fir or mixed conifer-hardwood forests, across Canada and the northern United States, extending southward in mountainous regions. During the non-breeding season, they migrate to Central America and the Gulf Coast of the United States.

HABITAT They favor cool, damp, and often boggy or swampy forested areas.

SIMILAR SPECIES Distinguishing the Yellow-bellied Flycatcher from other Empidonax species, such as the Acadian, Least, and Willow Flycatchers, can be challenging, relying on subtle differences in plumage, vocalizations, and habitat preferences.

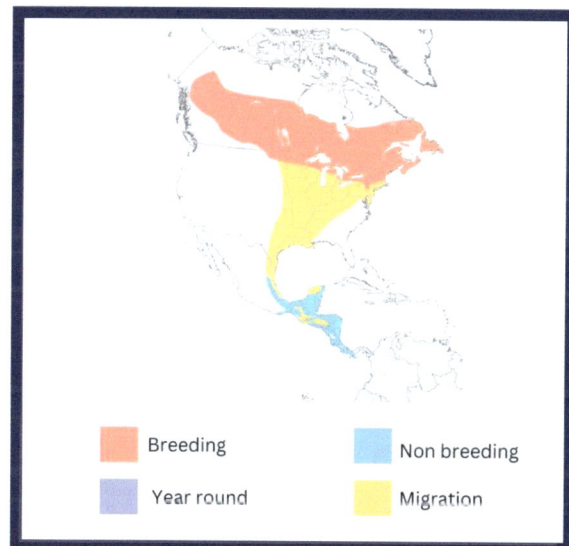

Adult

Adult

Juvenile

Breeding
Non breeding
Year round
Migration

Call 1   Call 2

DID YOU KNOW....

They have one of the shortest stays on their breeding grounds compared to other Neotropical migrant birds, often less than 70 days.

Unlike many flycatchers that nest in trees, Yellow-bellied Flycatchers build their cup-shaped nests on or very near the ground, often tucked into sphagnum moss in bogs or at the base of tree roots in damp, shady coniferous forests.

They are considered quite secretive and inconspicuous, often hiding in the lower shrubby layers of the forest, making them difficult to observe.

Alder Flycatcher - *Empidonax alnorum*

Alder Flycatcher is a small, rather indistinct olive-green flycatcher primarily found in wet thickets across northern North America. It is notoriously difficult to distinguish from other *Empidonax* flycatchers, particularly the Willow Flycatcher. General characteristics include dull greenish-olive upperparts, a whitish throat, and two pale wingbars. Males and females are visually very similar, and juveniles display brownish upperparts and yellowish underparts.

FEEDING These birds primarily feed on insects, which they catch in mid-air or glean from foliage.

SOUNDS Their distinctive song, a raspy "free-beer!", is a key identifier, along with their sharp "pip" call.

RANGE & MIGRATION They breed across much of Canada and Alaska, extending into the northeastern United States, and migrate south through the eastern United States, Mexico, and Central America to winter in South America.

HABITAT Their preferred habitat during the breeding season is wet, dense, shrubby thickets, especially those with alder, maple, or birch.

SIMILAR SPECIES Distinguishing the Alder Flycatcher from similar species like the Willow Flycatcher, Least Flycatcher, Eastern Phoebe, and Eastern Wood-Pewee often requires careful attention to vocalizations, habitat, and subtle plumage differences.

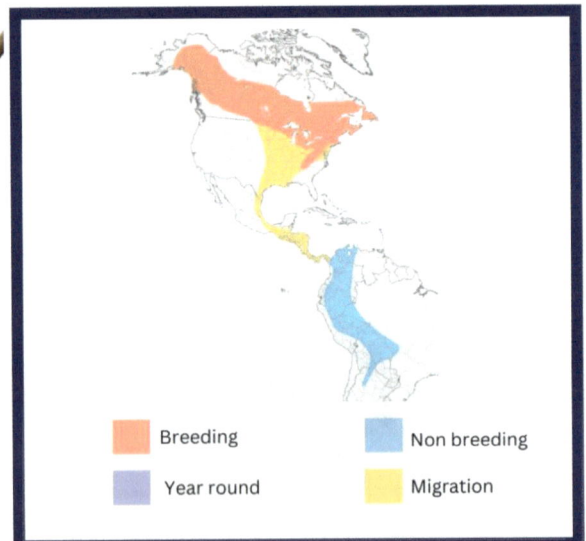

Adult

Adult

Juvenile

Breeding

Year round

Non breeding

Migration

Song

Call

DID YOU KNOW....

For many years, the Alder Flycatcher was considered the same species as the Willow Flycatcher (Empidonax traillii) and was collectively known as Traill's Flycatcher. It wasn't until 1973 that they were officially recognized as two distinct species due to differences in their songs and habitat preferences.

Because their plumage is virtually identical to the Willow Flycatcher, the most reliable way to identify an Alder Flycatcher in the field is by its distinctive song, often described as a harsh, burry "fee-BEE-o" with the second syllable strongly accented.

The Alder Flycatcher breeds farther north than any other member of the tyrant flycatcher family (Tyrannidae), nesting as far north as the Kenai Peninsula in Alaska

Olive-sided Flycatcher - *Contopus cooperi*

Olive-sided Flycatcher, a medium-sized flycatcher of North America, is characterized by its dark olive-gray upperparts, pale throat, and distinctive dark vest or "sides" that give it its name. Its strong, upright posture is also a key identifying feature. Males and females are virtually indistinguishable in plumage. Juveniles resemble adults but have buffy wingbars and tips to the secondary coverts.

FEEDING This flycatcher is an aerial insectivore, primarily feeding on flying insects caught on the wing, often from a prominent perch.

SOUNDS Its song is a loud, three-part "quick, THREE beers!" or "pip pip pip-squeer," while its call is a sharp "pip."

RANGE & MIGRATION During the breeding season, it inhabits coniferous forests, particularly along edges and in recently burned areas, across much of Canada, Alaska, and the western mountainous regions of the United States. It migrates long distances to winter in Central and South America.

SIMILAR SPECIES include other *Contopus* flycatchers, such as the Western Wood-Pewee, but the Olive-sided Flycatcher's dark vest and characteristic song help to differentiate it.

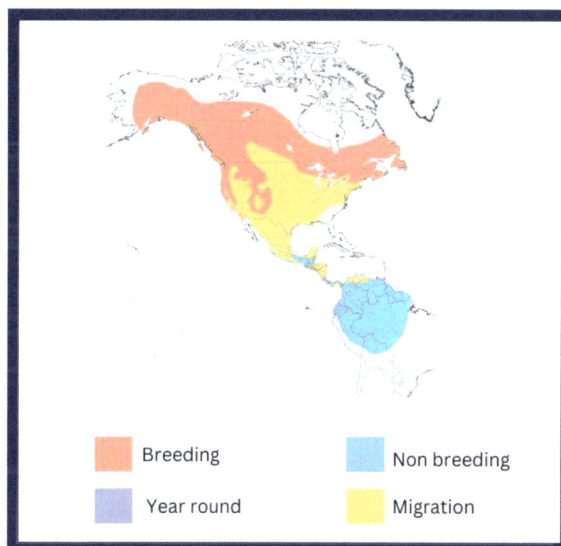

Adult

Adult

Juvenile

Breeding

Non breeding

Year round

Migration

Song

Call

DID YOU KNOW....

Among all flycatcher species that breed in the United States, the Olive-sided Flycatcher undertakes the longest migration, with some individuals traveling up to 7,000 miles between their breeding grounds in central Alaska and their wintering grounds in Bolivia.

Its plumage has a unique pattern where the deep brownish-olive sides of its breast contrast sharply with the white of its throat and belly, giving the appearance of the bird wearing a vest.

They are socially monogamous, and pairs can maintain strong bonds, sometimes lasting through failed nesting attempts and even across consecutive breeding seasons.

Least Flycatcher - *Empidonax minimus*

Least Flycatcher is a small, active flycatcher characterized by its grayish-olive upperparts, whitish underparts, and distinct white wing bars. It displays a prominent eye ring and a short, thin bill. Males and females are virtually indistinguishable in plumage, though males sing more frequently. Juveniles resemble adults but exhibit buffy wing bars and a slightly browner overall tone.

FEEDING These birds are primarily insectivorous, catching insects in mid-air or gleaning them from foliage.
SOUNDS Their song is a sharp, explosive "che-bek," and they also produce a dry, snapping "prit" call.

RANGE & BREEDING They breed across much of Canada and the northern United States, favoring deciduous and mixed forests, particularly those with open understories. In the fall, they migrate to wintering grounds in Central America and southern Mexico.

SIMILAR SPECIES include other *Empidonax* flycatchers, such as the Acadian, Willow, and Alder Flycatchers, requiring careful attention to subtle plumage details, vocalizations, and habitat preferences for accurate identification.

Adult

Adult

Juvenile

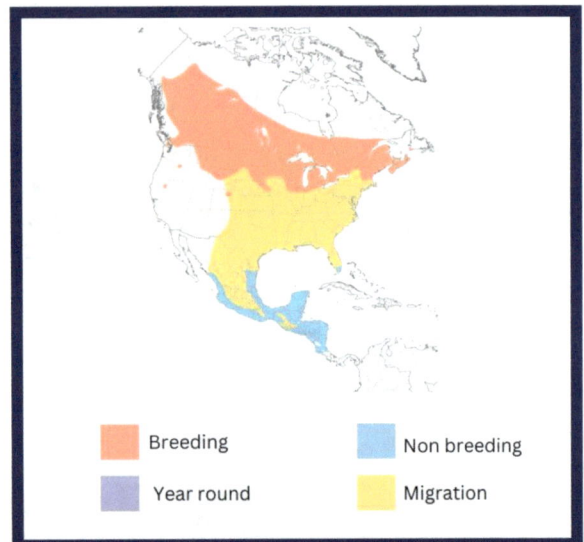

Breeding Non breeding

Year round Migration

Song

Call

DID YOU KNOW....

Unlike many other birds, Least Flycatchers often nest in loose "neighborhoods" or clusters, with anywhere from 2 to 30 territories in a small area of suitable habitat.

They have a relatively short stay on their breeding grounds, only about 64 days. This entire period is dedicated to finding a mate, building a nest, laying eggs, and raising their young to independence, leaving little extra time.

To reach their wintering grounds, Least Flycatchers can travel an average of 60 to 72 miles per day, making the journey in approximately 25 days.

Dusky Flycatcher - *Empidonax oberholseri*

Dusky Flycatcher, a small, unassuming bird of the *Empidonax* genus, is characterized by its grayish-olive upperparts and pale underparts, often with a faint olive wash across the breast. It displays two pale wing bars and a thin, light eye ring. Males and females are virtually indistinguishable in plumage, though males may be slightly larger. Juveniles resemble adults but typically have more distinct buffy wing bars.

FEEDING These flycatchers are primarily insectivorous, capturing their prey in mid-air or gleaning it from foliage.

SOUNDS Their song is a dry, buzzy "seep-seep-zeer," and their call is a sharp "whit."

RANGE & MIGRATION They breed in western North America, ranging from the southern Canadian Rockies down through the mountainous regions of the western United States, including the Great Basin. During the non-breeding season, they migrate to central Mexico.

HABITAT Their preferred habitat includes open coniferous forests, particularly those with a mix of mature trees and younger growth, as well as scrubby woodlands and riparian areas.

SIMILAR SPECIES Distinguishing the Dusky Flycatcher from other *Empidonax* flycatchers, such as the Gray Flycatcher or the Hammond's Flycatcher, can be challenging, requiring careful attention to subtle plumage details, vocalizations, and habitat preferences.

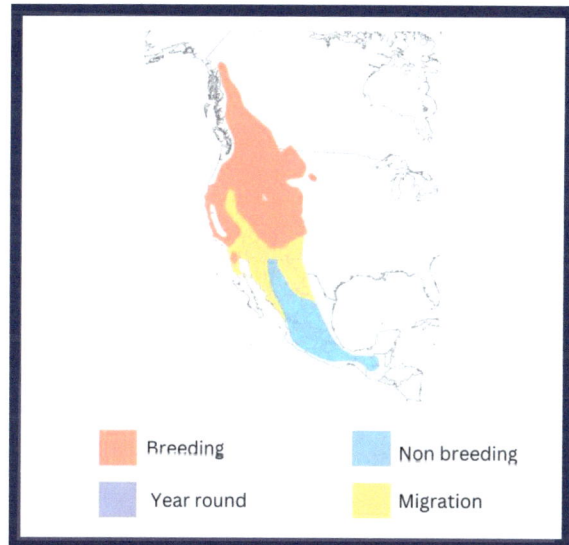

Breeding

Non breeding

Year round

Migration

Song

Call

DID YOU KNOW....

When visual identification is attempted, a key characteristic used to distinguish them from similar species like the Hammond's Flycatcher is the "primary projection." This refers to the length of the tips of the primary feathers that extend beyond the shortest flight feathers (tertials). In Dusky Flycatchers, this projection is noticeably short and stubby, giving them a relatively long-tailed appearance compared to Hammond's Flycatchers.

In areas where they coexist with Hammond's Flycatchers, Dusky Flycatchers primarily nest in shrubs, typically within a few meters of the ground. This contrasts with Hammond's Flycatchers, which exclusively nest in live, tall trees.

Dusky-capped Flycatcher - *Myiarchus tuberculifer*

Dusky-capped Flycatcher, a medium-sized flycatcher, is characterized by its olive-gray upperparts, a dusky cap, and a pale-yellow belly. It exhibits two pale wing bars and a rusty tail, particularly visible in flight. Males and females are virtually indistinguishable in plumage. Juveniles resemble adults but display buffy wing bars and a more subdued overall coloration.

FEEDING These flycatchers are primarily insectivorous, capturing insects in mid-air or gleaning them from foliage.

SOUNDS Their songs are typically a series of clear, descending whistles, and their calls include sharp "peep" or "wheep" notes.

RANGE & MIGRATION This species' range extends from the southwestern United States down through Central and South America. In North America, they are found primarily in wooded canyons and riparian areas of Arizona, New Mexico, and Texas. They are migratory, retreating southward for the winter.

HABITAT They favor habitats with dense foliage, including oak woodlands, pine-oak forests, and streamside thickets.

SIMILAR SPECIES include other Myiarchus flycatchers, such as the Ash-throated Flycatcher and Brown-crested Flycatcher, but differences in vocalizations and subtle plumage details help distinguish them.

Adult
Adult
Juvenile

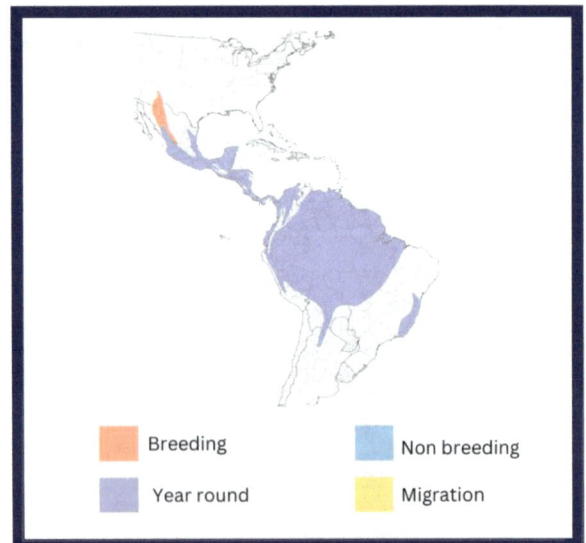

Breeding
Year round
Non breeding
Migration

Song

Call

DID YOU KNOW....

While they typically use common materials like moss, grass, and feathers to line their cavity nests, Dusky-capped Flycatchers have been recorded using more surprising items. These include things like shed snakeskin, lizard skin, spider egg sacs, and even owl pellets within their nests.

Unlike some flycatchers that perch conspicuously in the open to sally for insects, Dusky-capped Flycatchers often forage within the foliage of trees. They frequently change perches inside the vegetation, making short flights to glean insects or hovering briefly to snatch prey, rather than engaging in long, kingbird-like aerial pursuits.

Hammond's Flycatcher - *Empidonax hammondii*

Hammond's Flycatcher is a small, delicate songbird characterized by its grayish-olive upperparts, pale underparts, and distinct white eye-ring and wingbars. It is a member of the Empidonax flycatcher group, known for their similar appearances. Distinguishing between males and females visually is difficult, though subtle size differences may occur. Juveniles resemble adults but often exhibit more buffy wingbars.

FEEDING This flycatcher is primarily insectivorous, foraging by sallying out from perches to catch flying insects.

SOUNDS Its song is a short, abrupt series of notes, and its calls include sharp "peek" sounds.

RANGE & MIGRATION They breed in mature coniferous forests throughout western North America, favoring higher elevations. During migration, they move south to winter in the pine-oak woodlands of Mexico and Central America.

HABITAT Their habitat preference is typically mature and old-growth conifer forests.

SIMILAR SPECIES Distinguishing it from similar species like the Dusky Flycatcher can be challenging, but differences in primary projection, bill size, and vocalizations are key identifiers.

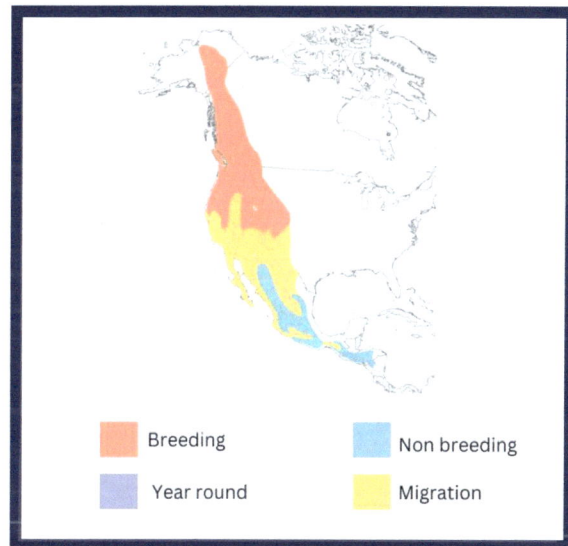

Breeding

Year round

Non breeding

Migration

Song

Call

DID YOU KNOW....

The Hammond's Flycatcher is named in honor of William Alexander Hammond, who was the Surgeon General of the U.S. Army. He collected the first specimens, which were then sent to ornithologist Spencer Fullerton Baird.

Interestingly, some Hammond's Flycatchers on Vancouver Island in British Columbia have shown a tendency to evolve longer and thicker bills in areas where the Western Flycatcher (which typically has a thicker bill) is absent. This suggests potential niche partitioning in the presence of a similar species.

THRASHERS

Thrashers are a fascinating group of New World passerine birds belonging to the family Mimidae, which also includes mockingbirds and catbirds. They are known for their often complex and varied songs, their generally larger size compared to their relatives, and their somewhat secretive habits.

General Characteristics:

- **Size and Shape:** Thrashers are generally medium to large-sized songbirds, often larger and more robust than their mockingbird and catbird relatives. They tend to have a somewhat slender body shape with relatively long tails.
- **Plumage:** Their plumage is typically muted and earthy-toned, often in shades of brown, rufous, gray, or white. Many species exhibit streaking or spotting on their underparts. Sexual dimorphism in plumage is usually minimal or absent.
- **Bill:** They possess a moderately long, slightly decurved (downward curving) bill. The bill is a versatile tool used for foraging, probing leaf litter, and catching insects.
- **Legs and Feet:** Thrashers have strong legs and feet adapted for ground foraging. They are often seen hopping or running on the ground while searching for food.
- **Vocalization:** This is a defining characteristic of thrashers. They are highly vocal birds with complex and varied songs. Their repertoire includes original phrases as well as accurate imitations of other bird songs, insect sounds, and even mechanical noises. Some species are known for their continuous and often repetitive singing.
- **Behavior:** Thrashers are often solitary or found in pairs, especially during the breeding season. They can be quite secretive and elusive, preferring dense vegetation. While capable of flight, they tend to spend a significant amount of time foraging on the ground.
- **Diet:** Their diet is typically omnivorous, consisting mainly of insects, other invertebrates, berries, and fruits. They use their bills to turn over leaf litter, probe the ground, and pluck fruit from bushes and trees.
- **Nesting:** Thrashers build cup-shaped nests in shrubs, thickets, or low trees. Both parents usually participate in nest building, incubation of eggs, and caring for the young.
- **Distribution:** Thrashers are exclusively found in the New World, with the greatest diversity occurring in North and Central America. Some species are migratory, while others are resident year-round.

Key Points:

- **Masters of Mimicry:** Their exceptional ability to imitate a wide range of sounds is a hallmark of the thrasher family. This mimicry likely serves various purposes, including attracting mates, defending territories, and potentially confusing predators.
- **Ground Foragers:** Thrashers are highly adapted for foraging on the ground. Their strong legs and slightly curved bills are ideal for searching through leaf litter and soil for insects and other invertebrates.
- **Diverse Song Repertoire:** Individual thrashers can possess an incredibly large song repertoire, often incorporating hundreds of different phrases and imitations.
- **Ecological Roles:** As omnivores, thrashers play a role in controlling insect populations and dispersing seeds through their consumption of fruits and berries.
- **Conservation Status:** While some thrasher species are common and widespread, others face conservation challenges due to habitat loss and degradation. Understanding their ecological needs is crucial for their long-term survival.
- **Distinguishing from Mockingbirds and Catbirds:** While related, thrashers generally tend to be larger, have longer tails, and often exhibit more rufous or brown coloration compared to mockingbirds and catbirds. Their songs, while also mimicking, often have a different quality or structure.

Brown Thrasher - *Toxostoma rufum*

Brown Thrasher, a large songbird found in North America, is recognized by its striking rusty-brown upperparts, heavily streaked underparts, and bright yellow eyes. Both male and female Brown Thrashers share a similar appearance, displaying no noticeable sexual dimorphism in plumage. Juveniles exhibit a somewhat duller coloration and less distinct streaking compared to adults.

FEEDING These birds are omnivorous, primarily foraging on the ground for insects, berries, nuts, and seeds.

SOUNDS Their songs are a rich, varied series of repeated phrases, often mimicking other bird species, while their calls include sharp "smacks" and "tchucks."

RANGE & MIGRATION Brown Thrashers occupy a broad range across eastern and central North America, extending from southern Canada to the Gulf Coast. They are migratory in the northern parts of their range, moving south for the winter, while southern populations may be resident year-round.

HABITAT They favor dense thickets, shrublands, and forest edges, often found in overgrown fields and suburban gardens.

SIMILAR SPECIES include other thrashers like the Long-billed Thrasher, but the Brown Thrasher's distinct plumage and song patterns help distinguish it.

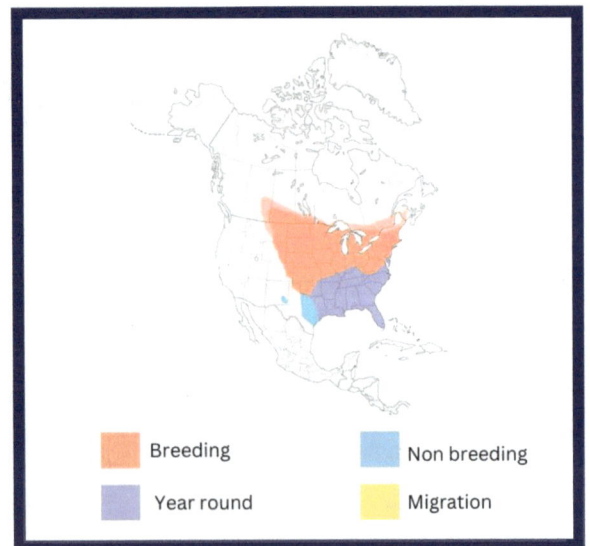

Adult

Adult

Juvenile

Breeding		Non breeding
Year round		Migration

Song

Call

DID YOU KNOW....

The Brown Thrasher possesses one of the largest song repertoires of any North American bird, with over 1,100 distinct song types documented. Some estimates suggest it might even exceed 3,000

It has been observed cracking open acorns by vigorously pounding them with its bill, a relatively unique behavior for a songbird of its size.

Its genus name, Toxostoma, means "curved bill," which it uses with a side-to-side sweeping motion to "thrash" through leaf litter and soil in search of food. This thrashing behavior is how it got its common name.

Curve-billed Thrasher - *Toxostoma curvirostre*

Curve-billed Thrasher is a medium-sized songbird readily identified by its long, distinctly down-curved bill. Its overall plumage is a grayish-brown, providing excellent camouflage in its arid habitats. Males and females are virtually indistinguishable in appearance, displaying similar plumage. Juveniles exhibit a somewhat mottled appearance compared to adults.

FEEDING These thrashers are primarily insectivores, foraging on the ground and probing with their curved bills for insects and spiders. They also consume berries and fruits, adapting their diet to seasonal availability.

SOUNDS Their song is a series of varied, musical phrases, often repeated, while their calls include sharp "chek" notes and harsher scolding sounds.

RANGE & MIGRATION They are found primarily in the southwestern United States and Mexico, favoring arid and semi-arid regions with shrubs and cacti. They are generally non-migratory, remaining within their territories year-round.

HABITAT Their preferred habitat consists of desert scrub, mesquite thickets, and areas with scattered cacti and shrubs.

SIMILAR SPECIES include other thrashers, such as the Bendire's Thrasher and the Gray Thrasher, but the Curve-billed Thrasher's distinct curved bill and song distinguish it from these relatives.

Adult

Adult

Juvenile

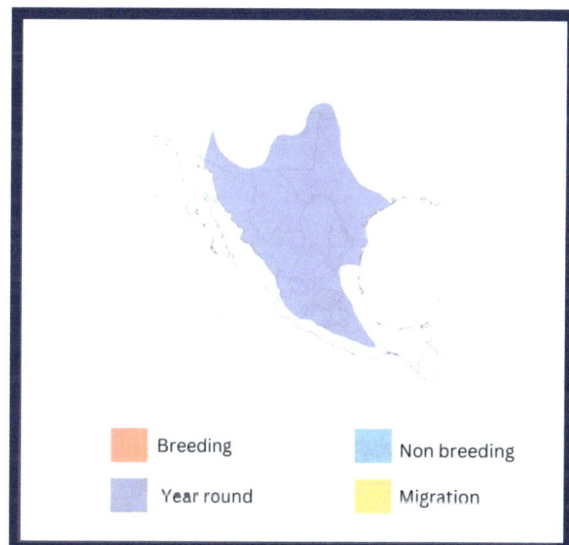

Breeding　　Non breeding

Year round　　Migration

Song　　**Call**

DID YOU KNOW....

While they inhabit various arid and semi-arid environments, Curve-billed Thrashers show a strong preference for nesting in certain types of cacti, particularly chain fruit and teddy bear cholla, using them in about 90% of cases. This has led some to suggest they should be called "Cactus Thrashers."

While not as prolific mimics as Northern Mockingbirds, Curve-billed Thrashers do sometimes incorporate imitations of other bird songs into their varied repertoire.

It's believed that the fruit of cacti, such as saguaro and prickly pear, provides an important source of water for Curve-billed Thrashers, especially during the hot, dry spring and early summer months before the late summer rains arrive.

California Thrasher - *Toxostoma redivivum*

California Thrasher is a large, slender songbird characterized by its long, curved bill and lengthy tail, a signature feature that aids in its ground foraging. Its plumage is a relatively uniform brownish-gray, with a paler underside. Distinguishing between males and females is difficult visually, as they exhibit similar plumage. Juveniles resemble adults but may display slightly less distinct coloration.

FEEDING These thrashers are primarily ground foragers, using their curved bills to "thrash" through leaf litter and soil, seeking insects, spiders, and other invertebrates; they also consume berries and fruits.

SOUNDS Their songs are complex and varied, often incorporating mimicry of other bird species, and are delivered in long, rambling phrases; their calls include harsh "chuck" notes.

RANGE & MIGRATION Found predominantly in California and a small portion of Baja California, they are non-migratory, remaining within their territories year-round.

HABITAT Their preferred habitat is dense chaparral, brushy areas, and oak woodlands, where they find ample cover.

SIMILAR SPECIES can include other thrashers or mockingbirds, but the California Thrasher's unique bill shape, habitat preference, and song help in identification.

Adult

Adult

Juvenile

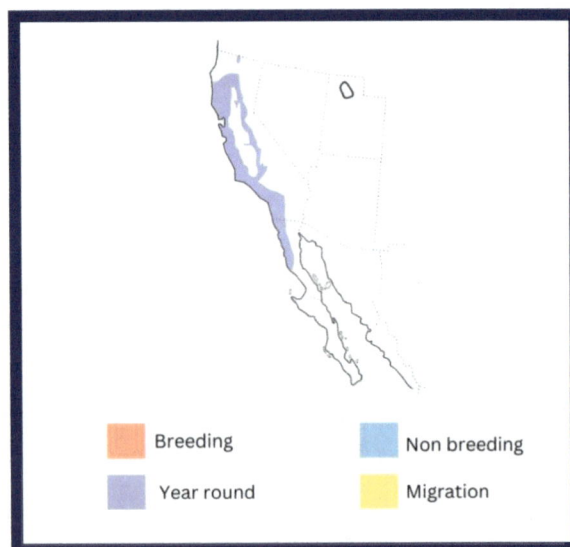

Breeding

Non breeding

Year round

Migration

Song

Call

DID YOU KNOW....

The California Thrasher is the largest species within the thrasher family. It can reach up to 32 cm (13 inches) in length and weigh around 78-93 grams (2.75-3.28 ounces).

Unlike many birds that peck or probe, the California Thrasher employs a distinctive sideways sweeping motion of its long, curved bill to sift through leaf litter and soil in search of insects, spiders, and other invertebrates. This "thrashing" behavior gives the bird its name

This species is strongly associated with chaparral habitat, a dense shrubland ecosystem found primarily in California and a small part of Baja California. It is considered a flagship species of this unique environment.

Sage Thrasher - *Oreoscoptes montanus*

Sage Thrasher, a slender and inconspicuous songbird, is characterized by its grayish-brown plumage, heavily streaked underparts, and pale-yellow eyes. It possesses a relatively long, slightly down-curved bill, well-suited for its ground-foraging lifestyle. Males and females are virtually identical in appearance, making it challenging to distinguish them visually. Juveniles exhibit a similar plumage pattern but tend to have less distinct streaking and a more mottled appearance.

FEEDING Sage Thrashers are primarily insectivorous, particularly during the breeding season, but they also consume berries and seeds, especially in the winter.

SOUNDS Their song is a continuous, varied, and often rapid series of warbles and trills, sometimes mimicking other bird species. Their calls include a sharp "check" or "chur."

RANGE & MIGRATION This species is found in arid regions of western North America, particularly in sagebrush steppe habitats. They are migratory, moving south to warmer areas of the southwestern United States and northern Mexico during the winter months.

HABITAT Their preferred habitat is characterized by expanses of sagebrush, where they find food and shelter.

SIMILAR SPECIES include other thrashers, such as the Brown Thrasher and Curve-billed Thrasher, but the Sage Thrasher's distinct habitat preference, plumage, and vocalizations help to differentiate it.

Adult

Adult

Juvenile

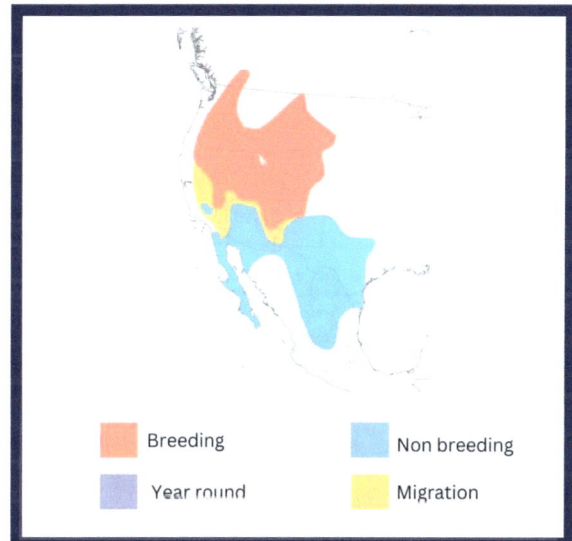

Breeding   Non breeding

Year round   Migration

Song   Call

DID YOU KNOW....

Its scientific name, Oreoscoptes montanus, translates to "mountain mimic," a fitting description because the Sage Thrasher is known for its impressive vocal abilities, often mimicking the songs of other birds in its habitat.

It is considered a "sagebrush obligate" species, meaning it is almost entirely dependent on sagebrush ecosystems for breeding. They prefer large, continuous stands of tall, dense sagebrush

The Sage Thrasher has a remarkably long and varied song. The longest recorded song lasted for approximately 22 minutes without a break, leading to the nickname "the poet of the lonesome sagebrush plain."

Bendire's Thrasher - *Toxostoma bendirei*

Bendire's Thrasher is a medium-sized songbird characterized by its overall pale grayish-brown plumage, a slightly decurved bill, and relatively short tail. It has a subtle, streaked breast and pale underparts. Male and female Bendire's Thrashers are virtually indistinguishable in appearance. Juveniles display a more heavily streaked breast and a slightly duller coloration compared to adults.

FEEDING These thrashers primarily forage on the ground, consuming insects, spiders, and berries.

SOUNDS Their song is a series of melodious warbles and phrases, less varied and often lower in pitch than that of the closely related Curve-billed Thrasher. Their calls include a sharp "check" or "chur."

RANGE & MIGRATION Bendire's Thrashers are found in arid regions of the southwestern United States and northern Mexico, favoring open desert scrub, grasslands with scattered shrubs, and mesquite thickets. They are migratory, moving south for the winter.

HABITAT Their preferred habitat includes areas with sparse vegetation, often with a mix of shrubs and open ground.

SIMILAR SPECIES include the Curve-billed Thrasher and the Sage Thrasher, but Bendire's Thrasher can be differentiated by its slightly shorter bill, less extensive streaking, and subtle plumage details.

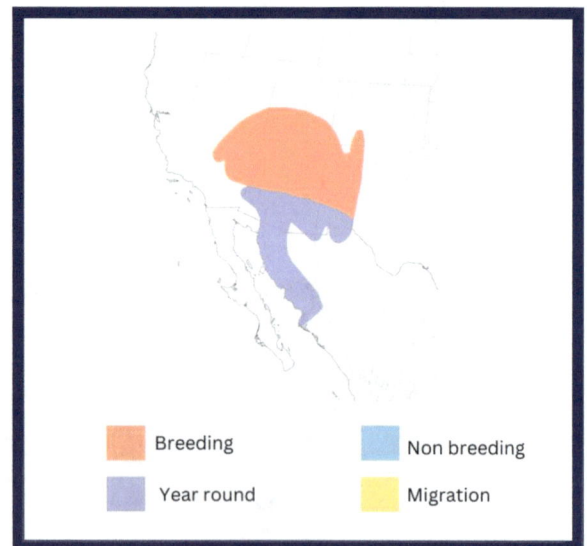

Adult

Adult

Juvenile

Breeding

Year round

Non breeding

Migration

Song

Call

DID YOU KNOW....

It was one of the last resident bird species in the southwestern United States to be discovered, only being recognized as distinct in the 1870s.

The species is named after U.S. Army Lieutenant Charles Bendire, who collected the first known specimen in Arizona.

It can be easily confused with the Curve-billed Thrasher due to similar coloration. A key distinguishing feature is its shorter bill and bright yellow eyes, as well as a pale base to its lower mandible.

Long-billed Thrasher - *Toxostoma longirostre*

Long-billed Thrasher is a relatively large thrasher species found in the dense, brushy areas of southern Texas and northeastern Mexico. It is characterized by its rich brown upperparts, heavily streaked white underparts, a grayish face, and distinctive orange eyes. While males and females appear very similar, juveniles display plumage that is generally less defined than that of adults.

FEEDING This thrasher forages primarily on the ground, utilizing its long bill to search for insects, other invertebrates, and berries.

SOUNDS Its song is a complex series of varied phrases, and it also produces a range of calls, including sharp notes and rattles.

HABITAT The Long-billed Thrasher inhabits dense thickets and woodlands, particularly in riparian areas.

RANGE & MIGRATION It is a resident species, meaning it does not typically undertake long migrations.

SIMILAR SPECIES The most similar species is the Brown Thrasher, but their ranges largely do not overlap, and the Long-billed Thrasher has a more grayish facial appearance.

Adult

Adult

Juvenile

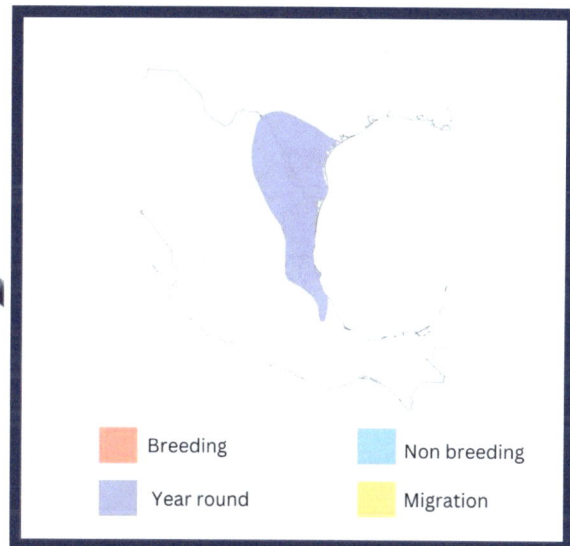

Breeding

Non breeding

Year round

Migration

DID YOU KNOW....

Unlike its close relative, the Brown Thrasher, which has a wide distribution across much of the eastern United States and southern Canada, the Long-billed Thrasher's range in the U.S. is almost entirely limited to South Texas.

Unlike most thrashers, the eggs in a Long-billed Thrasher nest tend to hatch at the same time, a process known as synchronous hatching.

They are strongly associated with dense, thorny brushlands and thickets, often with native plants like mesquite and acacia, providing both cover and nesting sites.

Song

Call

LeConte's Thrasher - *Toxostoma lecontei*

LeConte's Thrasher is a medium-sized, pale thrasher adapted to arid environments of the southwestern United States and northern Mexico. Its overall coloration is a light, sandy gray-brown, providing excellent camouflage in its desert habitat. Both male and female LeConte's Thrashers appear virtually identical, with subtle variations in size being the only distinguishing factor. Juveniles exhibit a slightly more mottled appearance compared to adults.

FEEDING These thrashers are primarily insectivorous, probing the ground with their curved bills to find insects and spiders, but they also consume seeds and berries.

SOUNDS Their song is a series of low, melodious warbles and trills, often delivered from a prominent perch, while their calls include sharp "chucks" and "wheeps."

RANGE & MIGRATION They are non-migratory, maintaining year-round residency within their range, which encompasses the deserts of southern California, Arizona, Nevada, and parts of northern Mexico.

HABITAT They prefer arid, sparsely vegetated habitats like creosote bush scrub and desert washes.

SIMILAR SPECIES include other thrashers such as the Curve-billed Thrasher and the Bendire's Thrasher, but LeConte's Thrasher can be distinguished by its pale coloration, relatively plain face, and preference for extremely arid landscapes.

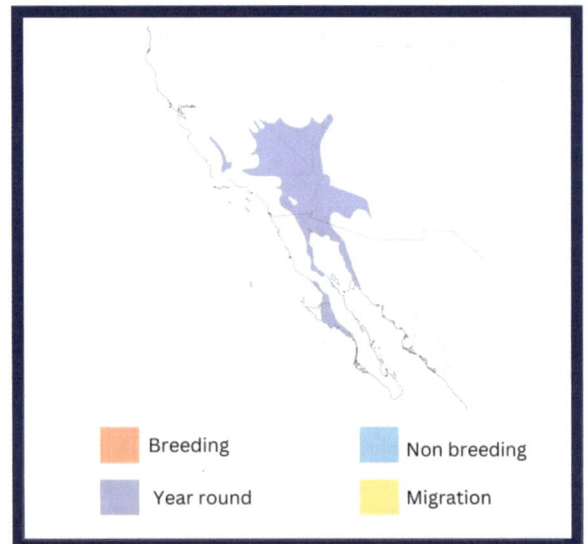

Adult

Adult

Juvenile

Breeding		Non breeding
Year round		Migration

Song

Call

DID YOU KNOW....

Unlike many other thrashers, the LeConte's Thrasher is primarily terrestrial. It spends most of its time on the ground, running swiftly with its tail held high rather than flying. It only takes to the air when closely pursued.

They obtain most of the water they need from their diet of insects and other arthropods. They rarely need to drink water directly, showcasing a physiological adaptation to their arid environment.

Despite their relatively large size (around 11 inches long), LeConte's Thrashers are often difficult to spot due to their inconspicuous pale coloration and preference for running on the ground in sparse vegetation.

Crissal Thrasher - *Toxostoma crissale*

Crissal Thrasher is a relatively large thrasher characterized by its long, deeply curved bill and dull yellow eyes. Its plumage is primarily a grayish-brown, with a striking feature being its bright cinnamon-colored undertail coverts, known as the crissum, which gives the bird its name. Distinguishing features also include a subtle black and white "mustache" mark. There's little to no visual difference between male and female Crissal Thrashers. Juveniles tend to have a paler and duller plumage compared to adults, with a browner undertail.

FEEDING This thrasher is primarily a ground feeder, using its long, curved bill to probe for insects, spiders, seeds, and fruits among leaf litter and under shrubs.

SOUNDS Its song is a melodious, rambling series of notes, often described as sweeter than those of other thrashers. Calls are less frequent but include sharp notes.

RANGE & MIGRATION The Crissal Thrasher's range spans the arid regions of the southwestern United States, including parts of Texas, New Mexico, Arizona, California, Nevada, and Utah, extending into central Mexico. It is generally a non-migratory bird, remaining within its territories year-round.

HABITAT It prefers habitats with dense brush, such as mesquite thickets, desert washes, and riparian areas, often near desert streams.

SIMILAR SPECIES include the Curve-billed Thrasher, which can be distinguished by differences in bill shape, plumage details, and vocalizations.

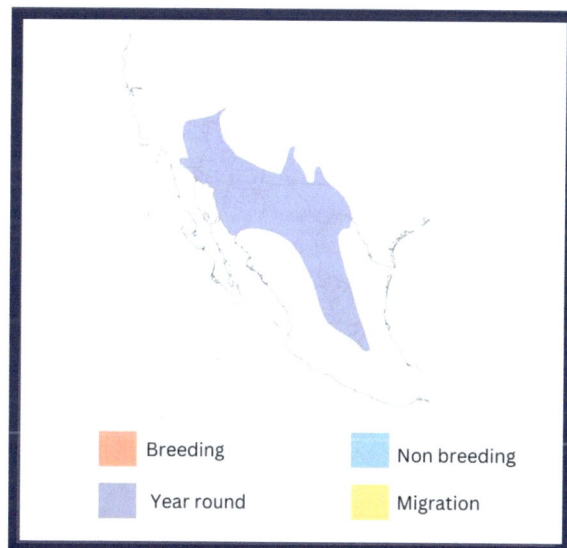

Adult

Adult

Juvenile

Breeding	Non breeding
Year round	Migration

Song

Call

DID YOU KNOW....

Unlike many other birds, the Crissal Thrasher is highly elusive and prefers to walk or run on the ground within dense vegetation rather than fly in the open. This behavior makes them difficult to spot.

One biologist has described the Crissal Thrasher as "reclusive and agoraphobic" due to its strong preference for staying hidden within dense thickets and its reluctance to venture into open areas.

The name "crissal" refers to the brightly colored undertail coverts (the feathers between the tail and vent), which are typically a rusty or cinnamon hue, providing a striking contrast to their otherwise muted grayish-brown plumage.

FINCHES

Finches are a diverse group of small to medium-sized passerine birds belonging to the family Fringillidae. They are found worldwide, with the greatest diversity occurring in the Northern Hemisphere.

General Characteristics:

- **Size and Shape:** Typically, small and stocky birds, ranging in size from about 10 to 25 cm (4 to 10 inches) in length. They generally have conical or stout beaks, well-suited for cracking seeds. Their bodies are compact with relatively short necks and forked tails.
- **Plumage:** Finch plumage is highly variable, both between species and within species (sexual dimorphism is common). Colors can range from dull browns and grays to vibrant yellows, reds, oranges, and blues. Males often exhibit brighter and more elaborate coloration than females, especially during the breeding season.
- **Beak Morphology:** A defining characteristic of finches is their strong, conical beak. The size and shape of the beak are closely related to their diet, with thicker, more powerful beaks adapted for larger, harder seeds, and finer beaks suitable for smaller seeds and some insects.
- **Diet:** The primary diet of most finches consists of seeds and grains. However, many species also consume fruits, buds, insects, and other invertebrates, especially during the breeding season when they need protein for themselves and their young.
- **Vocalization:** Finches are known for their often melodious and varied songs. Males use their songs to attract mates and defend territories. Calls are typically shorter and simpler, used for communication within a flock or family group.
- **Social Behavior:** Many finch species are social birds, often forming flocks, especially outside of the breeding season. These flocks can range in size from a few individuals to hundreds or even thousands. During the breeding season, they may become more territorial.
- **Nesting:** Finches typically build cup-shaped nests in trees, shrubs, or even on the ground, depending on the species and habitat. The female usually builds the nest, and both parents participate in incubating the eggs and feeding the young.
- **Reproduction:** They are typically monogamous during a breeding season. They lay a clutch of several eggs, which are usually pale in color and sometimes speckled. Incubation periods vary between species. The young are altricial, meaning they are born helpless and require significant parental care.
- **Flight:** Finches have strong, direct flight, often with undulating patterns. Their wings are relatively short and pointed, allowing for agility in maneuvering through vegetation.

Key Points:

- **Diversity:** The Fringillidae family is one of the largest bird families, encompassing hundreds of species with significant variations in appearance, behavior, and ecology.
- **Adaptation:** Finches exhibit remarkable adaptations to their specific environments and food sources, most notably in their beak morphology. The famous Galapagos finches, studied by Charles Darwin, are a prime example of adaptive radiation.
- **Ecological Roles:** Finches play important roles in their ecosystems, primarily as seed dispersers and sometimes as insect predators. They can influence plant populations and contribute to the food web.
- **Human Interaction:** Some finch species are popular as cage birds due to their attractive plumage and songs. However, this has also led to illegal trapping and trade, threatening some wild populations. Habitat loss and degradation also pose significant threats to many finch species worldwide.
- **Indicator Species:** Changes in finch populations can sometimes serve as indicators of environmental health and habitat quality. Their sensitivity to habitat changes and food availability can reflect broader ecological trends.
- **Evolutionary Significance:** Finches have been crucial in the study of evolution, particularly the processes of natural selection and speciation. The diversity within certain finch groups provides valuable insights into how species adapt and diverge over time.

American Goldfinch - *Spinus tristis*

American Goldfinch is a small finch characterized by its conical bill and notched tail. During the breeding season, males are easily identified by their vibrant yellow plumage, black forehead, and black wings with white markings. Females, in contrast, display a duller yellow-olive coloration. In winter, both males and females transition to a drabber, brownish plumage with distinct wingbars. Juveniles resemble winter females.

FEEDING These birds are primarily granivorous, feeding on seeds from plants like thistles, sunflowers, and asters.

SOUNDS Their song is a lively series of twitters and warbles, often incorporating mimicked sounds, while their flight call is a distinctive "po-ta-to-chip" sound.

RANGE & MIGRATION American Goldfinches are found throughout much of North America, with their range extending from southern Canada to the southern United States. They exhibit a partial migration, with some populations moving southward during the winter months, influenced by food availability.

HABITAT They prefer habitats with open fields, weedy areas, roadsides, and backyards, particularly those with abundant seed-bearing plants.

SIMILAR SPECIES include Pine Siskins and Lesser Goldfinches, which can be distinguished by differences in plumage and size.

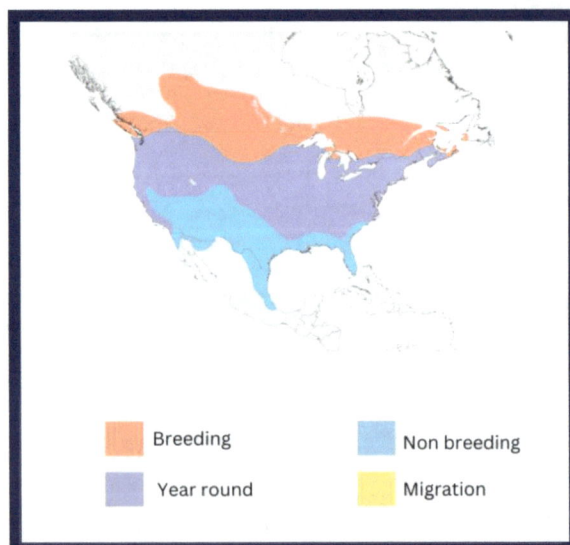

Non Breeding Male

Breeding Female

Juvenile

Breeding Male

Breeding | Non breeding
Year round | Migration

Song

Call

DID YOU KNOW....

Unlike many other songbirds that feed insects to their young, American Goldfinches are almost entirely vegetarian throughout their lives. They primarily eat seeds, even feeding a diet of regurgitated seeds to their nestlings. This makes them highly dependent on thistle and other seed-bearing plants.

They are one of the latest-nesting songbirds in North America. They typically wait until late June or July to begin nesting, coinciding with the peak availability of thistle seeds, which are a crucial food source for their young.

Male American Goldfinches undergo a complete molt twice a year, a relatively uncommon occurrence in songbirds. This results in their dramatic seasonal color change from bright yellow in the breeding season to a duller olive or brown in the winter.

House Finch - *Haemorhous mexicanus*

House Finch, a common sight across North America, is a small finch characterized by its conical bill and relatively long, square-tipped tail. Males are easily recognized by their bright red or orange plumage on the head, throat, and breast, though the intensity of the color can vary widely. Females and juveniles exhibit a more subdued appearance, with grayish-brown plumage streaked with brown underneath.

FEEDING House Finches are primarily seed-eaters, favoring small seeds and berries, and they also supplement their diet with buds and insects, especially during the breeding season.

SOUNDS Their songs are a cheerful, warbling series of notes, often delivered from a prominent perch. Their calls include a sharp "cheep" or "whit."

RANGE & MIGRATION They are widespread, inhabiting urban and suburban areas, as well as open woodlands, farms, and deserts, extending from southern Canada through Mexico. While some populations in northern regions may exhibit short-distance migration, many House Finches are year-round residents.

SIMILAR SPECIES that could cause confusion include Purple Finches and Cassin's Finches, but House Finches typically have more extensive streaking and a less distinct facial pattern. They thrive in areas with access to human-provided food sources and nesting sites.

Male

Female

Juvenile

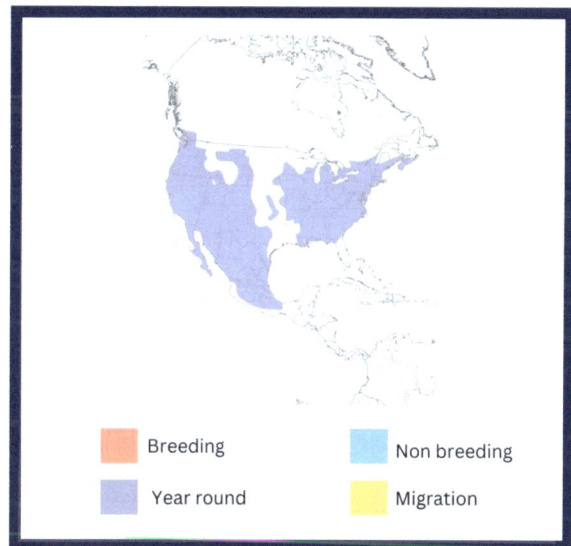

Breeding

Non breeding

Year round

Migration

DID YOU KNOW....

Unlike many bird species that naturally expanded their range, the House Finch's presence in eastern North America is due to a small number of birds being released in Long Island, New York, in 1940 after failed attempts to sell them as cage birds called "Hollywood Finches." These released birds thrived and rapidly spread across the eastern United States and southern Canada.

They are unusual in that they feed their nestlings exclusively plant-based foods, primarily regurgitated seeds. This is relatively rare in the bird world, as most adult vegetarian birds will still provide protein-rich insects to their fast-growing young

Song

Call

Purple Finch - *Haemorhous purpureus*

Purple Finch is a medium-sized finch that presents a striking difference between the sexes. Adult males are known for their vibrant, raspberry-red coloration across their head, breast, back, and rump, though their wings and tail are browner. Females, in contrast, exhibit a streaked brown and white plumage, with a distinctive bold facial pattern that includes a light eyebrow and dark whisker. Juveniles resemble females.

FEEDING These finches primarily feed on seeds, buds, blossoms, and fruits, and occasionally supplement their diet with insects.

SOUNDS Their songs are characterized by a cheerful, warbling melody, and they also produce a sharp "pik" call.

HABITAT They inhabit coniferous and mixed forests, and in winter, they can be found in woodlands, shrubby fields, and often visit backyard feeders.

RANGE AND MIGRATION Their range spans across southern Canada and the northern United States, with migration patterns that vary; northern populations migrate southward, while others may remain resident.

SIMILAR SPECIES One of the similar species that is often confused with the Purple Finch is the House Finch. Key differences help in distinguishing the two species. The House Finch has a less extensive red coloration, and differing facial patterns. Also, the bills are slightly different.

Male

Female

Juvenile

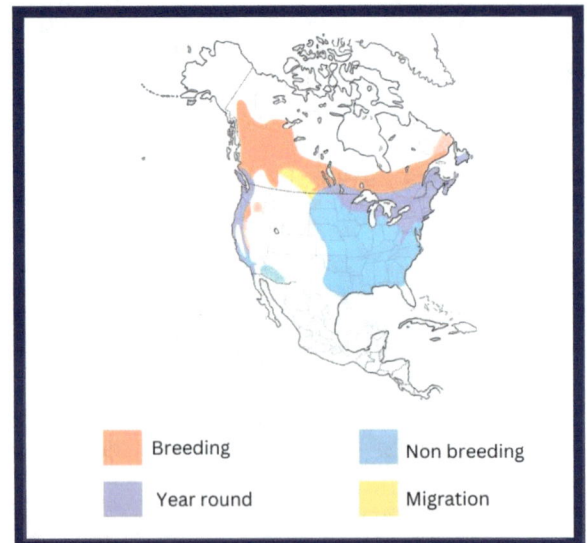

Breeding

Non breeding

Year round

Migration

Song

Call

DID YOU KNOW....

Despite their name, male Purple Finches aren't actually purple. Their vibrant plumage is a beautiful raspberry-red or rosy-crimson color, often described as "wine-stained." The name likely came from a more general 18th-century use of "purple" to describe reddish hues.

The coloration of the male is so distinctive that it's often poetically described as if the bird has been dipped in raspberry juice, with the color concentrated on the head, breast, and rump.

Unlike some finches that have predictable migration patterns, Purple Finch populations can be somewhat irruptive in winter.

Lesser Goldfinch - *Spinus psaltria*

esser Goldfinch is a small finch characterized by its vibrant yellow underparts and contrasting black wings with white wing bars. Males display a striking black cap and back, while females exhibit a duller olive-green back and a less intense yellow coloration. Juvenile birds are typically grayish-brown with faint wing bars, gradually developing their adult plumage.

FEEDING These finches are primarily seed-eaters, favoring small seeds from weeds and trees, and they also consume insects, especially during breeding season.

SOUNDS Their songs are a series of rapid, high-pitched twitters and trills, often interspersed with mimicry of other birds. Their calls include a sharp "chit" or "per-chick-o-ree" sound.

RANGE & MIGRATION The Lesser Goldfinch's range extends from the southwestern United States down through Mexico and into parts of Central America. They are generally resident in the southern parts of their range, with some northern populations exhibiting partial migration, moving southward during colder months.

HABITAT They prefer open woodlands, scrublands, and urban parks, particularly areas with an abundance of seed-bearing plants.

SIMILAR SPECIES include American Goldfinches, but Lesser Goldfinches are smaller and have a black cap in males and a darker overall appearance, and also Lawrence's Goldfinches, which have grey backs instead of black on the male.

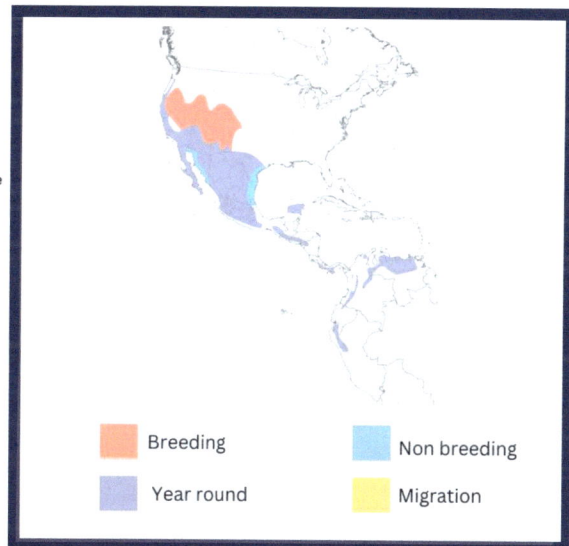

Male

Female

Juvenile

Breeding

Non breeding

Year round

Migration

Song

Call

DID YOU KNOW....

Male Lesser Goldfinches exhibit a distinct color variation across their range. Those in the eastern part of the US typically have black backs, while males along the West Coast usually have green backs.

Similar to American Goldfinches, Lesser Goldfinches often wait to begin breeding until the peak availability of thistle, dandelion, and other composite flowers are seeding, ensuring a plentiful food source for their young.

The female Lesser Goldfinch uses spiderwebs as a key component in binding their cup-shaped nests together, along with other plant materials like leaves, bark, and catkins.

Cassin's Finch - *Haemorhous cassinii*

Cassin's Finch is a medium-sized finch characterized by its conical bill and subtle, streaked plumage. Adult males exhibit a vibrant reddish-pink coloration on their crown, forehead, and breast, with a more subdued pinkish wash on their flanks. Females and juveniles display a grayish-brown plumage with distinct streaking, lacking the vibrant pink of the mature males.

FEEDING Their diet primarily consists of seeds, buds, and berries, supplemented with insects during the breeding season.

SOUNDS The Cassin's Finch's song is a melodious warble, often delivered from a prominent perch, and their calls include sharp "cheep" notes.

RANGE & MIGRATION These finches inhabit mountainous regions of western North America, ranging from British Columbia south to Baja California, typically residing in coniferous forests and subalpine woodlands. They exhibit altitudinal migration, moving to lower elevations during the winter months, and some populations undertake longer southward movements.

HABITAT Their preferred habitat includes open coniferous forests, forest edges, and areas with scattered trees.

SIMILAR SPECIES include the House Finch and Purple Finch; however, Cassin's Finch can be distinguished by its darker streaking, more prominent supercilium, and the male's darker red coloration, which is often confined to the crown.

Male

Female

Juvenile

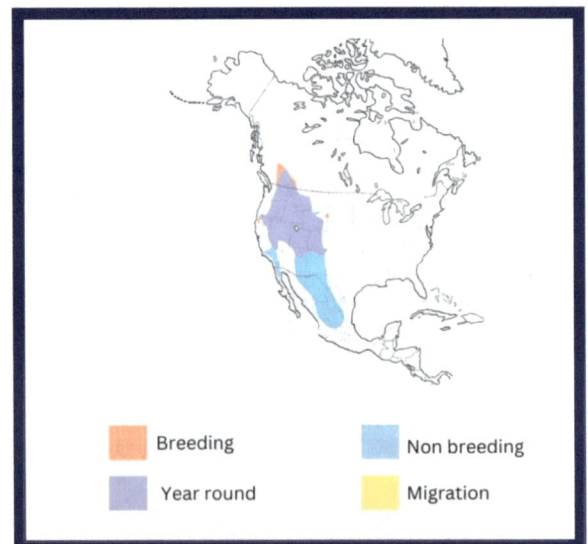

Breeding   Non breeding

Year round   Migration

Song

Call

DID YOU KNOW....

Unlike many other finches that might be found across a wider range of altitudes, Cassin's Finches are strongly associated with higher elevations, particularly coniferous forests in mountainous regions of western North America.[1] They often breed at elevations between 5,000 and 10,000 feet

Unlike some finches with predictable southward migrations, Cassin's Finch winter movements are often described as "irruptive" or irregular.

While they use typical materials like twigs, grasses, and rootlets for their cup-shaped nests, Cassin's Finches often incorporate a significant amount of conifer needles into the nest structure.

Brown-capped Rosy-Finch - *Leucosticte australis*

Brown-capped Rosy-Finch is a stocky, medium-sized finch inhabiting high-altitude regions of North America. Adult males display a rich brown coloration on their head, neck, and breast, with a rosy pink wash on the belly, rump, and wing edges. Females exhibit a similar pattern but with duller, less vibrant hues. Juveniles are characterized by a pale brown plumage with buffy edging on their wings and occasional hints of rosy coloration.

FEEDING These finches primarily feed on seeds and insects, particularly during the breeding season, and they forage on the ground, often near snowfields.

SOUNDS Their vocalizations include a series of low "cheep" notes for flock contact and a more elaborate song during mating flights.

RANGE & MIGRATION They have a localized range, primarily found in the high peaks of the Rocky Mountains, spanning from northern New Mexico to southeastern Wyoming and western Colorado. Their migration pattern is altitudinal, moving to lower elevations during the winter months.

HABITAT They are habitat specialists, breeding exclusively in alpine tundra near cliffs and rocky areas, and in winter they can be found in open areas, meadows, and sometimes visiting bird feeders.

SIMILAR SPECIES include the Black Rosy-Finch and Gray-crowned Rosy-Finch, but the Brown-capped Rosy-Finch can be distinguished by its uniformly brown head.

Non Breeding Adult

Breeding Adult

Juvenile

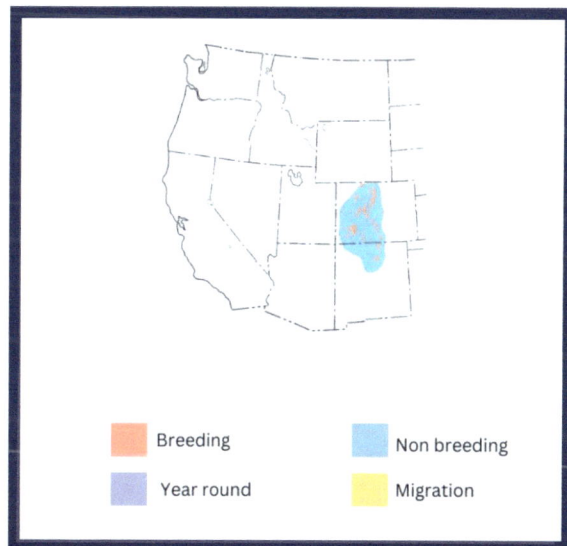

Breeding

Non breeding

Year round

Migration

Song   Call

DID YOU KNOW....

This species has a very restricted breeding range, found almost entirely in the high-altitude alpine regions of Colorado, with small populations extending into northern New Mexico and southeastern Wyoming. This makes it particularly vulnerable to habitat changes.

It breeds at higher elevations than almost any other North American songbird, sometimes nesting above 12,000 feet (3,650 meters).

A significant part of their summer foraging involves feeding on insects and seeds found along the edges and even on the surface of melting snowfields and glaciers.

Black Rosy-Finch- *Leucosticte atrata*

Black Rosy-Finch is a high-altitude specialist, found in the rugged mountains of western North America. This bird is characterized by its dark, sooty-black plumage, with vibrant crimson or pink patches on the wings, breast, and tail, particularly prominent in males. Males exhibit a more intense and extensive rosy coloration compared to females, who have a duller, browner overall appearance and less vivid pink markings. Juveniles are typically grayish-brown, lacking the bright pink accents of adults.

FEEDING These finches primarily feed on seeds and insects, foraging on the ground or among rocky outcrops.

SOUNDS Their songs are a series of sweet, warbling notes, and they produce short, sharp calls when alarmed.

RANGE & MIGRATION Their range is restricted to the high mountains of the western United States, specifically in areas of Montana, Idaho, and Wyoming. They are altitudinal migrants, moving to lower elevations during the winter months, although they remain within mountainous regions.

HABITAT Their preferred habitat consists of barren, rocky alpine slopes, talus fields, and snowfields at high elevations.

SIMILAR SPECIES include other rosy-finches, such as the Gray-crowned Rosy-Finch and Brown-capped Rosy-Finch, which can be differentiated by subtle plumage differences and geographic location.

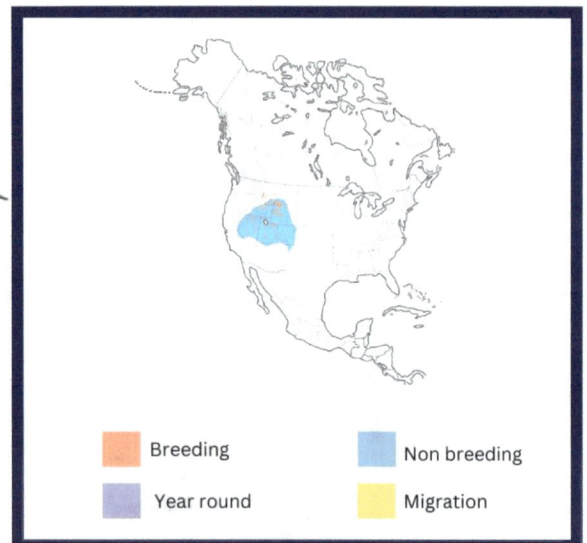

Non Breeding Adult

Breeding Adult

Juvenile

Breeding
Year round
Non breeding
Migration

Song

Call

DID YOU KNOW....

Among the three rosy-finch species found in North America, the Black Rosy-Finch has the most limited distribution, primarily breeding in the high-altitude alpine regions of the northern Great Basin.

They are true alpine specialists, typically breeding above the tree line in rocky, barren terrain, often near snowfields and cliffs. This makes them one of the least-familiar songbirds in North America as their breeding grounds are remote and difficult to access.

During courtship, the male Black Rosy-Finch will lower the front part of its body, tip its head far back with its bill held high, raise its tail almost vertically, and rapidly vibrate its slightly extended wings while emitting a high, continuous chirping sound. He often holds grass in his bill during this display.

Gray-crowned Rosy-Finch - *Leucosticte tephrocotis*

Gray-crowned Rosy-Finch is a robust, medium-sized finch inhabiting high-altitude regions of western North America. General characteristics include a chunky build, long wings, and a notched tail. Adult males exhibit a rich brown body with rosy hues, particularly on the wings, belly, and rump, a black forecrown, and a gray crown. Females are similar but display less vibrant pink coloration. Juveniles are duller, brownish overall, lacking the distinct gray crown and pink tones of adults.

FEEDING These finches primarily forage on the ground, consuming seeds and insects, especially those found near snowfields.

SOUNDS Their vocalizations consist of simple, twittering songs and various call notes.

HABITAT They occupy alpine environments, including rocky slopes, talus fields, and snowfields during the breeding season. In winter, they descend to lower elevations, inhabiting open areas like meadows and grasslands.

RANGE & MIGRATION Their range extends from Alaska down through the western mountain ranges of Canada and the United States. Migration patterns involve altitudinal shifts, moving to lower elevations in winter and returning to high-altitude breeding grounds in spring.

SIMILAR SPECIES include other Rosy-Finch variations such as the Black Rosy-Finch and the Brown-capped Rosy-Finch, differentiated by variations in coloring.

Adult

Adult

Juvenile

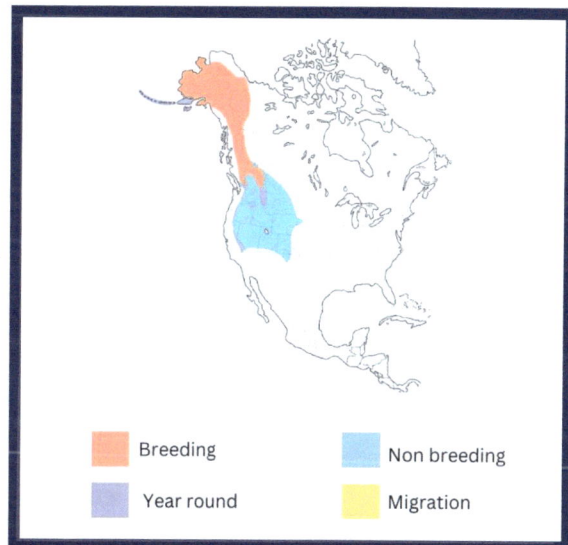

Breeding	Non breeding
Year round	Migration

Song

Call

DID YOU KNOW....

It's considered one of the highest-altitude breeding birds in North America, nesting in alpine areas often near snowfields and glaciers, sometimes reaching elevations of 14,000 feet.

Their diet changes significantly with the seasons. In the summer, they primarily eat insects, many of which get trapped and frozen on snowfields. In the winter, their diet shifts mainly to seeds from various grasses and weeds.

During the breeding season, adult Gray-crowned Rosy-Finches develop buccal (cheek) pouches that they use to carry significant amounts of food back to their young in the nest.

Lawrence's Goldfinch - *Spinus lawrencei*

Lawrence's Goldfinch is a small finch characterized by its gray plumage and bright yellow wing patches, particularly noticeable in flight. Males display a striking yellow face and breast, transitioning to a gray back and wings, while females have a duller, more subdued yellow wash on their face and breast. Juveniles are even more muted, with a streaky gray-brown appearance and less prominent yellow markings.

FEEDING These finches primarily feed on small seeds, particularly those of various weeds and forbs, and they are often seen foraging in open areas.

SOUNDS Their song is a rapid, high-pitched series of twitters and trills, and their calls include sharp, metallic notes.

RANGE & MIGRATION Lawrence's Goldfinch has a limited range, primarily found in California and parts of Oregon and Baja California, Mexico. They are known for their nomadic movements, following seed availability, and they may migrate short distances within their range or move to lower elevations during colder months.

HABITAT Their preferred habitat includes open woodlands, chaparral, and arid scrublands, where they find ample seed sources.

SIMILAR SPECIES include other goldfinches, such as the Lesser Goldfinch, which can be distinguished by its darker wings and more extensive black on the wings, and the American Goldfinch, when not in breeding plumage, which can be distinguished by the wing pattern and size.

Male

Female

Juvenile

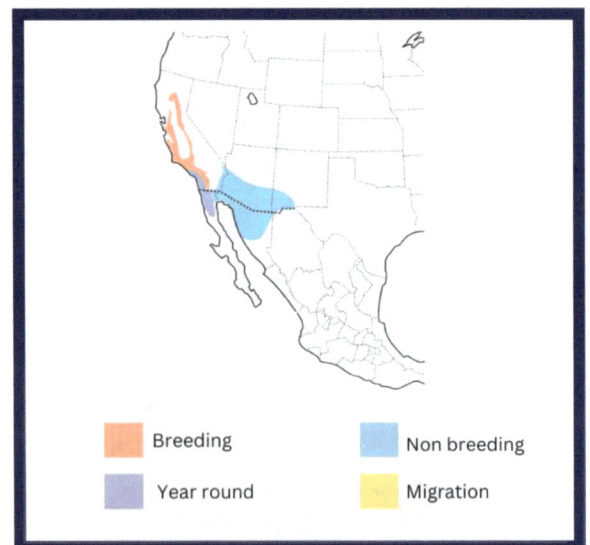

Breeding

Non breeding

Year round

Migration

DID YOU KNOW....

Unlike most other goldfinches which boast bright yellows, the Lawrence's Goldfinch has a predominantly soft gray body. This gives it a more subtle and elegant appearance.

The male doesn't acquire its lemon-yellow breeding plumage through molting. Instead, the brownish tips of its feathers wear away, revealing the yellow underneath. This unique way of gaining color is not seen in other goldfinch species.

This species is known for its highly erratic movements and can be abundant in one location one year and completely absent the next. These movements are likely tied to the availability of water and seed crops, making them difficult to reliably track.

CROWS, MAGPIES, JAYS

Crows, magpies, and jays belong to the *Corvidae* family, also known as corvids. This family is part of the order *Passeriformes*, which includes most songbirds. Corvids are widely distributed across the globe and are known for their intelligence, social behavior, and adaptability.

General Characteristics of Corvids:

- **Intelligence:** Corvids are considered some of the most intelligent birds, exhibiting problem-solving skills, tool use, and complex social structures. Their brain-to-body mass ratio is comparable to that of some primates and cetaceans.
- **Size and Build:** They are typically medium to large-sized birds with a robust build, strong legs, and feet.
- **Bill:** They possess strong, versatile bills adapted for their omnivorous diets. Most species have bristles covering their nostrils.
- **Plumage:** While crows and some magpies are often black, the family exhibits a variety of colors, including blues, greens, whites, and grays. Jays are particularly known for their colorful plumage.
- **Diet:** Most corvids are omnivorous, feeding on insects, seeds, fruits, nuts, small animals, eggs, and carrion. Many species also scavenge for food in human-populated areas and some store food for later consumption.
- **Social Behavior:** Many corvids are social birds, living in family groups, flocks, or communal roosts. They exhibit complex social hierarchies and communication. Some species engage in cooperative breeding, where non-parental birds help raise young.
- **Vocalizations:** Corvids are known for a wide range of vocalizations, from harsh calls and caws to more melodic songs and mimicry of other sounds.
- **Nesting:** They typically build relatively large, cup-shaped nests made of twigs and lined with softer materials, often in trees or shrubs.

Key Points about Crows:

- Generally larger, typically black birds, though some species have gray or iridescent feathers.
- Highly intelligent, known for problem-solving and tool use.
- Social birds, often found in family groups or flocks (sometimes called a "murder").
- Omnivorous and adaptable to various habitats, including urban areas.
- Distinctive harsh "caw" vocalizations.

Key Points about Magpies:

- Known for their striking black and white (or other contrasting colors) plumage and often have long tails.
- Also highly intelligent, exhibiting self-recognition in some species.
- Social birds, sometimes forming large flocks outside the breeding season.
- Omnivorous diet, including scavenging.
- Often build large, dome-shaped nests.

Key Points about Jays:

- Often brightly colored, with blue being a common color, but also greens, yellows, and grays.
- Intelligent birds with complex social behaviors.
- Many species are known for caching (storing) nuts and seeds, playing a role in seed dispersal.
- Diverse vocalizations, including mimicry of other birds' calls.
- Inhabit a variety of wooded and scrubland habitats.

Blue Jay - *Cyanocitta cristata*

Blue Jay, a vibrant and intelligent songbird, is a common sight across eastern and central North America. This medium-sized bird is easily recognized by its striking blue, black, and white plumage, including a prominent crest on its head. Males and females are virtually indistinguishable in appearance, sharing the same bright coloration. Juveniles display a duller, grayish-blue plumage and lack the distinct black necklace of adults.

FEEDING Blue Jays are omnivorous, consuming a wide variety of foods, including acorns, seeds, nuts, insects, and occasionally eggs and nestlings of other birds.

SOUNDS They are known for their diverse vocalizations, mimicking the calls of other birds, including hawks, and producing a variety of jay-like calls, such as the loud "jay-jay" and softer, melodic songs.

RANGE & MIGRATION Their range extends from southern Canada throughout the eastern and central United States. While some Blue Jays are year-round residents, others, particularly those in northern regions, undertake partial migrations, moving southward during the winter months.

HABITAT They prefer a variety of habitats, including deciduous and mixed forests, woodlands, parks, and suburban areas.

SIMILAR SPECIES include Steller's Jays, which are found in western North America and have a black head and crest, and other corvids like crows and ravens, which are typically larger and lack the Blue Jay's distinctive blue coloration.

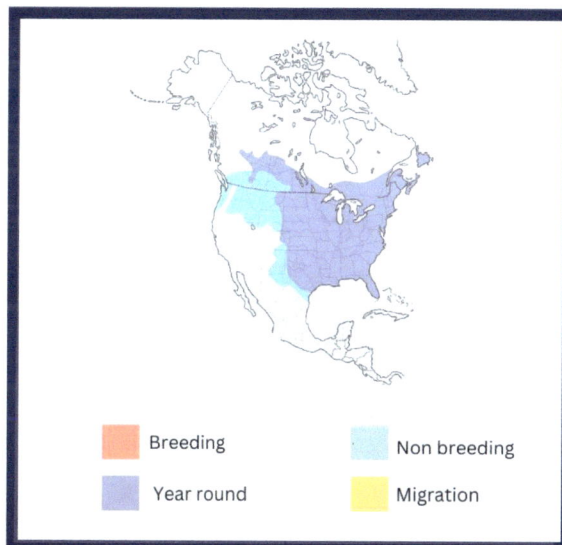

Adult

Adult

Juvenile

Breeding

Non breeding

Year round

Migration

Call 1

Call 2

DID YOU KNOW....

The vibrant blue of their feathers isn't due to a blue pigment. Instead, it's a result of the feather structure scattering light, a phenomenon called structural coloration. If you crush a blue jay feather, it will appear brown because the melanin pigment (which is brown) will be the only color visible without the light-scattering effect.

Blue Jays sometimes engage in a behavior called "anting." They rub ants on their feathers, which is thought to help remove parasites. The formic acid released by the ants during this process might act as a natural insecticide.

American Crow - *Corvus brachyrhynchos*

American Crow, is a large, all-black bird readily recognized across much of North America. It possesses a robust build, a strong bill, and a characteristic fan-shaped tail. Males and females are virtually indistinguishable in plumage, though males are typically slightly larger. Juveniles resemble adults but may display a duller, browner sheen to their feathers.

FEEDING American Crows are omnivorous, consuming a wide variety of foods, including seeds, grains, fruits, insects, carrion, and even garbage.

SOUNDS Their vocal repertoire is extensive, encompassing the familiar "caw-caw" call, as well as various rattles, clicks, and other sounds.

RANGE & MIGRATION They are found throughout most of North America, from southern Canada to northern Mexico. Some northern populations migrate southward for the winter, while southern populations tend to be resident year-round.

HABITAT They thrive in a variety of habitats, including woodlands, fields, agricultural lands, and urban areas.

SIMILAR SPECIES include the Fish Crow, which is smaller and has a nasal "caw" call, and the Common Raven, which is much larger and possesses a thicker bill and shaggy throat feathers.

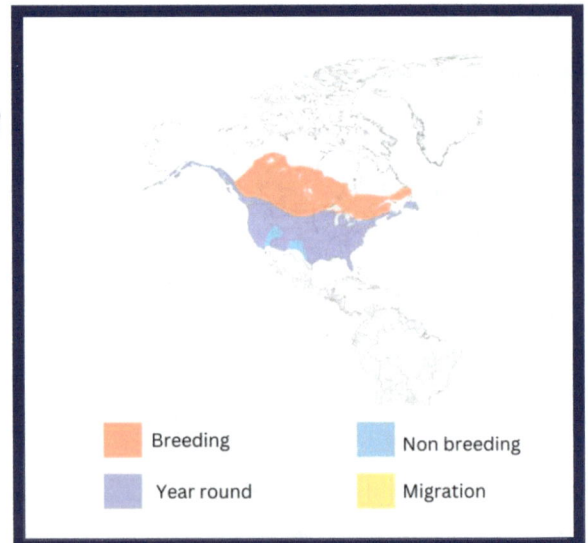

Adult

Adult

Juvenile

Breeding	Non breeding
Year round	Migration

Adult Call

Juvenile Call

DID YOU KNOW....

They have a sophisticated communication system beyond their familiar "caw." They use a variety of calls, body language, and even facial expressions to convey different messages, including warnings, threats, and even sounds of pleasure. They also have regional "dialects," with variations in calls between different populations

They possess remarkable facial recognition abilities and can remember individual humans who have threatened them. This memory can last for years, and they may even scold or mob those individuals in future encounters.

While not funerals in the human sense, crows gather around their dead. Research suggests this behavior allows them to learn about potential dangers or the circumstances surrounding the death

Common Raven - *Corvus corax*

Common Raven, North America's largest passerine, is a striking, all-black bird with a robust build, a thick neck, and a powerful bill. Adults of both sexes exhibit identical plumage, though females may be slightly smaller. Juveniles are distinguished by their duller, browner plumage.

FEEDING Common Ravens are opportunistic omnivores, feeding on a wide range of items, including carrion, insects, small mammals, birds, eggs, fruits, and grains.

SOUNDS Their vocalizations are diverse, encompassing deep, guttural croaks, rattles, and various other sounds; they are also capable of mimicking other animal calls.

HABITAT & MIGRATION They inhabit a wide range of environments, from deserts and forests to tundra and coastal cliffs, across much of North America, and are highly adaptable to human-altered landscapes. While they are primarily non-migratory, some individuals may undertake local movements in response to food availability or harsh weather.

SIMILAR SPECIES include the American Crow, but the raven is larger, has a thicker bill, a wedge-shaped tail, and a deeper, more varied vocal repertoire.

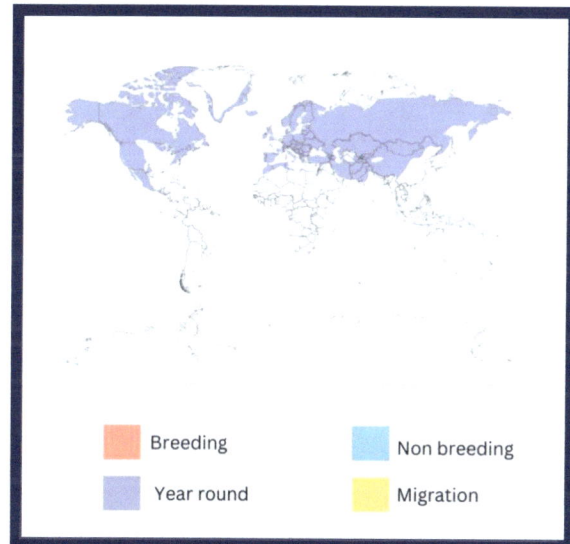

Adult

Adult

Juvenile

| Breeding | Non breeding |
| Year round | Migration |

Adult Call

Juvenile Call

DID YOU KNOW....

Common Ravens are surprisingly agile in the air, often performing rolls, somersaults, and even flying upside down, seemingly for fun.

They can plan for future needs, such as caching food when it's abundant and remembering where they stored it. They even take precautions to hide their caches from other ravens.

They sometimes hunt in pairs to flush out prey and have even been known to hunt animals larger than themselves using coordinated tactics.

Steller's Jay - *Cyanocitta stelleri*

Steller's Jay is a striking crested jay found in western North America, known for its dark blackish head and crest, transitioning into a vibrant blue body and wings. Both males and females exhibit similar plumage, making them difficult to distinguish visually. Juveniles have a duller coloration and a less pronounced crest compared to adults.

FEEDING These jays are omnivorous, consuming a diverse diet of seeds, nuts, insects, berries, eggs, and even small vertebrates.

SOUNDS Their vocalizations are varied and include harsh, raspy calls, mimicry of other birds, and softer, more musical notes.

RANGE & MIGRATION They are found primarily in coniferous forests, ranging from Alaska down through the western United States and into parts of Mexico. While some populations may move to lower elevations during harsh winters, Steller's Jays are generally considered non-migratory.

HABITAT Their preferred habitat is dense, mature forests, especially those with pine, fir, and oak trees.

SIMILAR SPECIES include the Blue Jay, which is found in eastern North America, but Steller's Jay is easily distinguished by its dark head and crest.

Adult

Adult

Juvenile

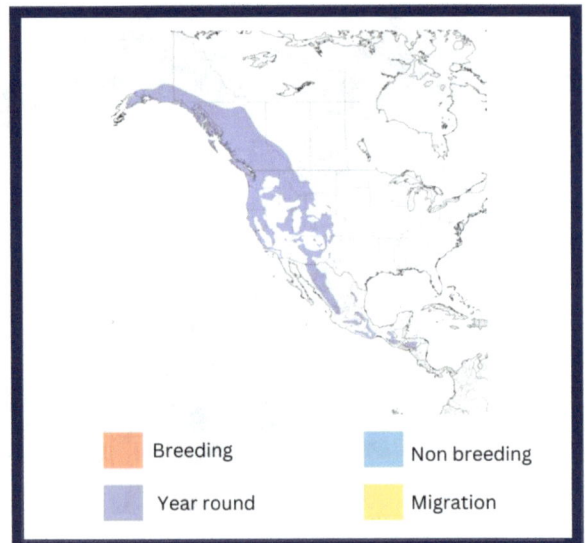

| Breeding | Non breeding |
| Year round | Migration |

Call 1

Call 2

DID YOU KNOW....

Unlike most jays, Steller's Jays often use mud to help construct their nests, which are typically bulky cups made of twigs, leaves, moss, and other materials. This mud helps to cement the nest together.

They exhibit slight variations in the color of the small spots on their forehead and near their eyes depending on their location. Inland birds tend to have whitish spots, while those closer to the coast often have blue spots.

In the eastern foothills of the Rocky Mountains, where their ranges sometimes overlap, Steller's Jays have been known to interbreed occasionally with Blue Jays (Cyanocitta cristata), producing intermediate-looking offspring.

158

Black-billed Magpie - *Pica hudsonia*

Black-billed Magpie, a striking corvid found across western North America, is easily recognized by its long, graduated tail, iridescent black plumage, and prominent white wing patches. Both males and females share this distinctive appearance, though males tend to be slightly larger. Juveniles resemble adults but have shorter tails and duller plumage.

FEEDING These intelligent birds are omnivorous, with a diet encompassing insects, carrion, eggs, nestlings, small mammals, and various plant matter.

SOUNDS Their vocalizations are a mix of harsh, chattering calls and squawks, rather than melodic songs.

HABITAT They inhabit open woodlands, riparian areas, grasslands, and agricultural lands, preferring areas with scattered trees and shrubs.

RANGE & MIGRATION Their range extends from Alaska and western Canada southward through the western United States. They are generally non-migratory, remaining within their territories year-round, although some altitudinal movements may occur in mountainous regions.

SIMILAR SPECIES include the Yellow-billed Magpie, which is restricted to California, and crows, which lack the magpie's long, graduated tail and white wing patches.

Adult

Adult

Juvenile

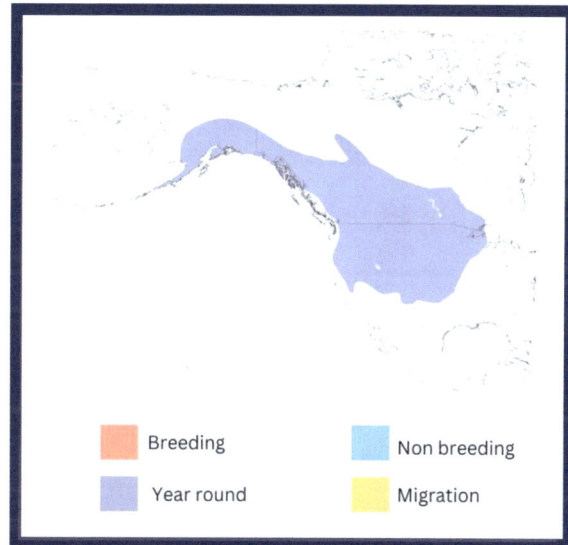

Breeding

Non breeding

Year round

Migration

Call 1

Call 2

DID YOU KNOW....

Unlike most jays, Steller's Jays often use mud to help construct their nests, which are typically bulky cups made of twigs, leaves, moss, and other materials. This mud helps to cement the nest together.

They are known to gather around the bodies of deceased conspecifics, engaging in loud calling. This behavior, often referred to as a "funeral," can involve up to 40 birds and last for 10-15 minutes.

They frequently land on the backs of large mammals like deer, moose, and cattle to pick off and eat ticks. This behavior provides a benefit to the mammals and a food source for the magpies. Historically, they likely performed this service for bison.

California Scrub-Jay - *Aphelocoma californica*

California Scrub-Jay, a striking bird of western North America, is characterized by its vibrant blue head and back, a gray-brown mantle, and a pale underbelly. Both male and female scrub-jays share similar plumage, making them difficult to distinguish visually. Juveniles exhibit a duller, grayer coloration compared to adults.

FEEDING They are omnivorous, with a diet that includes acorns, seeds, insects, fruits, and even small vertebrates. They are well-known for their caching behavior, hiding acorns for later retrieval.

SOUNDS Their vocalizations are diverse, ranging from harsh, raspy calls to softer, more musical notes, and they are adept at mimicking other bird sounds.

HABITAT They inhabit a range of environments, including oak woodlands, chaparral, and suburban gardens, primarily along the Pacific Coast from Washington to Baja California.

MIGRATION They are generally non-migratory, remaining within their territories year-round.

SIMILAR SPECIES include other scrub-jay varieties, such as Woodhouse's Scrub-Jay, which can be differentiated by subtle plumage differences and geographic range.

Adult

Adult

Juvenile

Breeding

Year round scarce

Year round

Call

Flock Call

DID YOU KNOW....

Until relatively recently (2016), the California Scrub-Jay was considered the same species as Woodhouse's Scrub-Jay (Aphelocoma woodhouseii) and collectively they were called the Western Scrub-Jay. They are now recognized as distinct species.

They are known for their role in seed dispersal, particularly of acorns. They gather and bury thousands of acorns each fall, often in damp soil, and sometimes forget where they've hidden them, allowing new oak trees to grow.

Some research suggests that California Scrub-Jays may possess a rudimentary "theory of mind," the ability to understand that others have their own thoughts and intentions.

Fish Crow - *Corvus ossifragus*

The Fish Crow, a medium-sized crow found in eastern North America, is nearly indistinguishable from the American Crow in appearance, sharing the same glossy black plumage. Distinguishing them visually is extremely difficult, and sexing them in the field is virtually impossible, as males and females share identical plumage. Juveniles are similar to adults, but may have slightly duller feathers.

FEEDING Fish Crows are omnivorous, but their diet leans heavily towards aquatic life, including fish, crustaceans, and other shoreline creatures, alongside typical crow fare like insects, carrion, and seeds.

SOUNDS Their most reliable distinguishing feature is their call: a nasal "cah-cah" or "uh-uh," in contrast to the American Crow's deeper "caw-caw."

HABITAT They inhabit coastal areas, river valleys, and wetlands, generally in proximity to water.

RANGE & MIGRATION Their range extends along the Atlantic and Gulf coasts of the United States, and they tend to be non-migratory or exhibit only short-distance movements.

SIMILAR SPECIES include the American Crow, from which they are best differentiated by their distinct vocalizations and habitat preferences, and in some areas, the smaller sized and more localized Tamaulipas Crow.

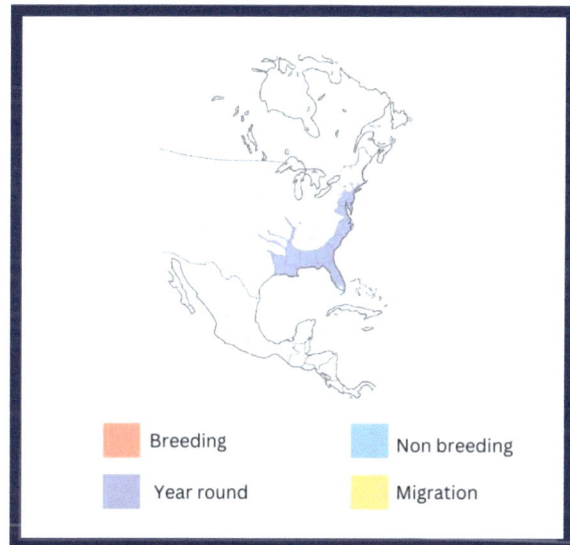

Adult

Adult

Juvenile

Breeding

Non breeding

Year round

Migration

Adult Call

Juvenile Call

DID YOU KNOW....

Unlike American Crows, which often have extended family units where young birds stay with their parents for several years, Fish Crows tend to have a more minimal territory holding time. Once their young can fly, the family often leaves the breeding site and joins larger social groups at food sources.

While not common, there have been documented instances of Fish Crows adopting fledgling birds of other species, such as Blue Jays, and feeding them.

They are slightly smaller than American Crows and tend to have a more slender bill and feet. Their plumage is also sometimes described as being smoother or silkier in appearance.

Canada Jay - *Perisoreus canadensis*

Canada Jay, also known as the Gray Jay, is a medium-sized songbird characterized by its soft, fluffy gray plumage with a paler face and underparts. Both male and female Canada Jays exhibit nearly identical plumage, making them difficult to distinguish visually. Juveniles, however, are a sooty gray color overall, transitioning to adult plumage as they mature.

FEEDING These opportunistic birds are omnivorous, consuming a wide range of foods including insects, berries, fungi, small mammals, and even cached food items.

SOUNDS Their vocalizations are varied, consisting of soft whistles, clicks, and chattering sounds, rather than elaborate songs.

RANGE & MIGRATION They are found throughout boreal and subalpine forests across Canada, Alaska, and the northern United States. Canada Jays are non-migratory, remaining within their territories year-round, even during harsh winter conditions.

HABITAT They prefer coniferous forests, particularly those with spruce and fir trees.

SIMILAR SPECIES include other jays, such as the Steller's Jay or Clark's Nutcracker, but the Canada Jay's uniform gray coloration and quiet demeanor set it apart.

Adult

Adult

Juvenile

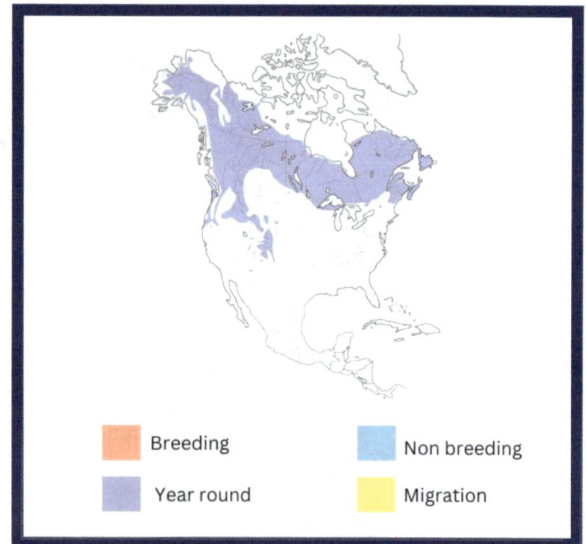

Breeding

Year round

Non breeding

Migration

Call 1

Call 2

DID YOU KNOW....

They use their sticky saliva to glue food caches to the bark, twigs, and crevices of trees. This helps them store food above the snow line for later consumption during harsh winters

Unlike most birds that breed in the spring or summer, Canada Jays nest and incubate their eggs during the late winter, often in temperatures well below freezing.

While often seen scavenging or eating berries, Canada Jays have been observed actively hunting and eating small animals, including landing on moose to eat blood-filled winter ticks or snatching baby bats.

Chihuahuan Raven - *Corvus cryptoleucus*

Chihuahuan Raven is a medium-sized raven, characterized by its glossy black plumage and a thick, heavy bill. It shares a similar appearance with other ravens but possesses a shorter, deeper bill and a slightly different vocalization. Males and females are visually indistinguishable, showing no noticeable differences in plumage or size. Juveniles have a duller, less glossy plumage than adults.

FEEDING These ravens are opportunistic feeders, primarily consuming carrion, insects, seeds, and fruits. Their diet also includes roadkill and garbage, reflecting their adaptability to human-altered landscapes.

SOUNDS Their calls are hoarse, croaking sounds, distinct from the deeper, resonant calls of the Common Raven, and they also produce a variety of other vocalizations, including rattles and clicks.

RANGE & MIGRATION The Chihuahuan Raven's range is primarily within the arid regions of the southwestern United States and northern Mexico, particularly within the Chihuahuan Desert. They are generally non-migratory, remaining within their range throughout the year.

HABITAT Their preferred habitat consists of open desert scrublands, grasslands, and areas with scattered trees or shrubs. They are often found near roadsides and human settlements.

SIMILAR SPECIES include the Common Raven, which is larger and has a deeper, more resonant call, and the American Crow, which is smaller and has a thinner bill.

Adult

Adult

Juvenile

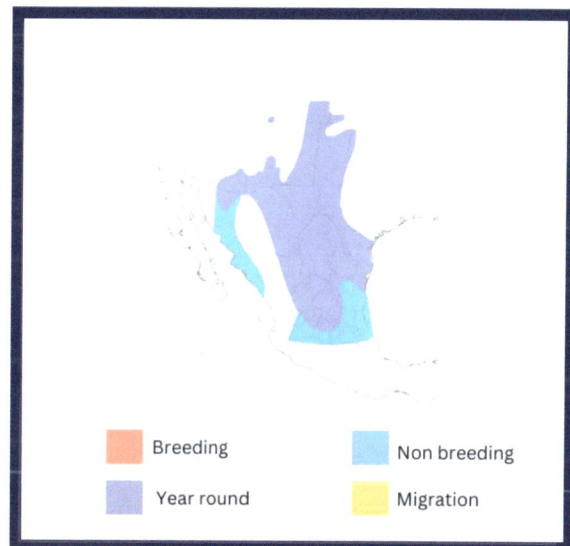

Breeding

Year round

Non breeding

Migration

Call

DID YOU KNOW....

Its scientific name, cryptoleucus, means "hidden white." This refers to the white bases of its neck and body feathers, a feature unique among North American crows and ravens.

They have unusually long nasal bristles that extend about two-thirds of the way down its upper bill. This is longer than in any other Corvus species.

In more arid environments, Chihuahuan Ravens tend to breed later in the year (around May) compared to some other corvids. This timing likely coincides with the emergence of a greater abundance of insects, which are a crucial food source for their young.

Florida Scrub-Jay - *Aphelocoma coerulescens*

Florida Scrub-Jay is a striking, medium-sized bird endemic to Florida, characterized by its blue head, wings, and tail, and a gray back and underparts, with a distinctive whitish forehead. Unlike its relative, the Blue Jay, it lacks a crest and black markings. Males and females exhibit similar plumage, though males may be slightly larger. Juveniles are generally grayer overall, lacking the vibrant blue of the adults.

FEEDING These birds are omnivorous, with a diet consisting primarily of insects, acorns, and other nuts, as well as small vertebrates like lizards and frogs. They are known for caching acorns, a vital behavior for their survival.

SOUNDS Their vocalizations include a variety of harsh, raspy calls and scolding notes, used for communication and territorial defense.

RANGE & MIGRATION The Florida Scrub-Jay's range is restricted to peninsular Florida, where it inhabits xeric oak scrub and scrubby flatwoods, habitats characterized by low-growing oak shrubs and sandy soils. They are non-migratory, remaining within their territories year-round.

HABITAT Their habitat specificity makes them vulnerable to habitat loss and fragmentation.

SIMILAR SPECIES include other jays, most notably the Blue Jay, from which it is easily distinguished by the lack of a crest and differences in color patterns.

Adult

Adult

Juvenile

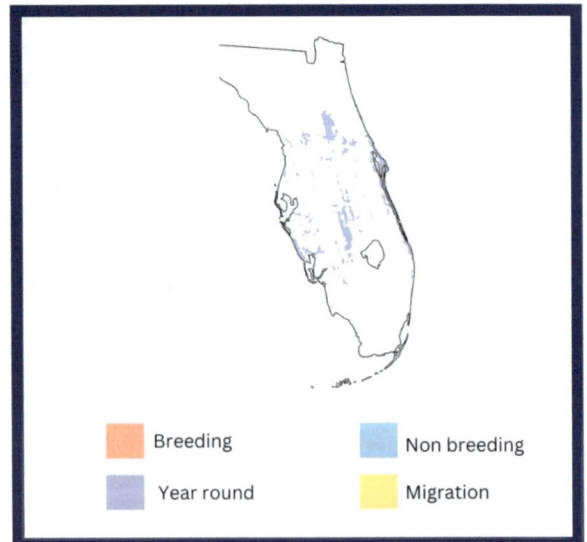

| Breeding | | Non breeding |
| Year round | | Migration |

Call 1

Call 2

DID YOU KNOW....

It is the only bird species found exclusively in the state of Florida, making it endemic to the region.

Florida Scrub-Jays live in close-knit family groups with a unique social structure. Offspring, known as "helpers," often stay with their parents for several years to assist in raising subsequent broods, defending territory, and protecting against predators.

Within the family group, individuals take turns acting as sentinels, perching in high spots to watch for predators and alerting others with specific calls.

Yellow-billed Magpie - *Pica nuttalli*

Yellow-billed Magpie, a striking bird endemic to California, is characterized by its sleek black plumage, white wing patches, and a long, graduated tail. Its most distinguishing feature is its bright yellow bill and bare skin around the eyes. Males and females are virtually indistinguishable in appearance, though males tend to be slightly larger. Juveniles have duller bills and less defined plumage than adults.

FEEDING These magpies are omnivorous, foraging on the ground for insects, seeds, fruits, carrion, and even small vertebrates.

SOUNDS Their vocalizations include a variety of harsh, chattering calls, as well as softer, more musical notes.

MIGRATION They are non-migratory and confined to the Central Valley and surrounding foothills of California, where they prefer open woodlands, savannas, and agricultural areas with scattered trees.

HABITAT They prefer open areas with scattered trees, and riparian zones.

SIMILAR SPECIES The Yellow-billed Magpie's range overlaps with that of the Black-billed Magpie, but the two species are easily distinguished by bill color.

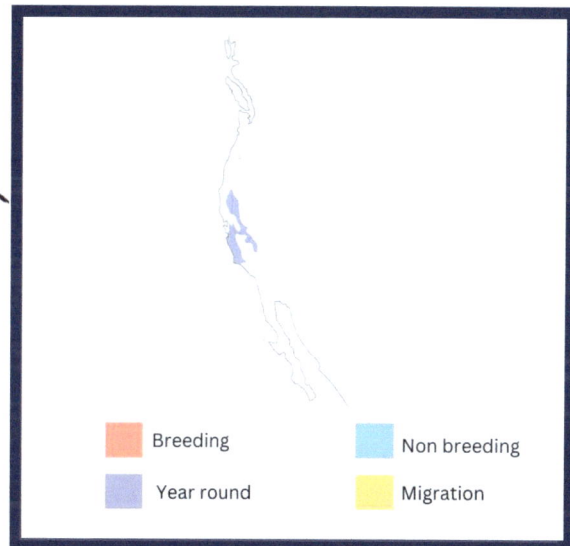

Adult

Adult

Juvenile

Breeding

Non breeding

Year round

Migration

Call 1

Call 2

DID YOU KNOW....

This striking bird is found nowhere else in the world but within the state of California. Its range is primarily limited to the Central Valley, the Coast Ranges, and the Sierra Nevada foothills.

Both male and female Yellow-billed Magpies work together for several weeks to construct a very large, dome-shaped nest, sometimes nearly 3 feet across. They use sticks for the base, cement them with mud and dung, and line the interior with soft materials.

In the spring, noisy groups of up to 20 magpies engage in chasing and calling in trees. This behavior is thought to be younger, non-breeding birds testing the territories of established pairs, potentially trying to take over if the opportunity arises.

Pinyon Jay - *Gymnorhinus cyanocephalus*

Pinyon Jay is a medium-sized, strikingly blue-gray bird endemic to western North America, known for its strong association with pinyon-juniper woodlands. Both male and female Pinyon Jays share a similar blue-gray plumage, making them difficult to distinguish visually, though males may be slightly larger. Juveniles are duller in color, displaying a browner hue before acquiring their adult plumage.

FEEDING These jays are specialized seed eaters, relying heavily on pinyon pine seeds, which they cache in large quantities for later retrieval; they also consume insects, berries, and other plant matter.

SOUNDS Their vocalizations are characterized by harsh, nasal calls and croaks, rather than melodic songs.

RANGE & MIGRATION They inhabit the pinyon-juniper woodlands of the interior western United States, from the Great Basin to the Rocky Mountains, and their range closely follows the distribution of pinyon pines. Pinyon Jays exhibit irruptive movements, meaning they may move in large numbers outside their typical range in response to fluctuations in pinyon pine seed availability, rather than following a predictable migration pattern.

HABITAT Their primary habitat is within pinyon-juniper woodlands, where they find their preferred food source and nesting sites.

SIMILAR SPECIES that might be confused with the Pinyon Jay include other blue jays, such as the Western Scrub-Jay, but the Pinyon Jay's overall blue-gray color, shorter tail, and specialized habitat preferences distinguish it.

Adult

Adult

Juvenile

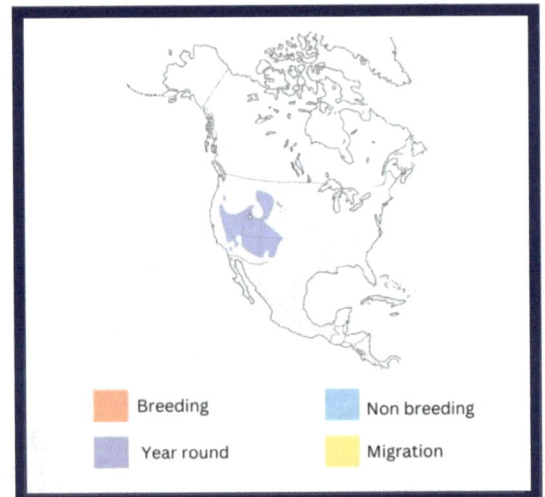

Breeding

Non breeding

Year round

Migration

Call 1

Call 2

DID YOU KNOW....

Unlike almost all other members of the corvid (crow and jay) family, the Pinyon Jay lacks feathers covering its nostrils. This is an adaptation that allows them to probe sticky pine cones for seeds without fouling their feathers with sap. Their scientific name, Gymnorhinus, even means "bare nostrils."

While they primarily form monogamous pairs that often mate for life, Pinyon Jays sometimes exhibit cooperative breeding. Young, non-breeding birds from previous years may help their parents raise the current brood, acting as "helpers at the nest."

They are among the earliest nesting songbirds in North America. They often begin nesting in late winter (February or March) if the pinyon pine seed crop is abundant, relying on their stored caches to feed themselves and their young.

Clark's Nutcracker - *Nucifraga columbiana*

Clark's Nutcracker is a medium-sized, pale gray bird with a pointed bill and black wings marked with white patches, primarily found in western North America's mountainous regions. Both male and female Clark's Nutcrackers share similar plumage, making them difficult to distinguish visually. Juveniles exhibit a duller gray coloration compared to adults.

FEEDING Their diet heavily relies on pine seeds, especially those of whitebark pine, and they also consume insects, berries, and carrion. They are known for their caching behavior, storing thousands of pine seeds for later retrieval, which aids in forest regeneration.

SOUNDS These birds are known for their harsh, grating calls and a series of raspy notes, rather than melodious songs.

HABITAT They inhabit high-elevation coniferous forests, particularly those with whitebark pine, and rocky alpine areas.

RANGE & MIGRATION Their range extends from the Rocky Mountains westward to the Sierra Nevada and Cascade ranges. While generally considered non-migratory, Clark's Nutcrackers may undertake altitudinal movements in response to food availability, moving to lower elevations during harsh winters.

SIMILAR SPECIES include other corvids, such as crows and ravens, but the Nutcracker's pale gray color, white-patched wings, and specialized bill make it relatively easy to identify in its preferred habitat.

Adult

Adult

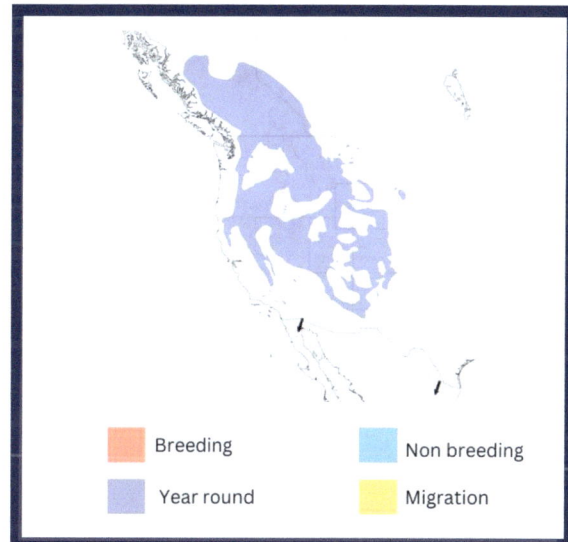

Breeding

Non breeding

Year round

Migration

Juvenile

Call 1

Call 2

DID YOU KNOW....

They have a keystone mutualistic relationship with several species of pine trees, most notably the whitebark pine. They are the primary seed dispersers for these trees, as the pines' cones don't open on their own to release seeds effectively.

They possess a unique sublingual pouch (a diverticulum under their tongue) that can hold a large number of pine seeds – sometimes as many as 50-150 depending on the seed size. This allows them to efficiently collect and transport seeds to their caching sites, acting like a built-in grocery bag.

Unlike most members of the crow and jay family (Corvidae), where only the female incubates the eggs, the male Clark's Nutcracker develops a brood patch and actively participates in incubating the eggs alongside the female.

Woodhouse's Scrub-Jay - *Aphelocoma woodhouseii*

Woodhouse's Scrub-Jay is a medium-sized jay characterized by its blue head and upperparts, a grayish-brown back, and a pale gray underside. Both males and females exhibit similar plumage, making them difficult to distinguish visually. Juveniles display a duller, more mottled appearance compared to adults.

FEEDING These jays are omnivorous, foraging on the ground and in trees for insects, seeds, nuts, berries, and occasionally small vertebrates.

SOUNDS Their vocalizations are varied, including harsh, raspy calls, as well as softer, more melodic songs and mimicry of other birds.

RANGE & MIGRATION They are non-migratory and primarily reside year-round in the arid and semi-arid regions of the western United States and northern Mexico.

HABITAT They favor habitats such as pinyon-juniper woodlands, scrublands, and oak woodlands.

SIMILAR SPECIES include the California Scrub-Jay, which has a more saturated blue coloration and a distinct blue bib, and the closely related Mexican Jay, which often forms larger social groups.

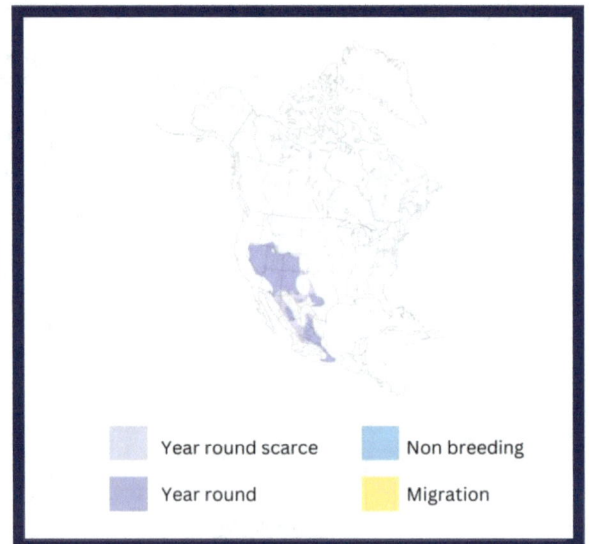

Adult

Adult

Juvenile

Year round scarce	Non breeding
Year round	Migration

Call 1   Call 2

DID YOU KNOW....

Unlike the California Scrub-Jay which has a stouter, more hooked bill for opening acorns, the Woodhouse's Scrub-Jay has a relatively thinner, straighter, and more pointed bill. This is an adaptation for efficiently extracting pine nuts from between the scales of pine cones, a preferred food source.

They are known for their intelligence and exhibit a behavior called "deceptive caching." If they sense another bird (especially a potential food thief) is watching them hide food, they may pretend to bury it in one spot while actually caching it in a different, concealed location.

They sometimes gather around a dead bird, including their own species, and vocalize loudly. This behavior, which some interpret as a type of "funeral," suggests a level of social complexity and awareness of death rarely seen in other bird species

Green Jay - *Cyanocorax yncas*

Woodhouse's Green Jay is a vibrant passerine characterized by its striking green and yellow plumage, with a blue crown and black mask. This jay exhibits no significant sexual dimorphism, making males and females visually indistinguishable. Juveniles are similar to adults but possess duller plumage and often lack the full intensity of the adult's coloration.

FEEDING Green Jays are omnivorous, consuming a diverse diet of insects, fruits, seeds, and occasionally small vertebrates.

SOUNDS Their vocalizations are varied and complex, including a range of harsh calls, chattering sounds, and melodic whistles.

RANGE & MIGRATION Their range in North America is restricted to the southern tip of Texas, where they inhabit dense woodlands, thickets, and riparian areas. Green Jays are non-migratory, remaining within their limited range year-round.

HABITAT They prefer habitats with dense vegetation that offers ample cover and foraging opportunities.

SIMILAR SPECIES include other jays, but the Green Jay's unique coloration and geographic location help distinguish it.

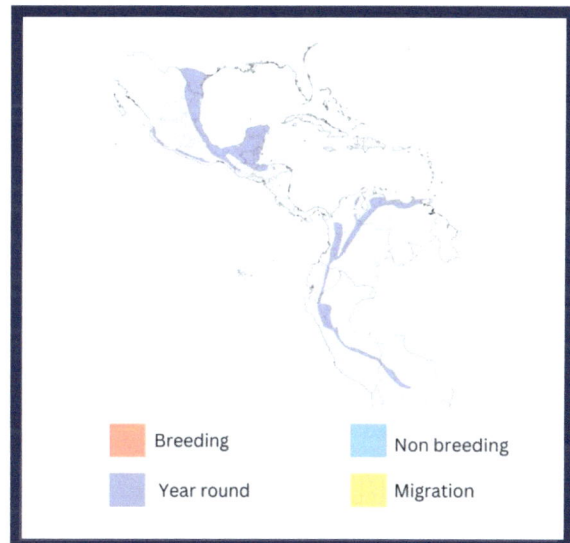

Adult

Adult

Juvenile

Breeding

Year round

Non breeding

Migration

Call 1

Call 2

DID YOU KNOW....

They are one of the few North American bird species known to use tools. They have been observed using sticks to pry up loose bark to find insects underneath.

Similar to their close relative the Blue Jay, Green Jays are excellent mimics. In Texas, they have been known to imitate the calls of hawks, potentially to scare away other birds from food sources.

While their diet primarily consists of insects, fruits, seeds, and small vertebrates, Green Jays are opportunistic eaters. They have been known to take advantage of human scraps and will even come to bird feeders.

Mexican Jay - *Aphelocoma wollweberi*

Mexican Jay, a vibrant member of the corvid family, is characterized by its striking blue plumage, particularly prominent on its head and back, with a gray-brown chest and underparts. Males and females are visually similar, exhibiting no significant differences in plumage. Juveniles display a duller, grayer coloration compared to adults.

FEEDING These jays are omnivorous, foraging for acorns, nuts, seeds, insects, and occasionally small vertebrates.

SOUNDS Their vocalizations are diverse, including harsh, nasal calls, as well as softer warbles and chatters used for communication within their social groups.

RANGE & MIGRATION They are found in mountainous regions of the southwestern United States and Mexico, primarily within oak and pine-oak woodlands. They are non-migratory, remaining within their territories year-round.

HABITAT Their preferred habitat is characterized by dense forests with an abundance of oak trees, which provide a crucial food source.

SIMILAR SPECIES include other *Aphelocoma* jays, such as the Western Scrub-Jay, which can be distinguished by subtle differences in plumage and range.

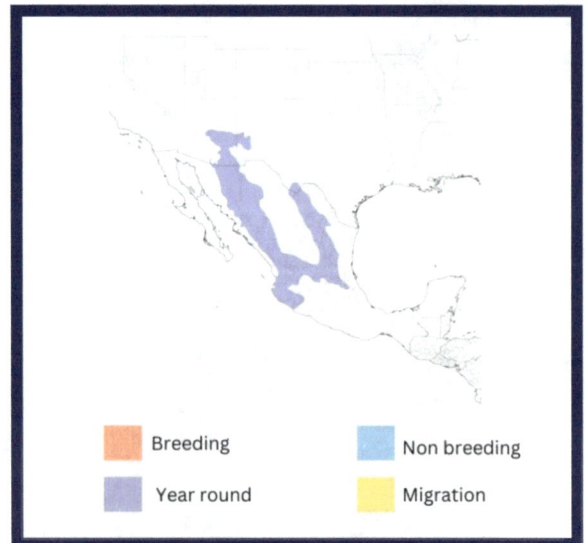

Adult

Adult

Juvenile

Breeding	Non breeding
Year round	Migration

Call 1

Call 2

DID YOU KNOW....

They live in social groups, sometimes as large as 25 individuals, with multiple active nests within a single territory. Uniquely, all group members, including non-breeding birds (often offspring from previous years), participate in raising the young.

DNA research has revealed that both males and females often mate with multiple partners within the group. The male that primarily helps a female raise her young is frequently not the biological father.

To open acorns, which they often do by stabbing with their lower mandible, Mexican Jays have evolved a specialized articulation in their lower jaw that acts as a shock absorber to withstand the force.

Tamaulipas Crow - *Corvus imparatus*

Tamaulipas Crow, a small, glossy black crow, is a resident of the extreme southern tip of Texas and much of northeastern Mexico. It is characterized by its relatively small size and slender bill compared to other crows. Males and females are visually indistinguishable, displaying a uniform glossy black plumage. Juveniles resemble adults but may exhibit a duller, less glossy appearance.

FEEDING Their diet primarily consists of insects, fruits, seeds, and carrion, reflecting an opportunistic feeding strategy.

SOUNDS Their vocalizations are described as higher-pitched and less harsh than those of the American Crow, often consisting of short, nasal "caws" and other varied sounds.

RANGE & MIGRATION The Tamaulipas Crow's range is restricted to coastal lowlands and adjacent scrublands, particularly in areas with thorny brush and open woodlands. They are generally non-migratory, remaining within their limited range throughout the year.

HABITAT Their preferred habitat includes thorn scrub, pastures, and open woodlands.

SIMILAR SPECIES include the American Crow and Fish Crow, but the Tamaulipas Crow's smaller size, slender bill, and distinct vocalizations help differentiate it.

Adult

Adult

Juvenile

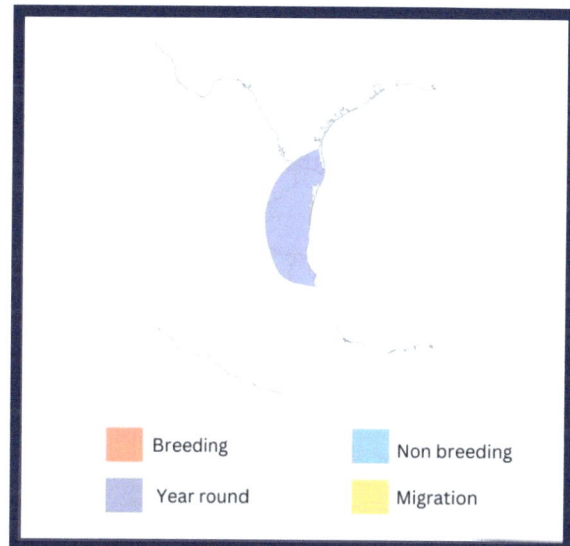

Breeding

Non breeding

Year round

Migration

Call

DID YOU KNOW....

Compared to other crow species, the Tamaulipas Crow is relatively small, measuring about 13-15 inches (34-38 cm) in length. This makes it a rather petite member of the Corvus genus.

Its feathers have a striking glossy dark blue sheen, which can appear soft and silky. This gives it a more elegant look compared to the matte black of some other crows.

Unlike the typical loud caw of many crows, the Tamaulipas Crow has an unusual low, croaking call that has been likened to the sound of a frog. It also has a soft "gar-lik" call.

Brown Jay - *Cyanocorax morio*

Brown Jay, a large and robust jay, is characterized by its uniform dark brown plumage, a strong black bill, and a long, rounded tail. There is minimal sexual dimorphism, with males and females appearing essentially identical in plumage. Juveniles are similar to adults but exhibit softer, duller plumage and often have a paler bill.

FEEDING Brown Jays are omnivorous, consuming a wide variety of foods, including insects, fruits, seeds, and small vertebrates, and are known to forage both on the ground and in trees.

SOUNDS Their vocalizations are diverse and complex, encompassing a range of harsh squawks, nasal calls, and melodious whistles, often used in social interactions within their cooperative breeding groups.

RANGE & MIGRATION They are non-migratory and their range in North America is restricted to the extreme southern tip of Texas, extending south through Mexico and Central America.

HABITAT They prefer habitats such as dense woodlands, forest edges, and semi-open areas with thick undergrowth.

SIMILAR SPECIES include other jays, but the Brown Jay's uniform brown coloration and large size, coupled with its distinct calls and social behavior, distinguish it from other jays in its limited North American range.

Adult

Adult

Juvenile

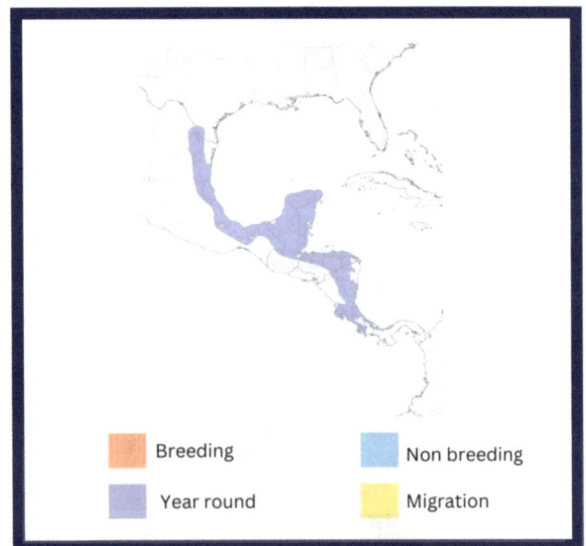

Breeding

Non breeding

Year round

Migration

Call 1

Call 2

DID YOU KNOW....

They exhibit a fascinating cooperative breeding system. Multiple adults within a social group, which can consist of 5-15 individuals, will contribute to raising a single brood of young in one nest. This includes feeding the incubating female and the chicks

Unusually, within a Brown Jay flock, several females might lay eggs in the same nest. All the adults in the group then participate in feeding the resulting young.

Offspring from previous breeding seasons often stay with their parents and help raise subsequent broods, acting as "helper birds." They assist in feeding the young and protecting the nest.

Cardinals, Grosbeaks and Buntings

Cardinals, Grosbeaks, and Buntings belong to the family Cardinalidae, a group of New World songbirds known for their vibrant colors, stout bills, and melodious songs.

General Characteristics:

- **Distribution:** Exclusively found in the Americas, ranging from Canada to South America.
- **Habitat:** Diverse habitats, including forests, woodlands, thickets, grasslands, and even urban areas.
- **Size:** Medium-sized songbirds, generally stocky with relatively short necks.
- **Bills:** Characterized by strong, conical bills adapted for cracking seeds. However, bill size and shape can vary within the family depending on diet.
- **Plumage:** Many species exhibit strong sexual dimorphism, with males displaying bright and colorful plumage (reds, yellows, blues) while females are typically duller in comparison (browns, grays, or muted versions of male colors).
- **Diet:** Primarily seed-eaters, but their diet often includes fruits, berries, and insects, especially during the breeding season when feeding young.
- **Vocalization:** Known for their clear, often whistled songs. In some species, both males and females sing.
- **Nesting:** Typically build open cup-shaped nests in shrubs or trees.
- **Behavior:** Many are monogamous breeders. Some species are migratory, while others are year-round residents. Males are often territorial, especially during the breeding season.

Key Points:

Cardinals (Genus *Cardinalis* and others):

- **Appearance:** Often associated with brilliant red plumage in males (e.g., Northern Cardinal), though other species and females exhibit different colorations (grays, browns with red tinges). Many have prominent crests.
- **Bill:** Stout, triangular, and typically bright orange or red.
- **Song:** Loud, clear whistles with repeated phrases. Both males and females sing.
- **Habitat:** Common in woodlands, gardens, and shrubby areas.
- **Notable Species:** Northern Cardinal, Pyrrhuloxia, Vermilion Cardinal.

Grosbeaks (Various Genera like *Pheucticus*, *Passerina*):

- **Appearance:** Diverse in coloration, with males often displaying bold patterns in black, white, yellow, blue, or rose. Females are usually less vibrant. Characterized by very thick, powerful bills.
- **Bill:** Large and conical, designed for crushing hard seeds.
- **Song:** Often described as rich warbles or clear, musical phrases, sometimes resembling a robin's song but more melodious.
- **Habitat:** Found in various wooded habitats, from deciduous forests to coniferous woodlands and thickets.
- **Notable Species:** Rose-breasted Grosbeak, Black-headed Grosbeak, Blue Grosbeak (taxonomically closer to buntings).

Buntings (Genus *Passerina* and others):

- **Appearance:** Typically, smaller than grosbeaks, with males often exhibiting striking blue, indigo, painted, or varied plumage. Females are usually brownish or duller versions of the male colors.
- **Bill:** Cone-shaped but generally smaller and less bulky than that of true grosbeaks.
- **Song:** Often characterized by rapid, sweet, and sometimes buzzy or warbling songs.
- **Habitat:** Tend to inhabit open woodlands, brushy areas, fields, and edges.
- **Notable Species:** Indigo Bunting, Lazuli Bunting, Painted Bunting, Varied Bunting.

Important Considerations:

- **Taxonomy:** The classification within Cardinalidae has been subject to change based on genetic studies. Some birds commonly called "grosbeaks" (like the Blue Grosbeak) are genetically closer to buntings.
- **Adaptations:** Their strong bills reflect their primary seed-based diet, allowing them to crack open tough seed coats.
- **Conservation:** While many species are common, some face threats due to habitat loss.
- **Birdwatching:** Their bright colors and distinctive songs make them popular subjects for birdwatching.

Northern Cardinal - *Cardinalis cardinalis*

Northern Cardinal, a vibrant and iconic North American songbird, is readily recognized by its striking plumage and prominent crest. Adult males are a brilliant crimson red overall, with a black face mask and a prominent red crest. Females, in contrast, display a more subdued brownish-olive coloration with reddish tinges on their crest, wings, and tail, and a reddish bill. Juveniles resemble females but are more mottled and have a grayish-brown bill.

FEEDING These birds are primarily seed-eaters, but they also consume fruits, berries, and insects, especially during the breeding season.

SOUNDS Their songs are rich, clear whistles and trills, often described as a series of descending notes, and they also produce sharp "chip" calls.

RANGE & MIGRATION They are non-migratory and have a wide range across eastern North America, extending westward into the Great Plains and southward into Mexico and Central America.

HABITAT Northern Cardinals favor habitats such as woodland edges, thickets, gardens, and urban parks.

SIMILAR SPECIES may include other red birds, like the Pyrrhuloxia, but the Northern Cardinal's distinctive crest, black face mask (in males), and song help distinguish it.

Male

Female

Juvenile

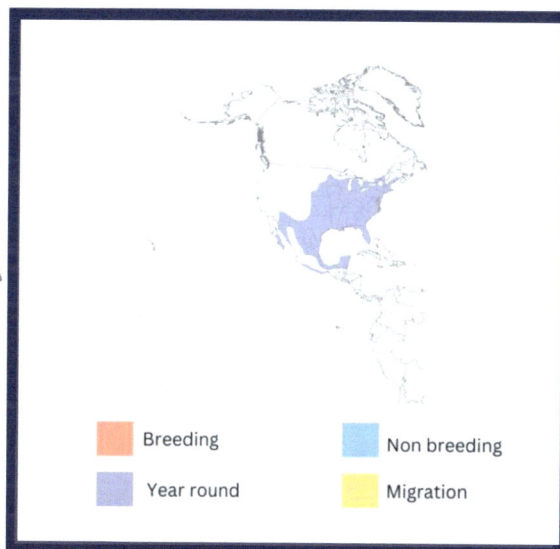

Breeding

Non breeding

Year round

Migration

Song

Call

DID YOU KNOW....

Unlike most songbirds where only the males sing, both male and female Northern Cardinals are accomplished singers. Females tend to sing more often when on the nest, possibly to communicate with their mate about food needs.

The male's vibrant red plumage comes from carotenoid pigments found in the berries and fruits they eat. If their diet lacks these pigments during feather molting, their feathers can appear more brownish.

During their late summer molt, Northern Cardinals can sometimes lose all of their head feathers at once, resulting in a temporarily bald appearance.

Indigo Bunting - *Passerina cyanea*

ndigo Bunting is a small finch renowned for the male's vibrant blue plumage during the breeding season. Males appear a striking, deep blue overall, though their coloration is actually a result of light refraction through modified feathers, appearing duller and browner in less direct light. Females are predominantly brown with subtle blue tinges, particularly on the wings and tail, making them resemble sparrows. Juveniles are similar to females, exhibiting brown plumage with faint streaking.

FEEDING These birds are primarily seed-eaters, supplementing their diet with insects, especially during the breeding season.

SOUNDS Indigo Buntings are known for their persistent singing, delivering high-pitched, paired notes from prominent perches, often repeating phrases. Their calls include sharp "chip" notes.

RANGE & MIGRATION They breed across eastern North America, from southern Canada down through the eastern and central United States. During the winter months, they migrate south to Central America, the Caribbean, and northern South America.

HABITAT Their preferred habitat includes brushy areas, forest edges, and open woodlands.

SIMILAR SPECIES include the Blue Grosbeak, which is larger and has a larger bill, and female or immature buntings may be confused with sparrows, but the subtle blue tones and distinctive song help in identification.

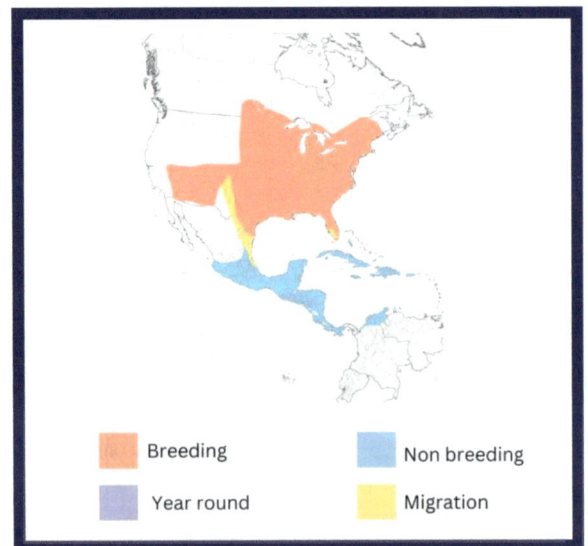

Breeding Male

Non- Breeding Male

Juvenile

Female

Breeding | Non breeding
Year round | Migration

Song

Flight Call

DID YOU KNOW....

Despite their brilliant blue appearance, male Indigo Buntings don't actually have blue pigments in their feathers. The vibrant color is a structural phenomenon.

They are nocturnal migrants and possess an incredible ability to navigate using the stars. They learn star patterns as nestlings and use them as a compass during their long-distance flights between breeding and wintering grounds.

Male Indigo Buntings learn their songs from other males in their vicinity during their first breeding season. This leads to the development of "song neighborhoods" where males within a few hundred yards of each other sing very similar songs, while songs can differ significantly across slightly larger distances.

Scarlet Tanager - *Piranga olivacea*

Scarlet Tanager, a vibrant neotropical migrant, is a medium-sized songbird known for the male's striking scarlet plumage with black wings and tail during the breeding season. Females are olive-yellow overall, with darker wings and a slight yellowish wash underneath. Juveniles resemble females, but often display a more mottled olive-green and yellowish coloration before acquiring adult plumage.

FEEDING These tanagers are primarily insectivorous, foraging for insects in the canopy, but they also consume fruits, especially during migration and in the non-breeding season.

SOUNDS Their song is a robin-like warble, but with a hoarser, more burry quality, and they also produce a distinctive "chip-burr" call.

RANGE & MIGRATION They breed throughout eastern North America, primarily in mature deciduous and mixed forests. They undertake long-distance migrations to their wintering grounds in South America, particularly in the Andean foothills.

HABITAT Their preferred habitat is mature forests with a dense canopy, often including oak and beech trees.

SIMILAR SPECIES include other tanagers, such as the Summer Tanager, but the Scarlet Tanager's unique plumage and song help distinguish it.

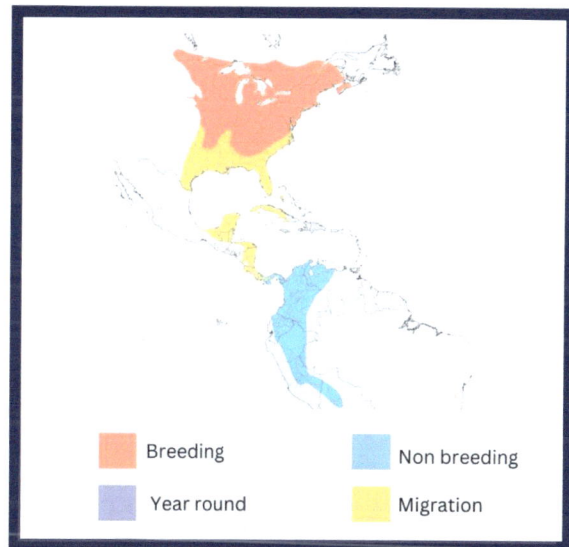

Breeding Male

Non- Breeding Male

Female

Juvenile

Breeding

Non breeding

Year round

Migration

Song

Call

DID YOU KNOW....

Despite the male's brilliant scarlet plumage, Scarlet Tanagers are often difficult to spot as they tend to stay high in the dense canopy of mature deciduous forests.

Until relatively recently, the Scarlet Tanager was classified within the tanager family (Thraupidae). However, genetic and morphological studies have led to its reclassification into the cardinal family (Cardinalidae), the same family as the Northern Cardinal and the Rose-breasted Grosbeak.

When Scarlet Tanagers catch bees, wasps, or hornets, they have a unique method of removing the stinger. They will rub or press the insect against a branch to dislodge the stinger before consuming it, avoiding being stung themselves.

Rose-breasted Grosbeak - *Pheucticus ludovicianus*

Rose-breasted Grosbeak is a striking medium-sized songbird, most easily recognized by the adult male's plumage. Males have a black head, back, and wings with white wing patches, and a vibrant rose-red breast patch. Females and juveniles display a brown and white streaked pattern, with a prominent white eyebrow and wing bars, and a yellowish wash under the wings.

FEEDING These birds possess a large, conical bill suited for cracking seeds. Their diet consists of insects, seeds, and berries, with a notable consumption of insects during the breeding season.

SOUNDS Rose-breasted Grosbeak's song is a rich, melodious warble, often compared to a robin's song but with a sweeter tone, and they also produce a sharp "chink" call.

HABITAT They predominantly inhabit deciduous and mixed woodlands, particularly along forest edges, parks, and gardens

RANGE & MIGRATION Their breeding range spans across eastern North America, and they undertake long migrations to wintering grounds in Central and South America. During migration they can be found in a wide variety of wooded areas.

SIMILAR SPECIES include the Black-headed Grosbeak, particularly challenging to differentiate in female and immature plumages, though range differences typically aid in identification.

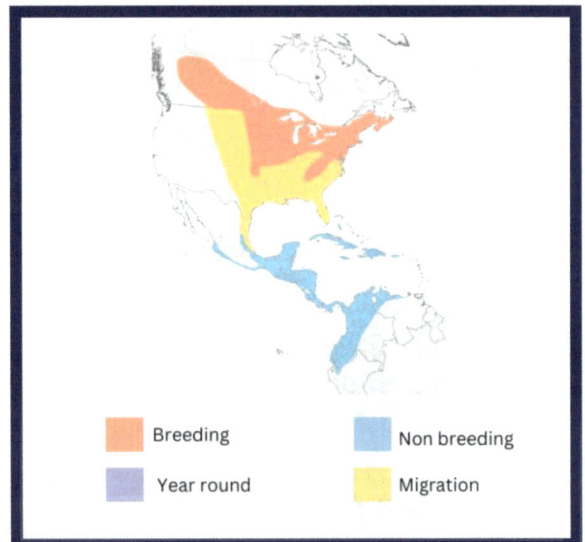

Female

Male

Juvenile

| Breeding | | Non breeding |
| Year round | | Migration |

Song

Call

DID YOU KNOW....

Due to the male's striking bright scarlet patch across its throat and upper breast, it was colloquially known as the "cut-throat" bird.

Unusually for songbirds, both the male and female Rose-breasted Grosbeak sing, even while incubating eggs on the nest. They often sing quietly to each other during incubation exchanges, and the male sometimes sings his full song from inside the nest.

Their nests are often so loosely constructed that the eggs can be visible from below through the bottom of the nest.

Painted Bunting - *Passerina ciris*

Painted Bunting is a small, vibrant finch renowned for the male's spectacularly colorful plumage. Adult males exhibit a striking combination of bright blue head, green back, and red underparts. Females and juveniles display a much more subdued appearance, with overall greenish-yellow plumage, making them resemble female goldfinches or other greenish finches.

FEEDING These buntings are primarily seed-eaters, supplementing their diet with insects, especially during the breeding season.

SOUNDS Their song is a series of rapid, high-pitched warbles, often delivered from a prominent perch. Calls include sharp "chip" notes.

RANGE & MIGRATION Painted Buntings breed in the southeastern United States, with a separate population in parts of Oklahoma and Texas. During the non-breeding season, they migrate south to southern Florida, the Caribbean, Mexico, and Central America.

HABITAT They prefer habitats with dense shrubbery, thickets, and woodland edges, often near open areas.

SIMILAR SPECIES include other *Passerina* buntings, such as the Indigo Bunting and Lazuli Bunting, but the male Painted Bunting's unique color pattern distinguishes it from all others. Females and juveniles, however, require careful observation to differentiate due to their more generalized plumage.

Male

Female

Juvenile

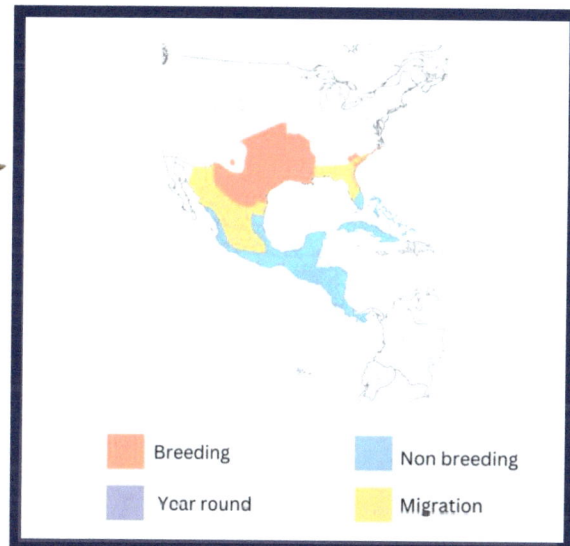

Breeding

Non breeding

Year round

Migration

Song

DID YOU KNOW....

Due to the male's vibrant plumage, the Painted Bunting is known as "siete colores" (seven colors) in Mexico and "nonpareil" (without equal) in French-speaking Louisiana.

Male Painted Buntings are fiercely territorial during the breeding season. Fights between males can be extremely aggressive, involving pecking, grappling, and striking with their wings, sometimes even resulting in death.

They have been observed raiding spiderwebs, not to eat the spider, but to steal insects that the spider has caught. They may even dive straight through the web to get the prey.

Western Tanager - *Piranga ludoviciana*

Western Tanager is a stocky songbird, noticeably larger than a warbler, with males exhibiting bright yellow bodies, black wings with two distinct wingbars (one yellow and one white), a black tail, and a striking orange-red head. Females are duller overall, displaying yellowish plumage with a grayish back and darker wings also featuring two yellowish-white wingbars. Juvenile Western Tanagers resemble adult females but may have a scalloped appearance on their back and less distinct head coloration.

FEEDING Their diet primarily consists of insects, which they glean methodically from foliage or catch in mid-air, supplemented with berries and fruits, especially during fall and winter, and they may occasionally feed on nectar.

SOUND The song of the Western Tanager is reminiscent of an American Robin's but is typically hoarser with short, fluty phrases separated by pauses; their call is a short, dry "pit-r-ick".

RANGE & MIGRATION These tanagers breed in open coniferous and mixed forests across western North America, from southern Alaska and the Northwest Territories south through the western United States, often at higher elevations. They undertake long migrations to wintering grounds in southern Mexico and Central America, with some individuals wintering in Southern California. During migration, they can be found in a wider variety of habitats, including deciduous woodlands, riparian areas, and even suburban gardens.

SIMILAR SPECIES that might be confused with the Western Tanager include the Summer Tanager, which lacks wingbars, and female orioles, which have thinner, more pointed bills.

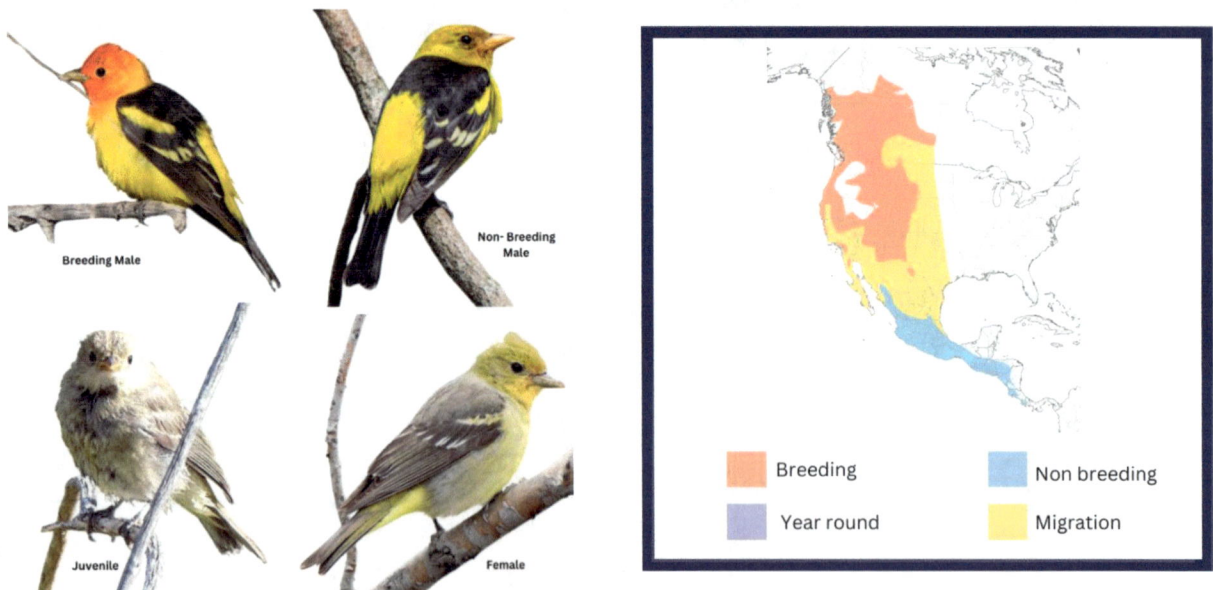

Breeding Male

Non- Breeding Male

Juvenile

Female

Breeding   Non breeding

Year round   Migration

Dawn Song   **Call**

DID YOU KNOW....

It breeds farther north than any other tanager species, with its breeding range extending up into southern Alaska and the Northwest Territories of Canada.

The bright red head of the adult male Western Tanager is not due to pigments found in fruits, as in many other red birds. Instead, they obtain a carotenoid pigment called rhodoxanthin by consuming insects that have fed on conifer needles.

Their pale, stout, and pointed bill is multi-purpose. They use it not only for catching insects and eating fruit but also for nest building, preening their feathers, and even digging small holes.

Summer Tanager - *Piranga rubra*

Summer Tanager is a medium-sized, chunky songbird with a noticeably large, thick, blunt-tipped bill. Adult males are a striking, brilliant rosy red all over, sometimes appearing slightly darker on their wings and tail, and they lack a crest. Females exhibit an olive-green coloration on their upperparts and mustard-yellow underparts, with a pale, horn-colored bill. Juvenile Summer Tanagers generally resemble adult females, but young males in their first spring may display a mix of yellow and red patches.

FEEDING This species primarily feeds on insects, with a particular fondness for bees and wasps, which they often catch in flight and subdue by beating them against a branch before consuming; they also eat a variety of other insects and will consume fruits, especially during migration and on their wintering grounds.

SOUNDS Their song is a melodious series of slurred whistles, often described as similar to a robin's song but softer and more drawn out, and they have a distinctive, dry, sharp "pit-ti-tuck" or "chi-ti-bit" call.

RANGE & MIGRATION Their breeding range extends across much of the southern and eastern United States, reaching as far north as Ohio and Pennsylvania and westward to southern California, with western populations also found in riparian areas. They are long-distance migrants, wintering from central Mexico south into South America as far as Bolivia and Brazil, with eastern populations often crossing the Gulf of Mexico during migration

HABITAT They inhabit open woodlands, including oak, hickory, and pine forests in the east and riparian cottonwood and willow woodlands in the west, and are sometimes found in orchards and parks.

SIMILAR SPECIES that might cause confusion include the Northern Cardinal, which has a crest and a black mask, the Scarlet Tanager, where males have black wings and tails, and females have darker wings, and the Western Tanager, which has blackish wings with wing bars.

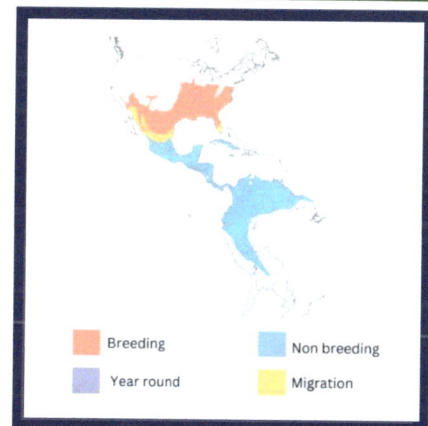

Breeding Non breeding Year round Migration

Song **Call**

DID YOU KNOW....

It is particularly adept at catching bees and wasps in flight. It subdues them by beating them against a branch and uniquely removes the stinger by wiping the insect on a branch before consuming it. This has earned it the nickname "Bee Bird." They even raid wasp nests to eat the larvae.

The adult male Summer Tanager is the only completely red bird found in North America, lacking any contrasting colors in its plumage.

Interestingly, there's a noted difference in nest construction between eastern and western populations. Eastern Summer Tanagers tend to build simple, flimsy nests, while those in the western part of their range construct well-made, sturdier nests.

Black-headed Grosbeak - *Pheucticus melanocephalus*

Black-headed Grosbeak is a stocky, medium-sized songbird characterized by its very large, conical bill. Adult males in breeding plumage are strikingly colored with a rich orange-cinnamon body, a black head, and black wings marked with white patches. Females and immature birds have a brown streaked back and warm orange or buff underparts with variable streaking on the sides, along with a prominent buffy eyebrow and neck. Juveniles resemble females but often have lighter scaling on their breast.

FEEDING Primarily foraging in trees and shrubs, the Black-headed Grosbeak feeds on a diverse diet of insects, seeds, and berries, and is one of the few birds capable of consuming monarch butterflies.

SOUNDS Its song is a melodious, warbling whistle, often described as sweeter and more continuous than that of an American Robin, and both males and females sing; a sharp "tick" or "chink" call is also common.

RANGE & MIGRATION This grosbeak breeds across western North America, from southwestern Canada through the western United States and into central Mexico. Birds breeding in the northern parts of their range are migratory, wintering in central Mexico, while more southern populations may be year-round residents.

HABITAT They favor deciduous and mixed woodlands, riparian areas, mountain forests, and even suburban gardens with adequate cover.

SIMILAR SPECIES include the Rose-breasted Grosbeak, with which it can hybridize in the Great Plains; female Rose-breasted Grosbeaks tend to have more streaking on a whiter breast compared to the Black-headed Grosbeak's buffy-orange underparts.

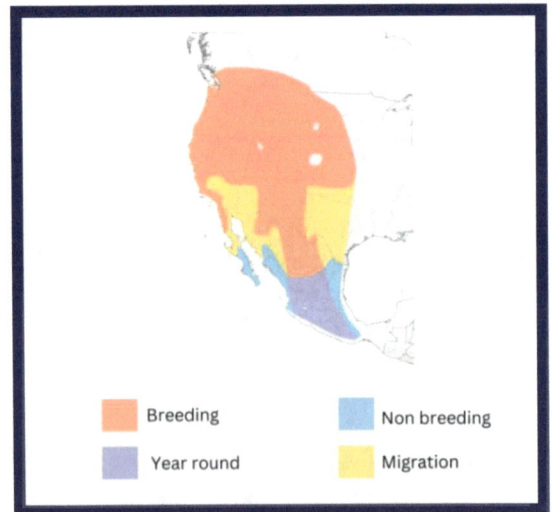

Adult Male

Young Male

Juvenile

Female

Breeding · Non breeding · Year round · Migration

Song

Female Call

DID YOU KNOW....

It is one of the few bird species capable of eating monarch butterflies without being harmed by their toxins.

While wintering in Mexico, their diet primarily consists of seeds. However, during their migration to California, approximately 60% of their diet shifts to animals like insects, spiders, and snails, with the remaining 40% being plant matter.

Both the male and female Black-headed Grosbeak share incubation duties. Unusually, they are also known to sing to each other from the nest as they exchange shifts incubating the eggs.

Blue Grosbeak - *Passerina caerulea*

Blue Grosbeak is a stocky songbird characterized by its very large, triangular, silvery bill. Adult males are a striking deep blue overall with noticeable chestnut wingbars and a small black mask around their eyes. Females exhibit a rich cinnamon-brown plumage, with a slightly richer color on the head and paler underparts, and also possess two wingbars, the upper being chestnut and the lower grayish to buffy; their tails have a bluish tinge. Juvenile Blue Grosbeaks tend to be a rich, dark chestnut brown with chestnut wingbars.

FEEDING Their diet consists mainly of insects, especially grasshoppers and crickets, along with other invertebrates, seeds of wild and cultivated grains, and occasionally fruits; they forage on the ground or in low vegetation, sometimes hovering to glean food.

SOUNDS The male's song is a pleasant, rich, warbling melody often sung from high perches in shrubs or small trees, and they have a loud, almost metallic "chink" call when disturbed, as well as a low, buzzy "bzzt" call.

RANGE & MIGRATION Blue Grosbeaks breed across much of the southern half of the United States and northern Mexico, migrating south to winter in Mexico, Central America, and the Caribbean, with some populations in central Mexico and Central America being year-round residents.

HABITAT They typically inhabit open, shrubby fields, hedgerows, forest edges, old fields beginning to grow back into woodland, and in more arid regions, shrubby growth along watercourses.

SIMILAR SPECIES include the Indigo Bunting, which is smaller with a smaller bill and lacks the obvious wingbars of the Blue Grosbeak, and the Lazuli Bunting, where the males have an orange breast and females have buffy wingbars and paler bellies compared to the Blue Grosbeak.

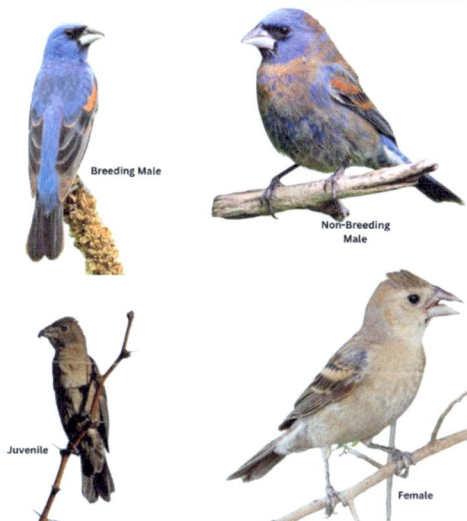

Breeding Male

Non-Breeding Male

Juvenile

Female

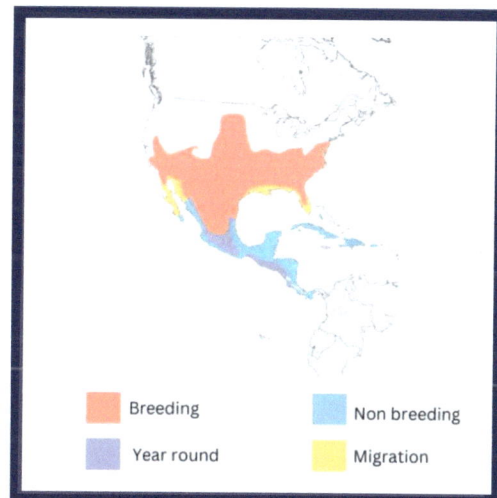

Breeding

Non breeding

Year round

Migration

Song

Call

DID YOU KNOW....

When Blue Grosbeaks feed insects to their young, they meticulously remove the head, wings, and most of the legs before offering the softened meal.

Female Blue Grosbeaks often incorporate surprising items into their nest construction, such as shed snakeskin, pieces of paper, string, cellophane, and even rags. The snakeskin might serve to deter predators.

Unlike most birds that hop or walk forward on branches, Blue Grosbeaks have been observed sidling or walking sideways along branches, a behavior more commonly seen in parrots.

Pyrrhuloxia - *Cardinalis sinuatus*

Pyrrhuloxia is a medium-sized songbird of North America characterized by its overall gray plumage accented with red or yellowish-orange markings and a distinctive short, stout bill with a curved upper mandible. Males are readily identified by their bright red plumage on the head, breast, back, and tail, with some gray on the back and wings, and a prominent peaked crest. Females exhibit a more subdued coloration, being primarily gray with red or yellowish-orange highlights on the crest, throat, breast, and tail, also possessing the characteristic crest. Juvenile Pyrrhuloxias resemble females but have browner plumage and lack the vibrant red or orange hues.

FEEDING Their diet mainly consists of seeds, fruits, and insects, which they forage for on the ground or in low vegetation.

SOUNDS The songs of the Pyrrhuloxia are varied and musical whistles, often described as sounding like "cheer-a-dilly" or "what-cheer," and their calls include sharp "chip" notes and softer "pyew" whistles.

RANGE & MIGRATION Their range is primarily in the southwestern United States and northern Mexico, where they are generally non-migratory, remaining within their territories throughout the year.

HABITAT Pyrrhuloxias favor arid and semi-arid habitats with thorny shrubs, mesquite thickets, and riparian areas.

SIMILAR SPECIES that might cause confusion include the Northern Cardinal, but the Pyrrhuloxia can be distinguished by its gray plumage, smaller bill, and peaked crest.

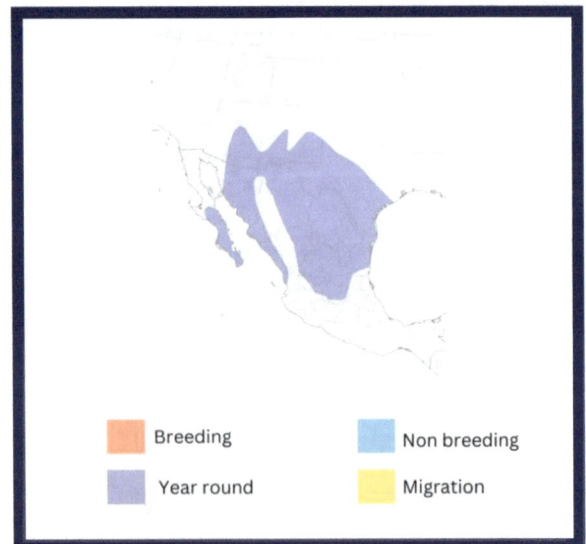

Adult Male

Female

Young Male

Juvenile

Breeding

Non breeding

Year round

Migration

Song

Call

DID YOU KNOW....

Unlike its close relative the Northern Cardinal, the Pyrrhuloxia is particularly well-adapted to arid and semi-arid environments of the southwestern United States and Mexico. This has earned it the nickname "desert cardinal."

It possesses a stout, slightly bulbous bill that is proportionally larger than that of the Northern Cardinal. This stronger bill is well-suited for cracking the hard seeds that make up a significant portion of its diet in the desert.

Pyrrhuloxias tend to be slightly shyer and less conspicuous than Northern Cardinals, often remaining in denser vegetation. This can make them a more prized sighting for birdwatchers.

Lazuli Bunting - *Passerina amoena*

Lazuli Bunting is a small, vibrant songbird found in western North America. Generally, it displays a conical bill suited for seed eating and a relatively short tail. The adult male is strikingly beautiful, exhibiting a bright turquoise blue head, back, and rump, contrasting with a rusty orange or cinnamon-colored breast and white belly. The female is much duller in comparison, presenting a plain grayish-brown plumage overall with a hint of blue on the wings and tail, often accompanied by a pale buffy wash on the breast. Juvenile Lazuli Buntings resemble the adult female but may have faint streaking on their underparts.

FEEDING Their diet primarily consists of seeds and insects, with insects becoming more important during the breeding season and for young birds.

SOUNDS The song of the Lazuli Bunting is a cheerful, warbling series of notes, often described as a jumble of musical phrases that varies considerably between individuals and can even incorporate elements learned from neighboring buntings. Their calls include sharp "chip" notes and a buzzy "zwee."

HABITAT During the breeding season, they inhabit open shrublands, chaparral, riparian thickets, and edges of woodlands in the western United States and southwestern Canada.

MIGRATION Lazuli Buntings are migratory, spending their winters in Mexico and Central America, and undertake long-distance journeys between their breeding and wintering grounds.

SIMILAR SPECIES that might cause confusion include the Western Bluebird, which has a different body shape and lacks the orange breast, and the Mountain Bluebird, which is uniformly blue. Female and juvenile Lazuli Buntings can be particularly challenging to distinguish from other drab finches or sparrows, but careful observation of subtle blue hints and habitat can aid in identification.

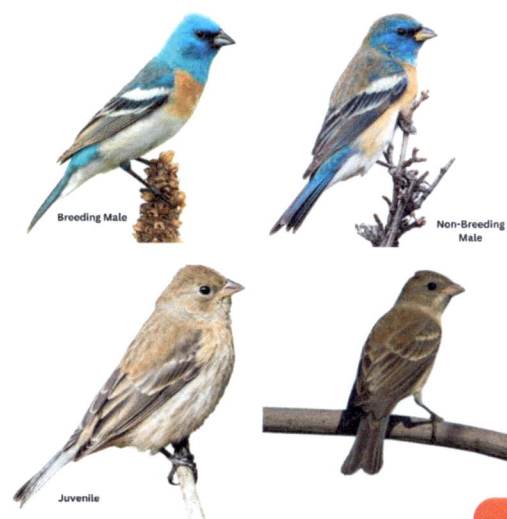

Breeding Male

Non-Breeding Male

Juvenile

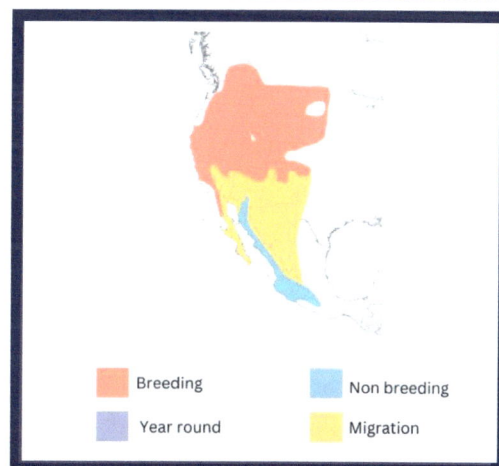

Breeding   Non breeding

Year round   Migration

Song

DID YOU KNOW....

Young male Lazuli Buntings learn their songs not just from their fathers, but by mimicking and rearranging syllables and song fragments from several older males in their vicinity. This leads to the development of distinct "song neighborhoods" where males in a specific area sing songs that sound similar to each other but different from those in other areas

Unlike most bird species that complete their molt (shedding and regrowing feathers) either on their breeding or wintering grounds, Lazuli Buntings interrupt their molt after breeding. They migrate to specific "molting hotspots" in the southwestern U.S. and northwestern Mexico, where they take advantage of abundant insects following monsoon rains to complete their molt before heading further south for the winter.

Blue Bunting - *Cyanocompsa parellina*

Blue Bunting is a small, relatively inconspicuous songbird found in North America as a rare visitor, primarily residing in Mexico and northern Central America. Adult males exhibit a striking dark blue plumage overall, with brighter blue highlights on the forehead, cheeks, and rump. Females and juvenile birds are a more subdued reddish-brown color.

FEEDING Blue Buntings forage singly or in pairs through low, dense vegetation, and their specific diet has not been extensively documented but is believed to consist of seeds and insects.

SOUNDS Their song is described as a sweet, somewhat sad warble, and they have a metallic "chink" or high "tsik" call note.

RANGE & MIGRATION In North America, they are very rare visitors to the far south of Texas, with occasional sightings extending as far east as Louisiana. They are generally considered permanent residents within their normal range and do not undertake long migrations, though some short dispersal after breeding may occur.

HABITAT Their preferred habitat includes dense vegetation such as scrubby areas, thickets, and the undergrowth and edges of tall forests, ranging up to moderate elevations.

SIMILAR SPECIES in North America could include the Indigo Bunting and the Blue Grosbeak; however, the Blue Bunting can be distinguished by its darker blue coloration in males, lack of wing bars, and the richer reddish-brown of the females compared to female Indigo Buntings, as well as its smaller size and bill compared to the Blue Grosbeak.

Male

Female

Juvenile

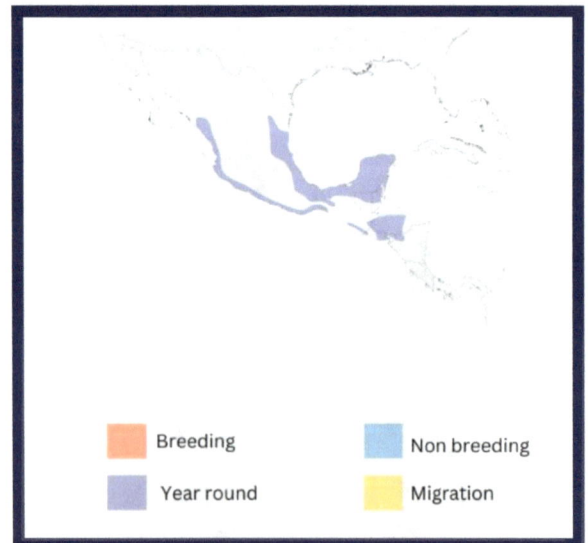

Breeding

Non breeding

Year round

Migration

Song

DID YOU KNOW....

The Blue Bunting is the sole species within the Cyanocompsa genus. This makes it unique within the Cardinalidae family.

The call note varies geographically. In western Mexico, it's described as a high "tsik," while in eastern Mexico, it's a metallic "chink."

While it prefers dense vegetation like scrubby areas, thickets, and forest undergrowth, the Blue Bunting seems capable of tolerating moderate habitat modification, which contributes to its "Least Concern" conservation status.

Dickcissel - *Spiza americana*

Dickcissel is a small, stocky songbird of North America characterized by a relatively large head and a short tail. Males in breeding plumage are quite striking, displaying a bright yellow breast, a black "V" on the throat, gray cheeks and crown, and brown streaked upperparts. Females are duller in comparison, exhibiting a yellowish breast with less distinct or absent black markings on the throat, and more heavily streaked upperparts. Juvenile Dickcissels resemble females but have buffier underparts and more extensive streaking.

FEEDING These birds primarily feed on seeds, especially during the non-breeding season and while foraging on the ground, but they also consume insects, particularly during the breeding season when feeding young.

SOUNDS The song of the male Dickcissel is a loud, buzzy "dick-dick-cissel-cissel," which gives the bird its name, and they also have various calls, including short chips and buzzy alarm notes.

RANGE & MIGRATION Their breeding range extends across the central United States and southern Canada, while they undertake a long migration to wintering grounds in northern South America, primarily Venezuela and Colombia.

HABITAT Dickcissels favor open grasslands, prairies, hayfields, and weedy fields as their habitat.

SIMILAR SPECIES might include some sparrows or meadowlarks, but the male Dickcissel's distinctive yellow breast and black throat, along with its characteristic song, usually make identification straightforward.

Breeding Male

Female

Juvenile

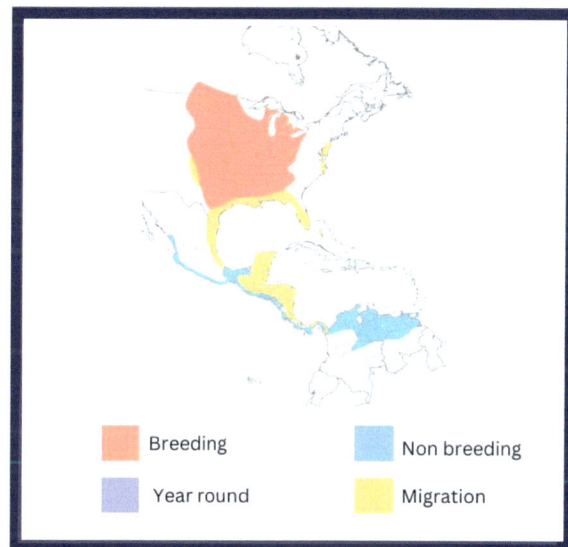

Breeding | Non breeding
Year round | Migration

Song | **Call**

DID YOU KNOW....

Beyond their namesake song, males have a diverse range of calls and songs used for territorial defense and attracting females.

They are one of the few songbirds considered truly polygynous. Males commonly have multiple female mates (up to six have been recorded) within their territory in a single breeding season.

Unlike some birds where males attract females primarily through displays, female Dickcissels primarily choose mates based on the quality of the territory the male holds, particularly the vegetation density which provides good nesting sites and foraging opportunities.

Flame-colored Tanager - *Piranga bidentata*

The Flame-colored Tanager is a medium-sized songbird characterized by two prominent white wingbars and a heavily streaked back. Adult males exhibit vibrant coloration ranging from flame orange to radiant red on their head and underparts, often with a blackish ear patch. Females share similar markings but are predominantly a rich yellow overall, sometimes with a hint of orange on the crown. Juvenile plumage is similar to the female's, often with some orange-red splotches appearing on young males.

FEEDING These tanagers primarily feed on insects and various berries, foraging in the middle to upper levels of trees, sometimes joining mixed-species flocks.

SOUNDS Their song is described as similar to a vireo's, a rich and musical series of notes, and their common call is a strong, rolled series of three notes, reminiscent of the Western Tanager.

RANGE & MIGRATION The range of the Flame-colored Tanager extends from Mexico through Central America to northern Panama, with occasional appearances in the mountains of the southwestern United States, particularly Arizona and western Texas. While largely resident, some populations may descend to lower elevations during the winter; those seen in the United States are generally considered wanderers.

HABITAT Their preferred habitat includes the canopy of humid montane forests, open oak and pine-oak woodlands, and large trees in semi-open areas like pastures and coffee plantations, typically in foothills and highlands.

SIMILAR SPECIES that might be confused with the Flame-colored Tanager include the Western Tanager, but the Flame-colored Tanager has bolder white wing markings and a streaked back, distinguishing it from the Western Tanager, especially in the case of females.

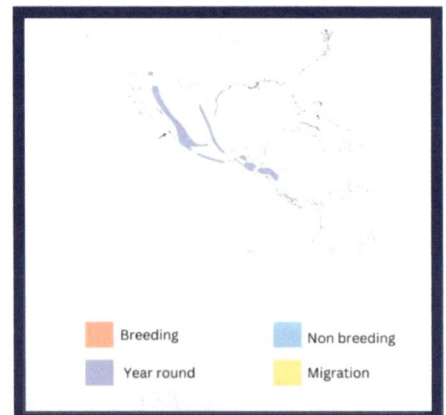

Male

Female

Juvenile

Song

Call

Breeding
Non breeding
Year round
Migration

DID YOU KNOW....

Unlike many tanagers that primarily feed on fleeing insects when following army ant swarms, the Flame-colored Tanager has been observed actively preying on the army ant "soldiers" themselves, as well as the wasp larvae and pupae the ants carry.

Although it looks and behaves like a typical tanager, in 2009, ornithologists reclassified the Flame-colored Tanager, along with other Piranga tanagers, from the Thraupidae (tanager family) to the Cardinalidae (cardinal and grosbeak family). This means it's more closely related to cardinals than to many other birds still called "tanagers."

Hepatic Tanager - *Piranga flava*

Hepatic Tanager is a medium-sized, stocky songbird with a relatively short, thick bill. Adult males are a distinctive grayish brick-red overall, with a grayish wash on their back and sides, and a noticeable gray cheek patch. Females exhibit an olive-yellow plumage above and yellowish below, also featuring a dusky or grayish cheek patch. Juvenile birds are grayish-olive above and buffy below with light streaking.

FEEDING Hepatic Tanagers primarily feed on insects and spiders, which they glean from foliage while hopping slowly through trees and shrubs, but they also consume berries, small fruits, seeds, flowers, and nectar.

SOUNDS Their song is a sweet, caroling series of clear phrases, often described as similar to an American Robin's song but sometimes with hoarser notes; they also have a low "chup" call and a rising "wheet" flight call.

RANGE & MIGRATION In North America, their breeding range is primarily in the mountainous regions of the southwestern United States, including Arizona, New Mexico, and parts of California, Colorado, and Texas, favoring open pine and pine-oak woodlands at higher elevations. They are generally short-distance migrants, with most U.S. breeders likely wintering in Mexico utilizing similar pine and pine-oak habitats as well as deciduous areas.

HABITAT Their preferred habitat during the breeding season is open pine or mixed pine-oak forests with a somewhat open canopy and understory.

SIMILAR SPECIES include the Summer Tanager, which in males is a brighter, more uniform red without gray cheeks and in females is a brighter yellow with a pinkish bill, and the Western Tanager, where the male has a distinct yellow, red, and black pattern, and the female has darker wings and usually shows wingbars, which the female Hepatic Tanager lacks.

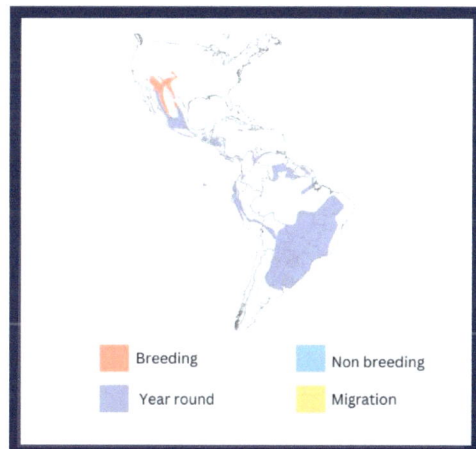

Male

Female

Juvenile

Song

Call

Breeding

Non breeding

Year round

Migration

DID YOU KNOW....

Despite their name, Hepatic Tanagers are not closely related to the true tanagers (family Thraupidae) found primarily in the tropics. Instead, along with the other Piranga tanagers in the US and Canada (Summer, Scarlet, and Western), they belong to the cardinal family (Cardinalidae), making them closer relatives to cardinals and grosbeaks.

The name "hepatic" refers to the liver-like (dusky reddish) color of the male's upperparts. However, male Summer Tanagers, which overlap in range, are actually a brighter, more vibrant red overall.

Varied Bunting - *Passerina versicolor*

The Varied Bunting, a small finch-like bird, presents a stunning display of color in mature males, exhibiting a vibrant mix of deep blue, purple, and red hues. Females, by contrast, possess a more subdued palette of grayish-brown to olive-brown tones. Juveniles resemble females, gradually acquiring adult plumage as they mature.

FEEDING These birds primarily forage on the ground, consuming seeds, insects, and berries.

SOUNDS Their song is a series of high-pitched, thin, warbled notes, often delivered from a prominent perch. Calls are typically sharp chips or metallic notes.

RANGE & MIGRATION The Varied Bunting's breeding range extends from the southwestern United States, particularly Texas, Arizona, and New Mexico, south into Mexico. They are migratory, moving south for the winter.

HABITAT Their preferred habitat includes dense thickets, scrublands, and woodland edges, particularly in arid or semi-arid regions.

SIMILAR SPECIES include other *Passerina* buntings, such as the Indigo Bunting and Lazuli Bunting, but the Varied Bunting's unique color pattern and range help distinguish it.

Male

Female

Juvenile

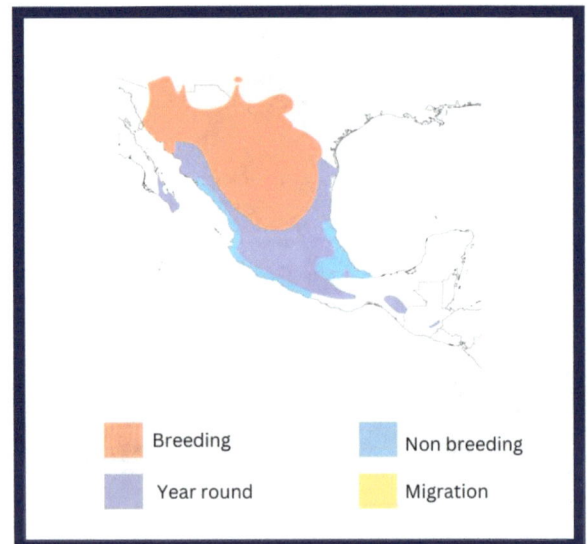

Breeding   Non breeding

Year round   Migration

Song

DID YOU KNOW....

While the male's vibrant mix of purple-blue and red is well-known, the "varied" in its name hints at more than just the male's appearance.

Unlike some other brightly colored buntings found in more lush environments, the Varied Bunting thrives in arid and semi-arid habitats, particularly dense, thorny brush, scrubby woodlands, and canyon washes. Their brilliance stands out against the often-drab desert landscape.

In some parts of their range, particularly Arizona, the Varied Bunting's nesting cycle is closely tied to the summer monsoon rains. They may delay singing and nest-building until the onset of significant rainfall, often as late as July or August.

Cuckoos, Roadrunners, Anis

These three groups of birds belong to the order Cuculiformes, a diverse group with worldwide distribution. While they share some common ancestry, they exhibit distinct characteristics and ecological roles.

General Characteristics:

- **Body Shape:** Most are slender birds with moderately long tails. Roadrunners, however, are more robust and have longer legs adapted for terrestrial locomotion.
- **Feet:** They possess zygodactyl feet, meaning the second and third toes point forward, and the first and fourth point backward. This arrangement is useful for grasping branches (in arboreal species) or gaining traction on the ground.
- **Bills:** Their bills vary in size and shape depending on their diet, but are generally slightly decurved. Anis have particularly heavy and ridged bills.
- **Plumage:** Their plumage varies greatly, from cryptic colors like browns and grays to bright and iridescent hues. Anis are typically black.
- **Diet:** The majority are carnivorous, feeding primarily on insects, especially caterpillars (including hairy and noxious ones avoided by other birds). Some species also consume other invertebrates, lizards, snakes, small mammals, and even eggs and nestlings of other birds. Some cuckoos and anis also eat fruits.

Cuckoos (Family Cuculidae - excluding roadrunners and anis in some classifications):

- **Arboreal or Terrestrial:** Most cuckoos are arboreal (tree-dwelling), but some are ground-dwelling.
- **Brood Parasitism:** A significant number of cuckoo species are brood parasites. This means they lay their eggs in the nests of other bird species (hosts), and the host parents raise the cuckoo young. This fascinating behavior has led to evolutionary "arms races" between cuckoos and their hosts, with cuckoos evolving egg mimicry and other adaptations to ensure their eggs are accepted.
- **Vocalizations:** Many cuckoos are highly vocal, with distinct calls used for territorial defense and mate attraction. The characteristic "cuckoo" call is well-known for some species.
- **Distribution:** Found worldwide, except for Antarctica, with a high diversity in tropical regions. Many temperate species are migratory.

Roadrunners (Genus *Geococcyx*):

- **Terrestrial Adaptation:** Highly adapted for running on the ground with strong legs and long tarsi. They are found in open and semi-arid habitats of North and Central America.
- **Limited Flight:** While capable of flight, they prefer to run and can reach impressive speeds (up to 30 km/h or 19 mph).
- **Predatory Behavior:** They are active predators, feeding on insects, rodents, lizards, snakes (including rattlesnakes), and other birds. They are known for their method of killing prey by repeatedly slamming it against the ground.
- **Nesting:** They build their own nests in low trees, thickets, or cacti. Both parents incubate the eggs and care for the young.
- **Cultural Significance:** Roadrunners and their tracks have inspired various beliefs and superstitions in indigenous cultures.

Anis (Genus *Crotophaga*):

- **Social Behavior:** Anis are unique within the Cuculiformes order for their social behavior. They live in groups and engage in cooperative breeding.
- **Communal Nesting:** Several females will lay their eggs in a single, communal nest, and all adults in the group participate in incubation and raising the young.
- **Distinctive Bill:** They have a heavy, laterally compressed bill with a prominent ridge on the upper mandible.
- **Plumage:** Anis are typically black or dark in color with a glossy sheen.
- **Habitat:** Found in warmer regions of the Americas, inhabiting open woodlands, savannas, and agricultural areas.
- **Diet:** They are omnivorous, feeding on insects, small vertebrates, and fruits. They are often seen foraging on the ground, sometimes following livestock to catch disturbed insects.

Greater Roadrunner - *Geococcyx californianus*

Greater Roadrunner, a large, terrestrial cuckoo, is a striking bird of the arid American Southwest, known for its long tail, crested head, and powerful legs. Its plumage is a mottled mix of brown, black, and white, providing excellent camouflage in its desert habitat. Males and females are virtually indistinguishable in appearance, though males may be slightly larger. Juveniles resemble adults but have a less defined crest and softer plumage.

FEEDING The roadrunner is a formidable predator, primarily feeding on insects, reptiles (including snakes and lizards), small mammals, birds, and even scorpions. It is famous for its ability to run at high speeds, often pursuing prey on the ground.

SOUNDS Its vocalizations are varied, including a series of low, guttural coos, clucking sounds, and a rapid, descending series of notes.

RANGE & MIGRATION Their range extends from the southwestern United States down into Mexico, inhabiting deserts, scrublands, and open woodlands. It is a non-migratory resident, remaining within its territory year-round.

HABITAT They prefer open, arid and semi-arid landscapes, typically with scattered brush and cacti.

SIMILAR SPECIES include other cuckoos, but the roadrunner's size, terrestrial habits, and distinctive appearance make it easily identifiable.

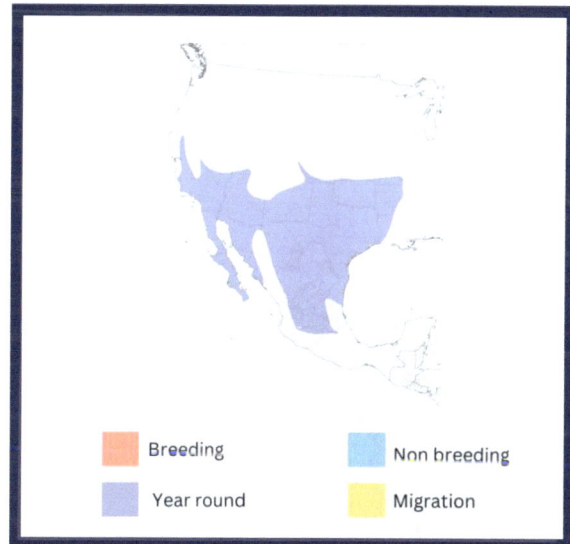

Breeding   Non breeding

Year round   Migration

Song   Call

DID YOU KNOW....

Their feet have a zygodactyl toe arrangement, meaning they have two toes pointing forward and two pointing backward. This creates an "X" shaped footprint, which can make it difficult to track the direction they are traveling.

Despite being a bird, they prefer to run and can reach speeds of up to 20 mph. They use their long tail as a rudder for balance and changing direction while running. They only fly for short distances when necessary

They have a remarkable adaptation that allows them to survive in arid environments without needing to drink water. They obtain most of the moisture they need from their prey and can excrete excess salt through a special gland near their eyes, similar to some seabirds. This conserves precious water.

Yellow-billed Cuckoo - *Coccyzus americanus*

The Yellow-billed Cuckoo is a slender, medium-sized bird characterized by its long tail, olive-brown upperparts, and whitish underparts. A key identifying feature is its large bill, with a bright yellow lower mandible. Males and females are virtually identical in appearance, exhibiting no significant plumage differences. Juveniles resemble adults but display buffy wing bars and less distinct yellow on the bill.

FEEDING These cuckoos are primarily insectivorous, specializing in caterpillars, but also consume other insects, fruits, and occasionally eggs of other birds.

SOUNDS Their vocalizations consist of a series of rapid, wooden "ka-ka-ka-kowlp-kowlp" notes, often described as a knocking sound, and various clucking or clicking calls.

RANGE & MIGRATION They breed across much of eastern and central North America, extending into parts of western North America, and winter in Central and South America. They are long-distance migrants, undertaking substantial journeys between their breeding and wintering grounds.

HABITAT Their preferred habitat includes deciduous woodlands, thickets, riparian areas, and orchards, particularly those with dense foliage.

SIMILAR SPECIES include the Black-billed Cuckoo, which can be distinguished by its entirely dark bill and slightly different vocalizations.

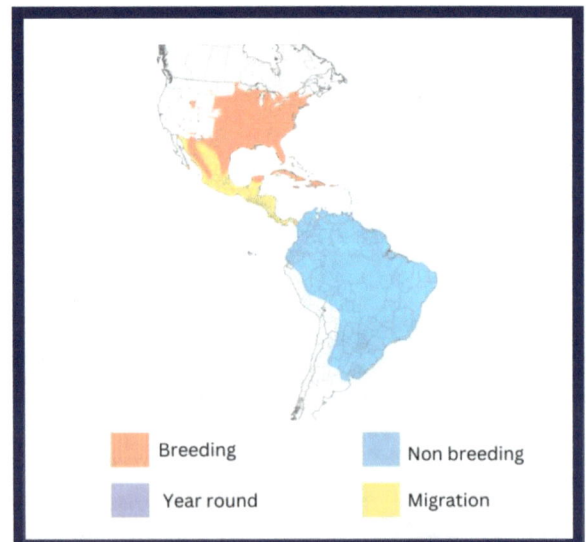

Adult

Adult

Juvenile

Juvenile

Breeding

Non breeding

Year round

Migration

Song

Call

DID YOU KNOW....

They are one of the few bird species that can digest hairy caterpillars, including tent caterpillars. In fact, during outbreaks, a single Yellow-billed Cuckoo can eat up to 100 tent caterpillars in one sitting. They have a specialized way of eating them, rolling the caterpillar in their bill to possibly remove some of the irritating hairs.

They are often called the "rain crow" or "storm crow" due to their tendency to call frequently on hot, humid days, often before a rainstorm.

They don't lay all their eggs at once. There can be several days (up to five) between laying each egg within a clutch. This leads to asynchronous hatching, where chicks in the same nest can be of different ages and sizes

Black-billed Cuckoo - *Coccyzus erythropthalmus*

Black-billed Cuckoo, a slender and secretive bird, is characterized by its long, narrow tail and relatively short, black bill. Its upperparts are a dull brown, while its underparts are a pale gray. Males and females are virtually indistinguishable in plumage. Juveniles resemble adults but have buffy wingbars and a less distinctly black bill.

FEEDING These cuckoos are primarily insectivorous, specializing in caterpillars, particularly tent caterpillars, and also consume other insects, fruits, and berries.

SOUNDS Their song is a series of quiet, hollow "cu-cu-cu" notes, often described as a wooden knocking sound, and they produce a variety of soft, clicking calls.

RANGE & MIGRATION They breed across eastern and central North America, extending into southern Canada, and winter in South America. They are long-distance migrants.

HABITAT Their preferred habitats include deciduous woodlands, forest edges, and thickets, particularly those with abundant caterpillars.

SIMILAR SPECIES include the Yellow-billed Cuckoo, which has a yellow lower mandible and a distinct, louder song, and the Mangrove Cuckoo in some overlapping coastal areas.

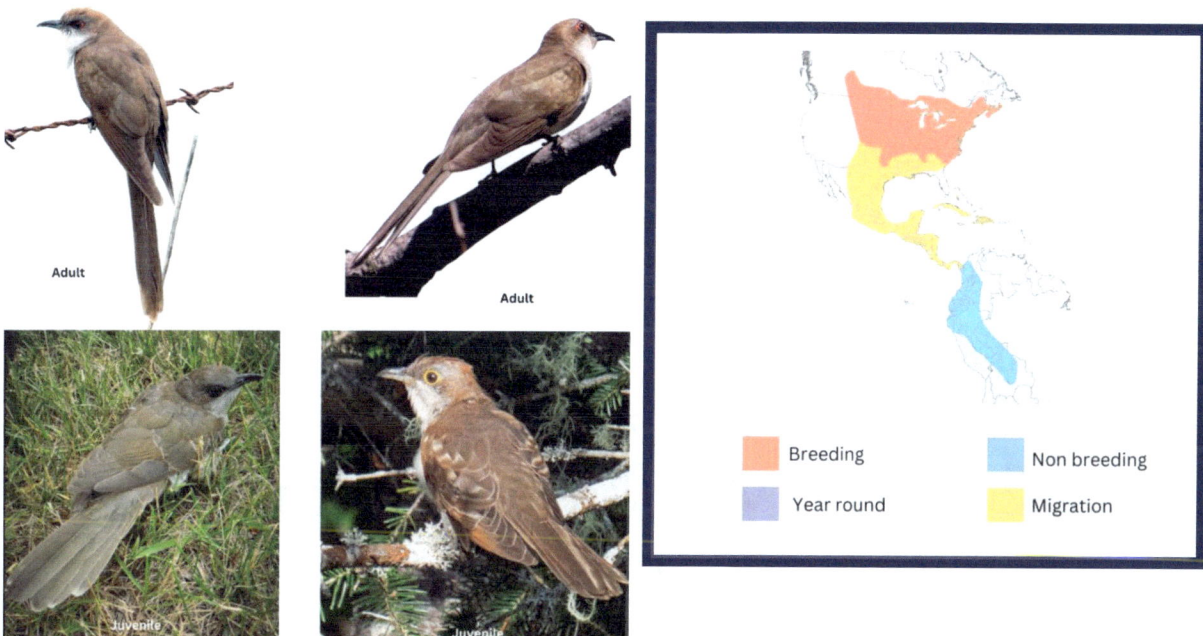

Adult

Adult

Juvenile

Juvenile

Breeding

Non breeding

Year round

Migration

DID YOU KNOW....

While they eat other insects, fruits, and occasionally eggs, Black-billed Cuckoos have a particular fondness for hairy caterpillars, including noxious species like tent caterpillars and gypsy moth larvae. To deal with the indigestible spines, they shed their stomach lining to expel the accumulated hairs, a rather unusual adaptation among birds.

The young develop incredibly quickly. The time from egg-laying to fledging (leaving the nest) is only about 17 days, one of the shortest periods for any bird.

At around 6 days old, before their feathers fully emerge, Black-billed Cuckoo nestlings have a spiky appearance due to their long, pointed feather sheaths, resembling tiny porcupines.

Song

Call

Groove-billed Ani - *Crotophaga sulcirostris*

Groove-billed Ani is a medium-sized, all-black bird characterized by its large, thick bill with distinct grooves along its upper ridge. Both male and female Groove-billed Anis share identical plumage, making them visually indistinguishable. Juveniles display a duller black coloration with less prominent grooves on their bill.

FEEDING These birds are opportunistic feeders, consuming insects, lizards, fruits, and seeds, often in open areas.

SOUNDS Their vocalizations include a variety of croaking and mewing sounds, as well as a distinctive, high-pitched "kee-ow" call.

RANGE & MIGRATION They inhabit open and semi-open habitats, including pastures, scrublands, and edges of woodlands, primarily in southern Texas and along the Mexican coast, extending into Central and South America. They are generally non-migratory within their North American range.

SIMILAR SPECIES include the Smooth-billed Ani, which lacks the grooves on its bill, and the Greater Ani, which is larger and has a different bill shape.

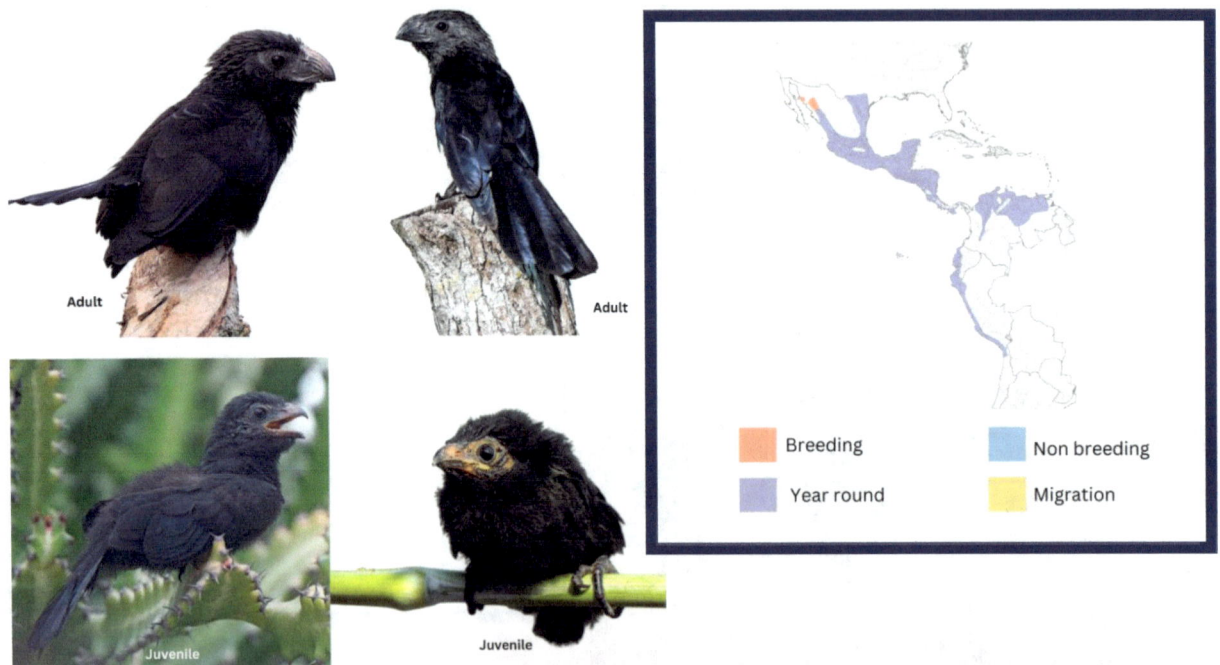

Adult

Adult

Juvenile

Juvenile

Breeding   Non breeding

Year round   Migration

Call

DID YOU KNOW....

Its most distinctive feature is its large, curved, and laterally compressed black bill, which has several parallel grooves running along the length of the upper mandible. This gives the bird its name and helps distinguish it from the similar Smooth-billed Ani.

They are highly social and live in groups of 1-5 breeding pairs. All the females in the group lay their eggs in a single, communal nest. This nest can contain a surprisingly large number of eggs, sometimes up to 20!

In addition to the breeding pairs, some groups may include non-breeding adult "helpers" from previous broods. These helpers also assist in raising the young.

WOOD WARBLERS

Wood warblers are a group of small, often colorful, passerine birds primarily found in the New World (Americas). They belong to the family Parulidae and are distinct from the Old-World warblers (Sylviidae).

General Characteristics:

- **Size and Shape:** Typically, small birds, ranging from 10 to 18 cm in length, with slender bills adapted for catching insects.

- **Plumage:** Many species, especially males in breeding plumage, exhibit bright and varied colors, including yellow, black, orange, red, blue, gray, and white. Females and non-breeding plumages are often duller, leading to the term "confusing fall warblers".

- **Diet:** Primarily insectivorous, feeding on a variety of small insects and insect larvae. Some species may also consume spiders, fruits, and nectar.

- **Behavior:** Generally active and agile birds, often flitting through foliage while foraging. Many are arboreal, feeding in trees, while some are more terrestrial.

- **Vocalization:** Known for a wide variety of songs and calls, which can be high-pitched, fast, and sometimes described as thin or buzzing. Songs are used for territorial advertisement and mate attraction.

- **Migration:** Most North American wood warblers are highly migratory, breeding in northern temperate regions and wintering in the tropics of Central and South America.

- **Nesting:** Nesting habits vary widely among species. Nests can be cup-shaped in bushes or trees, domed on or near the ground, or even in tree cavities.

- **Reproduction:** Typically monogamous, although some males can be polygynous. Females usually build the nest and do most or all of the incubation. Both parents typically feed the young. Clutch sizes are usually 2 to 5 eggs.

- **Habitat:** Occupy a wide range of wooded habitats, including forests (deciduous, coniferous, riparian), thickets, swamps, and early successional habitats. Different species have specific habitat preferences.

Key Points:

- **New World Endemic:** Wood warblers (Parulidae) are exclusively found in the Americas.

- **Diversity:** The family Parulidae comprises a significant number of species (around 120), with diverse plumages, behaviors, and ecological niches.

- **Migration Challenges:** Their long migrations make them vulnerable to habitat loss and degradation along their routes and in their wintering grounds.

- **Identification can be Difficult:** Due to their small size, active nature, and the variability in plumage (especially between sexes and seasons), identifying wood warblers can be challenging for birdwatchers.

- **Ecological Importance:** As insectivores, they play a role in controlling insect populations in their breeding and wintering habitats.

- **Conservation Concerns:** Several wood warbler species are facing population declines due to habitat loss, climate change, and other factors.

- **"Warbler Neck":** Birdwatchers often experience neck strain ("warbler neck") from looking up into the trees to observe these often canopy-dwelling birds.

- **Not True Warblers:** Despite their name, they are not closely related to the Old-World warblers (family Sylviidae). The name arose from superficial similarities in size and insectivorous habits.

Yellow Warbler - *Setophaga petechia*

Yellow Warbler, a vibrant songbird, is characterized by its overall bright yellow plumage, making it easily recognizable. Males are particularly striking, showcasing a vivid yellow body with distinctive reddish-brown streaks on their chest. Females, while still predominantly yellow, exhibit a slightly duller coloration, often with a greenish tinge and less prominent or absent chest streaks. Juveniles are even paler, displaying a yellowish-olive hue.

FEEDING These warblers are primarily insectivorous, feeding on a variety of small insects and spiders, which they glean from foliage.

SOUNDS Their songs are a series of sweet, rapid notes, often described as a descending "sweet-sweet-sweet, I'm-so-sweet" phrase. They also produce sharp chip notes for communication.

RANGE & MIGRATION The Yellow Warbler's breeding range spans across much of North America, from Alaska and Canada down through the United States, and they migrate south for the winter, reaching Central and South America.

HABITAT They prefer habitats with dense, shrubby vegetation, including wetlands, riparian areas, and thickets.

SIMILAR SPECIES include other yellow-colored warblers like the Prothonotary Warbler or the Pine Warbler, but the Yellow Warbler's consistent yellow plumage and distinct song aid in identification.

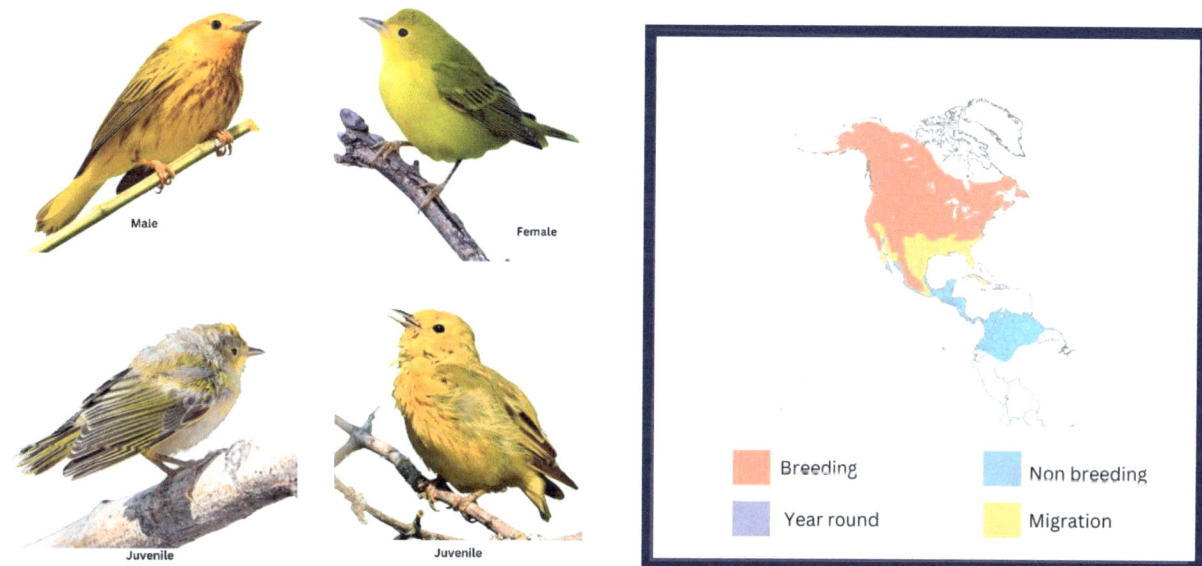

Male   Female   Juvenile   Juvenile

Breeding   Non breeding

Year round   Migration

Song

Chip Notes

DID YOU KNOW....

The Yellow Warbler is the most widespread species within the diverse Setophaga genus, breeding across almost the entire North American continent, the Caribbean, and even down to northern South America, including the Galápagos Islands.

It is sometimes colloquially called the "summer yellowbird" due to its bright plumage and its presence in many areas only during the breeding season.

They have a remarkable defense against brood parasitism by Brown-headed Cowbirds. If a cowbird lays an egg in their nest, the Yellow Warbler will often build a completely new nest directly on top of the old one, burying both its own and the cowbird's egg. They may do this multiple times in a single season, resulting in nests with several tiers.

Yellow-rumped Warbler - *Setophaga coronata*

The Yellow-rumped Warbler, a very common North American warbler, is known for its bright yellow rump patch, visible in all plumages. They are medium-sized warblers with a relatively robust build. During breeding season, males display a striking black mask, white wing bars, and a bright yellow crown, throat, and sides. Females have a more subdued plumage, showing a grayish-brown overall coloration with yellow rump and often yellow throat. Juvenile Yellow-rumped Warblers are streaky brown with a yellow rump, gradually acquiring adult plumage through molting.

FEEDING Their diet is highly adaptable, shifting from primarily insects during breeding to berries and seeds, especially wax myrtle berries, in winter.

SOUNDS Their songs are a series of trills, and their calls include sharp "check" notes.

RANGE & MIGRATION This warbler has a broad range, breeding across much of Canada and the northern United States, and wintering in the southern United States, Central America, and the Caribbean. They are highly migratory, moving south for the winter.

HABITAT They occupy a variety of habitats, including coniferous and mixed forests, shrublands, and even urban parks, particularly during migration and winter.

SIMILAR SPECIES include other warblers, but the Yellow-rumped Warbler is readily identified by its characteristic yellow rump patch and varied diet.

Male

Female

Juvenile

Juvenile

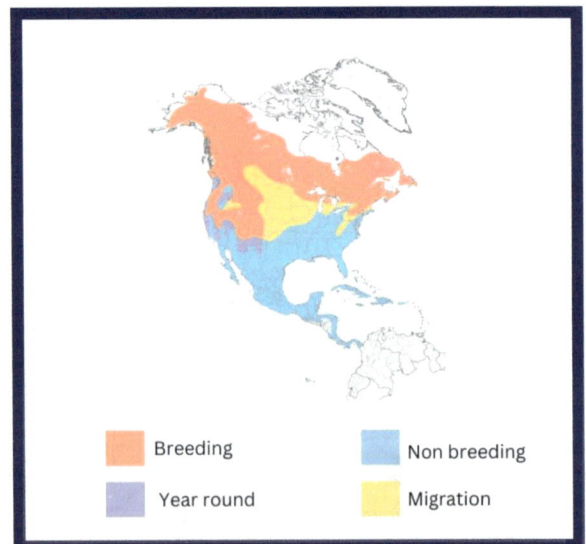

Breeding

Non breeding

Year round

Migration

Song

DID YOU KNOW....

It is the only warbler capable of efficiently digesting the waxy coatings found on berries like bayberries and wax myrtles. This unique ability allows them to winter much farther north than other warblers, as they can rely on these fruits when insects are scarce.

Birdwatchers call these birds "butterbutts" for their noticeable bright yellow rump, a consistent identifier in both sexes.

Unlike many warblers with specialized insect-based diets, the Yellow-rumped Warbler is an opportunistic generalist. They employ a wide array of foraging techniques, including gleaning insects from foliage, catching them in mid-air like flycatchers, picking them from spiderwebs, and even skimming them from the water's surface.

American Redstart - *Setophaga ruticilla*

American Redstart is a small, active warbler known for its vibrant plumage and energetic foraging behavior. Adult males are striking, with a jet-black body contrasted by bright orange patches on their wings, tail, and flanks. Females and immature males exhibit a more subdued palette, featuring olive-gray upperparts and yellow patches in similar locations to the males. Juvenile birds initially display a grayish-brown plumage with yellowish wing and tail patches.

FEEDING These warblers are primarily insectivorous, adeptly catching insects on the wing or gleaning them from foliage.

SOUNDS Their songs consist of a series of high-pitched, thin notes, often described as a buzzy or wiry melody, and they also produce sharp "chip" calls.

RANGE & MIGRATION They breed across much of North America, from southern Canada down through the eastern and western United States, favoring deciduous and mixed forests, particularly those with dense undergrowth. During migration, they travel to Central and South America, making them long-distance migrants.

HABITAT Their preferred habitats include forest edges, second-growth woodlands, and riparian areas.
SIMILAR SPECIES include other warblers, particularly those within the *Setophaga* genus, but the Redstart's unique plumage patterns and active, flycatching behavior help distinguish it.

Male

Female

Juvenile

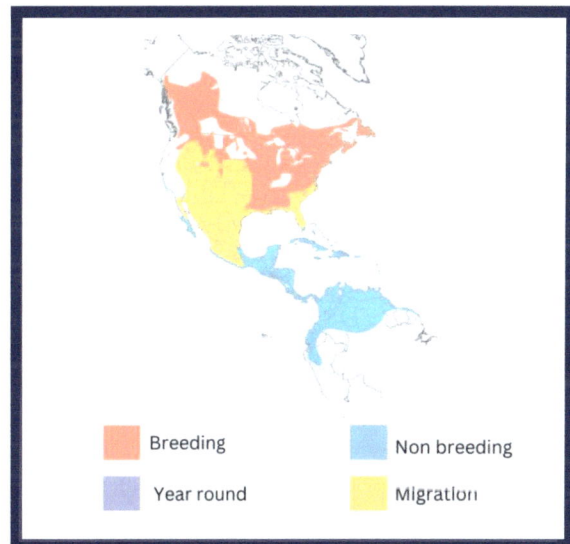

Breeding

Non breeding

Year round

Migration

Song

Female Song

DID YOU KNOW....

They are incredibly active foragers, constantly flitting and fluttering among leaves and branches. They often fan their brightly colored tails and droop their wings in a way that is thought to startle insects into flight, making them easier to catch. This energetic behavior and flashy plumage have earned them the nickname "butterfly of the bird world."

Their tail-fanning and wing-drooping displays aren't just for show. Scientists believe these "flash patterns" of orange and black (in males) or yellow and gray (in females) startle hidden insects, causing them to move and become visible to the redstart.

Black-and-white Warbler - *Mniotilta varia*

Black-and-white Warbler, a small, active songbird, is easily recognized by its striking black and white striped plumage, a pattern shared by both sexes and juveniles, though with subtle variations. Adult males possess a bold black and white streaked pattern across their entire body, while females and juveniles have a duller, more grayish-white streaking, often with buffy undertones. Juveniles further exhibit a browner cast to their plumage.

FEEDING This warbler specializes in foraging along tree trunks and branches, employing a creeper-like movement to glean insects and spiders from bark crevices.

SOUNDS Its song is a high-pitched, thin series of "wee-see, wee-see" notes, often described as a squeaky wheel, and its call is a sharp "chip."

RANGE & MIGRATION They breed across eastern North America, ranging from southern Canada down to the southeastern United States, and migrate to Central America, the West Indies, and northern South America for the winter.

HABITAT Their preferred habitat consists of deciduous and mixed forests, particularly those with mature trees.

SIMILAR SPECIES include other warblers, but the Black-and-white Warbler's unique striped pattern and foraging behavior make it relatively easy to identify.

Male

Female

Juvenile

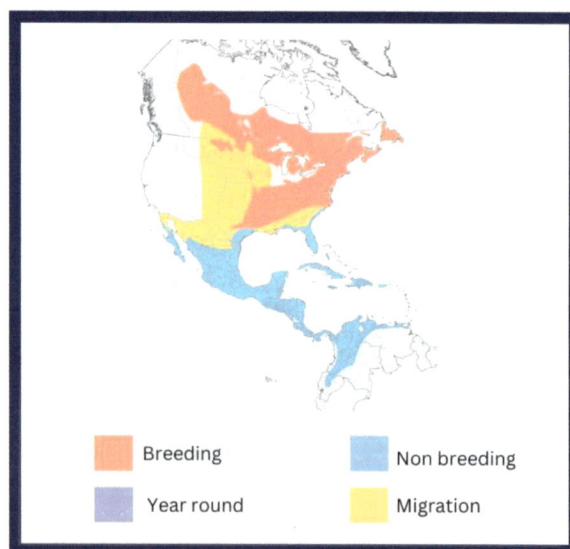

Breeding

Non breeding

Year round

Migration

Song

Call

DID YOU KNOW....

It is the sole species within the Mniotilta genus, making it a taxonomically unique warbler. The genus name Mniotilta means "moss-plucking," referring to its foraging habits.

Unlike most other warblers that primarily glean insects from leaves, the Black-and-white Warbler frequently forages on tree trunks and branches, moving in all directions (upwards, downwards, and sideways) like a nuthatch or creeper. This allows it to find insects hidden in bark crevices.

Its hind claw (hallux) is unusually long and strong compared to other wood-warblers. This adaptation, along with its heavier legs, provides a better grip for moving along and clinging to bark surfaces.

Common Yellowthroat - *Geothlypis trichas*

Common Yellowthroat is a small, vibrant warbler found throughout North America, characterized by its olive-brown upperparts and bright yellow underparts. Adult males are easily identified by their distinctive black facial mask and bright yellow throat, while females and juveniles exhibit a more subdued plumage, lacking the black mask and having a duller yellow throat and breast. Juvenile birds are generally browner overall.

FEEDING They are primarily insectivorous, foraging for insects and spiders in dense vegetation.

SOUNDS Their songs are a rapid, chattering series of notes, often described as "witchety-witchety-witchety," and they also produce sharp chip calls.

HABITAT They inhabit a wide range of habitats, including marshes, thickets, and woodland edges, favoring areas with dense, low-growing vegetation.

RANGE & MIGRATION Their breeding range extends across much of North America, and they are migratory, wintering in the southern United States, Mexico, and Central America.

SIMILAR SPECIES include other warblers, particularly those with yellow underparts, but the male's black mask and the Common Yellowthroat's preference for dense, low-lying habitats help distinguish it.

Male

Female

Juvenile

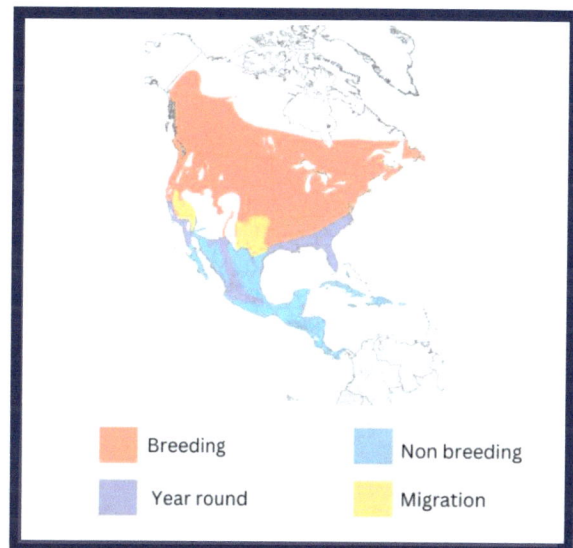

Breeding
Non breeding
Year round
Migration

Song

Call

DID YOU KNOW....

In the U.S. Midwest, the male Common Yellowthroat is sometimes referred to as the "yellow bandit" due to its distinctive black facial mask.

They are very secretive about their nests. They rarely fly directly to the nest. Instead, they will land some distance away and then walk or sneak through dense vegetation to reach it.

To further protect their nests from predators, parent birds often drop into the thickest vegetation near the nest, sneak over to feed their chicks, and then depart in a different direction.

Black-throated Blue Warbler - *Setophaga caerulescens*

Black-throated Blue Warbler is a small, striking warbler of North American forests, characterized by its compact build and relatively large eye. Adult males are easily identified by their deep blue-gray upperparts, black face and throat, and white underparts with a distinctive white wing patch. Females exhibit a much more subdued plumage, displaying olive-brown upperparts, a pale eyebrow stripe, and a small white wing patch, often with a hint of a dark cheek patch. Juvenile birds resemble female plumages but are typically duller and may have buffy or yellowish tones.

FEEDING They are primarily insectivorous, foraging for insects and spiders among foliage.

SOUNDS Their songs are thin, buzzy phrases, often described as a slow, rising "zwee-zwee-zwee," and they also produce sharp chip calls.

RANGE & MIGRATION They breed in mature deciduous and mixed forests across eastern North America, particularly in areas with dense undergrowth. During migration and winter, they travel to the Caribbean islands and Central America.

HABITAT Their preferred habitat includes forests with a well-developed understory.

SIMILAR SPECIES include other warblers with subtle plumage differences, such as the Black-throated Gray Warbler or female-plumaged Blackpoll Warblers, but the Black-throated Blue Warbler's distinct features, especially the male's coloration and female's wing patch, aid in identification.

Male

Female

Juvenile

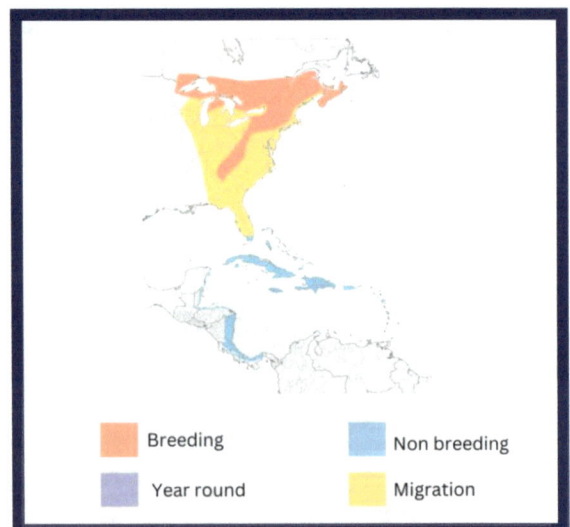

Breeding   Non breeding

Year round   Migration

Song

Call

DID YOU KNOW....

Males and females look so drastically different that they were originally described as two separate species. The striking, deep blue and black male contrasts sharply with the olive-brown and yellowish female.

Both males and females possess a distinctive small white square on their wings, often referred to as a "pocket handkerchief." This is a key identification mark, especially for distinguishing the less colorful female from other female warblers.

Unlike many other warblers where males have a duller "fall plumage," the male Black-throated Blue Warbler retains its vibrant black and blue coloration year-round

Ovenbird - *Seiurus aurocapilla*

Ovenbird, a small wood warbler, is known for its distinctive oven-shaped nest on the forest floor, giving it its name. It possesses an olive-brown upper plumage and a white underbelly with dark streaks, along with a prominent orange stripe down the center of its crown bordered by dark stripes. Males and females are virtually indistinguishable in plumage, with only slight variations in size. Juveniles resemble adults but display a buffy wash to their underparts and less distinct streaking.

FEEDING They are primarily insectivorous, foraging on the ground for insects, spiders, and other invertebrates.

SOUNDS Their song is a loud, ringing series of "teacher-teacher-teacher" notes, increasing in volume, and they also produce sharp "chip" calls.

They breed throughout eastern North America, extending into parts of Canada, and migrate to Central America and the Caribbean for the winter.

NESTING They favor mature deciduous or mixed forests with dense undergrowth, where they build their characteristic ground nests.

SIMILAR SPECIES include other ground-foraging warblers, such as the Northern Waterthrush, which shares habitat and foraging behaviors, but the Ovenbird's crown stripe and distinct song set it apart.

Adult

Adult

Juvenile

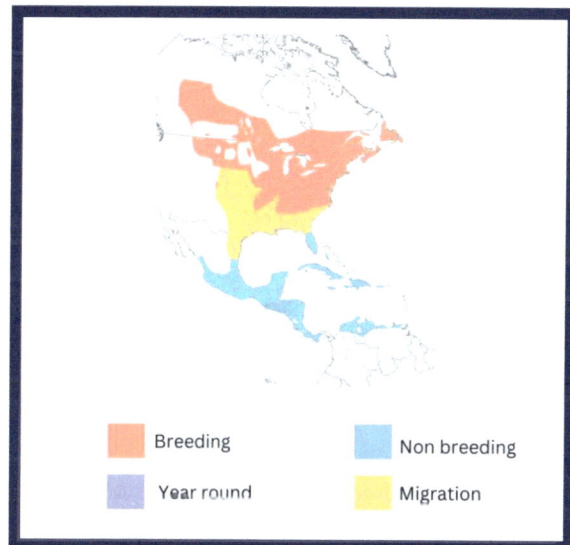

Breeding

Non breeding

Year round

Migration

Song

Chip Calls

DID YOU KNOW....

Unlike many other warblers that primarily forage in trees, the Ovenbird spends most of its time on the ground, walking rather than hopping as it searches for insects in the leaf litter. Its legs are longer and stouter than those of typical arboreal warblers, reflecting this terrestrial lifestyle.

It gets its name from its unique dome-shaped nest built on the forest floor. Constructed from dead leaves, grass, and other plant material, it has a side entrance, resembling a Dutch oven. The female weaves the cup, side entrance, and roof as a single integrated piece.

When foraging, Ovenbirds have a characteristic gait, walking with jerky steps and often bobbing their head and flicking their tail. This behavior is quite distinct from the hopping of more typical warblers.

Prothonotary Warbler - *Protonotaria citrea*

Prothonotary Warbler is a small, vibrant songbird known for its brilliant golden-yellow plumage, particularly prominent in males. Males display a striking golden-yellow head, breast, and belly, with bluish-gray wings and tail, and a black eye stripe. Females are duller, exhibiting a more olive-yellow coloration with less intense yellow on the head and breast. Juveniles are even more subdued, showing olive-brown upperparts and yellowish underparts, and lack the bright yellow of adults.

FEEDING These warblers are primarily insectivorous, foraging for insects and spiders in dense, swampy vegetation.

SOUNDS Their songs are a series of loud, ringing "tweet-tweet-tweet" notes, while their calls are sharp "chip" sounds.

RANGE & MIGRATION They breed in swampy, forested wetlands and bottomlands across the southeastern United States, extending northward along river systems. During the non-breeding season, they migrate to Central and South America.

HABITAT Their preferred habitat consists of flooded forests, cypress swamps, and other wetland areas with standing water and cavities for nesting.

SIMILAR SPECIES include other warblers, but the Prothonotary's bright yellow coloration and preference for swampy habitats make it relatively easy to identify.

Male

Female

Juvenile

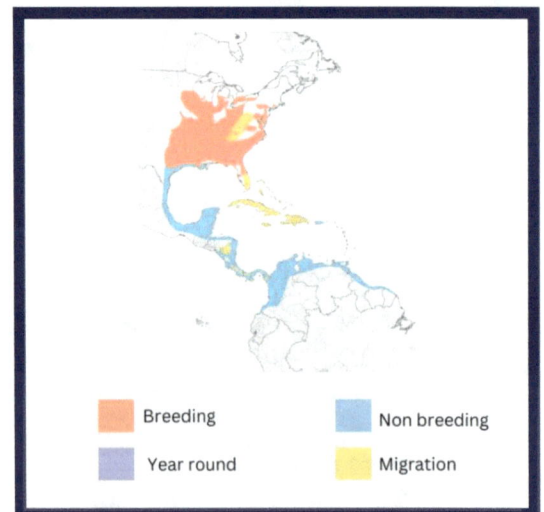

Breeding

Non breeding

Year round

Migration

Song

DID YOU KNOW....

Unlike most warblers that build open-cup nests in shrubs or trees, the Prothonotary Warbler is one of the few eastern North American warblers that nests in cavities.

Its vibrant golden-yellow plumage is said to resemble the bright yellow robes worn by prothonotaries, who were high-ranking clerks in the Roman Catholic Church.

Male Prothonotary Warblers often build several incomplete, non-functional nests within their territory. These "dummy" nests may serve to attract a mate or to confuse potential predators. The female is the one who builds the actual nest used for laying eggs.

206

Northern Parula - *Setophaga americana*

Northern Parula is a small, vibrant wood-warbler found across eastern North America. It displays a blue-gray upper plumage with a distinctive greenish-yellow back patch and two white wing bars. Males are particularly striking, showcasing a bright yellow throat and breast crossed by two bold bands: a black upper breast band and a reddish or rusty lower breast band. Females are generally duller, with less distinct breast bands, and often lack the reddish lower band altogether. Juvenile plumage is even more subdued, typically grayish-green with faint wing bars.

FEEDING They are primarily insectivorous, foraging among foliage for small insects and spiders.

SOUNDS Their song is a distinctive, buzzy trill that rises in pitch, often described as a zipping sound, culminating in a sharp, emphatic note. They also produce sharp chip calls.

RANGE & MIGRATION They breed in eastern North America, ranging from southern Canada down to the Gulf Coast, favoring mature forests with abundant hanging lichens or Spanish moss, which they use for nest construction. During the non-breeding season, they migrate south to the southeastern United States, the Caribbean, and Central America.

SIMILAR SPECIES include other small warblers, particularly other *Setophaga* warblers, which can be distinguished by subtle plumage details and vocalizations.

Male

Female

Juvenile

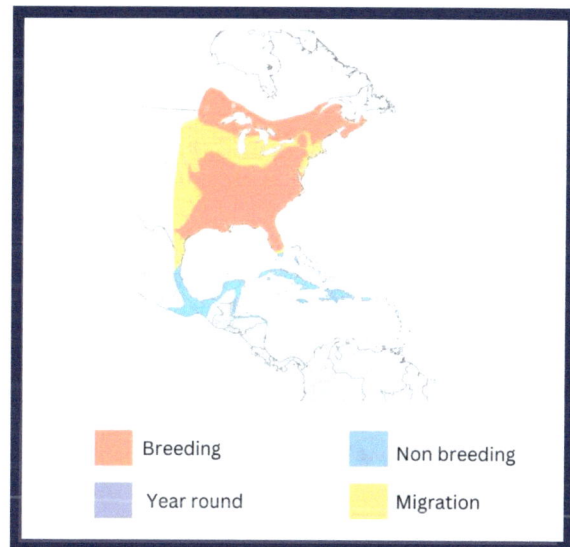

Breeding

Non breeding

Year round

Migration

Song

DID YOU KNOW....

They exhibit fascinating regional variation in their nesting habits. In the southern part of their breeding range, they primarily build their nests within hanging clumps of Spanish moss. Further north, they utilize beard lichen (Usnea) or lace lichen in a similar fashion, hollowing out the hanging vegetation to create a cup nest with a side entrance.

Birdwatchers often joke about getting "warbler neck" when trying to spot Northern Parulas. This is because they frequently forage and nest high in the canopy of trees, requiring observers to crane their necks upwards for extended periods.

Blackburnian Warbler - *Setophaga fusca*

Blackburnian Warbler is a small, vibrant songbird renowned for its striking plumage, particularly the male's brilliant orange throat. Adult males are easily identified by their black backs and wings, double white wing bars, white underparts with black streaks on the flanks, and a fiery orange-red throat and supercilium. Females have a more subdued coloration, with yellowish-orange to orange throats, a dark gray back, and yellowish underparts with dark streaks. Juvenile Blackburnian Warblers are generally olive-brown above and pale yellow below, with two pale wing bars and a hint of a yellowish face pattern.

FEEDING These warblers are primarily insectivorous, foraging actively in the canopy for insects and spiders.

SOUNDS Their songs are high-pitched, thin, and often described as a series of rapidly ascending notes, sometimes ending in a sharp, high-pitched "tsip." Their calls include sharp "chip" notes.

RANGE & MIGRATION The Blackburnian Warbler's breeding range extends across eastern North America, particularly in coniferous forests. They undertake long migrations, wintering in the Andean region of South America.

HABITAT Their preferred habitat during breeding season is mature coniferous and mixed forests, especially those with hemlock and spruce.

SIMILAR SPECIES include other small warblers, such as the Bay-breasted Warbler and Blackpoll Warbler, but the Blackburnian's distinctive orange throat (in males and to a lesser extent, females) and high-pitched song help distinguish it.

Male

Female

Juvenile

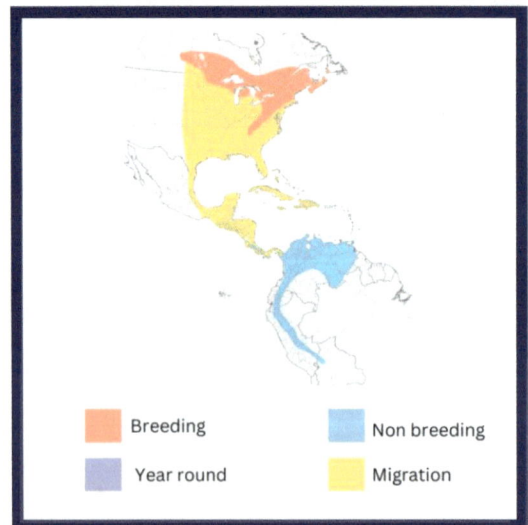

Breeding

Non breeding

Year round

Migration

Song

DID YOU KNOW....

The breeding male Blackburnian Warbler is unmistakable due to its brilliant, fiery orange throat and face, a feature that no other North American warbler shares. This vibrant coloration makes it a favorite among birdwatchers.

When establishing territories in the spring, rival male Blackburnian Warblers engage in dramatic aerial displays. These conflicts involve chasing each other through the treetops in looping flights, whirling descents through branches, and exaggerated slow flapping, resembling an aerial ballet

Unlike many other warblers that forage at various levels, Blackburnian Warblers are primarily canopy dwellers.

Orange-crowned Warbler - *Leiothlypis celata*

Orange-crowned Warbler is a small, active songbird characterized by its relatively plain plumage, typically olive-green to yellowish-green above and yellowish below, with faint streaking on the breast in some individuals. Males and females generally look alike, although the inconspicuous orange crown patch, which gives the bird its name, is typically larger and brighter in adult males but often concealed by other feathers. Juvenile Orange-crowned Warblers are duller in color, often more grayish-green, and lack the orange crown.

FEEDING They are primarily insectivorous, foraging actively in foliage for small insects and spiders, but they will also consume berries, especially during migration and in winter.

SOUNDS Their song is a trilling series of notes that descends in pitch and often ends with a lower, more distinct trill; their calls include a sharp "chip" and a softer "tsip."

RANGE & MIGRATION They have a broad breeding range across northern North America, extending from Alaska and Canada south into the western and northern United States. They are long-distance migrants, wintering primarily in the southern United States, Mexico, and Central America.

HABITAT Their breeding habitat consists of a variety of shrubby and open woodlands, including thickets, edges of forests, and riparian areas, while during migration and winter, they can be found in a wider range of habitats with sufficient foliage and food resources.

SIMILAR SPECIES that might cause confusion include other plain-colored warblers such as Tennessee Warblers or Hutton's Vireos, but subtle differences in plumage details, song, and behavior aid in distinguishing them.

Adult

Adult

Juvenile

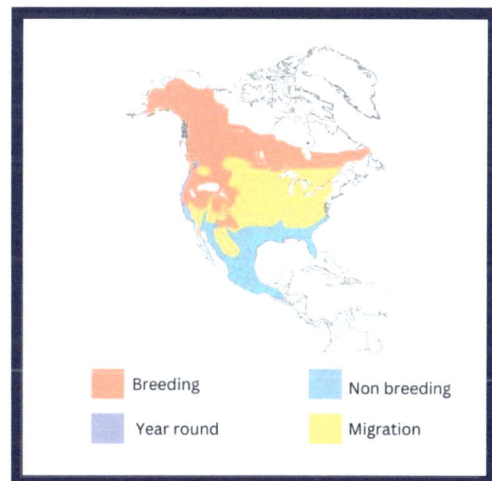

Breeding

Non breeding

Year round

Migration

Song

DID YOU KNOW....

Despite its name, the orange crown patch on this warbler is typically small and often entirely concealed by surrounding feathers. It is usually only visible when the bird raises its crown feathers, such as during territorial displays or when agitated. This makes it a rather inconspicuous namesake.

Most Orange-crowned Warblers nest on the ground, potentially as a strategy to avoid avian nest predators. However, the sordida subspecies, found on California's Channel Islands, is an exception. With fewer bird predators to worry about on these islands, they often nest in taller shrubs and trees, sometimes up to 20 feet high.

Yellow-throated Warbler - *Setophaga dominica*

Yellow-throated Warbler is a striking songbird characterized by its bright yellow throat and upper breast, sharply contrasting with a black mask that extends through the eye and onto the sides of the neck. Its back is typically gray, and it has black streaks on its flanks and two prominent white wing bars. Males tend to exhibit brighter yellow coloration, particularly on the throat, compared to females, which may have a slightly duller yellow or a whitish wash below the yellow throat. Juvenile Yellow-throated Warblers are less distinctly marked, with a paler yellow throat and breast, and their black markings are often dusky or incomplete.

FEEDING These warblers are primarily insectivorous, foraging actively in trees for insects and spiders, and they may occasionally consume berries.

SOUNDS Their songs are typically loud and musical, often described as a series of clear, whistled notes, while their calls include sharp chips and buzzy notes.

RANGE & MIGRATION The Yellow-throated Warbler's breeding range extends across the southeastern and central United States, with some populations reaching into southern Ontario. During the non-breeding season, they migrate south to the southeastern United States, the Caribbean, and Central America.

HABITAT Their preferred habitat during the breeding season includes mature deciduous or mixed forests, often with sycamore or pine trees, particularly near water sources.

SIMILAR SPECIES that might cause confusion include other warblers with yellow throats, such as the Prairie Warbler or Pine Warbler, but the Yellow-throated Warbler's distinctive black mask and gray back are key identifying features.

Adult

Adult

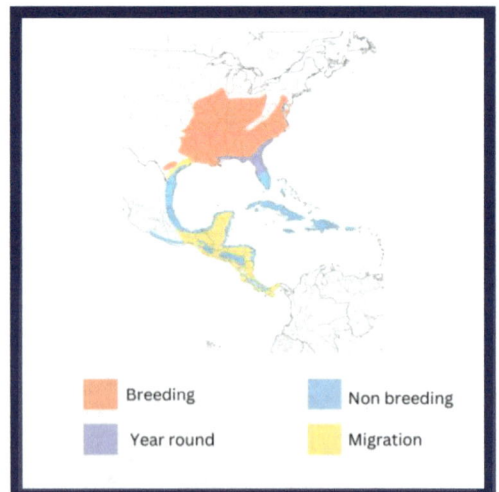

Breeding

Non breeding

Year round

Migration

Juvenile

Song

DID YOU KNOW....

Early naturalist Mark Catesby, one of the first to illustrate this species, called it the "Yellow-throated Creeper" due to its habit of deliberately creeping along branches and trunks while foraging, much like a Brown Creeper or Black-and-white Warbler.

They spends most of its time high in the canopy of trees, making it a challenge for birdwatchers to observe closely. They probe bark crevices, pine cones, and Spanish moss with their long, narrow bills for insects.

They often build cup-shaped nests in Spanish moss or high branches of various trees, sometimes very high up.

Pine Warbler - *Setophaga pinus*

Pine Warbler is a relatively large warbler with a stout bill that is closely associated with pine trees throughout the year. Adult males exhibit olive upperparts and a bright yellow throat and breast, along with two prominent white wingbars. Females and immature birds have duller yellow underparts and more olive-brown upperparts, sometimes appearing grayish. Juveniles resemble adults but are typically less brightly colored.

FEEDING Pine Warblers primarily feed on insects, which they glean from pine needles and branches, but they are unique among warblers for also consuming significant amounts of seeds, especially pine seeds, and occasionally berries and suet at feeders.

SOUNDS Their song is a musical, even trill, often likened to that of a Chipping Sparrow or Dark-eyed Junco but typically slower and more musical; they also have sharp "chip" calls and a softer "tseet" call.

RANGE & MIGRATION This warbler's range spans across eastern North America, with some populations being year-round residents in the southeastern United States, while northern breeders migrate to the south, northeastern Mexico, and the Caribbean for the winter. Their preferred habitat is open pine woods, pine-oak forests, and mature pine plantations, and they are rarely found far from pine trees, even during migration.

SIMILAR SPECIES that could be confused with the Pine Warbler include the Yellow-throated Vireo, which has a thicker bill and yellow "spectacles," and fall plumaged Blackpoll and Bay-breasted Warblers, which typically show streaking on their backs and other distinguishing features.

Male

Female

Juvenile

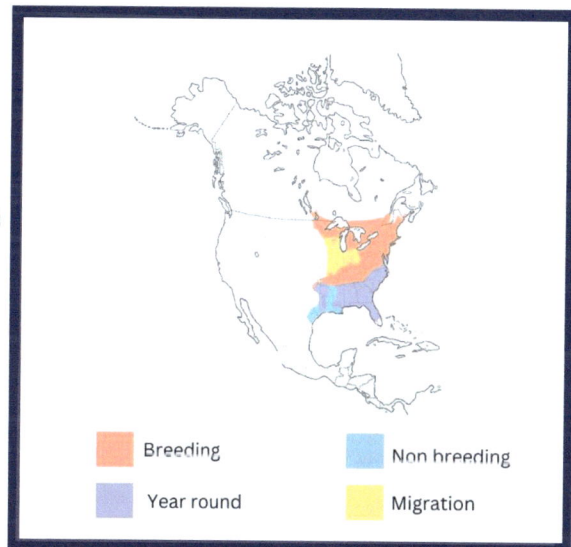

Breeding

Non breeding

Year round

Migration

Song

DID YOU KNOW....

Unlike most other warblers that primarily feed on insects, the Pine Warbler is the only warbler that regularly eats seeds, especially pine seeds.

Due to their seed-eating habits, Pine Warblers are occasional visitors to bird feeders, especially in winter. They will eat suet, sunflower seeds, cracked corn, millet, and peanuts – a behavior quite uncommon among most warbler species.

In the southern part of their range, male Pine Warblers may begin singing on breeding territories as early as February, and they are often the earliest nesting warbler in these areas, sometimes starting nest building in mid-March.

Cerulean Warbler - *Setophaga cerulea*

Cerulean Warbler is a small, active songbird typically found high in the canopy of mature deciduous forests. Adult males are strikingly blue on their back with black streaks along the sides and a distinctive dark blue or black band across their white chest, also exhibiting two white wing bars.

Females are duller in comparison, displaying a bluish-green coloration on their upperparts and a yellowish wash on their underparts, while still retaining the two white wing bars and often showing a pale eyebrow stripe. Juvenile Cerulean Warblers are brownish-gray above with a pale central crown stripe and entirely white underparts.

FEEDING These warblers are primarily insectivorous, foraging actively in the canopy for caterpillars, moths, and other insects.

SOUNDS The male's song is a distinctive rapid series of buzzy notes on one pitch, often ending with a rising "zeeeeee," while their call is a sweet "chip."

RANGE & MIGRATION Their breeding range extends across eastern North America, from the Great Lakes region and southern Quebec down to the Gulf Coast states. They are long-distance migrants, wintering in the Andean forests of South America.

HABITAT Their preferred habitat during the breeding season is mature deciduous forests with tall trees and an open understory, sometimes near water.

SIMILAR SPECIES that might be confused with the Cerulean Warbler include other small, canopy-dwelling warblers, but the male's azure blue and the presence of two white wing bars on both sexes are key identifying features.

Male   Female

Juvenile

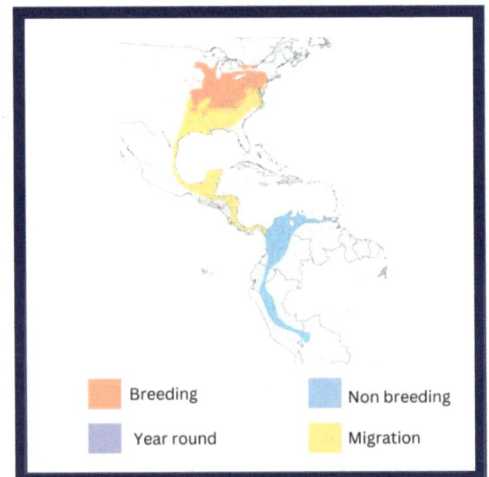

Breeding   Non breeding

Year round   Migration

Song 1   Song 2

212

Chestnut-sided Warbler - *Setophaga pensylvanica*

Chestnut-sided Warbler is a moderately sized warbler known for the distinctive chestnut stripe along its flanks during the breeding season. Breeding males are striking with a yellow crown, black facial markings including an eye stripe and malar stripe, a white throat and belly, and a gray back streaked with black. Females in breeding plumage are duller, exhibiting a greenish crown, less prominent black markings, and less extensive chestnut on their sides. Juvenile birds resemble fall adults, with a greenish-yellow crown and back, grayish cheeks and underparts, and a white eye-ring, often lacking or having minimal chestnut coloration.

FEEDING They primarily feed on insects, including caterpillars, fly larvae, moths, and spiders, which they glean from the undersides of leaves in shrubs and small trees.

SOUNDS The male sings two main song types: a common, accented-ending song often described as "pleased-pleased-pleased-to-meetcha," and an unaccented song that can sound similar to a Yellow Warbler's song; their call is typically a rich, sweet "chip."

RANGE & MIGRATION Their breeding range extends across southern Canada and the northeastern United States, south along the Appalachian Mountains. They are Neotropical migrants, wintering in Central America and northern South America, migrating primarily east of the Rocky Mountains.

HABITAT Their preferred breeding habitat is shrubby second-growth deciduous forests, forest edges, and overgrown fields, often in areas that have undergone recent disturbance.

SIMILAR SPECIES might include the Bay-breasted Warbler, which also has chestnut flanks but with different head and throat coloration in breeding plumage, and non-breeding plumaged birds could potentially be confused with the Yellow Warbler or Pine Warbler, though subtle differences in plumage details and calls can aid in identification.

Breeding Male

Nonbreeding Male

Breeding Female

Juvenile

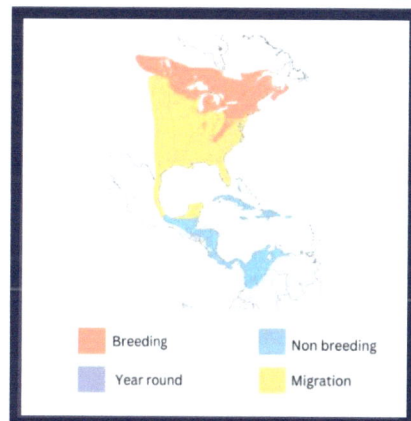

Breeding

Non breeding

Year round

Migration

Song 1

Song 2

DID YOU KNOW....

Chestnut-sided Warblers favor young forests and thickets from natural or human disturbances, thriving due to increased early-successional habitats.

When foraging for insects, this warbler frequently holds its tail cocked upwards at a jaunty angle, a behavior that makes its tail appear longer. They actively hop along slender branches, often inspecting the undersides of leaves for caterpillars and other prey.

They can quickly colonize new patches of suitable habitat, often moving into regenerating areas just a few years after a disturbance.

Blackpoll Warbler - *Setophaga striata*

Blackpoll Warbler is a medium-sized warbler characterized by its relatively plain appearance outside of breeding plumage. During the breeding season, the male is strikingly marked with a black cap, white cheeks, a black throat and upper breast, and a white belly with black streaks on the flanks. Females in breeding plumage have a grayish-blue crown and back, streaked sides, and a pale throat and breast. Juvenile Blackpoll Warblers are typically olive-green above with yellowish underparts and faint streaking.

FEEDING This species is primarily insectivorous, feeding on a variety of insects and spiders, especially during the breeding season, and will also consume berries during migration.

SOUNDS Its song is a series of high-pitched, thin, buzzy notes, often described as a monotonous "tsi-tsi-tsi-tsi-tsi." The call is a sharp "chip" or "tsip."

RANGE & MIGRATION The Blackpoll Warbler breeds across boreal forests of Canada and the northeastern United States. It undertakes one of the longest migrations of any songbird in North America, flying southeast over the Atlantic Ocean to its wintering grounds in northern South America.

HABITAT Its breeding habitat consists mainly of coniferous forests, particularly spruce and fir.

SIMILAR SPECIES might include other fall warblers, but the Blackpoll Warbler in fall plumage is often identifiable by its yellowish legs, pale underparts, and faint streaking, and in breeding plumage, the male's black cap and throat are distinctive.

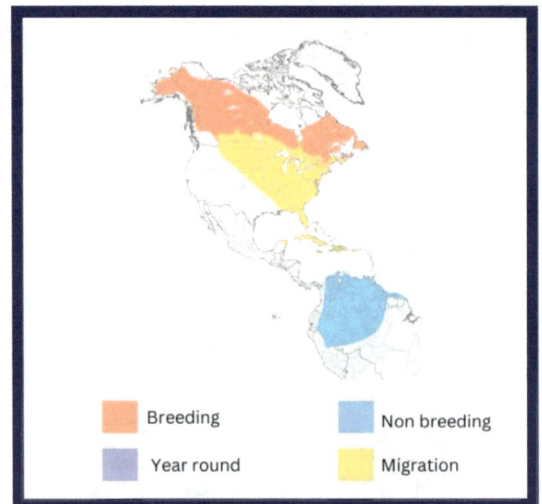

Breeding Male

Nonbreeding Female

Breeding Female

Juvenile

Breeding

Non breeding

Year round

Migration

Song

DID YOU KNOW....

This small songbird undertakes one of the longest overwater migrations of any land bird relative to its size. In the fall, it flies non-stop over the Atlantic Ocean from northeastern North America to its wintering grounds in South America, a journey of approximately 3,000 kilometers (1,900 miles) that can take 72-88 hours.

Unlike many other migratory birds, Blackpoll Warblers from western breeding populations winter in eastern South America, while those from eastern breeding areas travel westward across the Atlantic.

To fuel their epic transatlantic flight, Blackpoll Warblers nearly double their body mass before departure, storing large amounts of fat.

Golden-winged Warbler - *Vermivora chrysoptera*

Golden-winged Warbler is a small, active songbird characterized by its silvery gray body, prominent golden wing patches, and yellow crown. Adult males exhibit a striking black mask and throat bordered by white stripes on the face, while females have a similar pattern but with a gray throat and cheek, and a less sharply defined black mask. Juvenile Golden-winged Warblers resemble adult females.

FEEDING These warblers primarily feed on insects and spiders, actively foraging in the leaves and branch tips of low, shrubby vegetation, sometimes even hanging upside down to reach prey.

SOUNDS The male's song is typically a buzzy, two-parted phrase consisting of a high-pitched note followed by several lower buzzy notes; they also have a rapid, stuttering song used in territorial defense. Their calls include "tzip" notes used during courtship and a "zeee" note given to young.

RANGE & MIGRATION The breeding range of the Golden-winged Warbler is fragmented, with populations concentrated in the Great Lakes region and the Appalachian Mountains, extending into southeastern Canada. They are long-distance migrants, wintering in Central America and the northern Andes of South America.

HABITAT Their preferred breeding habitat is shrubby, young forest areas found in deciduous forests, such as regenerating clearcuts, abandoned fields, utility corridors, and wetlands.

SIMILAR SPECIES include the closely related Blue-winged Warbler, which is more yellow overall and has blueish wings with white wingbars, and their hybrids, Brewster's and Lawrence's Warblers, which display intermediate plumage characteristics.

Male

Female

Juvenile

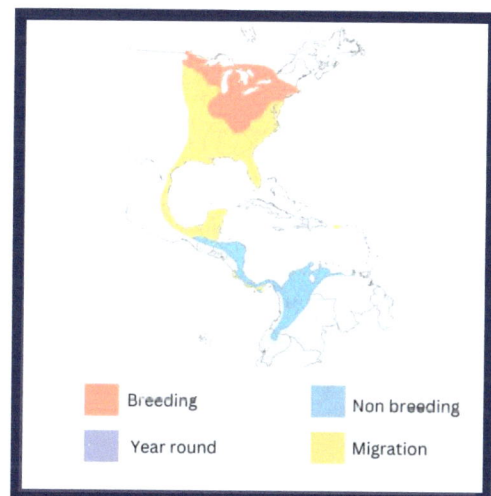

Breeding   Non breeding

Year round   Migration

Song 1   **Song 2**

DID YOU KNOW....

They readily interbreed with their close relatives, Blue-winged Warblers (Vermivora cyanoptera), where their ranges overlap. This hybridization produces two distinct hybrid forms known as "Brewster's Warbler" and "Lawrence's Warbler," which can further complicate identification.

Unlike many other warblers that build nests in trees or shrubs, the Golden-winged Warbler typically builds its cup-shaped nest on or very near the ground, often concealed at the base of a shrub or in a clump of grasses.

After their young fledge (leave the nest), the parent Golden-winged Warblers may divide the brood, with each parent taking responsibility for feeding and caring for a subset of the fledglings for up to a month.

Canada Warbler - *Cardellina canadensis*

Canada Warbler is a small, active songbird characterized by its bluish-grey upperparts and bright yellow underparts, with a prominent white or yellowish-white eyering that gives the appearance of spectacles. The adult male is particularly striking with a well-defined necklace of black streaks across its yellow chest and black on its forehead and cheeks. The adult female has a similar pattern but with duller grey upperparts and a less distinct, often grayish, necklace. Juvenile Canada Warblers resemble adult females with duller plumage and a very faint necklace, lacking the strong black markings of the adult male.

FEEDING These warblers are insectivorous, actively foraging in the understory by hopping and fluttering among branches to glean insects and spiders, and they also frequently catch flying insects in mid-air.

SOUNDS The song of the Canada Warbler is a loud and clear series of warbling notes, often beginning with a chip sound and typically ending on a higher pitch, with significant variation between individuals. They also have a "chip" call.

RANGE & MIGRATION Their breeding range extends across southern boreal and northern temperate forests of Canada and the northeastern United States, southward along the Appalachian Mountains. Canada Warblers are long-distance migrants, wintering primarily in the highlands of northern South America.

HABITAT Their preferred breeding habitat consists of moist, mixed deciduous-coniferous forests with a dense understory of shrubs, often near water, and they also utilize riparian thickets and regenerating forests.

SIMILAR SPECIES that might be confused with the Canada Warbler include the Kentucky Warbler, which has a half eyering and lacks chest markings, the Northern Parula, which has white wing bars and a white belly, and the Magnolia Warbler, which has wingbars and a streaked back.

Male

Female

Juvenile

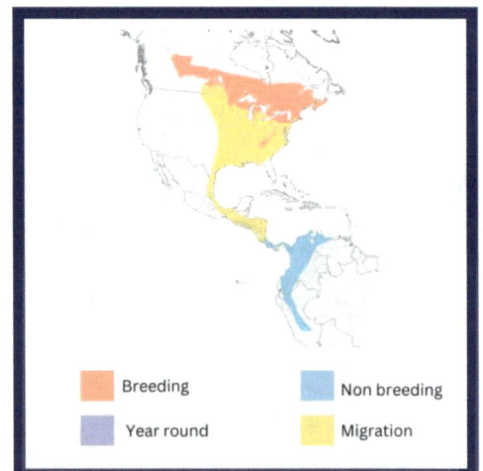

Breeding		Non breeding
Year round		Migration

Song

216

DID YOU KNOW....

The male Canada Warbler sports a distinctive and bold black band of streaks across its bright yellow chest, resembling a necklace. This feature is less pronounced in females and immature birds.

Approximately 80% of the global Canada Warbler population breeds within Canada, giving the country significant responsibility for its conservation.

Unlike many other warblers that nest in trees, the Canada Warbler usually builds its nest on or very close to the ground, often concealed in dense shrubs, ferns, or near upturned tree roots or mossy areas.

Bay-breasted Warbler - *Setophaga castanea*

Bay-breasted Warbler is a medium-sized warbler characterized by its relatively plain appearance outside of its breeding plumage. During the breeding season, the male is strikingly marked with a rich chestnut crown, throat, breast, and flanks, contrasting with a black face mask, gray back, and two white wing bars. The female in breeding plumage is duller, exhibiting a paler chestnut wash on her breast and flanks, a grayish crown and back, and a less distinct face mask. Juvenile Bay-breasted Warblers are even plainer, typically greenish above and whitish below with faint streaking on the breast and two pale wing bars.

FEEDING These warblers are primarily insectivorous, especially favoring spruce budworm larvae during outbreaks, but they will also consume other insects and some berries.

SOUNDS Their song is a high-pitched, thin series of "see-see-see-see-see" notes, often difficult to hear. Their call is a sharp "chip" or "tsip."

RANGE & MIGRATION They breed in the boreal forests of central and eastern Canada and the northeastern United States. This species is a long-distance migrant, wintering in northwestern South America.

HABITAT Their breeding habitat is primarily mature coniferous forests, especially those dominated by spruce and balsam fir.

SIMILAR SPECIES In their non-breeding plumage, they can be confused with other fall warblers, particularly the Blackpoll Warbler, but subtle differences in leg color (dark in Bay-breasted, yellowish in Blackpoll) and overall coloration can aid in identification.

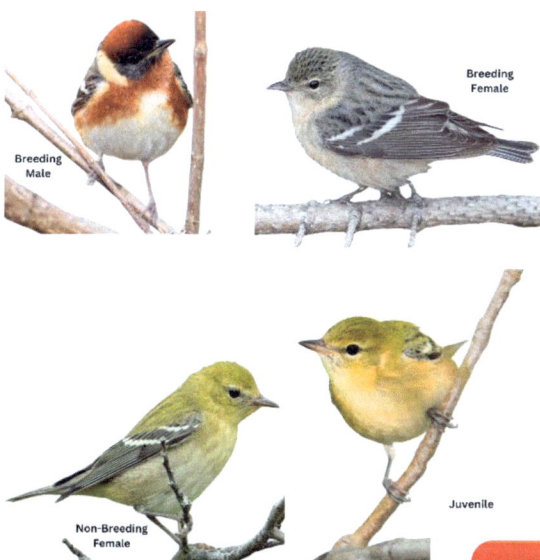

Breeding Male

Breeding Female

Non-Breeding Female

Juvenile

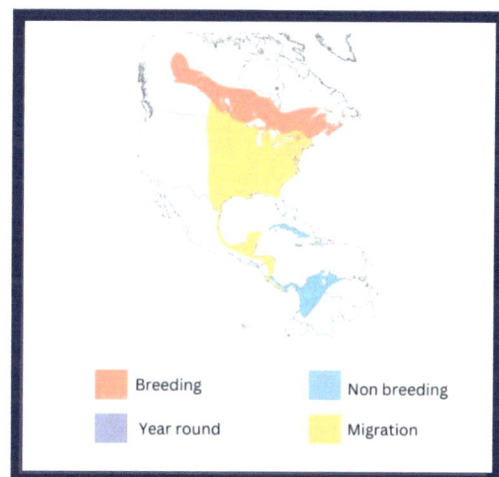

Breeding | Non breeding
Year round | Migration

Song

DID YOU KNOW....

While they readily consume other insects and spiders, the Bay-breasted Warbler exhibits a strong numerical response to outbreaks of the spruce budworm. Their populations can dramatically increase during these infestations due to the abundant food supply.

Bay-breasted Warblers have blackish/grayish feet, distinguishing them from Blackpoll Warblers with their yellowish feet, especially in fall.

Adult Bay-breasted Warblers tend to follow a more westerly migration route in the fall, west of the Appalachian Mountains. In contrast, first-year (juvenile) birds are more frequently observed along the Atlantic Coast during their southward migration.

Painted Redstart - *Myioborus pictus*

Painted Redstart is a striking warbler characterized by its glossy black plumage, a vibrant red lower breast and belly, prominent white patches on its wings, white outer tail feathers, and a distinct white crescent below each eye. Males and females exhibit similar plumage, though males tend to be slightly larger. Juvenile Painted Redstarts have a sooty brownish-gray coloration, lacking the bright red belly of adults, but retain the white wing patches and eye crescents.

FEEDING These active birds primarily feed on insects, employing a dynamic foraging technique that involves hopping, pivoting, and flashing their white wing and tail feathers to startle prey, which they then glean from foliage, snatch in mid-air, or pick from surfaces.

SOUNDS Their songs are described as sweet, even, and cheerful warbles, often rendered as "weeta weeta weeta wee" or "weeta weeta chilp chilp chilp," and both males and females sing. Their calls include a harsh "sreeu" reminiscent of a Pine Siskin's flight call.

RANGE & MIGRATION The Painted Redstart's breeding range in North America is primarily limited to mountainous regions of Arizona, New Mexico, and parts of West Texas, typically in pine-oak, oak, and oak-juniper forests, often near streams and canyons. While some individuals may overwinter at lower elevations in the southern parts of their US range, most migrate south into Mexico and Central America for the non-breeding season, where they inhabit similar forest types.

HABITAT They favor shady forests with lush undergrowth, and their nests are typically built on the ground in sheltered spots.

SIMILAR SPECIES in their range might include the Red-faced Warbler and the American Redstart, but the Painted Redstart's unique color combination and foraging behavior help distinguish it.

Adult

Adult

Juvenile

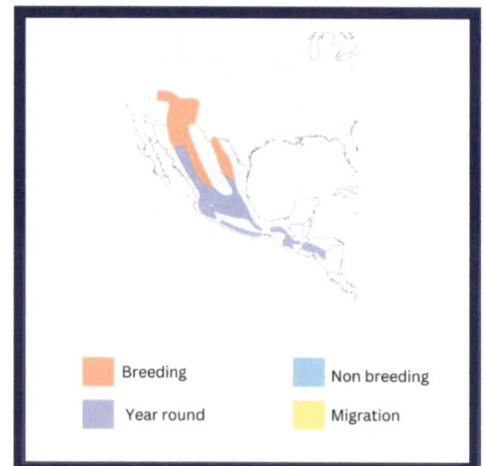

Breeding

Non breeding

Year round

Migration

Song

Call

DID YOU KNOW....

Despite its common name, the Painted Redstart is not closely related to the familiar American Redstart (Setophaga ruticilla). It belongs to a different genus, Myioborus, which means "fly glutton" in Greek, referring to its insectivorous diet.

In some parts of the world, particularly among ornithologists, it's also known as the Painted Whitestart. This name highlights its relationship to other Myioborus species found further south and is fitting because of the significant white markings on its wings and tail.

Unusually for warblers, female Painted Redstarts sing as well as males. Pairs often sing duets during courtship, which strengthens their bond.

GULLS AND TERNS

Gulls and terns belong to the family Laridae, within the order Charadriiformes. While they share similarities as seabirds, they also have distinct characteristics.

General Characteristics

- **Habitat:** Both are typically found near water, including seacoasts, lakes, and rivers. Some gull species can also be found inland, especially near human settlements.
- **Diet:** Both groups are generally carnivorous, feeding on fish, insects, crustaceans, and other small animals. Gulls are often more opportunistic scavengers, while terns are typically more specialized fish hunters.
- **Nesting:** Most species of both gulls and terns are colonial breeders, often forming large and noisy colonies. They typically nest on the ground, sometimes using simple scrapes or built-up nests of vegetation.
- **Vocalizations:** Both groups are vocal birds, with a variety of calls used for communication within the colony and with their young. Gull calls are often described as harsh cries or squawks, while tern calls can be high-pitched and sometimes more musical.
- **Plumage:** Adult gulls typically have plumage in shades of white, gray, and black, with variations depending on the species and season. Terns also exhibit white and gray plumage, often with black caps, and some species have more colorful bills and legs during breeding season. Immature birds in both groups often have mottled brown plumage.
- **Flight:** Both are strong fliers. Gulls often soar and glide extensively, using their broad wings to their advantage. Terns are typically more agile and buoyant in flight, often hovering before diving to catch prey.

Key Points about Gulls

- **Robust Build:** Gulls tend to be sturdier and heavier-bodied than terns, with broader wings and legs.
- **Bill Morphology:** They have stout, hooked bills adapted for tearing food and scavenging.
- **Feet:** Gulls have fully webbed feet, except for the hind toe, which aids in swimming and walking on soft substrates.
- **Tail Shape:** Most gulls have squared-off or rounded tails.
- **Behavior:** Gulls are known for their adaptability and opportunistic feeding habits, including scavenging from human sources. Some species exhibit complex social structures and communication.
- **Maturity:** Larger gull species can take up to four years to reach full adult plumage.
- **Lifespan:** Many large gull species are long-lived, with some individuals recorded living for several decades.

Key Points about Terns

- **Slender Build:** Terns are generally smaller and more streamlined than gulls, with a more delicate appearance.
- **Bill Morphology:** They possess slender, sharply pointed bills adapted for catching fish.
- **Feet:** Terns have webbed feet, but their legs are often shorter than those of gulls, and they are not as adept at walking.
- **Tail Shape:** Many tern species have long, forked tails, which contribute to their graceful flight and have earned them the nickname "sea swallows."
- **Flight Behavior:** Terns are known for their agile, often buoyant flight, frequently hovering and then plunging into the water to catch fish. They typically flap their wings more continuously than gulls.
- **Migration:** Many tern species are long-distance migrants, with some, like the Arctic Tern, undertaking the longest migrations of any bird.
- **Diet Specialization:** While some terns eat insects and crustaceans, their primary diet is usually small fish caught by diving.

American Herring Gull - *Larus smithsonianus*

American Herring Gull is a large gull with a robust body and a somewhat large but slim yellow bill that has a red spot on the lower mandible. Breeding adults exhibit a clean white head and underparts with pale gray backs and wings, along with pale pink legs and yellow eyes. Males and females appear similar in plumage, though females are typically smaller. Juvenile American Herring Gulls are mottled brown overall with a dark bill and dark eyes, gradually acquiring adult plumage over four years through a series of intermediate stages with increasing amounts of gray on the back and white on the head and underparts.

FEEDING This species is an omnivorous scavenger, feeding on a wide variety of items including fish, marine invertebrates, insects, other birds, carrion, and garbage found in diverse habitats such as shorelines, open water, mudflats, plowed fields, and refuse dumps.

SOUNDS They do not have a true song but possess a variety of calls, including a quick "hahaha" alarm call, a louder "keow" alarm, a "long call" used in display, and a "choking" call associated with courtship and territorial disputes.

RANGE Their breeding range extends across Alaska and northern Canada, south to the Great Lakes and along the Atlantic Coast to North Carolina, while they winter from southern Alaska south to Mexico, the Great Lakes south to the Caribbean and Central America.

HABITAT They inhabit a variety of areas near water, including coasts, islands, beaches, mudflats, fields, and even urban environments like parking lots and garbage dumps, often nesting in colonies near water on the ground or sometimes on rooftops.

SIMILAR SPECIES include the European Herring Gull, which can be differentiated by subtle plumage and wing marking differences, as well as other large gulls such as the Great Black-backed Gull, which is larger with darker upperparts, and the Ring-billed Gull, which is smaller with a black ring around its bill and yellow legs in adults.

Breeding Adult

Non-Breeding Adult

Juvenile

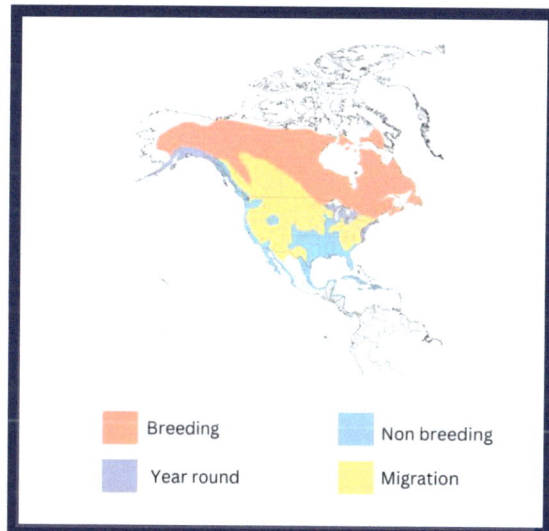

Breeding		Non breeding	
Year round		Migration	

Call 1

Call 2

Ring-billed Gull - *Larus delawarensis*

Ring-billed Gull is a medium-sized gull with a pale gray back and wings, a white head, body, and tail, and distinctive black wingtips spotted with white. Adults have yellow legs and a yellow bill with a prominent black ring around it; non-breeding adults show brown streaking on their heads. Males and females are generally similar in appearance. Juvenile Ring-billed Gulls exhibit a mottled brown and gray plumage with a dark bill that has a pink base.

FEEDING These opportunistic feeders consume a wide variety of food, including fish, insects, earthworms, rodents, grain, and garbage, often foraging in urban, suburban, and agricultural areas as well as near water.

SOUNDS Their vocalizations are typically high-pitched, scratchy, and squealing, with a common call being a rising squeal followed by short, exclamatory notes.

RANGE & MIGRATION Ring-billed Gulls breed near lakes, rivers, or the coast across much of Canada and the northern United States, nesting colonially on the ground, often on islands, and they are migratory, with most moving south to the United States and northern Mexico for the winter, although some remain in milder areas of their breeding range or near the Great Lakes.

HABITAT Their habitat includes inland waterways, coastlines, marshes, and open areas, and they are commonly found in human-modified environments like parking lots and landfills.

SIMILAR SPECIES may include other medium-sized gulls, but the characteristic black ring on the bill is a key identifying feature.

Breeding Adult

Non-Breeding Adult

Juvenile

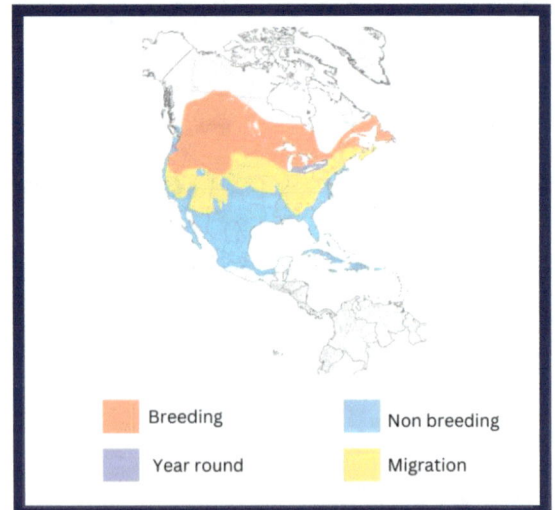

Breeding
Non breeding
Year round
Migration

Call

Juvenile Call

DID YOU KNOW....

Unlike many other gull species that primarily stick to coastal areas, the Ring-billed Gull is remarkably adaptable to urban and suburban environments. They are commonly found in parking lots, around shopping malls, agricultural fields, and even scavenging at garbage dumps far inland.

Some Ring-billed Gull nests have been observed containing pebbles that closely resemble the size and shape of their own eggs. It's believed the parents mistakenly incorporate these pebbles into their nests.

Their nesting colonies sometimes include pairs of two females. These pairs, after mating with a male, can produce "superclutches" containing 5-7 eggs, with each female contributing.

Black Tern - *Chlidonias niger*

Black Tern is a small, graceful tern characterized in breeding plumage by its black head and underparts contrasting with dark gray wings and back, and a pale gray underwing. Males and females in breeding plumage have a similar appearance, although the female may exhibit slightly grayer tones. Juvenile Black Terns resemble non-breeding adults but have dark gray-brown upperparts with faint paler bars, a white forehead, a black cap, and a dark ear mark.

FEEDING These terns primarily feed on insects during the breeding season, which they catch in flight or by dipping to the water's surface, and they also consume small fish, tadpoles, and frogs when available; during migration and winter, their diet shifts mainly to small fish.

SOUNDS Their most common vocalization is a clipped "kik" sound, and nesting birds may produce longer "kyew" calls.

RANGE & MIGRATION The Black Tern breeds in freshwater marshes across north-central United States and southern Canada, extending west to California and east to the Atlantic coast. They undertake long migrations to winter along the coasts of northern South America, often traveling in flocks and sometimes over open ocean.

HABITAT Their preferred breeding habitat is shallow freshwater wetlands with emergent vegetation, while during migration they can be found in various wetland habitats and in winter along coastal lagoons, marshes, and open ocean waters.

SIMILAR SPECIES include Forster's Tern, which is larger and paler gray, and non-breeding Common Terns, which have more extensive black on the head.

Breeding Adult

Non-Breeding Adult

Juvenile

Call

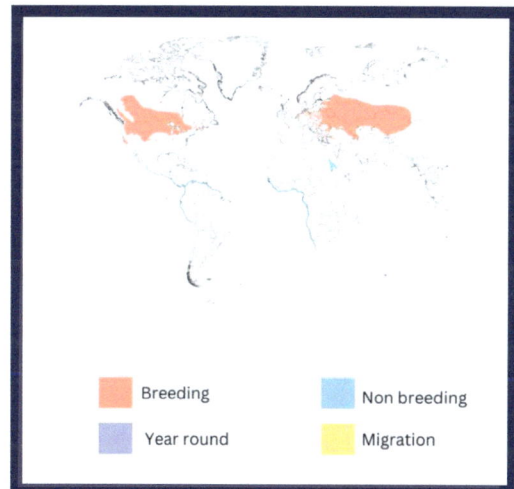

Breeding

Non breeding

Year round

Migration

DID YOU KNOW....

Unlike most other terns that are primarily seabirds, the Black Tern is strongly associated with freshwater marshes and wetlands during its breeding season. This has earned it the nickname "marsh tern," a trait it shares with the White-winged Tern and Whiskered Tern.

It leads a "double life" by inhabiting freshwater wetlands during the summer breeding season and then migrating to tropical coastlines and even far out to sea during the non-breeding season.

This tern forages uniquely with buoyant, erratic flight, dipping for surface food or snatching aerial insects, sometimes even stealing fish from fishermen.

Short-billed Gull - *Larus brachyrhynchus*

Short-billed Gull is a small and somewhat dainty gull with a notably short and slender yellow bill and a round, almost dove-like head. Adult Short-billed Gulls in breeding plumage exhibit a white head, pale eyes with red orbital skin, and yellow legs. Non-breeding adults are similar but show light brown mottling on the head and neck, and their bill and eye-ring become duller. Males are generally slightly larger than females with a longer and stouter bill, though their plumage is identical. Juvenile Short-billed Gulls are brownish overall with dark wingtips and appear darker and more smudged on the head and neck; they gradually acquire gray back feathers during their first winter, and their bill becomes pink at the base with a black tip.

FEEDING These gulls are omnivorous, foraging along shorelines by dipping to seize marine organisms, wading, swimming, or even dropping hard-shelled prey onto rocks; they also feed in fields and freshwater environments on insects, small fish, crustaceans, and other invertebrates, and may consume berries and grains.

SOUNDS Their calls are typically high-pitched, scratchy, and squealing, often described as a short "ka," "kyew," or "kia," with a repeated series of these calls forming their "long call" used in displays; they also make lower-pitched, guttural sounds on their breeding grounds.

RANGE & MIGRATION The Short-billed Gull breeds in northwestern North America, primarily in Alaska and northern Canada, nesting in colonies near coastal areas and inland wetlands, sometimes even in trees. Most individuals migrate south for the winter along the Pacific Coast, reaching as far as the Sacramento Valley, and are less common inland or further south to Baja California.

HABITAT Their habitat includes coastal waters in winter and lakes in summer, frequenting shorelines, estuaries, mudflats, and occasionally wet fields and landfills.

SIMILAR SPECIES include the Ring-billed Gull, California Gull, and American Herring Gull, all of which are larger with stouter bills; the Short-billed Gull also differs in its smaller size, more delicate bill, and often darker eye.

Breeding Adult   Non-Breeding Adult

Juvenile

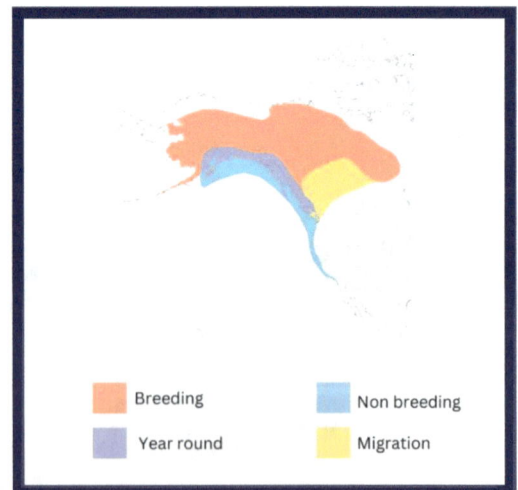

Breeding   Non breeding

Year round   Migration

Call

DID YOU KNOW....

Until 2021, the Short-billed Gull was considered the North American subspecies of the Common Gull (Larus canus) and was often referred to as the "Mew Gull". It was officially recognized as a distinct species based on genetic, plumage, morphological, and vocalization differences.

In flight, adult Short-billed Gulls show a "string of pearls" pattern on their wing primaries due to white tips transitioning to a broad white edge.

Unlike most other white-headed gulls, the Short-billed Gull is known to sometimes nest in trees, similar to Bonaparte's Gulls, particularly in their Alaskan and Canadian breeding grounds. They may build platform nests in low spruce trees up to 20 feet above the ground.

Franklin's Gull - *Leucophaeus pipixcan*

Franklin's Gull is a medium-sized gull characterized in breeding plumage by a complete black hood, prominent thick white eye arcs, a deep red bill and legs, and medium-gray upperparts with black wingtips that have large white spots. The underparts are typically white, often with a pinkish hue during the breeding season. Outside of breeding, the black hood is reduced to a grayish smudge on the back of the head, and the bill and legs become darker. Males and females are generally similar in appearance. Juvenile Franklin's Gulls have browner upperparts and a less distinct hood.

FEEDING These gulls are primarily insectivorous, especially during the breeding season, feeding on a variety of terrestrial and aquatic insects, earthworms, and occasionally small vertebrates. They often forage in fields, sometimes following plows to catch disturbed insects, and can also be seen hawking insects in flight or picking them from the water's surface.

SOUNDS Their songs are described as shrill, laughing calls, often a "kuk-kuk-kuk" that is higher pitched than that of a Laughing Gull. They also have other calls.

RANGE & MIGRATION Franklin's Gulls breed in large colonies in freshwater prairie marshes across the north-central United States and central Canada. They construct floating nests of vegetation anchored to emergent plants in relatively deep water. This species is strongly migratory, undertaking long journeys to winter along the Pacific coast of South America, primarily from Peru to Chile. During migration, they can be found across the interior of North America and along both coasts.

HABITAT Their habitat during the breeding season is primarily prairie freshwater marshes with emergent vegetation. In winter, they utilize coastal areas, including beaches, bays, and estuaries, and can also be found on inland lakes and agricultural fields.

SIMILAR SPECIES that could be confused with Franklin's Gull include the Bonaparte's Gull, which is smaller with a thinner dark bill and lacks the bold white eye arcs in breeding plumage, and the Laughing Gull, which is slightly larger with a longer, often drooping bill and has almost entirely black wingtips without the distinct white spots of the Franklin's Gull. Non-breeding Bonaparte's Gulls also have a distinct dark ear spot rather than the more extensive grayish hood of a non-breeding Franklin's Gull.

Breeding Adult

Juvenile

Non-Breeding Adult

First Winter

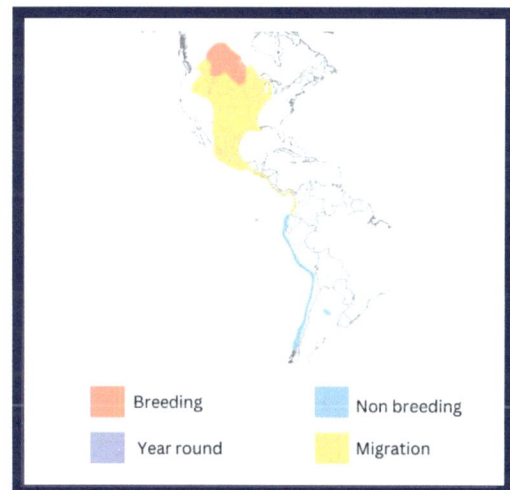

Breeding   Non breeding

Year round   Migration

Call

DID YOU KNOW....

Unlike most gulls that undergo one complete molt per year, the Franklin's Gull has two complete molts annually – one after breeding and another upon reaching its wintering grounds. This is unusual for gulls.

They are strongly associated with the prairies of North America for breeding, often called the "Prairie Dove" due to this preference. They nest in large colonies in freshwater marshes with emergent vegetation.

They undertake a remarkable long-distance migration from their breeding grounds in central North America to their wintering grounds along the Pacific coast of South America, from Peru to Chile. This makes them one of the more significant migratory birds in the region.

Western Gull - *Larus occidentalis*

Western Gull is a large and stocky gull primarily found along the Pacific Coast of North America. Adult Western Gulls have a white head, neck, and underparts, with dark slate-gray upperparts and bright pink legs. They possess a large yellow bill with a distinctive red spot near the tip. Males are typically larger than females, but their plumage is identical. Juvenile Western Gulls go through several plumage stages over about four years, starting mostly brown and gradually acquiring the adult white and gray coloration.

FEEDING They are opportunistic feeders with a varied diet consisting mainly of fish and marine invertebrates, which they obtain through foraging at sea, in intertidal zones, and along beaches. They are also known to scavenge carrion and refuse, and will readily take eggs and chicks of other seabirds.

SOUNDS Their vocalizations include a low, piercing "keow" call, a lower "cow-cow-cow" sound, and a longer series of higher-pitched notes in their "long call," which is used in courtship and territorial displays.

RANGE & MIGRATION The range of the Western Gull is almost exclusively coastal, extending from southern Washington south to central Baja California. While they are present year-round throughout much of their breeding range, some individuals, particularly subadults, may disperse southward after nesting, and adults may move slightly north or south outside the breeding season. They are rarely found far inland, typically inhabiting coastal waters, estuaries, beaches, and offshore islands where they nest in colonies on the ground or on rocky cliffs.

SIMILAR SPECIES include the California Gull, Glaucous-winged Gull, and Yellow-footed Gull, and hybridization with the Glaucous-winged Gull in the northern part of their range can create identification challenges due to intermediate plumages.

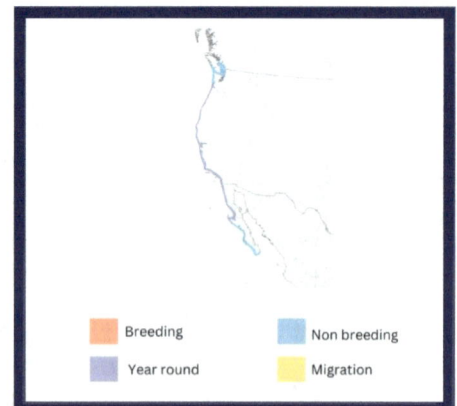

Breeding Adult

Juvenile

Non-Breeding Adult

Third Winter

Breeding   Non breeding
Year round   Migration

Call 1   **Call 2**

DID YOU KNOW....

They have been observed stealing milk directly from the teats of sleeping, lactating female elephant seals on rookeries.

Unlike some gull species that reach adult plumage in three years, the Western Gull takes a full four years to achieve its characteristic gray back and white head and underparts.

In the Pacific Northwest, they hybridize so extensively with Glaucous-winged Gulls (Larus glaucescens) that in some areas, hybrids are more common than pure Western Gulls. Interestingly, females paired with these hybrid males have shown higher breeding success in certain habitats.

Yellow-footed Gull - *Larus livens*

Yellow-footed Gull is a large gull with a dark slate-gray back and wings contrasting with a white head and underparts. Adults possess a thick yellow bill with a reddish spot near the tip and, most distinctively, bright yellow legs. Males and females exhibit similar plumage. Juvenile Yellow-footed Gulls are overall brown with pinkish legs in their first year, gradually developing the gray back and yellow legs over several years, reaching full adult plumage in about three years.

FEEDING This species is primarily a scavenger and forager, feeding on fish, invertebrates, carrion, and sometimes preying on seabird eggs and chicks; they are also known to scavenge around docks and refuse areas.

SOUNDS Their vocalizations are described as similar to those of the Western Gull but deeper and less harsh, including flat, raucous calls and screams.

RANGE & MIGRATION The Yellow-footed Gull is primarily found in the Gulf of California in Mexico, with some post-breeding dispersal north to the Salton Sea in California. They are mostly non-migratory within their core range.

HABITAT Their typical habitat includes sandy and rocky coasts and islands, often with sparse vegetation, where they nest in colonies on the ground near the high tide line.

SIMILAR SPECIES include the Western Gull, but the Yellow-footed Gull is distinguished by its consistently yellow legs in adults; the Lesser Black-backed Gull also has yellow legs but is smaller with a less robust bill.

Adult

Juvenile

Adult

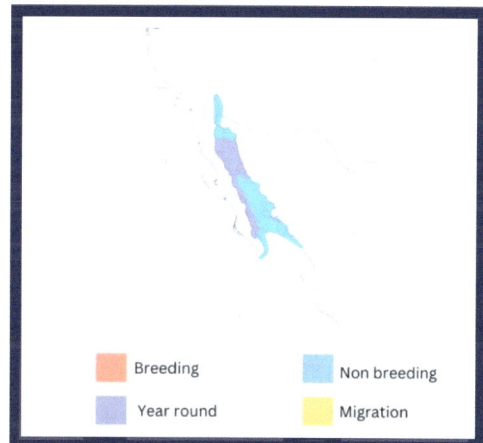

Breeding

Non breeding

Year round

Migration

Call

DID YOU KNOW....

This large gull has a restricted breeding range, found almost exclusively on islands within the Gulf of California in Mexico. This makes it a truly regional species.

Compared to many other widespread gull species, the Yellow-footed Gull has a relatively small global population, estimated at around 40,000 breeding individuals.

While it scavenges and forages for fish and invertebrates, the Yellow-footed Gull is also a notable predator. It actively preys on the eggs and chicks of other seabirds, including species like Heermann's Gull, Brown Pelican, and cormorants.

Bonaparte's Gull - *Chroicocephalus philadelphia*

Bonaparte's Gull is a small and graceful gull, often appearing more tern-like in flight than other gulls, with a slender black bill and relatively narrow, pointed wings. During the breeding season, the adult male and female develop a striking black head, contrasting with their otherwise white body and gray upperparts, and they have red legs. In non-breeding plumage, their head becomes white with a distinctive dark smudge behind the eye, and their legs turn pinkish. Juvenile Bonaparte's Gulls have a patchy brown head and scalloped brown feathers on their back, with a black bar across the wings and a black tip on the tail; they gradually molt into their first-winter plumage, which resembles the non-breeding adult but retains the dark bar on the wings and a black tail band.

FEEDING These gulls primarily feed on insects during the breeding season, often catching them in flight, and switch to a diet of small fish and invertebrates in coastal and wintering areas, which they often capture by dipping and diving into the water.

SOUNDS Their calls are typically harsh and scratchy, often described as a "cherrr" or "kheh," somewhat lower in pitch than a Forster's Tern.

RANGE & MIGRATION They breed in the boreal forests across southern Alaska and much of interior western Canada, favoring open areas near water and uniquely nesting in trees, usually conifers. They are migratory, with most birds moving southeast or southwest to winter along the coasts of North America, including the Great Lakes and open ocean.

HABITAT Their habitat during migration and winter includes a variety of aquatic environments such as ocean coasts, bays, harbors, estuaries, mudflats, rivers, lakes, and ponds.

SIMILAR SPECIES that could be confused with Bonaparte's Gulls include the Little Gull and the Black-headed Gull, both of which are also small hooded gulls, but they possess subtle differences in size, bill color, leg color, and wing patterns. Franklin's Gull is another similar species, particularly in breeding plumage with its black head, but it has a reddish bill and white eye crescents, and in flight, Bonaparte's Gull shows a distinctive white wedge on the leading edge of the wing.

Breeding Adult

Non- Breeding Adult

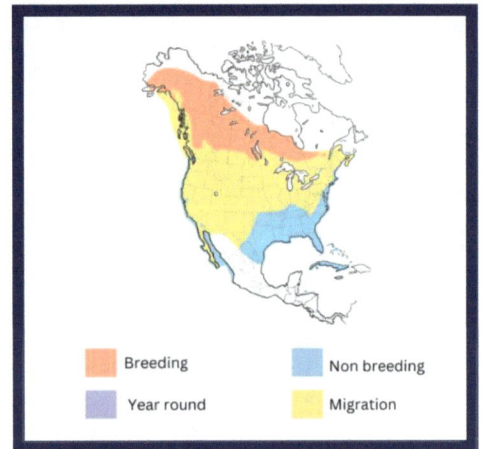

Juvenile

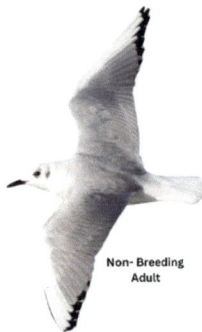

Breeding   Non breeding

Year round   Migration

Call

DID YOU KNOW....

Unlike most other gull species that nest on the ground, the Bonaparte's Gull is the only one that regularly builds its nests in trees, typically in boreal forests near water. They construct small stick nests, often in conifers like spruce or tamarack.

The common name honors Charles Lucien Bonaparte, a nephew of Napoleon Bonaparte, who made significant contributions to American ornithology in the 1820s.

Adult Bonaparte's Gulls have a striking white wedge on the leading edge of their upperwing during flight, contrasting with their gray wings and black wingtips. This pattern is a key identification feature.

Laughing Gull - *Leucophaeus atricilla*

Laughing Gull is a medium-sized gull characterized by its dark gray back and wings with black wingtips, and white underparts. During the breeding season, adults develop a distinctive black head, thin white eye crescents, and a reddish bill, while in the non-breeding season, the black head is replaced by a white head with a grayish smudge behind the eye, and the bill turns blackish. Males and females are largely similar in appearance, although males tend to be slightly larger in all measurements. Juvenile Laughing Gulls have an entirely warm brown plumage with pale edgings on the upperwing coverts and a dark terminal band on their white tail, gradually acquiring adult plumage over two to three years.

FEEDING These opportunistic feeders consume a wide variety of items, including fish, crustaceans, insects, and often scavenge for garbage and steal food from other birds like pelicans.

SOUNDS Their most recognizable vocalization is a loud, strident series of "ha-ha-ha" calls, reminiscent of laughter, along with shorter alarm calls.

RANGE & MIGRATION The Laughing Gull's breeding range extends along the Atlantic coast of North America, the Caribbean, and northern South America, with northern populations migrating south in the winter as far as Central and South America, while some southern populations may be year-round residents.

HABITAT They primarily inhabit coastal areas such as salt marshes, beaches, and bays, but can also be found inland near rivers, fields, and landfills.

SIMILAR SPECIES include Franklin's Gull, which has a darker hood extending further down the neck in non-breeding plumage and a different wing pattern, and Bonaparte's Gull, which is smaller with a thinner bill and whiter in the wings during the non-breeding season.

Breeding Adult

Juvenile

Non- Breeding Adult

Call

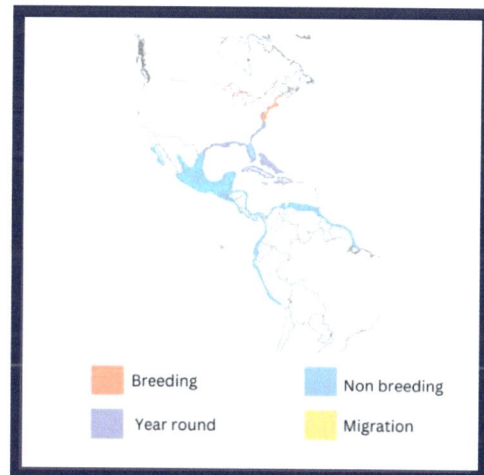

Breeding

Non breeding

Year round

Migration

DID YOU KNOW....

The Laughing Gull is named for its loud, high-pitched "ha-ha-ha" calls that genuinely sound like laughter, making it one of the most audibly distinctive gulls

While they forage for their own food (fish, insects, mollusks, and even garbage), Laughing Gulls are notorious for their kleptoparasitic behavior, frequently stealing food from other birds, especially Brown Pelicans. They will boldly land on a pelican's head and snatch fish from its pouch.

Unlike some coastal birds that suffer from human development, the Laughing Gull seems to thrive in proximity to humans. They are commonly seen scavenging for scraps on boardwalks, parking lots, and landfills.

California Gull - *Larus californicus*

California Gull is a medium-sized gull, intermediate in size between the Ring-billed Gull and the Herring Gull, with which it can be easily confused. Breeding adults have a white head, a medium gray back and upper wings, yellow legs, and a dark eye; nonbreeding adults develop brown streaking on their head. Both sexes have a yellow bill with a black ring and a red spot near the tip, which is brighter in breeding birds. Juvenile California Gulls are mottled brown and white with a pink bill that has a black tip and pinkish legs, gradually acquiring adult-like plumage over four years. Males are typically larger than females, possessing a larger bill, head, and tarsi.

FEEDING These opportunistic feeders forage while flying, swimming, walking, or wading, consuming a varied diet of insects, fish, eggs and young of other birds, small mammals, and even scavenging from garbage dumps and agricultural fields; they are also known to eat fruits like cherries.

SOUNDS California Gulls are quite vocal, especially in their breeding colonies, with a repertoire of scratchy, hoarse calls described as a series of "aow" and "uh-uh-uh" notes; they do not possess true songs but have distinct "long calls," "choking calls," "warning calls," and "alarm calls" associated with specific behaviors.

RANGE & MIGRATION Their breeding range is in the interior of western North America, around lakes and marshes from the Northwest Territories south to eastern California and Colorado, where they nest in colonies. Most California Gulls are migratory, moving west or southwest to the Pacific Coast for the winter, from southern British Columbia to western Mexico, where they inhabit seacoasts, estuaries, beaches, and other open areas; some younger birds may remain along the Pacific Coast throughout the summer, and a few winter inland near major lakes and rivers.

HABITAT They can be found in various open habitats, including lakes, marshes, seacoasts, offshore islands, rivers, agricultural lands, and garbage dumps.

SIMILAR SPECIES include the Ring-billed Gull and Herring Gull, but the California Gull can be distinguished by subtle differences in size, bill shape and markings, leg color, and eye color, as well as the extent of black in the wingtips.

Breeding Adult

Non- Breeding Adult

Juvenile

Breeding	Non breeding
Year round	Migration

Call

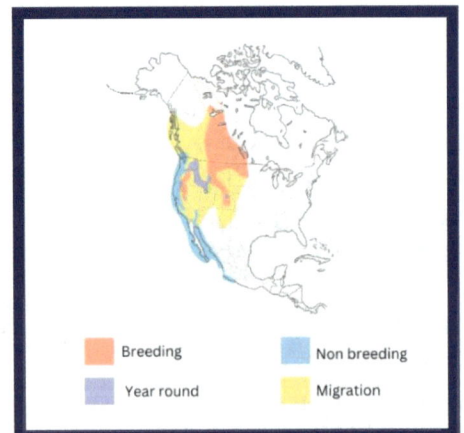

DID YOU KNOW....

Uniquely, California Gull chicks develop individual "begging calls" even before hatching. The parents learn to recognize these calls and will preferentially feed their own chick based on its specific vocalization, even within a crowded colony.

Beyond simply scavenging, California Gulls employ various clever foraging techniques. They have been seen "paddling" in shallow water with their feet to stir up invertebrates, and even dropping hard-shelled prey like clams and mussels from a height to break them open.

In times of food scarcity, California Gull parents can exhibit facultative brood reduction. This means they may preferentially feed stronger chicks, indirectly leading to the starvation of weaker siblings.

BLACKBIRDS AND ORIOLES

While the term "blackbird" might bring to mind the common Eurasian Blackbird (Turdus *merula*) of the thrush family, in the Americas, "blackbird" refers to a group of birds primarily belonging to the family Icteridae. Orioles also belong to this New World blackbird family (Icteridae), making them relatives, though distinct groups. It's important to distinguish between Old World blackbirds (true thrushes) and New World blackbirds (icterids). This note will focus on the characteristics of New World blackbirds and orioles within the Icteridae family.

General Characteristics of New World Blackbirds (Family Icteridae):

- **Diversity:** This is a highly diverse family of passerine birds, encompassing not only birds called "blackbirds" and "orioles" but also meadowlarks, grackles, cowbirds, bobolinks, caciques, and oropendolas.
- **Size:** They range considerably in size, from relatively small orioles to the larger grackles and oropendolas.
- **Bill Shape:** Most have sharply pointed, starling-like bills, although the shape can vary depending on diet (e.g., conical bills in seed-eaters, slender bills in nectar feeders).
- **Plumage:** Many species exhibit black plumage, often with a glossy sheen. However, the family also includes brightly colored birds with yellow, orange, and red. Sexual dimorphism in color and size is common, with males often being more brightly colored and larger than females.
- **Habitat:** They occupy a wide variety of habitats across the Americas, including forests, grasslands, marshes, and urban areas.
- **Diet:** Their diet is generally omnivorous, consisting of insects, seeds, fruits, and sometimes nectar, eggs, and nestlings of other birds. Foraging techniques vary depending on the species and their primary food source.
- **Social Behavior:** Many icterids are social, forming flocks, especially during migration and in winter roosts. Some species nest in colonies.
- **Vocalizations:** They have a diverse range of vocalizations, including songs and calls that vary significantly between species.

Key Points about Blackbirds (within Icteridae):

- **Appearance:** Typically characterized by black plumage in males, often with iridescent qualities. Females may be brown or streaked. Some species have brightly colored patches (e.g., red-winged blackbird).
- **Habitat:** Commonly found in open areas such as marshes, fields, and woodland edges.
- **Diet:** Primarily eat insects during the summer and seeds during the winter. Some species, like grackles, have a broader diet.
- **Nesting:** Nesting habits vary, with some species nesting on the ground, in marsh vegetation, or in trees.
- **Sociality:** Often form large flocks, especially during migration and at roosting sites, which can sometimes cause agricultural issues.

Key Points about Orioles (Genus *Icterus* within Icteridae):

- **Appearance:** Known for their striking and often contrasting plumage, typically involving combinations of black with vibrant yellow or orange. Females are usually less brightly colored. They have long tails and long, pointed bills.
- **Habitat:** Prefer tall trees in open woodlands, forest edges, parks, and backyards.
- **Diet:** Primarily feed on insects, fruits, and nectar. Some species have specialized feeding behaviors, like "gaping" to extract juice from fruits.
- **Nesting:** Many oriole species build distinctive, hanging, woven nests suspended from slender tree branches.
- **Migration:** Many oriole species are migratory, breeding in North America and wintering in Central and South America.
- **Attraction to Feeders:** Orioles can be attracted to backyard feeders offering sugar water, fruit (especially oranges), and jelly.

Baltimore Oriole - *Icterus galbula*

Baltimore Oriole is a striking medium-sized songbird known for its vibrant orange and black plumage in adult males. These birds have a black head, throat, back, and tail, sharply contrasting with the brilliant orange underparts, shoulder patch, and rump. Adult females exhibit a duller coloration, typically with grayish-brown on their backs and head, and yellowish-orange on their breast and rump, often with some dusky streaking on the breast. Juvenile Baltimore Orioles resemble females but tend to have paler yellow-orange underparts and a greenish-yellow wash on their backs.

FEEDING Their diet is varied, consisting of insects, berries, nectar, and occasionally fruit, which they sometimes obtain by "gaping," a unique feeding behavior where they insert their bill into a fruit and then open it to create a feeding surface.

SOUNDS The songs of the Baltimore Oriole are rich, musical whistles with varied phrases, often described as fluting or warbling. Their calls include a sharp "chack" or "hew-hew" and a scolding chatter.

RANGE & MIGRATION During the breeding season, they are found across eastern North America, from southern Canada south to the central United States. They are long-distance migrants, wintering primarily in Central and South America.

HABITAT Their preferred breeding habitat includes deciduous woodlands, especially those with tall trees, open forests, forest edges, and even suburban areas with mature trees.

SIMILAR SPECIES that might cause confusion include other orioles such as the Orchard Oriole, which is smaller and has a chestnut-red rather than orange coloration in the male, and the Hooded Oriole, which has a more westerly distribution and a different head pattern.

Male

Female

Juvenile

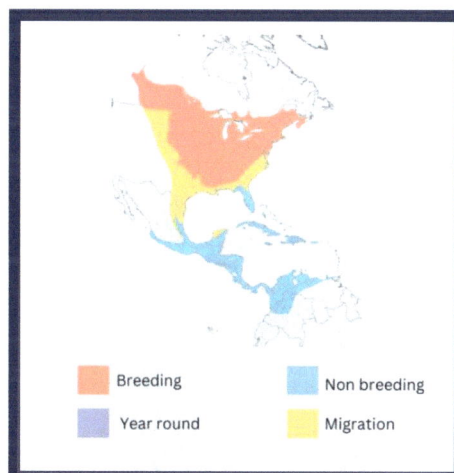

Breeding

Non breeding

Year round

Migration

Song

DID YOU KNOW....

For 20years, the Baltimore and Bullock's Orioles were "lumped" as the Northern Oriole due to interbreeding. Research later revealed key differences, leading to their re-separation.

Female Baltimore Orioles are the primary nest builders, and their creations are truly remarkable. They weave intricate, sock-like hanging nests, often 3-4 inches deep, from slender fibers like grasses, weeds, animal hair, and even artificial materials like string and yarn they find.

While they are voracious insect eaters, especially during the breeding season, Baltimore Orioles have a notable sweet tooth. They are attracted to ripe fruit, especially oranges and dark-colored berries, as well as nectar and even grape jelly offered in backyard feeders.

Red-winged Blackbird - *Agelaius phoeniceus*

Red-winged Blackbird is a medium-sized songbird with a stocky build and a conical bill, widely distributed across North America. Adult males are easily recognizable by their glossy black plumage and striking red shoulder patches, often edged with yellow. Females exhibit a heavily streaked brown plumage, sometimes with a hint of reddish color near the throat. Juvenile birds resemble females, displaying brown streaking, and gradually acquire adult plumage through subsequent molts.

FEEDING Red-winged Blackbirds are omnivorous, with their diet varying seasonally; they primarily consume insects during the breeding season and switch to seeds and grains in the fall and winter.

SOUNDS Males possess a diverse repertoire of songs, often described as a liquid "conk-la-ree!" or a musical trill, used for territorial defense and attracting mates. They also have a variety of calls, including sharp "check" notes and softer "chit" sounds.

RANGE & MIGRATION These birds have an extensive range, breeding from Alaska and Canada south throughout the United States and into parts of Mexico and Central America. They are generally migratory, with northern populations moving south for the winter, often forming large flocks.

HABITAT Their preferred habitats include wetlands such as marshes and swamps, but they can also be found in open fields, grasslands, and even suburban areas.

SIMILAR SPECIES might include other blackbirds, but the male's distinctive red shoulder patches and the female's heavy streaking are key identifying features.

Male

Female

Juvenile

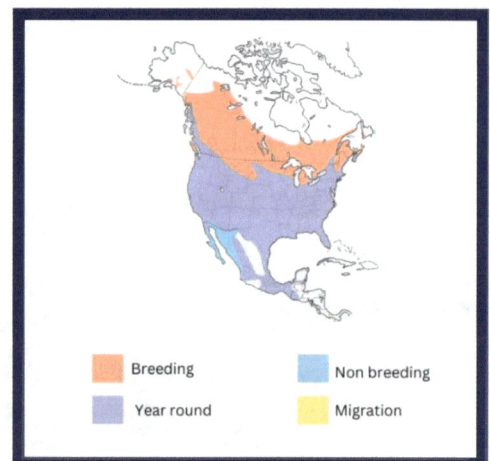

Breeding		Non breeding
Year round		Migration

Song **Call**

DID YOU KNOW....

Male Red-winged Blackbirds are highly polygynous. A single male can have up to 15 different females nesting within his territory. On average, a male will have around five mates.

During the breeding season, males are fiercely territorial, spending over a quarter of their daylight hours defending their territory. They are known to aggressively dive-bomb intruders, including much larger animals like horses and even humans, to protect their nests.

They can learn to avoid new foods simply by watching another blackbird get sick after eating it, even without tasting the food themselves.

Common Grackle - *Quiscalus quiscula*

Common Grackle is a large, lanky blackbird with long legs, a long tail, and a long, slightly curved bill. Adult males are typically glossy black with an iridescent sheen that can appear bluish on the head and bronzy on the body, along with bright yellow eyes. Females are similar in shape but are generally duller and browner overall with a shorter, straight tail. Juvenile Common Grackles are brownish with dark eyes and lack the glossy iridescence of adults.

FEEDING These omnivorous birds forage on the ground, in shallow water, or in shrubs, consuming a varied diet of insects, seeds, grains, berries, and even small vertebrates.

SOUNDS Their songs are characterized by a harsh, guttural squeak often accompanied by high-pitched whistles, sometimes likened to the sound of a rusty gate, and they also have a short, harsh "chlack" call.

RANGE & MIGRATION Common Grackles are widely distributed across North America east of the Rocky Mountains, inhabiting open and semi-open areas including woodlands, parks, farm fields, and suburban environments. Northern populations are migratory, typically moving in flocks to the southeastern United States for the winter, while birds in the central and southern parts of their range may be year-round residents.

SIMILAR SPECIES include the larger Great-tailed Grackle and Boat-tailed Grackle, as well as Brewer's Blackbird, Rusty Blackbird, and Brown-headed Cowbird, which can be distinguished by differences in size, tail length, bill shape, and plumage details.

Adult Male

Female

Juvenile

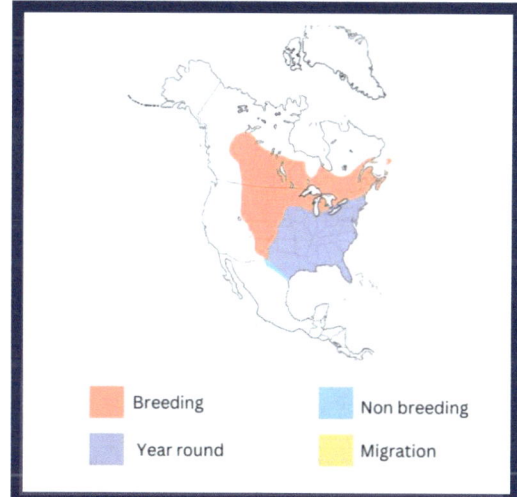

Breeding

Year round

Non breeding

Migration

DID YOU KNOW....

They possess a hard, keel-like ridge inside their upper beak. This specialized structure allows them to saw open acorns, a valuable food source, especially in fall and winter. They typically score the outside of the narrow end before biting the acorn open.

They have a magnetic mineral called magnetite in their heads, beaks, and necks. This is believed to aid them in detecting the Earth's geomagnetic fields, which they likely use for navigation during migration.

While not as skilled as mockingbirds, Common Grackles have been known to mimic the calls of other bird species and even human-made sounds.

Song

Call

Brown-headed Cowbird - *Molothrus ater*

Brown-headed Cowbird is a stocky, blackbird-like species found throughout much of North America, notable for its brood parasitic behavior. Adult males are characterized by their glossy black plumage and a distinctive chocolate-brown head. Females are a plain, dull gray overall with subtle streaking on their underparts and a slightly darker head. Juvenile cowbirds resemble adult females but often have faint streaking on their breasts and backs.

FEEDING These birds have a varied diet, consuming seeds, insects, and grains, often foraging in open areas like fields and pastures, frequently associating with grazing livestock which stir up insects.

SOUNDS Male Brown-headed Cowbirds possess a unique repertoire of liquid, gurgling songs and a variety of short calls, including sharp "check" notes and high-pitched whistles.

RANGE & MIGRATION Their range spans from southern Canada south through the United States and into central Mexico. They are migratory, with northern populations moving south for the winter, often forming large flocks.

HABITAT Their habitat preferences include open or semi-open country, grasslands, agricultural fields, and the edges of forests.

SIMILAR SPECIES might include other blackbirds, but the Brown-headed Cowbird's characteristic head color in males and its typical open-country foraging behavior help in identification.

Male

Female

Juvenile

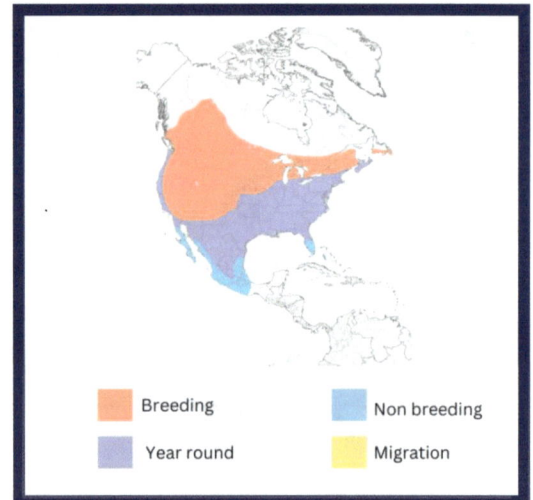

Breeding

Non breeding

Year round

Migration

Song

Call

DID YOU KNOW....

They are North America's most common obligate brood parasite. This means they only reproduce by laying their eggs in the nests of other bird species and never build their own nests or raise their own young.

Unlike most birds, Brown-headed Cowbird parents have no role in raising their offspring. The female lays the egg and leaves, and the male does not participate in any parental care.

A single female can lay a surprisingly large number of eggs in a breeding season, sometimes as many as 30-40, and in exceptional cases, even up to 70. This high reproductive output compensates for the low survival rate of their young.

Bullock's Oriole - *Icterus bullockii*

Bullock's Oriole is a striking medium-sized songbird characterized by its vibrant orange and black plumage in males. Males possess a brilliant orange body, a black throat and back, a black eye-line extending to the nape, and a patch of white on the wing. Females are more subdued, displaying grayish-brown on their backs and dull yellow-orange on their breasts and bellies, often with a hint of a dark throat. Juvenile Bullock's Orioles resemble females but tend to be paler overall.

FEEDING These birds have a varied diet, feeding on insects, fruits, and nectar, often foraging in the canopy.

SOUNDS Their songs are a series of rich, whistled notes and chatters, and they have a sharp "chek" call.

RANGE & MIGRATION The Bullock's Oriole's breeding range extends across the western half of North America, from southern Canada south through the United States to northern Mexico. They are migratory birds, typically wintering in Mexico and Central America.

HABITAT Their preferred habitats include open woodlands, riparian areas, orchards, and suburban gardens with deciduous trees.

SIMILAR SPECIES that might cause confusion include the Baltimore Oriole, particularly in areas of overlap, but Bullock's Orioles tend to have more orange coloration and different song patterns.

Adult Male

Female

Juvenile

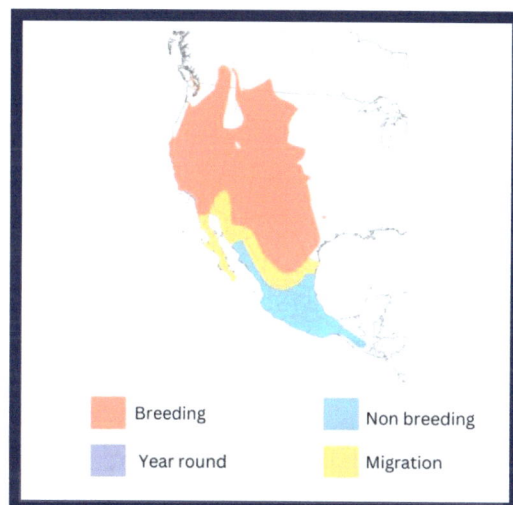

Breeding

Non breeding

Year round

Migration

Song

Call

DID YOU KNOW....

They employ a unique feeding technique called "gaping." They insert their closed bill into soft fruits or even tough-skinned caterpillars and then pry their bill open inside to create a wider opening, allowing them to lap up the juices with their brushy tongue

When Bullock's Orioles prey on honeybees, they exhibit a careful behavior of extracting and dropping the stinger before consuming the bee.

While the female typically takes on the primary role of weaving the intricate hanging nest, the male may occasionally assist in the process, with one partner working on the inside and the other bringing nest materials from the outside.

Bobolink - *Dolichonyx oryzivorus*

Bobolink is a striking migratory songbird found in North America, renowned for the dramatic seasonal differences in plumage between the sexes. During the breeding season, the male Bobolink is unmistakable with its black underparts, white scapulars and rump, and a buffy nape, a pattern sometimes described as wearing a tuxedo backward. Females in breeding plumage are buffy yellow with dark streaks on their back and flanks. Juvenile Bobolinks resemble females and maintain this cryptic coloration through their first fall migration.

FEEDING These birds are primarily insectivorous during the breeding season, feeding on a variety of insects and their larvae, but switch to a diet of seeds, particularly rice and other grains, during migration and in their wintering grounds.

SOUNDS The male Bobolink's song is a complex, bubbly, and melodious warble, often delivered in flight, while their calls include a sharp "pink" or "tink."

RANGE & MIGRATION Their breeding range spans across the northern United States and southern Canada, favoring open grasslands, hayfields, and meadows. They undertake one of the longest migrations of any North American land bird, traveling thousands of miles to their wintering grounds in South America, primarily in Argentina, Paraguay, and Bolivia.

HABITAT Their preferred habitat during the breeding season is tallgrass prairie and similar open fields.
SIMILAR SPECIES might include meadowlarks or longspurs, but the male Bobolink's unique breeding plumage and the female's distinct streaked appearance help distinguish them.

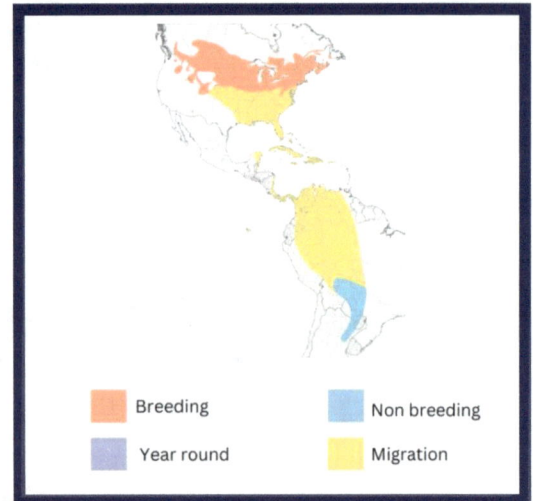

Breeding Male

Female

Juvenile

Breeding

Non breeding

Year round

Migration

Song

Call

DID YOU KNOW....

Its scientific name, oryzivorus, means "rice-eating," referring to its habit of feeding on grains, especially rice, during migration and in its wintering grounds. This has also earned it the nickname "Rice Bird."

The breeding male Bobolink is the only North American songbird that is black underneath and white on its back, resembling a "backwards tuxedo."

They are long-distance migrants, traveling roughly 12,500 miles (20,000 kilometers) round-trip each year from their breeding grounds in North America to their wintering grounds in South America.

Yellow-headed Blackbird - *Xanthocephalus xanthocephalus*

Yellow-headed Blackbird is a striking North American icterid characterized by its medium size and bold coloration. Adult males are easily recognized by their brilliant yellow head and chest, contrasting sharply with their black body. Females exhibit a more subdued appearance, typically displaying a brown or dusky gray body with a yellow throat and breast, often showing some yellow streaking on the head. Juvenile birds resemble females but tend to have less distinct yellow markings and more extensive streaking.

FEEDING These blackbirds primarily forage in wetlands and agricultural fields, consuming a diet that varies seasonally but includes insects, seeds, and grains.

SOUNDS Their songs are a distinctive and somewhat harsh mix of croaks, gurgles, and whistles, often described as sounding like a rusty hinge. Their calls include sharp "check" notes and nasal "kleck" sounds.

RANGE & MIGRATION The Yellow-headed Blackbird's breeding range is concentrated in the western and central parts of North America, typically in freshwater marshes and wetlands with emergent vegetation. They are migratory, with most populations moving south for the winter, often forming large flocks in agricultural areas of the southern United States and Mexico.

HABITAT Their preferred habitat during the breeding season is characterized by the presence of cattails or bulrushes over water, where they build their nests.

SIMILAR SPECIES that might be confused with the Yellow-headed Blackbird include other blackbird species, particularly the Brewer's Blackbird and the Tricolored Blackbird, but the male's bright yellow head and the female's distinct yellow throat and breast are key distinguishing features.

Adult Male

Female

Juvenile

Breeding

Non breeding

Year round

Migration

Song

Call

DID YOU KNOW....

Its genus and species name, Xanthocephalus xanthocephalus, literally translates from Greek to "yellow head, yellow head," a very direct reference to the striking coloration of the adult male.

While visually stunning, the male's song is often described by humans as harsh, grating, and sounding like a rusty hinge or a saw grating metal. This unmusical song serves to attract females and defend territory within the noisy marsh colonies.

Unlike many other blackbird species that readily adapt to various habitats, Yellow-headed Blackbirds are strongly tied to freshwater marshes for breeding. They build their nests exclusively over water, attached to emergent vegetation like cattails and bulrushes.

Hooded Oriole - *Icterus cucullatus*

Hooded Oriole is a slender songbird with a slightly downcurved bill, with males exhibiting striking plumage that varies regionally from brilliant yellow in the west to flame orange in Texas and eastern Mexico, always featuring a black throat extending to the eye, a black back, wings, and tail, and two white wingbars. Females are olive-yellow overall with grayer backs and thin white wingbars. Juvenile males resemble females but develop a black throat patch.

FEEDING These acrobatic foragers primarily feed on insects, nectar from flowers, and fruits, and are known to visit hummingbird feeders.

SOUNDS Their songs are a variable series of whistles, chatters, and warbles, sometimes including mimicry of other birds, while their calls include a whistled "wheet" and a chattering alarm.

RANGE & MIGRATION They breed in open woodlands with scattered trees, especially favoring palms in the southwestern United States and northern Mexico, and often attach their woven, pouch-like nests to the underside of large leaves, particularly palm fronds. Most Hooded Orioles migrate south to Mexico for the winter, though some may overwinter in the southern United States, especially near feeders.

SIMILAR SPECIES can include other orioles such as the Orchard Oriole, but differences in size, bill shape, and plumage details help in identification.

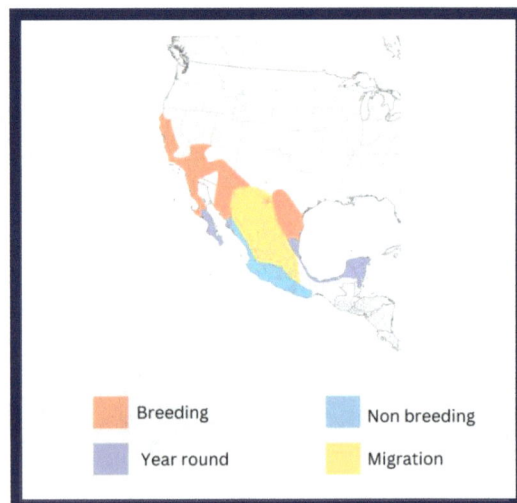

Adult Male

Female

Juvenile

Breeding
Non breeding
Year round
Migration

Song

Call

DID YOU KNOW....

Hooded Orioles, though nectar consumers, often "rob" flowers by piercing their bases with sharp bills to access nectar, bypassing pollination.

The color of the adult male Hooded Oriole varies significantly across its range. Males in the southwestern United States and northwestern Mexico tend to be a bright yellow, while those in southern Texas and eastern Mexico are a more vibrant flame orange.

They are particularly known for their nesting habits, especially when using palm trees. The female will weave her hanging pouch nest and then "sew" it to the underside of large palm fronds by poking holes in the leaf and pushing plant fibers through to secure it. This has earned them the nickname "palm-leaf oriole" in some areas.

240

Orchard Oriole - *Icterus spurius*

The Orchard Oriole is the smallest North American oriole, with the adult male exhibiting a striking plumage of black on the head, throat, back, and tail, contrasting with rich reddish-chestnut underparts and a patch on the wing. Females are distinctly different, displaying an overall greenish-yellow coloration with two white wing bars and lacking any black markings. Juvenile males resemble females but develop a black throat patch during their first year.

FEEDING These orioles primarily forage for insects, especially during the breeding season, but also consume fruits, nectar, and spiders.

SOUNDS Their songs are characterized as lively, warbling series of whistles, often ending with a slurred note, and their calls include a soft "chuck" or a dry chatter.

RANGE & MIGRATION They breed across much of the eastern United States and southern Canada, favoring open woodlands, orchards, parks, and areas with scattered trees, particularly near water. Orchard Orioles are migratory, spending their winters in Central and South America.

HABITAT They typically inhabit semi-open areas with deciduous trees.

SIMILAR SPECIES might include other orioles or even some warblers, but the Orchard Oriole's size, color patterns, and vocalizations help in its identification.

Adult Male

Female

Juvenile Male

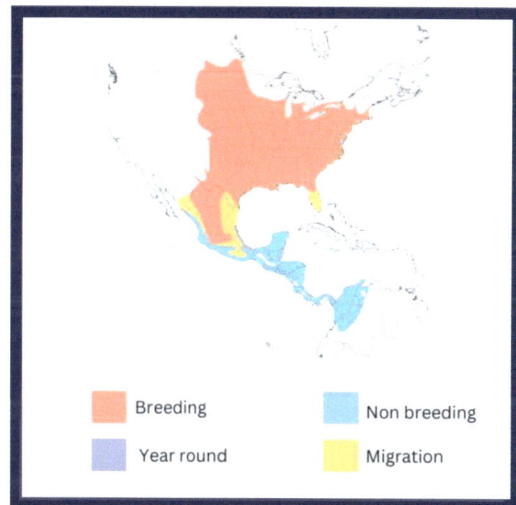

Breeding

Non breeding

Year round

Migration

Song

Call

DID YOU KNOW....

It holds the title of the smallest oriole species found in North America.

Its species name, spurius, comes from the Latin word for "illegitimate." This refers to an early misidentification where it was mistaken for a female Baltimore Oriole by early ornithologists.

Unlike many birds where the adult male has a consistent plumage, the Orchard Oriole male has two distinct breeding plumages. First-year breeding males resemble females with a black throat patch, while older males develop the rich chestnut-brown body with a black head, throat, and upper breast. Both plumages are capable of attracting mates.

Eastern Meadowlark - *Sturnella magna*

Eastern Meadowlark is a medium-sized songbird characterized by its bright yellow underparts boldly marked with a prominent black "V" across the chest. Its upperparts are a mottled brown and black, providing excellent camouflage in its grassland habitat. Males and females exhibit similar plumage, although the black "V" may be slightly less distinct in females, especially outside of the breeding season. Juvenile Eastern Meadowlarks are duller in coloration with more streaking and less vibrant yellow on their undersides.

FEEDING Their diet primarily consists of insects, particularly grasshoppers and crickets, which they forage for on the ground, though they also consume seeds and berries, especially during the winter months.

SOUNDS The song of the Eastern Meadowlark is a series of clear, flute-like whistles, often described as "spring is here," while their calls include a short, sharp "dzert" and a chattering alarm call.

RANGE & MIGRATION This species has a wide range across eastern North America, extending west to the Great Plains and south into Central and South America. Northern populations are migratory, typically moving south to the southern United States and beyond for the winter, while southern populations may be year-round residents.

HABITAT They favor open grasslands, meadows, pastures, and hayfields with relatively tall vegetation.

SIMILAR SPECIES that might cause confusion include the Western Meadowlark, which overlaps in range in some areas but has a different song and subtle plumage differences, and various longspurs, which are smaller and lack the bright yellow underparts and black "V".

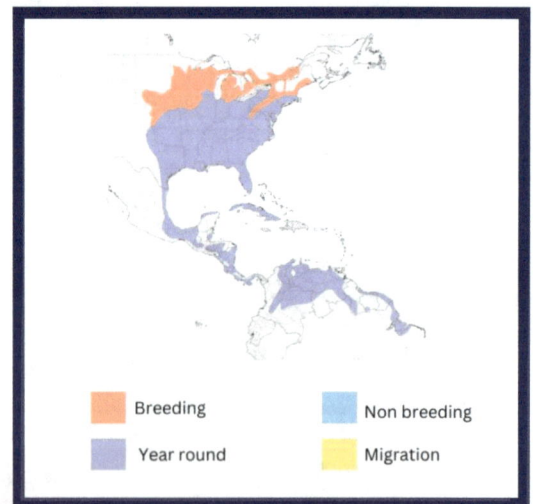

Breeding Adult

Non-Breeding Adult

Juvenile

Breeding   Non breeding
Year round   Migration

Song   Call

DID YOU KNOW....

Males are often polygynous, meaning one male will have two or three female mates within his territory. Each female, however, typically mates with only one male per breeding season.

Male Eastern Meadowlarks have a repertoire of several different songs, which are typically clear, flute-like whistles. They often sing one song repeatedly before switching to another. They even have a distinct "flight song" sung while in the air.

The female Eastern Meadowlark builds her nest on the ground, often in a shallow depression well-concealed by dense vegetation. Uniquely, some nests can have a partial or even complete woven grass roof with a side entrance, offering extra protection and camouflage.

Brewer's Blackbird - *Euphagus cyanocephalus*

Brewer's Blackbird is a medium-sized blackbird with a glossy, iridescent plumage. Adult males are entirely black with a striking violet or purplish iridescence on their heads and necks, and they possess bright yellow eyes. Females are a duller, uniform gray or brownish-gray, also with yellow eyes. Juvenile Brewer's Blackbirds are generally brownish and have dark eyes in their first year, gradually developing the yellow eyes and glossy plumage.

FEEDING These birds are omnivorous, foraging on the ground for insects, seeds, grains, and occasionally small fruits and berries.

SOUNDS Their songs are a somewhat unmusical mix of squeaks, whistles, and gurgling notes, often described as rusty or creaky. Their calls include a sharp "check" or "chuck."

RANGE & MIGRATION They have a wide range across western and central North America, extending into parts of the Great Lakes region. They are migratory, with most birds breeding in the northern parts of their range and wintering in the southern United States and Mexico.

HABITAT Their preferred habitats include open woodlands, grasslands, agricultural fields, marshes, and suburban areas.

SIMILAR SPECIES can include other blackbirds like the Common Grackle or Rusty Blackbird, but Brewer's Blackbirds are typically smaller and have a slenderer bill, along with the distinctive eye color in adults.

Male

Female

Juvenile

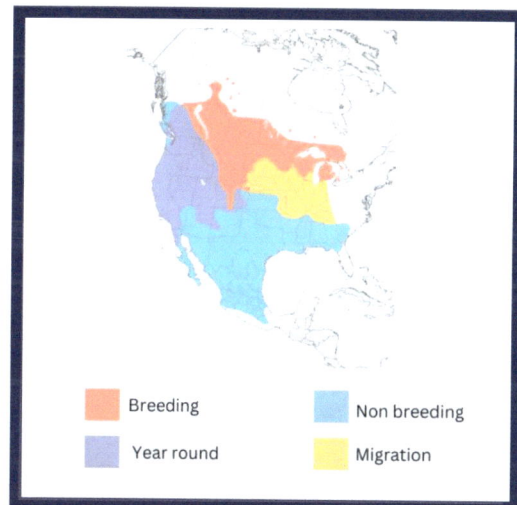

Breeding

Non breeding

Year round

Migration

Song

Call

DID YOU KNOW....

The female Brewer's Blackbird builds the nest alone in 5-10 days and fiercely defends it against other females and intruding males.

Their eggs exhibit extreme variability in color and pattern. This is thought to be an adaptation to help camouflage the eggs by matching the background pattern of the specific nest.

The Brewer's Blackbird has a common name honoring the American ornithologist Thomas Mayo Brewer, who first identified it as a new species. However, it was scientifically described earlier by a German herpetologist, Johann Georg Wagler, who gave it the species epithet cyanocephalus, referring to its bluish glossy head. Thus, its scientific name reflects an earlier observation, while its common name recognizes a later contribution

Great-tailed Grackle - *Quiscalus mexicanus*

Great-tailed Grackle is a large, slender blackbird characterized by its long legs, flat-headed profile, and stout bill. Adult males are striking with iridescent black plumage that often shimmers with bluish-purple hues, and they possess a remarkably long, V-shaped tail and piercing yellow eyes. Females are considerably smaller, exhibiting a dark brown coloration above and a paler brown below, with a buff-colored throat and a stripe above the eye. Juvenile Great-tailed Grackles have a similar dark brown plumage to adult females but feature streaked underparts and dark eyes.

FEEDING These highly adaptable birds have a broad omnivorous diet, feeding on a variety of items including insects, spiders, worms, snails, crustaceans, tadpoles, frogs, lizards, snakes, small mammals, bird eggs and nestlings, as well as grains, seeds, fruits, and even human refuse.

SOUNDS Their vocalizations are diverse and often loud, encompassing a range of whistles, clacks, squeals, and harsh, grating sounds, sometimes described as sounding like a rusty hinge or badly lubricated machinery; they also have specific calls for mating, alarm, and territorial defense.

RANGE & MIGRATION The Great-tailed Grackle's range extends across the southern and southwestern United States, throughout Mexico and Central America, and into parts of South America, with a notable expansion northward and westward in recent history. While largely a permanent resident in the southern portions of its range, populations in the northernmost areas may exhibit some southward migration during harsh winter conditions, often following river valleys.

HABITAT They thrive in a variety of open and semi-open habitats, including agricultural fields, feedlots, suburban areas, parks, golf courses, and wetlands, generally favoring locations near water sources and trees or hedgerows for roosting and nesting.

SIMILAR SPECIES that might be confused with the Great-tailed Grackle include the Boat-tailed Grackle, which overlaps in range along the Gulf Coast and differs by having a more rounded head and darker eyes in both sexes where their ranges intersect, as well as the smaller Common Grackle, Brewer's Blackbird, and Bronzed Cowbird, which have different size proportions and tail lengths.

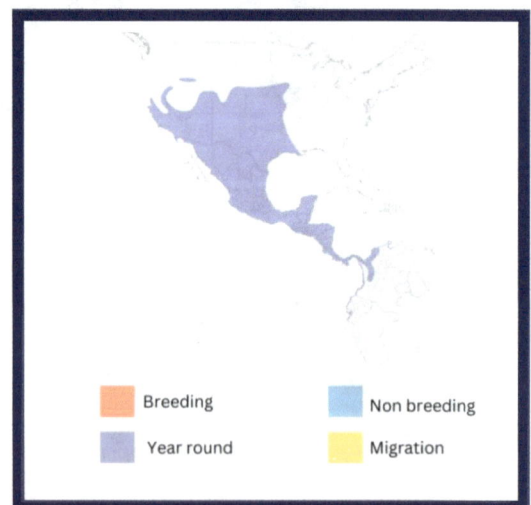

Breeding

Non breeding

Year round

Migration

Song

Call

DID YOU KNOW....

According to a Mexican legend, the voiceless Zanate (Great-tailed Grackle) cunningly stole seven songs embodying life's passions from a wise sea turtle.

It is one of the fastest-expanding native bird species in North America. Since the 1960s, they have dramatically increased their range northward and westward, following the spread of irrigated agriculture and urban development.

Female Great-tailed Grackle chicks have a higher survival rate to fledging than males because they are smaller and require less food. This can also lead to adult populations with more females than males, meaning females may outlive males.

Rusty Blackbird - *Euphagus carolinus*

Rusty Blackbird is a medium-sized blackbird characterized by its relatively long tail and pale yellow or whitish eye. Adult males in breeding plumage are a glossy black with a faint greenish or bluish sheen, while in fresh fall plumage, they exhibit rusty edges to their feathers, giving them their name.

Females are typically a slaty gray or brownish overall, with rusty tinges, particularly on the head and breast, and often have a paler throat. Juvenile Rusty Blackbirds are generally dark brownish with buffy or rusty feather edges and dark eyes that gradually lighten to the adult pale yellow.

FEEDING These birds are omnivorous, foraging in shallow water or on the ground for insects, seeds, berries, and occasionally small fish or amphibians.

SOUNDS Their song is a somewhat squeaky, liquid series of notes, often described as sounding like a rusty hinge, and their most common call is a sharp "chuck."

RANGE & MIGRATION Rusty Blackbirds breed primarily in the boreal forests and taiga across Canada and Alaska, extending into the northern United States. They are long-distance migrants, wintering in the eastern and southeastern United States, often in swampy woodlands, bottomland forests, and agricultural fields.

SIMILAR SPECIES include other blackbirds such as the Brewer's Blackbird and Common Grackle, but the Rusty Blackbird's pale eye and distinctive rusty fall plumage help to distinguish it. Their populations have experienced significant declines in recent decades, making them a species of conservation concern.

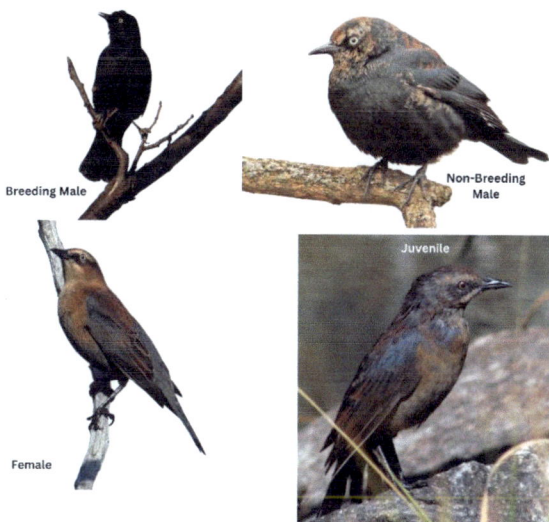

Breeding Male

Non-Breeding Male

Juvenile

Female

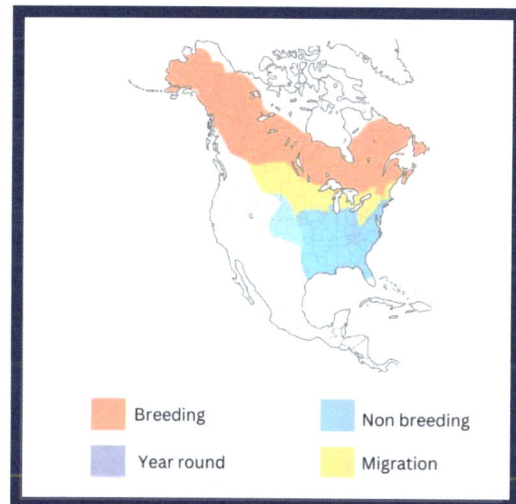

Breeding

Non breeding

Year round

Migration

Song

Flock Calls

DID YOU KNOW....

The "rusty" in their name comes from the rust-colored edges on their feathers, most visible in their non-breeding (winter) plumage. Breeding males turn glossy black, while females become uniform slate-gray.

The Rusty Blackbird has experienced one of the most significant population declines of any North American bird species in recent decades, with estimates ranging from an 85% to 95% decrease since the mid-20th century. This steep decline remains largely unexplained, making it a high conservation concern.

Unlike many blackbirds that primarily forage on the ground, Rusty Blackbirds frequently forage in shallow water or on very wet ground. They have a unique habit of flipping over leaves and debris in shallow water with their bills to find aquatic insects and other invertebrates.

Tricolored Blackbird - *Agelaius tricolor*

Tricolored Blackbird is a medium-sized songbird with a stocky build, often appearing somewhat hunchbacked when perched, and a slender, pointed bill. Adult males are glossy black with a striking red shoulder patch bordered by a crisp white band. Females exhibit a sooty dark gray-brown plumage with subtle grayish streaks, a paler throat, and may have a reduced reddish shoulder patch. Juvenile birds resemble females but tend to be browner overall with some mottling.

FEEDING Tricolored Blackbirds are opportunistic feeders, consuming primarily insects, especially during the breeding season, and switching to seeds and grains at other times of the year; they often forage in flocks in agricultural fields, pastures, and wetlands.

SOUNDS Their songs are described as nasal and low-pitched, less musical than that of the Red-winged Blackbird, and they have various calls including buzzy notes and sharp "check" sounds, with males sometimes producing a distinctive cat-like mewing call.

RANGE & MIGRATION The Tricolored Blackbird's range is largely restricted to California, with smaller populations in Oregon, Washington, and Nevada, and they are generally not long-distance migrants, though they may move locally in response to food availability and breeding conditions.

HABITAT Their preferred breeding habitat historically included freshwater marshes with dense vegetation like cattails, but they now frequently nest in agricultural fields, particularly silage fields, and require a nearby water source and foraging areas.

SIMILAR SPECIES to be aware of include the more widespread Red-winged Blackbird, which in males has a yellow or buffy border below the red shoulder patch and females that tend to be more reddish-brown with more distinct streaking.

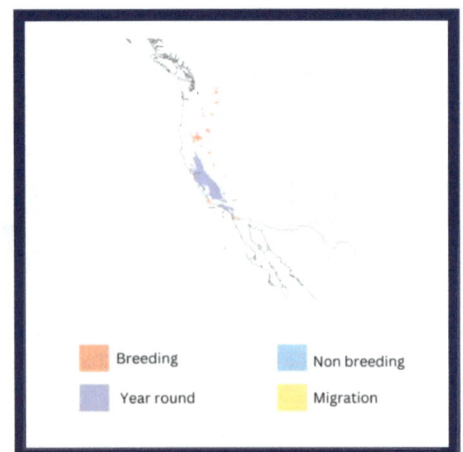

Breeding Male

Non-Breeding Male

Female

Juvenile

Breeding
Year round
Non breeding
Migration

Song

Call

DID YOU KNOW....

Female Tricolored Blackbirds collect dry leaves, soak them in water until wet, and then weave them into their nests.

They form the largest breeding colonies of any extant land bird in North America. These colonies can be incredibly dense, with nests sometimes only a foot or two apart and historically reaching hundreds of thousands of birds.

This species exhibits a unique breeding behavior where individuals may breed twice in a single year but in two different locations. They might have an initial nesting effort in the San Joaquin Valley (early March to late April) and then move north to breed again in the Sacramento Valley, Sierra foothills, or northeastern California.

Bronzed Cowbird - *Molothrus aeneus*

Bronzed Cowbird is a stocky, blackbird-like species found in open country, characterized by its robust build and relatively long bill. Adult males are a glossy black with a bronze or greenish sheen, particularly noticeable on their back and rump, and they possess striking red eyes and a distinctive erectile ruff on their neck. Females are typically dull black or grayish-brown, depending on the subspecies, and also have red eyes, though sometimes brownish outside the breeding season. Juvenile Bronzed Cowbirds resemble adult females but have darker eyes.

FEEDING These birds primarily forage on the ground in flocks, feeding on seeds, grains, and insects, and may associate with livestock to catch flushed insects.

SOUNDS The male's song is a distinctive, somewhat wheezy series of whistles and gurgling notes, while their calls include various squeaks and whistles.

RANGE & MIGRATION Bronzed Cowbirds inhabit the southern United States, from California to Louisiana, extending south through Central America to Panama. They are generally considered short-distance migrants, with some populations in the northern parts of their range moving southward in winter, although they remain year-round residents in much of their range.

HABITAT Their preferred habitat includes open fields, pastures, scrubby grasslands, agricultural areas, and lightly wooded canyons.

SIMILAR SPECIES include the Brown-headed Cowbird, which is smaller and has a brown head on the male, and the Shiny Cowbird, which is also expanding its range in North America; careful attention to size, plumage details, and eye color is needed for accurate identification. As brood parasites, Bronzed Cowbirds lay their eggs in the nests of other bird species, leaving the host parents to raise their young.

Adult Male

Female

Juvenile

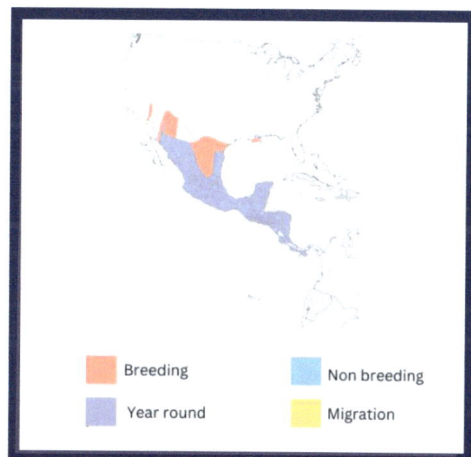

Breeding
Non breeding
Year round
Migration

Song

Call

DID YOU KNOW....

Unlike many bird species where eye color is relatively consistent, the Bronzed Cowbird exhibits variation in eye color across its subspecies

Their eggs are known to have relatively thick and strong shells compared to some of their host species. This might be an adaptation to prevent host birds from easily damaging or ejecting the foreign egg from their nest

While native to parts of the Americas, the Bronzed Cowbird has undergone a significant northward range expansion in recent decades, particularly in the United States. This expansion is still being studied and is likely influenced by factors such as habitat changes and the availability of new host species.

Scott's Oriole - *Icterus parisorum*

Scott's Oriole is a striking medium-sized songbird with a long tail and a slightly curved, pointed bill. Adult males are vividly lemon yellow on their underparts and velvety black on their upperparts, featuring a black throat and chest, a yellow shoulder patch bordered in white, and one white wingbar; their tail is black with a yellow base. Adult females exhibit a duller plumage, being yellowish-olive above and dull yellow below, often with faint wingbars and some dark stippling on the head. Juvenile birds resemble adult females but are typically duller overall.

FEEDING Scott's Orioles primarily feed on insects, which they actively seek in various locations, including foliage, bark, and even inside flowers, often employing acrobatic maneuvers; they also consume nectar from flowers, especially yucca, agave, and ocotillo, and will eat fruits and berries.

SOUNDS Their song is a series of rich, melodious, flute-like whistles that carry well, often resembling the song of a Western Meadowlark, and their common call is a harsh, nasal "chuk," with a softer, rising "wheet" also heard.

RANGE, HABITAT & MIGRATION These orioles breed in the arid and semi-arid regions of the southwestern United States and into Mexico, favoring habitats with abundant yucca, agave, pinyon pine, juniper, and live oak, typically at higher elevations but also in desert oases with taller trees; they are uncommon in chaparral unless tall yuccas are present. Scott's Orioles are migratory, with the populations breeding in the United States moving south to winter in Mexico and southern California, generally arriving on breeding grounds in March or April and departing in July and August; some populations in central Mexico are non-migratory.

SIMILAR SPECIES that might be confused with Scott's Oriole include Hooded Oriole, Bullock's Oriole, Orchard Oriole, and Audubon's Oriole, but differences in coloration patterns, especially on the head, back, and underparts, along with variations in wing markings and tail color, help distinguish them.

Male

Female

Juvenile

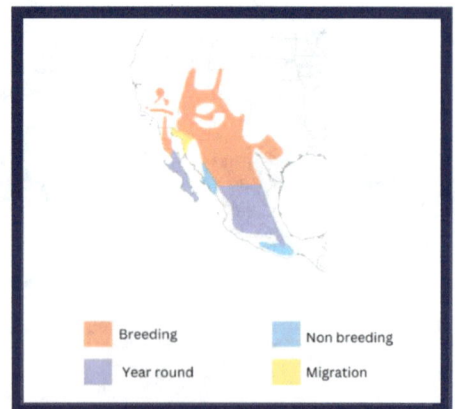

Breeding
Non breeding
Year round
Migration

Song

Call

248

DID YOU KNOW....

The male Scott's Oriole is often one of the first birds to begin singing each day, even before sunrise. Their song is a sweet, clear warble that can be heard over considerable distances.

They have a strong association with yucca plants. They frequently build their woven, pendant-like nests using the tough fibers from dried yucca leaves. The color of these fibers can camouflage the nest effectively.

The current common name commemorates General Winfield Scott, who was involved in the Trail of Tears. This has led to proposals to rename the species "Yucca Oriole" to better reflect its ecology and avoid the negative historical connotations. The scientific name parisorum was given by a French naturalist to honor the Paris brothers, who financed a French exploratory expedition.

Boat-tailed Grackle - *Quiscalus major*

Boat-tailed Grackle is a large, glossy blackbird found in the southeastern United States. Males are particularly striking with their iridescent black plumage that can show hints of purple, blue, or green, and they possess a long, keel-shaped tail that is often held cocked. Females are considerably smaller and have a duller brown to dark brown coloration with a less pronounced tail. Juvenile Boat-tailed Grackles are typically dark brown and gradually acquire the adult plumage.

FEEDING These omnivorous birds have a varied diet consisting of insects, crustaceans, small fish, eggs, and seeds, often foraging in wetlands, coastal areas, and even urban parks.

SOUNDS The songs of Boat-tailed Grackles are a complex mix of whistles, clicks, and harsh notes, while their calls can include a sharp "check" and various chattering sounds.

RANGE & MIGRATION Their range extends along the Atlantic and Gulf Coasts of the United States, from North Carolina south to Florida and west to Texas. While generally considered non-migratory, some northern populations may undertake short-distance movements, especially in response to harsh weather.

HABITAT They inhabit a variety of wetland and coastal habitats, including marshes, swamps, mangroves, and also readily adapt to human-modified environments.

SIMILAR SPECIES might include the Common Grackle, but the Boat-tailed Grackle is notably larger, especially the male, and has a more pronounced boat-shaped tail.

Adult Male

Female

Juvenile

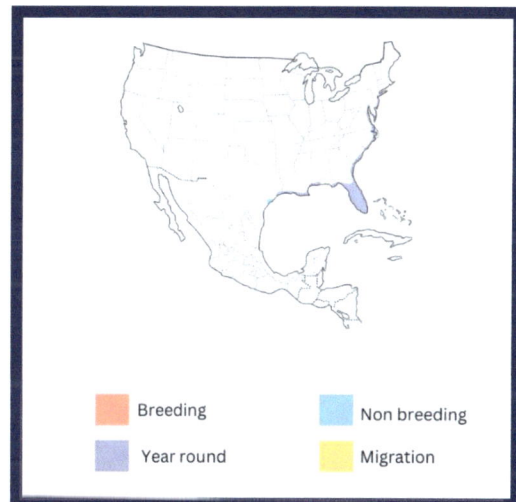

Breeding

Non breeding

Year round

Migration

Song

Call

DID YOU KNOW....

Young Boat-tailed Grackles that fall into the water are surprisingly capable swimmers for short distances, using their wings as paddles to propel themselves.

They are known to dunk hard or dry food items like bread, dog food, and even rice in water before eating them, a behavior that softens the food and makes it easier to swallow.

They exhibit a unique mating system where dominant males defend clusters of nesting females (harems) from other males. While the dominant male does most of the mating within the colony, DNA fingerprinting has revealed that many females also mate with males away from the colony, meaning the dominant male is not the sole father of all the young.

CONCLUSION

This guide, encompassing 201 of North America's avian treasures, has aimed to do more than simply catalog birds. It has sought to illuminate the intricate lives of these creatures, fostering a deeper appreciation for their beauty, behaviors, and the vital roles they play in our ecosystems. From the vibrant tapestry of plumages – the subtle differences between male, female, and juvenile – to the detailed range maps charting their seasonal journeys, and the unique soundscapes of their songs and calls, each page has been crafted to enhance your birdwatching experience.

We've journeyed together through diverse habitats, encountering iconic species and hidden gems alike. The "Did You Know?" sections have, hopefully, added layers of intrigue, transforming simple observations into captivating stories of survival, adaptation, and the sheer wonder of evolution. The detailed bird descriptions, combined with visual aids, have equipped you with the tools to confidently identify and appreciate the nuances of each species.

But this guide is not an end point. Rather, it is an invitation. An invitation to step outside, to raise your binoculars, and to immerse yourself in the dynamic world of birds. North America's avifauna is a constantly evolving spectacle, shaped by the changing seasons, ecological shifts, and the enduring power of natural selection. There is always something new to discover, a different song to learn, a fresh plumage to admire.

As you continue your birdwatching journey, remember that you are not just an observer, but also a steward. By understanding and appreciating these birds, we become more invested in their conservation and the preservation of their habitats. Let this guide be a companion in that endeavor, a resource you return to time and again as you explore the rich tapestry of North American birdlife. May your path be filled with the joy of discovery, the thrill of identification, and the satisfaction of contributing to a greater understanding of the avian world. The symphony of feathers awaits.

Made in United States
Troutdale, OR
05/19/2025

31511825R00144